African Placenames

African Placenames

Origins and Meanings of the Names for Over 2000 Natural Features, Towns, Cities, Provinces and Countries

by Adrian Room

McFarland & Company, Publishers
Jefferson, North Carolina and London

British Library Cataloguing-in-Publication data are available

Library of Congress Cataloguing-in-Publication Data

Room, Adrian.
African placenames : origins and meanings of the names for over 2000 natural features, towns, cities, provinces and countries / by Adrian Room.
p. cm.
Includes bibliographical references.
ISBN 0-89950-943-6 (lib. bdg. : 50# alk. paper)
1. Africa—Gazetteers. 2. Names, Geographical—Africa. I. Title. II. Title: African place names.
DT2.R66 1994
916′.003—dc20 93-40261
CIP

Manufactured in the United States of America

McFarland & Company, Inc., Publishers
Box 611, Jefferson, North Carolina 28640

"We all belong, ultimately, to Africa."
(Roland Oliver, *The African Experience,* 1991)

Contents

Preface

The present work evolved from an earlier dictionary of the placenames of southern Africa that I was planning with my South African coauthor, Julie Wilcocks. We were preceded to publication, however, by Peter Raper, who brought out the first edition of his *Dictionary of Southern African Place Names* in Johannesburg in 1987, after we had already gathered our own material. We therefore held our fire, even though our own material, as it turned out, represented southern Africa much more fully than Dr. Raper's book.

Instead, and building on the basis of our accumulated material, I now offer a work that aims to represent the whole African continent rather than simply the southern portion of it.

It has been a difficult task, since information on the placenames of some African countries is hard to come by, to say the least. Or if one can come by it, it often turns out to be of dubious authority. There is the added problem of the hundreds of different languages that need to be tackled. (For more on this aspect, see the last section of the Introduction, p. 8.) One is here working in very much a specialized linguistic and ethnic area.

Even so, it has been possible to determine with reasonable confidence the origins of most of the major names of Africa, the ones that almost everyone has heard of, such as the names of countries and their capitals, of the largest rivers, lakes, and mountains, and of familiar deserts, islands, and capes. At the same time, by means of assiduous delving in academic publications in various European languages (English, French, German, Italian, Portuguese, Russian and Spanish) it has been possible to compose entries for a number of less well-known and relatively minor placenames, such as those of villages, oases, and even individual wells.

However, although the coverage is geographically continental, I am aware that some countries are more fully represented than others, and that it would be misleading to claim uniform treatment for all parts of Africa. (Southern Africa is well documented, North Africa reasonably well, but East, West, and Central Africa less fully than I would have liked.) This is not so much because information is difficult to obtain in some cases, but simply because nothing is known about certain names, even of important places. Or if something is known, it is known only to a handful of specialists. The present work cannot yet claim to be *the* dictionary, although so far as I am aware it is the only one that aims to be reasonably comprehensive. (There are entries for just over 2000 places.)

Although my original coauthor was in the end not the coauthor of this book, I am considerably indebted to Julie Wilcocks for all the work she put into our aborted enterprise. That she was more than qualified to undertake it is proved by the inclusion of a title of her own in the Bibliography.

Adrian Room
Stamford, England
December 1993

Introduction

Africa. . . . Was there ever a more resonant name? In the 19th century the name evoked among Europeans and North Americans an unknown and virginal land with commercial and missionary potential. It was a land begging to be explored. The actual exploration—and exploitation—that ensued was the "scramble for Africa," a vigorous but disparate bid among whites to appropriate the continent's vast and varied resources.

That was then. Now, at the end of the 20th century, the concept of "Africa" is rather different. Most countries have broken free from colonial ties and gained independence of a kind. But there is hardly a country without some kind of strife or some sort of economic difficulty. Civil unrest, ethnic conflict, even full-scale war, continues in Algeria, Angola, Chad, Djibouti, Ethiopia, Kenya, Liberia, Mali, Morocco, Niger, South Africa, Sudan, Togo, and Zaïre. The names of certain countries evoke particular associations: Angola, Ethiopia, and Sudan are lands of famine; Somalia is a country of anarchy; South Africa is a state still torn by racially divided forces and still racked by dashed hopes of true democracy and harmony. The names less often in the news, such as Benin, Botswana, Gambia, Mauritius, Namibia, and Zambia, are those of stabler countries where something approaching true democracy has been achieved, and where economic growth has been more successfully sustained.

But this rather misleadingly negative image is just one side of the coin. The continent's true face, that of the real Africa, is more authentically and vividly seen in her placenames, as is true in any other country or continent. The names themselves generally reveal a much more positive picture.

From a linguistic point of view, African placenames range from the classical and biblical in the north to the modern European in the south, and are found in an array of different languages, spoken by a host of different peoples.

To the European or Westerner, the familiar but apparently meaningless names may cause some confusion. The countries themselves have names that are disconcertingly similar. There is a need to distinguish between *Libya* and *Liberia, Mali* and *Malawi, Niger* and *Nigeria, Mauretania, Mauritania* and *Mauritius, Guinea, Equatorial Guinea,* and *Guinea-Bissau, Zambia, Zaïre,* and *Zimbabwe.* Among all these exotic Zs, where does *Zanzibar* fit in, and the *Zambezi,* and *Tanzania,* and *Azania*?

The modern map of Africa has changed significantly in the final four decades of the century. Many European names have now been replaced by indigenous ones. *Gold Coast* is now *Ghana, Rhodesia* is part *Zambia* and part

Zimbabwe, Nyasaland is *Malawi.* The city *Salisbury* is now *Harare, Lourenço Marques* is *Maputo, Bathurst* is *Banjul.* The name change process works right down to city streets, as any visitor to a renamed town in Africa will know. In Harare, for example, *North Street* is now *Josiah Tongogara Avenue, Gordon Avenue* is *George Silindika Avenue, Stanley Avenue* is *Jason Mayo Avenue,* and *Rhodes Avenue* is *Herbert Chitepo Avenue.* All these changes were made in 1990, bidding farewell to such famous British colonial names as those of General Gordon, Sir H. M. Stanley, and Cecil Rhodes.

The African continent is traditionally divided into five main geographical regions. It would be as well at this point to define these, as used both here in the Introduction and in the dictionary proper. (Other books may of course have slightly different definitions.)

By *North Africa* is meant the countries of (from west to east) Mauritania, Western Sahara, Morocco, Algeria, Tunisia, Libya, Egypt, and Sudan. In some general contexts, however, the name includes countries whose northern regions lie in the Sahara, such as Mali, Niger, and Chad. Moreover, *Sudan* has an older sense that is much more wide-ranging than the present one.

By *West Africa* is meant (from north to south, coastal countries first, land-locked last) Senegal, Gambia, Guinea-Bissau, Guinea, Sierra Leone, Liberia, Côte d'Ivoire, Ghana, Togo, Benin, Nigeria, Mali, Burkina Faso, and Niger.

By *East Africa* is meant (from north to south) Eritrea, Ethiopia, Djibouti, Somalia, Uganda, Kenya, Rwanda, Burundi, Tanzania, and Zambia.

By *Southern Africa* (as distinct from the country of South Africa, whose name may one day change with the advent of black rule) is meant (from north to south) Mozambique, Zimbabwe, Namibia, Botswana, South Africa, Swaziland, and Lesotho.

The remaining countries comprise *Central Africa,* that is (from north to south), Chad, Cameroon, Central African Republic, Equatorial Guinea, Gabon, Congo, Zaïre, and Angola. Some sources refer to this region as *Equatorial Africa,* since the countries lie across the Equator. Another general name for the same region still sometimes found is *Tropical Africa,* since all of Central Africa (and most of the continent, for that matter) is located between the tropics of Cancer and Capricorn. (Morocco and Tunisia are the sole countries wholly to the north of Cancer, while only Swaziland and Lesotho lie wholly to the south of Capricorn.)

Africa's islands are not usually comprehended in these regions, although the Canaries, for example, could be said to be part of North Africa, the Cape Verde Islands to belong to West Africa, and Madagascar to be included in Southern Africa. The present dictionary casts its net rather generously in this respect, taking in islands some distance from the African continent, such as the Azores in the North Atlantic, Tristan da Cunha in the South Atlantic, and the Seychelles in the Indian Ocean.

North Africa, as mentioned, has in the main the continent's oldest place-names. Many of them have been well documented in ancient writings. As one goes farther south, however, placename documentation is more uncertain and unreliable. Several names of West and Central Africa, for example, have been preserved in a corrupt form. These two regions are supremely those of the great explorers, who themselves recorded the names as best they could, but without the accuracy that linguists would demand today. This was not their fault: they knew little or nothing of African languages, and frequently devised their own often rudimentary methods of transcription.

It is worth noting, in this connection, that although 19th century explorers bestowed a number of European names, they also did their best to record and interpret the indigenous ones. They did not Europeanize at every opportunity, as sometimes supposed. Britain's David Livingstone, for example, is known to have taken pains to preserve the African names he found, and he himself gave only two European names: those of Africa's largest lake (*Lake Victoria*) and greatest waterfall (*Victoria Falls*).

It was thus the colonists, rather than the explorers, who gave the greatest number of European names. The Portuguese, Africa's earliest European colonists in post-Roman times, were responsible for the colorful coastal names in the Gulf of Guinea: *Grain Coast* (modern Liberia), *Gold Coast* (Ghana), *Ivory Coast* (Côte d'Ivoire), *Slave Coast* (Nigeria, Benin, Togo). The names are so familiar that they still appear on modern maps. They are not only evocative, but descriptive in an entirely commercial sense: from one stretch of coast our ancestors got grain (more precisely, pepper); from another, gold; from a third, ivory; from a fourth, slaves.

While North Africa has in the main retained its original names, even if in altered form, Central and Southern Africa have known three types of names over the centuries. First, there were the indigenous or native names. Then, there were the European names. Finally, there was a reversion to indigenous names, either the original ones or those that were entirely new.

Herewith, following a trail from north to south, is an examination in rather more detail of what sorts of names are to be found in this vast and varied continent.

1. North Africa. Most placenames of North Africa are either Arabic in origin or, especially in the west of the region, Berber. However, along the Mediterranean coast are found arabicized or berberized versions of names that were originally Latin, Greek, or Phoenician. Examples are *Awjidah* (originally *Augila*), *Cherchell* (*Caesarea*), *Gabes* (*Takape*), *Labdah* (*Leptis Magna*), *Nabeul* (*Neapolis*), *Sbeïtla* (*Sufetula*), *Sfax* (*Safaqis*), *Tangier* (*Tingis*), *Tolmeta* (*Ptolemaïs*), and *Tunis* (*Tunes*). The Graeco-Latin name *Hippo Regius* can be still just detected behind that of *Bône* (now *Annaba*), while the Greek *Hippo Diarrhytus* came to give modern *Bizerta*. In some cases the meaning of the earlier form of the name is known, in which case that of the present name is also known. In other cases it is not, and the present form of the name must equally remain uninterpreted. *Africa* itself was originally the name of a Roman province formed in the 2nd century BC from territory around Carthage. (The name itself dates from much earlier than this, however.)

The true Berber or Arabic original names appeared next. They include such names of towns and cities as *Agadir, Algiers, Fès, Marrakech, Oran, Rabat,* and the many names of rivers (beginning *Oued* or *Wadi*) and mountains (beginning *Jebel, Jabal* or *Gebel*).

Most of the modern European names along the Mediterranean seaboard have now reverted to Arabic. Among them were a number of French names, such as *Ferryville* (now *Menzel Bourguiba*), *La Goulette* (*Halq El-Oued*), *Louis Gentil* (*Youssoufiya*), *Orléansville* (*El-Asnam*), *Petitjean (Sidi Kacem*), and *Philippeville* (*Skikda*).

In Egypt the situation is somewhat similar. The oldest names are either ancient Egyptian, classical Greek, or Coptic. Ancient Egyptian names, like the classical names of other North African countries, now often appear in altered form. Among them are *Aswan* (originally *Syene*) and *Asyut* (*Siut*). Some apparently Greek names are actually of ancient Egyptian origin. One famous example is *Memphis* (originally *Mennefer*).

Greek names appeared after the 4th century BC. Examples are *Alexandria, Busiris, Cynopolis, Heliopolis,* and *Philae.* They were followed by Coptic names, such as *Coptos* (modern *Qift*), *Faiyûm, Girga,* and *Isna.* Finally, after the 10th century, came the Arabic names of Egypt, such as *Cairo, El Mansura, El Minya, Luxor,* and *Port Said.*

Most of Egypt's oldest names appear in the Nile valley (Upper Egypt) and delta (Lower Egypt), as one would expect. In the rest of the country, Arabic names predominate, many beginning with *Ain* (spring, well), *Bir* (oasis), *Gebel* (mountain, especially between the Nile and the Red Sea), and *Wadi* (watercourse). Egypt's newest names include those of towns and ports that have developed along the Suez Canal: *Ismailia, Port Fuad, Port Said, Port Taufiq.* These are all regnal names.

Further south, the placenames of the Sahara are again distinctive. Unsurprisingly, they mainly apply to natural features such as deserts and oases, and in the south of the region are mostly Arabic, in the west are Berber (often Tuareg, a dialect of Berber), and in the east are Sudanic (Mande, Hausa, and the like). Examples of Berber names are *Adrar, Ahaggar, Aïr* (mountains), *Tamanrasset, Tekouyat, Tesaret* (watercourses), *Tamandouririt* (well), *Tabankurt, Tin Tires, Tin Zouatene* (oases and villages).

The many Arabic names in the Sahara can readily be recognized by the generic words that begin them, such as *Ain, Bir* and *Hassi,* denoting various types of spring or well. As mentioned, watercourses often have names beginning *Oued* or *Wadi,* and mountains begin with *Jabal* or *Gebel.* (Hence, though not in Africa, the name of *Gibraltar,* "mountain of Tariq.")

The few French names in the Sahara, mainly those of military posts, have now almost all become Arabic or Berber, such as *Fort Charlet* (now *Djanet*), *Fort de Polignac* (*Illizi*), *Fort Flatters* (*Bordj Omar Driss*), and *Fort Gouraud* (*Fdérik*).

2. West Africa. Where North Africa is generally ancient and historic, West Africa is relatively recent and "young." The colonial history of countries such as Senegal and Sierra Leone dates from the 15th century, when they were invaded by the Portuguese. Liberia's colonial history began only in the 19th century, as did that of Burkina Faso, formerly Upper Volta.

Many placenames of West Africa are Sudanic, a term that includes languages that are both mutually related and those that have little or nothing in common. Even so, despite their bewildering variety, several languages, or language groups, spoken in the region share common features. They include Fula, Fulbe, Hausa, Mande, Wolof, Yoruba, and many others.

A particular feature of West Africa is the high proportion of settlement names derived either from natural features such as rivers and mountains, or from ethnic groups such as races and tribes. *Kaduna* and *Sokoto,* in Nigeria, are thus names of both a town and a river. The original name is frequently also extended to an administrative region, whether historic, such as a kingdom or sultanate, or modern, such as a province. *Sokoto* is a case in point. The town of the name existed as early as the 12th century. It was then applied to the caliphate established in 1814 (and existing until 1903), and in modern times is the name of a state. *Bukuru,* also in Nigeria, is similarly a settlement that took its name from a mountain. It is not always easy to determine whether a natural feature gave its name to a people or tribe, or the other way around. Again in Nigeria, *Ankwe* is the name of both a river and tribe (and of its language). Although the expected transfer of a name is from a natural object to the people who live by it, as for many of the aboriginal peoples of America, there is no logical reason why the transfer should not be from people to place, especially when, as usually, one group of people is named by another, who then name the river that flows through their territory for that same people.

Berber names are also found in West Africa, though not commonly. Two of the most familiar names in the region, *Niger* and *Timbuktu,* are Tuareg in origin.

There are still a number of European names in West Africa, especially in coastal countries. *Sierra Leone, Liberia,* and *Côte d'Ivoire* are three contiguous countries that have all retained their European names. Liberia itself still has many names of English (more precisely, American) origin, especially along its coast, such as *Buchanan, Greenville, Harper, Marshall, Maryland, Monrovia,* and *Robertsport.* Ports with European names in neighboring countries are Sierra Leone's *Freetown,* Côte d'Ivoire's *Bingerville,* Ghana's *Cape Coast,* Benin's *Novo Porto,* and Niger's *Lagos* and *Port Harcourt.* Inland, however, only African names are found.

A distinctive feature of West Africa is the representation of Muslim placenames, many of them imported from holy Islamic cities in Arabia and the Middle East. Islam spread south of the Sahara from the 11th century, and remains the dominant religion in West Africa today. The name of *Medina,* Islam's second holiest city, is found in many parts of West Africa, such as *Médina* in Senegal, *Meedine* in Mali, and *Madina* in Guinea-Bissau. (Many North African towns have *Medina* as the name of their oldest quarter, often surrounding a Great Mosque, with more recent districts still retaining their European colonial name, such as *Franceville* and *Lafayette,* Tunis.) The Arabic name of Egypt, *miṣr,* is represented in *Missira* and *Missirah,* Senegal, while *Kairouan,* a holy Muslim city in Tunisia, is represented by *Kerewan,* Gambia, and *Kérouané,* Guinea. *Basra,* in Iraq, has had its name transferred to West Africa and preserved in *Boussoura,* Guinea. Examples of general names given under Islamic influence are those of *Darsalami,* Burkina Faso (identical with *Dar es Salaam,* Tanzania), and *Yélimané,* Mali.

3. East Africa. In Eritrea, Ethiopia, Djibouti, and Somalia there are very few European placenames. Most names here are either Ethiopic, in such languages as Amharic and Tigrinya, or Cushitic, in such languages as Somali and Beja.

Ethiopic and Cushitic placenames have still not been widely researched, though Cushitic languages have certain features in common with Arabic. Ethiopia's capital, *Addis Ababa,* is a well-known example of an Amharic name, as is *Djibouti.* Cushitic names in Somalia are, among others, *Buqda Kosar, El-Berde, Garba Harre, Semmade,* and *Wargalo.*

The proximity of these countries to the Arab world means that there are a fair number of Arabic names in this part of Africa. Among them are the various coastal names beginning *Ras* (point, cape), such as *Ras el Bir,* Djibouti, and names such as *Bender Beila* and *Bender Kassim,* Somalia, and *Ali Sabieh,* Djibouti. *Ethiopia* and *Eritrea* are both Greek names.

In most other countries of East Africa, as also in Central and Southern Africa, the prevailing language group is Bantu. One of the most familiar Bantu languages in Swahili, spoken in Kenya and Tanzania. Others are Rwanda, spoken in Rwanda and Burundi (in which it is known as Rundi), and Bemba, Tonga, and Nyanja, spoken in Zambia, where the official language is actually English. Typical well-known Swahili names are *Dodoma, Kampala, Kilimanjaro,* and *Nairobi.* As in West and Central Africa, many towns are named for the rivers on which they lie or the mountains by which they arose. *Dodoma* is one of the latter type. Similarly, many places are named for their indigenous peoples. *Uganda* is named for the *Ganda* people, as is that country's former kingdom and present administrative region, *Buganda.* (*U-* and *Bu-* in these names are Bantu prefixes meaning "land." The latter prefix is also seen in the name of *Burundi,* and in that of its capital, *Bujumbura,* formerly *Usumbura.*)

Arabic names are occasionally found in these southern countries of East Africa, two well-known examples being *Dar es Salaam* and *Zanzibar.* European names are not widely found, though *Lake Victoria*'s quintessentially English name remains, together with a scattering of other English names around it, such as *Port Victoria* in Kenya, *Speke Gulf* in Tanzania, and *Port Bell* in Uganda.

4. Southern Africa. Southern Africa contains the highest proportion of European names, almost all of them in South Africa. The two European languages most obviously represented here are English and Afrikaans, the latter being a form of Dutch. There are also a number of German names. Until relatively recently, European names were also commonly found in other countries of Southern Africa, notably Portuguese in Mozambique, and English in what are now Zimbabwe and Zambia (the former Rhodesia). Several German names are still on the map in Namibia.

Examples of familiar English names in Southern Africa include *East London, Kimberley, Ladysmith,* and *Port Elizabeth,* all in South Africa. In Zimbabwe a few English names remain for less important places, such as those of several settlements in the vicinity of the capital, Harare (formerly *Salisbury*): *Bromley, Concession, Glendale, Maryland, Trelawney, Wellesley,* and others.

Well-known places with Afrikaans names in South Africa include *Bloemfontein, Johannesburg, Pietermaritzburg, Stellenbosch,* and *Witwatersrand. Cape Town,* with its English name, is equally known by its Dutch name, *Kaapstad.* Some names were imported direct from the Netherlands, such as *Dordrecht, Middelburg,* and *Utrecht.* Others came from Germany: *Hamburg, Hanover, Heidelberg.* German names still current in Namibia include *Lüderitz, Maltahöhe, Mariental, Steinhausen,* and *Warmbad.* Here also, however, there are Afrikaans names, such as *Fransfontein, Keetmanshoop,* and *Windhoek,* the capital.

The oldest names in South Africa are the non-Bantu ones of the San (Bushmen) and Khoikhoin (Hottentots). These are mainly found in the west of the country, such as *Kakamas, Keimoes, Koekanaap, Nababeep,* and the well-known *Karoo,* the semidesert region in Cape Province. Bantu names are mostly in the center and east of South Africa, and include Sotho names such as *Clocolan* and *Mahwelereng,* and Xhosa names such as *Umtata* and *Umzimkulu.* There are also Zulu names in the southeast, such as *Amanzimtoti, Empangeni, Eshowe, Ixopo,* and *Umlazi.* Expectedly, Bantu names are most common in the various bantustans, or Bantu homelands, so that Tswana names such as *Mafikeng, Mmabatho, Pudumong,* and *Taung* are in *Bophuthatswana,* a name that itself means "gathering of the Tswana." Tswana names also predominate in *Botswana,* as the country's name implies. Rare exceptions are English *Francistown* and Afrikaans *Kalkfontein.*

Swaziland and Lesotho, as their names similarly indicate, have mainly Swazi and Sotho names. Examples of Swazi names are *Hlatikulu, Manzini,* and *Siteki*; Sotho names include *Maseru, Matsieng,* and *Thaba Putsoa.*

Mozambique has a preponderance of Bantu names, such as *Inhambane, Manica* (a tribal name), and *Nampula* (the name of a chief). Most placenames in Zimbabwe are also Bantu in origin, such as Ndebele *Bulawayo* or Shona *Gweru.*

5. Central Africa. In the heterogeneous region that is Central Africa, Bantu names are also predominant. Most names that are obviously African, not European, will be found to have originated in a Bantu language. Here belong Angola's *Huambo, Lubango,* and *Moxico,* Cameroon's *Douala* and *Yaoundé* (both ethnic names), and many more in Congo, Zaïre, and other parts of the region. For such a patently "African" territory, it is strange that a handful of major European names have persisted to this day, although most have been superseded by indigenous names. Thus, *Cameroon* itself has a Portuguese name; Congo's capital, *Brazzaville,* is French in origin; and the same country's main seaport, *Pointe-Noire,* is also obviously French. Most curious of all, *Central African Republic* (or *République Centrafricaine,* to give it its French name), actually adopted a European name in place of an African one, *Ubangi-Shari,* on gaining independence in 1958.

* * *

Africa's largest island, Madagascar, has the most esoteric placenames. They are Malagasy in origin, in the language brought to the island by Indonesian traders some time in the first millennium AD. The names are thus not strictly African at all. Many are remarkable for their length. The country's capital is *Antananarivo* (formerly familiar as *Tananarive*), and other names to rival and surpass this are *Fianarantsoa, Amparafarovola,* and *Ambatofinandrahana.* These lengthy names arose as an agglutination of individual words. The elements *Am-* or *An-* that begin many names represent an abbreviation of the demonstrative adverb *any* meaning "[place] where there is" followed by words such as *ràno,* "water," *vàto,* "rock," or *vòhitra,* "mountain," "village." The few European names that remain in Madagascar are those given by French colonists. As on the African continent, they are mostly on coastal sites. They include *Faux Cap* in the south and *Hell-Ville* in the north. Even these do not appear on some modern maps.

Elsewhere round the continental coast, São Tomé e Príncipe and the Cape Verde Islands have retained many Portuguese names, while insular (but not mainland) Equatorial Guinea still has some Spanish ones. The Canary Islands, on the other hand, as provinces of Spain, have mainly Spanish names, such as *Gran Canaria, Las Palmas,* and *Santa Cruz. Tenerife,* on the other hand, has a Guanche, pre–Spanish name.

The 19th century map of colonial Africa was full of territories with European possessive names denoting their particular national tie. Much of West and Central Africa was *French: French West Africa, French Equatorial Africa, French Guinea, French Congo.* Down the eastern side of Africa, from Egypt to South Africa, came other nationalities, such as *Anglo-Egyptian Sudan, British Somaliland, Italian Somaliland, German East Africa.* In the center of the continent was *Belgian Congo;* in West Africa there were *Portuguese Guinea* and *Spanish Guinea.* All these names (as the English equivalents of the national original) were still on the map of Africa in 1914. Today not one such colonial possessive name remains, although a few endured surprisingly long: *Portuguese Guinea* became *Guinea-Bissau* only in 1973. (The other names do not necessarily neatly correspond to those of modern territories.) Where a European country still has an African possession, the territory name will now not indicate as much. This disguises some unsuspected realities. Spain, for example, not only has two provinces in insular Africa (*Canary Islands*) but two toeholds on the continent itself (*Ceuta* and *Melilla,* both on the Moroccan coast).

The Languages of Africa

The many European languages that are still in evidence in some placenames in Africa are easily outnumbered by the hundreds of indigenous African languages that exist, or that are believed to exist.

Informed estimates give a total of 1000 to 2000 languages in Africa. The disparity between these figures is great simply because little is known about many of the languages. It is not even certain whether some of them are true languages, as differentiated from dialects of other languages. Again, a number of languages are known simply by name. Moreover, a single language can be known by different names, given either by its speakers, by neighbors of its speakers, or by Europeans. Thus the language usually known as Fula, spoken in Nigeria, Guinea, and Senegal, is also known as Ful, Fulfulde, or (after the name of its speakers) Fulani. It is also known as Peul, the term favored by the French.

Dated or "politically incorrect" names for languages also persist, as they do for their speakers. What were once known as Hottentots are now usually known as the Khoikhoin, and the Bushmen as the San. Both these peoples speak languages that are part of the Khoisan group, found chiefly around the Kalahari Desert in countries such as Angola and South Africa. Khoisan languages are famous for their "click" consonants, represented in written form by symbols such as "!" and "≠." Hence the unusual appearance of some Southern African placenames when written or printed in these languages.

Bantu languages appear widely in Central and Southern Africa. They number from 300 to 500, and include such familiar languages as Swahili, spoken (as mentioned above) mainly in Tanzania and Kenya, Xhosa, spoken chiefly in the Transkei territory of South Africa, and Zulu, spoken mainly in Natal, South Africa (in Zululand, in fact). Xhosa and Zulu are mutually intelligible though they are usually regarded by their speakers as distinct languages.

In the matter of African language families, one could continue here with terms such as "Benue-Congo" and "Nilo-Hamitic," but these would almost certainly require explanation and illustration. Such terms are anyway themselves subject to modification or supersession. What were formerly spoken of somewhat biblically as "Hamito-Semitic" languages (evoking Ham and Shem, sons of Noah) are now usually referred to ethnically as "Afro-Asiatic," for example. At least this is more readily meaningful.

In the entries that follow, therefore, it is individual languages that are mostly cited, especially when they are the more familiar ones. Where a less familiar African language is involved, or there is uncertainty even about *which* language is involved, reference will often be made to a "local" or "indigenous" language (though not normally a "native" one, as this term, too, is now out of favor).

In the final analysis, what matters is the actual origin and meaning of the name. But since it will have originated in *some* language or other, the matter of language cannot be overlooked altogether. (See also Appendix III, page 222.)

Arrangement of Entries

The entries are designed to be as accessible as possible. They are in alphabetical order, with cross-references part of this order. (Cross-references are provided both for former names that were established for several years, and for alternate spellings or forms of a current name.)

The entry headings give the placename itself followed by a brief descriptive phrase stating its country and, in most cases, geographical location within that country (northern, central, and so on). In the sizeable country of South Africa, the unit for locational purposes is the province. When it comes to the status of an inhabited place, such as a town, city, or village, the descriptor is only general. It uses "city" for a large and important town, "town" for a place of average size, and "village" for a less important or smaller place. Administratively the term may not be correct, so that the place is really a "township," "settlement," "commune," or the like. But the present work is not a geographical gazetteer, and is not designed as such.

The rest of the entry is the account of the name's origin and meaning, as far as it is known, with appropriate historical, topographical, and biographical references. Some names, such as *Cairo,* have a complex history, and in such cases I have aimed to tease out the various chronological and linguistic strands as clearly as possible. Where the origin of the name appears to be anecdotal, I have related the anecdote. Although such origins should be treated with caution (in some entries I have said as much), there is little doubt that some African placenames actually *are* anecdotal—that is, they have evolved from an account of some kind of incident. Even a spoken remark can produce a placename, such as the answer to a (sometimes misunderstood) question.

Spellings and forms of names are in the main those in either *The Times Atlas of the World* or *Webster's New Geographical Dictionary* (see Select Bibliography, page 231).

The Placenames

Abbai. See **Nile.**

Abengourou. *Town, southeastern Côte d'Ivoire.* The name of the town is a French form of *n'pekro,* "I don't like talking." This was the name applied by the Agni people to the peaceful hunting country here, where the town was founded some time in the late 19th century. It later became the capital of the Agni kingdom of Indénié.

Abeokuta. *Town, southwestern Nigeria.* The town, on the east bank of the Ogun River, was founded in about 1830 by Sodeke (Shodeke), a hunter and leader of the Egba, a Yoruba people, as a settlement for refugees from slave hunters in the disintegrating Oyo Empire (see **Oyo**). The fugitives originally gathered in a cave under a mass of porphyry. Hence the name, meaning "refuge among rocks."

Abercorn. See (1) **Mbala,** (2) **Shamva.**

Aberdare Range. *Mountain range, central Kenya.* The mountains were so named in 1884 by the Scottish explorer Joseph Thomson for Henry Austin Bruce, 1st Baron *Aberdare* (1815–1895), president of the Royal Geographical Society and chairman of the National African Company. He took his title from the Welsh town of *Aberdare,* Glamorganshire. The Kikuyu name for the mountains is *Nyandarua,* "drying hide," with reference to their outline.

Aberdeen. *Town, southern Cape Province, South Africa.* The town arose round a church in 1856. The settlement was named in honor of the local minister, the Rev. Andrew Murray, who was born in *Aberdeen,* Scotland.

Abidjan. *City and port, southern Côte d'Ivoire.* The city, the country's capital from 1960 to 1983, was founded in 1903. The story goes that when the first French colonists arrived here, they met some women and asked them where they were. The women, mistaking their question, replied "*T'chan m'bi djan,*" from *m'bi,* "leaves," and *djan,* "to tear," "to cut," that is, "I am coming from cutting leaves" in their Abidji language. The Frenchmen noted the name and wrongly gave it to the new town. The country's present capital is **Yamoussoukro.**

Aboisso. *Town, southeastern Côte d'Ivoire.* The name is a corrupt form of the local name *Ebouisso,* "on the pebbles." At this point the Bia River crosses rapids.

Abomey. *Town, southern Benin.* The town was founded in about 1600 and was the capital of the historic kingdom of the same name. In 1730 the kingdom was renamed **Dahomey,** a name subsequently adopted for the country that is now Benin. The two names may therefore be related, with that of the town perhaps a corruption of *Agbomi,* meaning "inside the rampart," from *agbo,* "rampart," and *mi,* "inside."

Aboukir. *Village, northern Egypt.* The historic locality, famous for its battles of 1799 (when Napoleon defeated the Turks) and 1801 (when Sir Ralph Abercromby defeated the French), has an Arabic name, representing *abū qīr,* from *abū,* "father of," and *qīr,* a man's name. Some authorities, however, see the name as a corruption of its former Libyan name, *Apugit,* of uncertain meaning. The village gave the name of *Aboukir Bay,* also noted for its battles.

Abuja. *Capital of Nigeria.* Transfer of the Nigerian capital from **Lagos** to Abuja, a new city in the center of the country, was completed in 1992. It takes its name from the historic Hausa emirate of *Abuja,* whose own name came from the fortified settlement founded in 1828 near Zuba by *Abu Ja* ("Abu the Red").

Abukir. See **Aboukir.**

Abu Mīna. *Ruined city, northern Egypt.* The ancient site, a historic place of Christian pilgrimage southwest of Alexandria, has an Arabic name meaning literally "father Mīna," with reference to the popular Egyptian saint *Minas,* said to be buried here.

Abu Simbel. *Historic locality, southern Egypt.* The site is famous as that of two temples of Rameses II, which were moved to higher ground in 1966 before the area behind the Aswan Dam was flooded. Its name represents Arabic *abū sunbuli,* from *abū,* "father of," and *sunbuli,* a Muslim man's name meaning "ear of corn."

Abydos. *Ancient town, central Egypt.* The historic site, famous for its many temples and tombs, has a name that ultimately evolved from Egyptian *Ābdūt,* of uncertain meaning. An ancient Greek colony on the Asiatic side of the Hellespont has the same name.

Abyssinia. *Former or alternate name of* **Ethiopia.** The name represents a latinized form of Amharic *hăbăŝa,* itself said to come from the root element *ḥbŝ,* "mixed," referring to the mixed black and white races in this region of Africa. However, this origin has been disputed by some Amharic scholars.

Accra. *Capital of Ghana.* The city, founded in the 16th century, has a name representing a local (Akan) word *n'kran,* "ant," referring to the teeming black ants found in the forests here. The name came to be that of the local people, with the ants probably assuming a totemic function. (The ants bite painfully when attacked: hence the people's adoption of this symbolic warning to outsiders.)

Achoueir. *Village, western Mauritania.* The village, east of the capital, Nouakchott, derives its name from Zenega *achour,* "closure." The reference is to a place that "closes" a valley.

Acorn Hoek. *Village, eastern Transvaal, South Africa.* The name appears to have evolved as a misunderstanding of the original Afrikaans name *Eekhoornhoek,* meaning "squirrel corner."

Adamawa. *Region, West Africa.* The region, in modern Nigeria and Cameroon between the Bight of Bonny and Lake Chad, takes its name from the Fulani warrior and scholar Moddibo *Adama* (died 1848), who founded an emirate here in 1806. (His first name means "learned one," while *Adama* represents the Christian name *Adam,* "man.") The name is also that of the plateau here, and the French form of the name, *Adamoua,* is that of a province in Cameroon (see **Littoral** for the others).

Ad Dakhla. *Town and port, western Western Sahara.* The capital of former Río de Oro was originally known as *Villa Cisneros,* named for the Spanish cardinal and inquisitor Francisco Jiménez de *Cisneros* (1436–1517), who promoted the Spanish campaigns in North Africa of 1505–1510 and who aimed to conquer all North Africa. (His own name came from the small town of *Cisneros,* in north central Spain.) Spanish *villa* here means "commune," "borough," rather than "town" (which is *ciudad*). In 1976 the town assumed its present Arabic name, meaning "the inner." The town is on a peninsula to the west of the inlet (the "inner" sea) known as Bahía de Río de Oro. The name is sometimes found simply as *Dakhla.*

Addis Ababa. *Capital of Ethiopia.* The name represents Amharic *ăddis ăbăba,* "new flower," from *ăddis,* "new," and *ăbăba,* "flower." This was the auspicious name given the settlement by Empress Taitu, wife of Emperor Menelik II, when in 1887 she persuaded her husband to build a new capital near the hot springs at the center of the country in place of the former capital, Entoto, which had been located on a cold, exposed site.

Addo. *Town, southern Cape Province, South Africa.* The town, with its famous elephant national park, has a name that is a European corruption of Khoikhoin (Hottentot) *kadouw,* "river passage," referring to a ford here over the Sundays River.

Adelaide. *Town, southeastern Cape Province, South Africa.* The town arose in 1834 as a military post named *Fort Adelaide* in honor of Queen *Adelaide* (1792–1849), wife of King William IV of England.

Adendorp. *Village, southern Cape Province, South Africa.* Just south of Graaff-Reinet, the village has a name derived from that of N. J. *Adendorff,* the landholder on whose farm it arose in the 1950s.

Ado-Ekiti. *Town, southwestern Nigeria.* The town takes its name from its founders, the *Ekiti* people, a subgroup of the Yoruba.

Adoumri. *Village, northern Cameroon.* The name means "*Adoum*'s village," from a personal name, presumably that of a local (Hausa) chief or leader.

Adrar. *Mountainous region, Sahara Desert, northwestern Africa.* The name, actually that of several different regions, is simply the Berber word for "mountain." Individual mountain chains so named are frequently followed by a distinguishing word, such as *Adrar Souttouf,* "black Adrar," in Western Sahara. See also **Atlas Mountains.**

Afars and Issas. See **Djibouti.**

Africa. *Continent.* The name directly derives from Latin *Africa* or Greek *Aphrikē,* as applied not to the whole present continent but to a region that originally corresponded to modern Tunisia. The ultimate source of the name remains uncertain. Possible etymologies include the following: (1) from Latin *Afer,* plural *Ifri,* the Hamitic name of a Berber tribe; (2) from Arabic *ʿafar,* "dust," "earth"; (3) from the name of *Ifrikos,* the mythical son of the biblical Goliath; (4) from Punic *faraqa,* "share," "colony," a word related to Hebrew *paroq,* "to loose" and Arabic *faraqa,* "to separate." This last origin is supported by the fact that the name was originally applied by the Carthaginians to their territory. Under Roman rule there were three provinces of the name. First, in 146 BC, the Romans replaced the empire of Carthage, in what is now Tunisia, with their own province of *Africa.* This was renamed *Africa Vetus,* "old Africa," when

Caesar conquered Numidia in 46 BC and out of it formed *Africa Nova,* "New Africa." Both provinces were united in 29 BC by Augustus to form a larger province again simply named *Africa.* In AD 297 Diocletian split this province into three: **Byzacium** (or Byzacena), in what is now southern Tunisia, **Tripolitania,** in what is now western Libya, and (once again) *Africa,* corresponding to northern Tunisia. In 320 Tripolitania and Byzacium, though retaining their autonomy, combined as the larger colony of *Africa Proconsularis,* "proconsular Africa." (Latin *proconsul* was the title of the governor of a province.) In 439 the Roman *Africa* that remained was lost to the Vandals.

Africa Nova. See **Africa.**

Africa Proconsularis. See **Africa.**

Africa Vetus. See **Africa.**

Aftout. *Region, western Mauritania.* The name is that of various stretches of sand dunes, usually with a distinguishing addition, such as *Aftout de Faye* or *Aftout de Tassaret. Aftout* itself is a Zenaga word for a broad valley, or extended plain bordered by sand dunes.

Agadez. *Town, central Niger.* The town, founded by the Tuaregs in the early 15th century, has a Tuareg name that translates as "visiting place," from the root word *egdez,* "to visit." The overall sense is "meeting place for travelers." In 1430 it became the capital of the native kingdom of Aïr.

Agadir. *Town and port, southwestern Morocco.* The name may represent either Tuareg *ağādir,* "wall," "bank," or else Phoenician *gadir,* "wall," "fortress," though even these are borrowed words. (If the latter, the name has the same origin as that of the Spanish city of *Cadiz.*) The original name applied to the natural slope on which the old town was built, above the modern port and harbor. See also **Tlemcen.**

Agbokpa. See **Bopa.**

Agulhas, Cape. *Cape, southern Cape Province, South Africa.* Africa's southernmost point takes its name from Portuguese *agulhas,* "needles," referring either to its many sharp rocks and reefs or, according to some accounts, to a magnetic anomaly observed nearby. (A compass needle is said to have pointed due north, without any magnetic deviation, off the coast here.)

Ahaggar. *Mountains, southern Algeria.* The high plateau region in the central Sahara takes its name from the *Ihaggaren,* a Tuareg people who inhabit this part of the desert. Their own name means simply "members." An alternate form of the name is *Hoggar.*

Aha Hills. *Hills, northwestern Botswana.* The name is a San (Bushman) one meaning "small rocks," referring to the terrain here.

Aigams. See **Windhoek.**

Aïn Beïda. *Town, northeastern Algeria.* The town is famous for its springs, the largest of which gave its name, meaning "white spring," from Arabic *ʿain,* "spring," and *bayḍāʾ,* feminine of *abyaḍ,* "white." The present town was founded in 1848 as a French military post under the name *Daoud.*

Aïn Draham. *Village, northwestern Tunisia.* The Arabic name of the village means "spring of money," from *ʿain,* "spring," and *darāhem,* "money." The reference is not to a wishing well but to a spring that is a source of fertility and (relative) prosperity.

Aïn Sefra. *Town, northwestern Algeria.* The town was founded in 1881 as a French garrison and lies either side of the usually dry *Aïn Sefra* River, whose own Arabic name means "yellow spring," from *ʿain,* "spring," and *aṣfar,* feminine *ṣafra,* "yellow." (The Arabic word is not the source of English *saffron,* despite the similarity.)

Ain Sukhna. *Town and port, northern Egypt.* The seaside resort, on the northwestern shore of the Gulf of Suez, has an Arabic name meaning "hot spring," from *ʿain,* "spring," and *sukhn,* feminine *sukhna,* "hot." The reference is to the hot sulfur spring here.

Aioun Abd el Malik. *Village, northern Mauritania.* The name means "springs of Abd el Malik," from Arabic *ʿayūn,* plural of *ʿain,* "spring," "well," and the name of their owner, *Abd el Malik* (literally "servant of the king").

Aioun el Atrouss. *Town, southern Mauritania.* The name means "springs of the goat," from Arabic *ʿayūn,* plural of *ʿain,* "spring," "well," and *ʿatrūs,* "goat."

Aiyetoro. *Town, southwestern Nigeria.* The town arose as a religious settlement of the Nigerian Holy Apostles' Community in 1947, founded by Yorubas. Its name is Yoruba for "the happy city."

Akchar. *Region, western Mauritania.* The region, an expanse of sand dunes, takes its name from *Akchar,* the ancestor of a local desert tribe.

Akhmīm. *Town, east central Egypt.* The town, on the east bank of the Nile, stands on the site of the ancient Egyptian settlement of *Khente-Mim* and takes its present name from this. The reference is apparently to the god *Min,* who was the town's protective deity. Under the Greeks the place was known as *Panopolis,* "city of *Pan.*"

Akjoujt. *Town, western Mauritania.* The name of the town probably means "the little well," from the local word *ghūjuten,* plural of *ghawj,* a term for a small ditch dug to prevent rainwater from seeping into tents.

Aksum. *Town, northern Ethiopia.* The ancient town, former capital of the Aksumite Empire, has a name representing Amharic *ăksum.* The meaning of this is unknown.

Al-Araish. See **Larache.**

Al-Arish. See **El-Arish.**

Albert, Lake. See **Mobutu Sese Seko.**

Albert Edward Nyanza. See Lake **Edward.**

Albertinia. *Town, southern Cape Province, South Africa.* The town was founded in 1900 and takes its name from the Rev. Johannes Rudolph *Albertyn,* a Dutch Reformed Church minister, who planned the establishment of the local church community here.

Albert National Park. See **Virunga Mountains.**

Albert Nile. See **Nile.**

Alberton. *Town, southern Transvaal, South Africa.* The town was established in 1904 and was named for General Hendrik Abraham *Alberts,* chairman of the syndicate of developers.

Alcazarquivir. *City, northern Morocco.* The historic town, famous for the battle of 1508 in which King Sebastian of Portugal was defeated and slain by the Moors, is today also known as *Ksar el Kebir.* This more accurately reflects its original Arabic name, which has become distorted by the Spanish. Its full version is *al-qaṣr al-kebīr,* "the great castle," from *al,* "the," *qaṣr,* "castle," "palace" (from Latin *castrum,* "castle," "fort"), and *kebīr,* "great."

Aleg. *Town, western Mauritania.* The name means "hill slope," from Zenaga *adyeg,* "climbing path."

Alexander Bay. *Town and port, western Cape Province, South Africa.* The town takes its name from the bay here at the mouth of the Orange River. This is itself named for Sir James Edward *Alexander* (1803–1885), the British army officer who in about 1852 mined copper in Namaqualand, floating ore down the river in barges.

Alexandra. *Township, southern Transvaal, South Africa.* The black township, near Johannesburg, developed soon after Johannesburg itself arose in the early 20th century, and is probably named for Queen *Alexandra* (1844–1925), wife of King Edward VII of England.

[1]**Alexandria.** *Port, northern Egypt.* The chief port of Egypt, on the Nile Delta, takes its name from its founder in 332 BC, *Alexander* the Great. Before his time the settlement here was known as *Rhacōtis* or *Rhacōtēs,* of uncertain meaning. The current Arabic form of the city's name is *al-iskandariyya.*

[2]**Alexandria.** *Town, southeastern Cape Province, South Africa.* The town arose in the early 19th century under the name of *Olifantshoek,* "elephants' corner," for the abundance of these animals here. In 1973 the present name was adopted in honor of the Rev. *Alexander* Smith, the Dutch Reformed Church minister who had had charge of the congregation here since 1823.

Al-Fashir. *Town, western Sudan.* The town, now the capital of Darfur province, became that of the Darfur Sultanate in 1790. Its name represents Arabic *al-fāshir,* "the capital."

Algeria. *Republic, northwestern Africa.* The name was introduced only in 1839, following the French possession in 1830 of territory here formerly held by the dey of **Algiers**. This territory was itself named for the city that was its capital and that today is that of the republic.

Algiers. *Capital of Algeria.* The name of the ancient Mediterranean port represents Arabic *al-jazā'ir*, "the islands," from *al,* "the," and *jazā'ir,* plural of *jazīra,* "island." The reference is to the former small islands off the northwest coast of the Bay of Algiers. All but one (La Marine) have now either been connected to the mainland or else obliterated by harbor works and jetties. The city gave the name of its country, **Algeria**. The Roman name of the city was *Icosium,* deriving from the original name of the Phoenician settlement, itself of unknown meaning. *Algiers* was also the name of the former Barbary state here, the predecessor of modern **Algeria**. Hence the same name for city and republic in some languages still today, such as Russian *Alzhir.*

Algoa Bay. *Bay, southern Cape Province, South Africa.* The Portuguese navigator Bartholomeu Dias entered the bay here in 1488 and named it *Angra da Roca*, "rock bay." This name was then superseded by a new Portuguese name, *Bahia da Lagoa*, "lagoon bay," which in turn was corrupted to the present name. For a similar name, see **Maputo**.

Al-Ḥammadah al-Ḥamrā'. *Plateau, northwestern Libya.* The Arabic name is that of a rocky plateau of the Sahara. It means "the red plateau," from *al*, "the," *ḥammadah,* "plateau," and *ḥamra*, feminine of *aḥmar*, "red." The name is also found in the form *Hamada el Homra*.

Alice. *Town, Ciskei, South Africa.* The settlement that had been here since at least 1824 was so named in 1847 in honor of Princess *Alice* (1843–1878), daughter of Queen Victoria.

Alicedale. *Village, southern Cape Province, South Africa.* The village, an important railroad junction, was named for *Alice* Slessor, née *Dale*, wife of the engineer in charge of railway construction here.

Aliwal North. *Town, northeastern Cape Province, South Africa.* The town was founded in 1849 by Sir Harry Smith, governor of the Cape of Good Hope, and named by him to commemorate his victory over the Sikhs in 1846 at *Aliwal*, India. The second word of the name was added later when *Aliwal South* was adopted as the name for what is now **Mossel Bay**.

Aliwal South. See **Mossel Bay**.

Al-Jadida. See **El-Jadida**.

Al-Kharga. See **El-Kharga**.

Al-Kharijah. See **El-Kharga**.

Allanridge. *Town, northwestern Orange Free State, South Africa.* The gold-mining town was laid out in 1950 and takes its name from *Allan* Roberts, a pioneer of the goldfields in the region and the engineer who sank the first borehole for gold on the ridge here.

Almadies, Cape. *Cape, western Senegal.* The cape, as the extreme tip of the peninsula forming Cape Vert, is the westernmost point of Africa. It was discovered by the Portuguese in the 15th century, and takes its name from Portuguese *almadia*, "canoe," presumably with reference to its shape.

Al-Marj. *Town, northeastern Libya.* The present town grew around a Turkish fort built in 1842 on the site of the 6th century BC Greek colony of *Barca* (known to the Italians, who developed the modern town, as *Barce*). This was captured by the Arabs in about AD 642 and given its present name, meaning "the meadow," from Arabic *al*, "the," and *marj*, "meadow." The name properly relates to the plain near the Mediterranean coast where the town is located.

Al-Qantara. See **El Qantara**.

Alto Molocue. *Town, northern Mozambique.* The second word of the name is that of the river here, and is based on the Makua word *moloki*, meaning simply "river." The first word is Portuguese *alto*, "high," "upper," referring to the location of the town on the upper reaches of the river.

Amabele. *Village, southeastern Cape Province, South Africa.* The name means "breasts," from Xhosa *ama-*, a plural indicator, and *i bele*, "the breast." The reference is to two round hills nearby.

Amalia. *Town, southwestern Transvaal, South Africa.* The town was founded in 1927 and named for Mrs. *Amalia* Faustmann, a well-known local church figure.

Amanzimtoti. *Town, southern Natal, South Africa.* The coastal town is said to take its name from a remark made by the Zulu chief Shaka in 1828 when camping with his army nearby: "*kanti amanza mtoti*," "So, the water is sweet." The name was originally that of the river here and was subsequently transferred to the town.

Amarna. See **Tell el Amarna.**

Amatikulu. *Town, eastern Natal, South Africa.* The name probably derives from the old Lala word *matigulu*, literally "water that scrapes away." The reference is to the eroding or washing away of crops here by the waters of the Tugela River when they flood.

Amatole Range. *Mountain range, Ciskei, South Africa.* The name represents the plural of Xhosa *i tole,* "the weaned calf," referring to the outlines of the peaks here.

Ambatofinandrahana. *Village, south central Madagascar.* The village lies in a mountainous region and takes its Malagasy name from its location. The meaning is "[place] where there is chiselled rock."

Ambatolampy. *Town, central Madagascar.* The town, on the eastern heights of the Ankaratra mountains, has a Malagasy name describing its location, meaning "[place] where there are flat rocks."

Ambohimanga Atsimo. *Village, southwestern Madagascar.* The name means "southern place of the blue mountain," with *Ambohi-* a contraction of Malagasy *any vòhitra*, "where the mountain is which [is]," followed by *mànga*, "blue," and *atsìmo*, "south." This last word distinguishes the place from another *Ambohimanga*, the former capital, 11 miles (17 km) north of the present capital, Antananarivo.

Amboseli National Park. *National park, southern Kenya.* The game reserve, on the border with Tanzania, takes its name from the lake at its center. The lake's own name derives from the Maasai word for "salt dust." The lake is a seasonal one, and for much of the year is a dried-up alluvial bed of soda deposits.

Ambriz. *Town and port, northwestern Angola.* The name appears to be connected in some way with that of **Nzeto**, further up the coast, which was originally known as *Ambrizete*. Ambriz arose from the fort built by the Portuguese here in 1790.

Ambrizete. See **Nzeto**.

Amersfoort. *Town, southeastern Transvaal, South Africa.* The town arose round a church built here in 1876 and was named for *Amersfoort* in the Netherlands, perhaps because it was located southeast of the capital, Pretoria, as its Dutch namesake is with regard to Amsterdam.

Aminuis. *Village, eastern Namibia.* The name is of Khoikhoin (Hottentot) origin and is said to mean "ostrich cloaca," presumably for a local waterhole thought to resemble one.

Amirante Islands. *Island group, southwest of Seychelles, Indian Ocean.* The islands were discovered in 1502 by an expedition led by the Portuguese navigator Vasco da Gama, appointed admiral that year, and named for him as *Ilhas de Almirante*, "admiral's islands."

Amoukrouz. *Region, western Mauritania.* The region is a plain to the east of the capital, Nouakchott. Its name means literally "sorrowful," and refers to an inhospitable stretch of land, where the soil is barren and the water salty.

Amparafaravola. *Village, north central Madagascar.* The name represents Malagasy words meaning literally "where a silver bedstead is," referring to a prominent local rock.

Amsterdam. *Town, southeastern Transvaal, South Africa.* The town was founded as a settlement for Scottish immigrants in 1867 and was originally called *Roburnia,* for Scotland's national poet, *Robert Burns.* In 1882 the name was changed to its present form, for the Dutch capital, "in recognition of the old Motherland's sympathetic attitude towards the Republic during the first Anglo-Boer War."

Androy. *Region, southern Madagascar.* The Malagasy name of the upland region means "[place] where there are thorn bushes."

Aného. *Coastal town, southern Togo.* The town was earlier known by the name of *Petit Popo,* by contrast with **Grand Popo**, to the east in southwest Benin. Its present name means "*Ane* dwellings." The Ane, a local people, came here from what is now Cape Coast in southern Ghana.

Anfa. See **Casablanca.**

Anglo-Egyptian Sudan. See **Sudan.**

Angoche. *Town, southeastern Mozambique.* The coastal town is named for the island of *Angoche* that lies to the south of it. This takes its own name from the local *Akoti* people, who themselves were named for *Akote*, the sheikh who held power here in medieval times. The town, with its Portuguese form of the name, was founded in 1685 and in the late 19th century was renamed *Vila António Enes*, for the Portuguese dramatist *António Enes* (1848–1901). In the 1970s the original name was readopted.

Angola. *Republic, southwestern Africa.* The country is named for *N'gola*, the hereditary title of the local Bantu ruler of the territory of Ndongo (former southern modern Angola) in the 15th century, when the region was colonized by the Portuguese. Portuguese West Africa was named *Angola* in 1914.

Angra do Heroísmo. *Town and port, Terceira, Azores.* The town, on the south coast of the island, has a Portuguese name that was originally just *Angra*, "bay." The words *do Heroísmo*, "of heroism," were added subsequently to commemorate the island's resistance to the Spanish invasion of 1580–1582.

Angra Pequena. See **Lüderitz.**

Annaba. *Town and port, northeastern Algeria.* The present name has evolved from Arabic *madīnat al-ʿunnāb*, "town of the jujube" (a spiny tree with dark red, edible fruits), given the settlement in the 13th century. The surrounding region was long covered by a small forest of jujube trees. The French colonial name of the city was *Bône*. This was a corruption of the Roman name, *Hippo*, genitive *Hipponis*, which represented Greek *Hippōn*, from *hippōn*, "stable," in turn from *hippos*, "horse." Its full Roman name was *Hippo Regius*, "royal Hippo," with reference to the royal stables of Numidian princes formerly here.

Annobón. *Island, Equatorial Guinea.* The island, in the Gulf of Guinea, was discovered by the Portuguese in 1471. It takes its name from Old Portuguese *anno bom*, "New Year" (literally "good year"), since the Portuguese first landed here on New Year's Day, January 1, 1474. From 1973 to 1979 it was known as *Pagalu*, a Creole name meaning "papa cockerel," from Spanish *papá*, "papa," "daddy," and *gallo*, "cockerel," "rooster." The cockerel was the symbol of Equatorial Guinea's president Francisco Macías Nguema in the presidential elections of September 1968. The name reverted to its Portuguese original in the year of his execution (1979).

Antananarivo. *Capital of Madagascar.* The name is Malagasy in origin, and means "town of the thousand," from *an-*, placename prefix (standing for *any*, literally "where there is"), *tanàna*, "town," and *arìvo*, "thousand." The reference may be to a thousand inhabitants, or to a thousand homesteads or compounds, originally detached settlements on the slopes of the long ridge on which the city stands. "Thousand" here, in a typical Oriental style, simply means "many."

Antongil Bay. *Inlet, northeastern Madagascar.* The bay is said to take its name from that of *Antonio Gil*, the Portuguese captain who discovered it in the early 16th century.

António Enes. See **Angoche.**

Antseranana. *Town and port, northern Madagascar.* The Malagasy name of the town means literally "[place] where there is a port," from *an-*, placename prefix (See **Antananarivo**) and *serànana,* "port." The town's former name (to 1977) was *Diégo-Suarez,* a combination of the names of *Diego* Dias, the Portuguese captain who discovered Madagascar in 1500, and Hernán *Suárez,* the Spanish admiral who landed here in 1506.

Antsirabé. *Town, central Madagascar.* The Malagasy name means "[place] where there is much salt." The thermal springs here have made the town a popular health resort.

Aouker. *Region, south central Mauritania.* The extensive desert region derives its name from Zenaga *éouguer,* "great sand dune."

Apollinaris Magna. See **Edfu.**

Arabian Desert. *Desert, eastern Egypt.* The name applies to the northeastern part of the Sahara, between the Nile, the Gulf of Suez, and the Red Sea. It is so called for its proximity to *Arabia,* the great peninsula between the Red Sea and the Persian Gulf. This is itself named for the *Arabs,* the Semitic people who spread throughout the Middle East, North Africa and Spain during the 7th and 8th centuries AD. Their own name is traditionally interpreted as "tent-dweller," implying a nomadic people.

Aranos. *Village, eastern Namibia.* The original name of the village was *Arahoab.* This was then altered to its present form in order to avoid confusion with **Aroab.** The new name is a blend of *Arahoab* and *Nossob,* the latter being the name of the river here.

Arguin. *Island, western Mauritania.* The name is that of an island, cape *(Cap d'Arguin),* and bay *(Baie d'Arguin)* to the south of Nouadhibou, near the border with Western Sahara. It may well be a form of the Tuareg word meaning "fortified wall" that gave the name of **Agadir,** Morocco, although some authorities relate it to *argan,* the oil-yielding seeds of a hardwood tree native to Morocco. The island was discovered by the Portuguese in 1443.

Argungu. *Town, northwestern Nigeria.* The town, originally known as *Birnin Lelaba dan Badau* ("walled town of Lelaba dan Badu") was renamed as now in 1827 when it became the capital of the emirate of the same name. The name is said to represent the Fulani (Peul) words *a yi gungu,* "let us regroup," or *ar sunyi gungu,* "alas, they have regrouped," referring to the frequent invasions made by these people, and their equally frequent repulsions. But these explanations are almost certainly apocryphal.

Ariamsvlei. *Village, southeastern Namibia.* The first part of the name represents Khoikhoin (Hottentot) *≠ari am,* "raisin bush" *(Grewia).* (The unusual character denotes a click.) The second part is Afrikaans *vlei,* "swamp."

Aribinda. *Village, northern Burkina Faso.* The name derives from the Songhay words *har,* "man," and *windi,* "enclosure." The local people had come here from a village near Gao, a walled town. They therefore built a wall round their new home and gave it a name describing them as the "people of the enclosed place."

Aris. *Village, central Namibia.* The village, south of the capital, Windhoek, has a name of Khoikhoin (Hottentot) origin said to refer to a type of edible root found locally.

Aroab. *Village, southeastern Namibia.* The name is a Khoikhoin

(Hottentot) one, representing *≠aro,* "thorn-tree" *(Ziziphys mucronatus)* and *!ab,* "river." (The unusual characters denote clicks.)

Arsinoë. See **El Faiyûm.**

Artur de Paiva. See **Matala.**

Arusha. *Town, northern Tanzania.* The name is that of the *Arusha* tribe, indigenous to the region. The meaning of their own name is uncertain. The region here was established as an administrative unit in 1963 as the *Northern Region.* It was then renamed for the town as the *Arusha Region.*

Aruwimi. *River, northern Zaïre.* The river, a tributary of the Congo (Zaïre), has a local name that probably means "big open water," from *ba,* "big" (literally "father of"), *ru* or *uru,* "open" (literally "outstanding" or "sunny"), and *hime,* "water."

Asab. *Village, south central Namibia.* The name is of Khoikhoin (Hottentot) origin and means "new place."

Ascension. *Island, South Atlantic.* The island was discovered by the Portuguese navigator João da Nova Castela on June 1, 1508, *Ascension* Day, and is named for this festival. Ascension lies northwest of **St. Helena**, an island that da Nova had already discovered and named six years previously. Ascension remained uninhabited until claimed by Britain in 1815.

Asfi. See (1) **Fès,** (2) **Ifni,** (3) **Safi.**

Ashanti. *Region, central Ghana.* The administrative region, a former kingdom, takes its name from its indigenous people, the *Ashanti,* their own name meaning "united in war."

Asilah. *Town and resort, northern Morocco.* The seaside resort, south of Tangier, was founded by the Phoenicians and was long known as *Zili,* from a Semitic root word meaning "beauty."

Asir, Ras. *Headland, eastern Somalia.* The northeasternmost (but not quite easternmost) cape in the African continent has a name that means "*Asir* headland," *Asir* being a name for southern Arabia (now southwestern Saudi Arabia and Yemen), opposite which it lies. The cape's former name was *Guardafui,* which through an association with Portuguese *guarda,* "protection," or French *gardez-vous,* "look out," was popularly taken to refer to the dangers to shipping here. However, the name in fact represents Arabic *ghard,* a word for a stretch of sand dunes, and *Hafun,* the name of the district here, preserved in that of Ras **Hafun**, to the south (the actual easternmost cape). A poetic name for the headland was *Cape of Perfumes,* for the spices found here. See also **Cinnamon Coast**.

Asmara. *Capital of Eritrea.* The city has an Amharic name, from *āsmăra,* meaning "flowering wood" in the Tigrinya language.

Assegaaibos. *Town, southern Cape Province, South Africa.* The town, near the coast west of Humansdorp, has a name that is a corruption of *Assegai Bosch.* This was the name of the farm on which the town arose. The meaning is "assegai wood," from *assegai,* the tree *Curtisia faginea,* the wood of which is used for making spears, and Afrikaans *bosch,* "wood."

Aswan. *Ancient town, southeastern Egypt.* The present form of the name represents its Egyptian original, *Suānit,* "market." The historic town is mentioned in the Bible as *Syene* (Ezekiel 29:10). It was this town that gave the name of the famous *Aswan* Dam, built on the Nile River in 1902. In 1971 the Aswan High Dam (Arabic *as-sudd al-ʿalī,* literally "the dam the high") was opened 4 miles (6 km) above it.

Asyut. *City, central Egypt.* The city, on the west bank of the Nile, stands on the site of the ancient Egyptian settlement of *Syut,* a name presumably referring to a local deity. It was a center of the worship of the wolf-headed god Wepwawet, as a result of which it was known to the Greeks as *Lycopolis,* "wolf city."

Atar. *Town, western Mauritania.* The name represents Berber *adrar,* "mountain." The town lies at the southern end of the **Adrar** mountains.

Athiémé. *Village, southwestern Benin.* The village has a local name meaning "under the white trees," from Fon *ati hié,* "white trees," and *mé,* "under." The reference is to the *samba (Triplochiton scleroxyton).*

Atlas Mountains. *Mountain system, North Africa.* The mountains, between the Mediterranean and the Sahara, have a name that is generally associated with that of *Atlas,* the mythological giant who held up the sky, since that is what the peaks themselves appear to do. In late mythology, Atlas is said to be the king of this part of northwestern Africa, which is also not far from the supposed submerged land of *Atlantis,* said to have sunk in the *Atlantic* to the west of the Straits of Gibraltar. All these names are thus apparently interrelated. However, the arabicized Berber name for the mountains is *Daren,* representing a shortened form of Berber *adràr n'idràren,* "mountain of mountains," and this may possibly lie behind the name, since *atl-* and *adr-* are phonologically related. Cf. **Adrar**.

Auas Mountains. *Mountain range, central Namibia.* The range, south of the capital, Windhoek, has a name of Khoikhoin (Hottentot) origin said to refer to a type of tree growing locally and bearing small red berries.

Augrabies. *Village, western Cape Province, South Africa.* The village takes its name from the falls on the Orange River here near the border with Namibia. The origin is in Khoikhoin (Hottentot) *aughrabies* or *aukoerebis,* meaning "place of noise." The missionary George Thompson came on the falls in 1824 and proposed calling them *King George's Cataract.* The name never caught on, however. Also here is the *Augrabies Falls National Park.*

Augusto Cardoso. See **Metangula.**

Auob. *River, Namibia.* The seasonal river, a tributary of the Nossob in the east of the country, has a name of Khoikhoin (Hottentot) origin meaning "bitter river." The former German name for the watercourse, translating this, was *Gross Bitter Fluss.*

Aurora. *Village, southwestern Cape Province, South Africa.* The village, north of Cape Town, was founded in 1906 and romantically named for the Roman goddess of the dawn.

Aus. *Village, southwestern Namibia.* The village, east of Lüderitz, has a Nama name meaning "place of snakes," referring to the snakes kept here by the Khoikhoin (Hottentots).

Avontuur. *Town, southern Cape Province, South Africa.* The village takes its name from the farm on which it was founded. The word is Afrikaans for "adventure," denoting a pioneering enterprise.

Azania. See **South Africa.**

Azemmour. *Town and port, northwestern Morocco.* The historic town, which played an important part in the Portuguese occupation of neighboring El-Jadida, has a name of Berber origin meaning "wild olive tree."

Azores. *Island group, North Atlantic.* The archipelago, comprising ten volcanic islands off the coast of Portugal, takes its name from Portuguese *açor,* "goshawk" *(Accipiter gentilis),* a bird found in abundance here by the Portuguese when they discovered the islands in 1427. See also individual islands: **Corvo, Faial, Flores, Formigas, Graciosa, Pico, Santa Maria, São Jorge, São Miguel, Terceira.**

Azrou. *Town, north central Morocco.* The town has a name of Berber origin, meaning "rock," referring to the massive outcrop of rock that still stands near the town's main square.

Babanango. *Village, northeastern Natal, South Africa.* The name has the following legendary origin. The young child of a Zulu chief strayed from his parents' kraal and became missing. A search party was sent out, and one of its members, sighting him, exclaimed *"Baba, nango!"* "Father, there he is!" The village was actually founded near the kraal of the Zulu chief Dingane.

Bab el Mandeb. *Strait connecting Red Sea with Gulf of Aden.* The strait, between the Arabian peninsula and East Africa, opposite the border between Ethiopia and Djibouti, has a name representing Arabic *bāb al-mandab,* "gate of the tears," from *bāb,* "gate," *al,* "the," and *mandab,* "tears," "lamentations," from *nadaba,* "to weep." The reference is to the potential danger to shipping here.

Bab el Oued. *Northern district of Algiers, Algeria.* The name represents Arabic *bāb al-wād,* "gate of the river," from *bāb,* gate, *al,* "the," and *wād,* "river," "river bed." This is descriptive of the district's original location, at the mouth of a small stream.

Badoumbé. *Village, western Mali.* The village is on the Bakoy River, upstream from **Bafoulabé.** Its Mande name means "meeting-place of the depth of the river," referring to its location at the point where the river becomes navigable.

Badplaas. *Town, eastern Transvaal, South Africa.* The Afrikaans name means "bathing place," and refers to the hot sulfur springs here that also gave the indigenous name of the place: *Emanzana,* "healing waters."

Bafata. *Town, central Guinea-Bissau.* The town is located at the confluence of two rivers, as its name indicates, from Mande *ba,* "river," and *fata,* "confluence." Cf. **Bafoulabé.**

Bafilo. *Town, northern Togo.* The town is said to take its name from the following incident. In the late 18th or early 19th century, Gonja warriors were returning to Tamale, now in northern Ghana. Although tired, they dared not ask their chief if they could stop to rest. The chief's horse then stopped to urinate. The warriors took the chance to rest, and finding the location pleasant, set up a camp which they called *Gobangafol,* from *banga,* "horse," and *mbofol,* "urine." This subsequently became *Gobafilo* then finally *Bafilo,* as now.

Bafing. *River, western Mali.* The river, a headstream of the **Bafoulabé,** has a Bambara name meaning "black river." Cf. **Bakoy; Baoulé.**

Bafoulabé. *Town, western Mali.* The town is on the Senegal River at the confluence of its headstreams, the Bafing and the Bakoy, the latter having the Baoulé as its chief tributary. The Bambara name refers to this location, and means "confluence of two rivers," from *ba,* "river," *foula,* "two," and *bé,* to meet." Downstream from Bafoulabé is **Badoumbé.**

Bagamoyo. *Town and port, northeastern Tanzania.* The town, on the coast opposite Zanzibar, has a name said to represent the local (Kisaramo) words *buwaga mioyo,* "peaceful heart." The reference is supposedly to travelers, who were grateful to reach the coast here after difficult and dangerous journeys through the hinterland.

Bagoé. *River, southern Mali.* The river, rising in Côte d'Ivoire as a tributary of the **Bani,** has a name that means "white river." It is thus of the same origin as that of the **Bakoy.**

Bahr al-Ghazal. *River, southwestern Sudan.* The river, the chief western affluent of the Nile, has a name that represents Arabic *baḥr al-ghazāl,* "river of the gazelles," from *baḥr,* "sea," "river," *al,* "the," and *ghazāl,* "gazelle." (The English word for the animal derives from the Arabic, through Old French.) The name is also that of a province here.

Bahr al-Jebel. *River, southern Sudan.* The name is used for that section of the Nile between Nimule, in the south, on the border with Uganda, and Malakai, in the east. It represents Arabic *baḥr al-jabal,* "river of the mountain," from *baḥr,* "sea," "river," *al,* "the," and *jabal,* "mountain." The reference is to the mountains in the southern Sudan.

Bahr az-Zaraf. *River, south central Sudan.* The river, a tributary of the Nile, has a name representing Arabic *baḥr az-zarāf,* "river of the giraffes," from *baḥr,* "sea," "river," *al,* "the" (here *az* before *z*), and *zarāfah,* "giraffe." (The English word for the animal derives from the Arabic, through Italian.)

Bahr Yusef. *Canal, northern Egypt.* The Arabic name is that of a lengthy irrigation channel running parallel with the Nile on its western side. Its meaning is "river of *Joseph,*" traditionally referring to the biblical son of Jacob who was sold into slavery in Egypt.

Baia dos Tigres. *Bay, southwestern Angola.* The Portuguese name means "tiger bay." The reasons for the name are uncertain. There are no tigers in Africa. Possibly the sandhills on the shore here were blown into stripes suggesting those on a tiger's coat.

Bailundo. *Town, west central Angola.* The name may represent local words *bai,* "to receive," and either *mbalundu,* "inhabited place" or *elundo,* "height." If the latter, the overall meaning could be "place at a height," which would suit the elevated location of the town. In the 1930s the name was changed to *Vila Teixeiro da Silva,* for the Portuguese explorer Pedro *Teixeiro da Silva* (1575–1640), but the original name was readopted in the late 1970s.

Bakel. *Town, northeastern Senegal.* The story goes that when the local people first came here they frequently longed for their former homeland. Whenever this happened, they would say to their minstrel, "*Bakalene,*" "Beat the tomtom."

Bakenskop. *Mountain, Bophuthatswana, South Africa.* The mountain, on the western border of the bantustan, has an Afrikaans name meaning "beacon hill." A beacon must have been lit here at some time, perhaps to demarcate a territory.

Bakoy. *River, western Mali.* The river, a headstream of the **Bafoulabé,** has a Bambara name meaning "white river." Cf. **Bafing; Baoulé.**

Bakwanga. See **Mbuji-Mayi.**

[1]**Balfour.** *Town, southern Cape Province, South Africa.* The town

arose as a mission station in 1828 and was named for Dr. Robert *Balfour,* secretary of the Glasgow Missionary Society.

[2]**Balfour.** *Town, southern Transvaal, South Africa.* The town, southeast of Johannesburg, was originally known as *McHattiesburg,* for Frederick Stuart *McHattie,* on whose farm it was founded in 1898. In 1905 it was given its present name, for the British prime minister Arthur *Balfour* (1848–1930), who visited South Africa that year.

Balombo. *Town, western Angola.* The town was founded as a military post in 1902 and given a local name said to mean "tattoo." In the 1920s the town was renamed *Norton de Matos,* for the Portuguese colonial administrator, José *Norton de Matos,* governor-general of Portuguese West Africa (now Angola) from 1912 to 1915. The original name was re-adopted in the late 1970s.

Bamako. *Capital of Mali.* The name of the city on the Niger River in the southwest of the country has two generally favored origins. One takes it from Bambara *Bamma-ko,* "behind Bamma," the latter a man's name, implying a settlement that lay behind his village, itself said to be Moribadougou, 6 miles (10 km) downstream. The other derives it from *bamma-ko,* "crocodile affair," alluding to a custom, now happily historic, of offering a live victim annually to the crocodiles in the Niger. A third story is also sometimes told to explain the name. A hunter from Kong (modern Côte d'Ivoire) named Bamba Sanogo received permission from a Bambara chief to found a town on the spot where he had killed an elephant. He therefore named it *Bamba-Kong* for himself and his land of origin. This was later shortened to *Bamako.*

Bambouk. *Region, western Mali.* The region, near the border with Senegal, has a Mande name meaning "land of back-carriers," from *bāmbu,* "back-carrier," and *ko,* "country." The reference is to the region where loads are carried on the back (as more usual in the west), not the head (as more usual in Africa).

Banamba. *Village, western Mali.* The village, northeast of Bamako, the capital, has a Mande name meaning "the great cheesemaker," from *banā,* "cheesemaker," and *mba,* "big." The reference is to a place renowned for someone who made and sold cheese.

Bancroft. See **Chililabomwe.**

Bandundu. *Town, western Zaïre.* The town, at the junction of the Kwango and Kwilu rivers where they flow into the Kasai, adopted its present Bantu ethnic name in 1966. Before this date its colonial name, coincidentally similar but entirely unrelated, was *Banningville,* for the Belgian official Émile *Banning* (1836–1898), an active participant in the creation of the Congo Free State in 1885. *Bandundu* is also the name of the region here.

Bangui. *Capital of Central African Republic.* The word is Bobangui for "the rapids." The town was founded in 1889 as a French military post above the first great rapid on the *Ubangi* River.

Bangweulu, Lake. *Lake, northeastern Zambia.* The shallow lake with its extensive swamps has a Bantu name meaning "large water."

Banhine National Park. *National park, south central Mozambique.* The game reserve takes its name from the village of *Banhine* here. The village's own name is said to mean either "that which is seen from afar" or "land of white sand."

Bani. *River, southern Mali.* The river, a tributary of the Niger, has a

Mande name meaning "little river," with the initial *ba* ("river") found in many other river names here. Cf. **Bafoulé.**

Banjul. *Capital of Gambia.* The name became official only in 1973, but was in local use long before this. The story goes that when the first Portuguese colonists arrived here, in the 15th century, they asked the local people what the name of the place was. The latter misunderstood the question, thinking they were being asked what they were making. They therefore replied *"bangjulo,"* "rope matting." The colonists noted the name and gave it to their settlement. In 1816 British colonists founded the modern city, naming it *Bathurst,* for Henry *Bathurst,* 3d Earl Bathurst (1762–1834), British colonial secretary.

Banket. *Village, northern Zimbabwe.* The village, northwest of Harare, was so named for the gold-bearing rock here, which resembled the Dutch candy known as *banket,* a kind of almond hardbake. The word was later adopted generally for this type of rock, with its appearance of almond-shaped pebbles.

Banningville. See **Bandundu.**

Bantustan. *Black homeland, South Africa.* The name, sometimes (as in this book) spelled with a small *b,* is that of one of the regions set aside in South Africa for black Africans from the 1970s with the aim of gaining self-government. Those that have so far achieved nominal independence, although unrecognized outside South Africa itself, are **Bophuthatswana, Ciskei, Transkei,** and **Venda.** The others are currently as follows: **Gazankulu, KaNgwane, KwaNdebele, KwaZulu, Lebowa,** and **Qwaqwa.** The name is unofficial, and "homeland" or (more formally) "National State" is often preferred instead. Its origin is in *Bantu,* the nationality of the people, and the group of languages that they speak, and *-stan,* the word for "home" or "land" found in the names of various Asian countries, such as *Pakistan* and *Hindustan. Bantu* itself means "men," "people," from the root word *ntu,* "man," "person," with the plural prefix *ba-* (as for *Basuto:* see **Lesotho**). The name was devised in about 1860 as a term to replace "African," as applied to the language group, by the German–South African philologist Wilhelm Heinrich Immanuel Bleek (1827–1875). Many black Africans dislike both names, associating them with oppression. However, *Bantu* has an established linguistic and ethnic application, and in this sense makes *Bantustan* a more precise term than simply "homeland" or "National State."

Banzyville. See **Mobayi-Mbongo.**

Baoulé. *River, western Mali.* The river, a tributary of the **Bakoy,** has a Bambara name meaning "red river." Cf. **Bafing, Bakoy,** and see also **Bagoé.**

Barbary. *Coastal region, North Africa.* The region, named *Barbaria* on 16th century maps, extended along the whole Mediterranean coast from western Egypt to the Atlantic. Its name derives from its original inhabitants, the *Berbers,* whose own name, from Arabic *barbar,* is probably related to, but not derived from, Greek *barbaros,* "foreign," "not Latin or Greek," which in turn gave modern English *barbarous.* All these words almost certainly go back to a meaningless imitation of foreign babble ("bar-bar") of speech that cannot be understood. When the Mediterranean shore here became a center of piracy against European shipping in the 16th century, the name *Barbary Coast* appeared.

Barberspan. *Village, western Transvaal, South Africa.* The village takes its name from the salt pan here, its own name meaning "barbel pan," for the fish in its waters.

Barberton. *Town, eastern Transvaal, South Africa.* The town arose as a gold-mining center, and takes its name from the goldminer Graham Hoare *Barber,* from Natal, who in 1884 found a rich gold-bearing reef here. ("Reef" in this South African sense refers to a rock deposit that is not expected to yield gold or diamonds.) The resulting town was at first called *Barber's Reef,* but later adopted the shorter name.

Barca. See **Al-Marj.**

Barce. See **Al-Marj.**

Barkly East. *Town, eastern Cape Province, South Africa.* The town was founded in 1874 and named for Sir Henry *Barkly* (1815–1898), governor of the Cape from 1870 to 1877. *East* distinguished it from **Barkly West,** which at first was simply *Barkly.*

Barkly West. *Town, northeastern Cape Province, South Africa.* The town arose from the gold diggers' camp that was set up on the site here in 1869, originally with the Afrikaans name of *Klipdrift* ("rock ford"). In 1870 the settlement received its present name, for Sir Henry *Barkly* (1815–1898), governor of the Cape from 1870 to 1877. (It was at first simply *Barkly,* but later added *West* to be distinguished from **Barkly East.**)

Barotse. *Former province, western Zambia.* The province took its name from its indigenous inhabitants, the *Barotse* (or *Lozi*) people, whose empire here was founded in the mid 16th century. Their own name means "river people," referring to the Congo River basin from which they originally migrated. (They were earlier known as the Aluyi.) The province was formed in 1964 in territory earlier known as *Barotseland.* In 1969 it was renamed *Western,* an unusual example of an African name progressing to a European one.

Basutoland. See **Lesotho.**

[1]**Bathurst.** *Town, southeastern Cape Province, South Africa.* The town was founded in 1820 and named for Henry *Bathurst,* 3d Earl Bathurst (1762–1834), British secretary for the colonies. See also **Banjul.**

[2]**Bathurst.** See **Banjul.**

Battlefields. *Village, central Zimbabwe.* The name alludes to the many mining claims here, their own names deriving from European battles.

Beaconsfield. *District of Kimberley, eastern Cape Province, South Africa.* The name was originally that of a separate town to the south of Kimberley. It was at first named *Dutoitspan,* for the diamond mine (pan) owned by A. P. *du Toit.* It was later renamed for the British prime minister, Benjamin Disraeli, 1st Earl of *Beaconsfield* (1804–1881), who took his title from the town in Buckinghamshire. In 1912 Beaconsfield was incorporated into Kimberley.

Beatrice. *Village, east central Zimbabwe.* The village was named for *Beatrice* Borrow, sister of Captain Henry John Borrow (1865–1893), who held the claims to the gold mine here.

Beaufort West. *Town, south central Cape Province, South Africa.* The town was founded in 1818 and named for the 5th Duke of *Beaufort,* father of the then governor of the Cape, Lord Charles Henry Somerset (1768–1831). In order to avoid confusion with **Fort Beaufort** and *Port Beaufort,* also named for his family, the original name of *Beaufort* was suffixed with *West,* referring to its location with regard to the other places.

Bechuanaland. See **Botswana.**

Bedford. *Town, southeastern Cape Province, South Africa.* The town was founded in 1854 on the farm owned by Sir Andries Stockenström, who named it for his friend, Francis Charles Hastings Russell, 9th Duke of *Bedford* (1819–1891).

Beheira. *Region, northern Egypt.* The region, a governorate in the western part of the Nile Delta, has a name representing Arabic *al-buḥayrah,* a diminutive of *baḥr,* "sea," "Nile."

Beira. *Port, eastern Mozambique.* The Portuguese named the port commemoratively for their province of the same name, in north central Portugal. It means "edge," "brink," from Portuguese *ribeira,* "river," with the first syllable of this dropped by confusion with the prefix *re-*. This is also an appropriately descriptive name for the African port, which lies southwest of the Zambezi estuary.

Bejaïa. *Port, northeastern Algeria.* The name represents Arabic *bijāya,* which is possibly a corruption of *baqāyā,* "survivors," plural of *baqayya,* alluding to some people or tribe who sought refuge here. Under French influence the name was altered to *Bougie,* which gave modern French *bougie,* "candle," with reference to the wax candles that the town introduced in medieval times when trading with Europe. (The candles were at first called *chandelles de Bougie,* "candles from Bougie," then just *bougie,* a word that now also means "sparkplug.") The ancient Roman name of the settlement here was *Saldae.*

Bela Vista. *Town, southern Mozambique.* The town, south of the capital, Maputo, has a Portuguese name meaning "beautiful view," referring to the panoramic view here over the Maputo River.

Belfast. *Town, east central Transvaal, South Africa.* The town is named for *Belfast,* Northern Ireland, the hometown of John O'Neill, whose son Richard founded the original village here in 1890.

Belgian Congo. See **Zaïre.**

Bellville. *Town, southwestern Cape Province, South Africa.* The town, just east of Cape Town, arose on a site known as *Hardekraaltje,* "hard ground." When the railroad reached the area, the name became *Twaalfde Mylpaal,* "twelfth milestone," referring to its distance from Cape Town. Finally, in 1861, the settlement was given its present name, in honor of Charles Davidson *Bell,* surveyor-general of the Cape Colony from 1848 to 1872 (and designer of the famous "Cape triangular" postage stamps).

Bendougou. *Village, central Guinea.* The village has a name that means "place of the meeting," from Mande *be,* "meeting," and *dougou,* "place."

Benghazi. *City and port, northern Libya.* The name probably represents Arabic *banghāzī,* from *banī ghāzī,* "sons of the conqueror," from *banī,* "sons," the plural of *ibn,* and *ghāzī,* "conqueror," from the verb *ghaza,* "to invade" (hence French and English *razzia* as a historic term for a raid for plunder or slaves). However, tradition ascribes the name to a locally venerated marabout (holy man), *Banī ghāzī,* whose tomb lies to the north of the city. The Greeks of Cyrenaica founded the original settlement here in the 7th century BC and named it *Hesperides* or *Euhesperides,* for the mythological Islands of the Blessed. Later, when Cyrenaica was ruled by the Ptolemies in the 4th century BC, the town took the additional name of *Berenice,* in honor of the wife of Ptolemy III.

Benguela. *Town and port, western Angola.* The town is said to have a local name meaning "defense," although it has also been derived from a word *bayuella* (or some similar spelling) meaning "highland." The name is also that of the province here.

Beni Hasan. *Village, northern Egypt.* The Nile village, famous for its ancient rock tombs, has an Arabic name meaning "sons of *Hasan,*" from *banī,* "sons," and *ḥasan,* "Hasan," a name meaning "good," "beautiful." The reference is to the leader of an Arab tribe who formerly lived in this region.

Beni Mellal. *Town, central Morocco.* The town lies on the northern foothills of the Middle Atlas Mountains, and has a spring that is famous for the volume and freshness of its water. The name refers to this, as a combination of Arabic *banī,* "sons," and a Berber root word *mell* meaning "white." Cf. **Melilla.**

Benin. *Republic, West Africa.* The present country takes its name from its indigenous inhabitants, the *Bîni,* who were themselves named for a former kingdom here on the Gulf of Guinea. The people are now more closely associated with southern Nigeria, hence the name of **Benin City** in that country. Until 1975 Benin was known as **Dahomey.**

Benin City. *City, southern Nigeria.* The city, also known simply as *Benin,* arose in medieval times as the capital of the *Bîni* people who gave the name of **Benin.** It was ransacked (for its famous bronzes) and burned down by the British in 1897, but subsequently rebuilt.

Benoni. *City, southern Transvaal, South Africa.* The city, now effectively an eastern suburb of Johannesburg, was founded in 1904 and given the biblical name *Ben-Oni* (Genesis 25:18). This means "son of sorrow," and referred to the difficulty of developing the settlement as a result of the awkward contour of the area.

Bensonville. *Town, western Liberia.* The town is named for Stephen A. *Benson,* president of Liberia from 1856 to 1864.

Benue. *State, southeastern Nigeria.* The state takes its name from the river, a tributary of the Niger, that forms part of its northern border. The river's own name means "mother of waters," from Batta *be,* "water," and *nue,* "mother."

Beoumi. *Village, central Côte d'Ivoire.* The name of the village is said to be a contraction of Baule *m'békoumi,* "he kills me." The sinister appellation is supposed to refer to the judgment passed on malefactors by a local Kode chief, whose capital the village was.

Berbera. *Town and port, northern Somalia.* The historic town was founded by Ptolemy II Philadelphus in about 300 BC and has a name ultimately deriving from Greek *barbaros,* "foreign," "not Greek." Cf. **Barbary.**

Berea. *District, northwestern Lesotho.* The name was originally that of a French mission station set up here in 1843. It is biblical in origin, from *Berea* (Acts 17:10), the city to which Paul and Silas were sent.

Berenice. See **Benghazi.**

Bergville. *Town, western Natal, South Africa.* The town, founded in 1897, has a name referring to its location in the foothills of the Drakens*berg* mountains.

Berkane. *Town, northeastern Morocco.* The town takes its name from a local Muslim holy man, Muhammad *Aberkane.* His own name derives from the Berber word for "black."

Berlin. *Village, southeastern Cape Province, South Africa.* The village, east of King William's Town, was founded in 1857 by settlers from the British-German Legion and was named for what was then (and is now once again) the German capital.

Berseba. *Village, southern Namibia.* The village was founded as a German mission station in 1850 and was named for the biblical *Beersheba.*

Bethal. *Town, southeastern Transvaal, South Africa.* The town was founded in 1880 and named for the two sisters Eliza*beth* Du Plooy and *Al*ida Naudé, whose husbands were the original landowners here. The name also happens to suggest the biblical *Bethel.*

Bethanien. *Village, southern Namibia.*The original Nama name of the village, east of Lüderitz, was *Uigantes,* meaning "fountain that cannot be closed by a stone." The reference is to the strong springs here. In 1814 the place was renamed by a German missionary for the biblical town of *Bethany* (Mark 11:1).

Bethlehem. *Town, northeastern Orange Free State, South Africa.* The town was founded in 1860 and named for its biblical counterpart, the common link being the abundance of wheat in the region. (*Bethlehem* means literally "place of bread.") The river that flows through the South African town was appropriately named the *Jordan.*

Bethulie. *Town, southern Orange Free State, South Africa.* The town arose in 1829 as a missionary station at a site already bearing the Afrikaans name of *Groot Moordenaarspoort,* "great murderers' gateway," referring to the murder of Bushmen by the Basuto here. In 1833 the settlement was renamed *Caledon,* for the river. As there was already a **Caledon** in the Cape, the name was further changed to *Verhuellpolis* in 1835, in honor of Admiral C. H. *Verhuell,* president of the Paris Mission, *-polis* meaning "town" (as in *metropolis*). Missionary directors, however, preferred a biblical name, so chose *Bethulia,* from the Apocrypha (Judith 8:3), taking this to mean "maiden of God." But when a town was officially proclaimed on the site in 1863, the name was changed once again to *Heidelberg.* This in turn caused confusion with the existing Heidelberg, so that finally in 1872 the name of *Bethulie* was adopted. The Basuto name of the town is *Masimo,* "gardens."

Betsiboka. *River, Madagascar.* The river rises in central Madagascar and flows northwest to enter the Mozambique Channel at Majunga. Its Malagasy name means "big [river] that is not brackish."

Betsimisaraka. *Region, eastern Madagascar.* The Malagasy name, that of an escarpment parallel with the coast, means "many that are not separated," itself the name of the people who live here.

Beyla. *Town, southern Guinea.* The name is said to represent Arabic *billāh,* "by God!," serving as an Islamic propitious statement.

Bhunya. *Town, western Swaziland.* The name of the forestry town is said to derive from Siswati *ukubhunya,* "to give off smoke," referring to the spray thrown up by a local waterfall. By coincidence, the town's many pulp factories have chimneys that disgorge large quantities of smoke, thus giving the name a modern application.

Biafra. *Region, eastern Nigeria.* The former independent republic takes its name from the Bight of *Biafra* (now the Bight of Bonny), which extends from the Niger Delta to Cape Lopez, on the western coast of Gabon. Its own name is a European alteration of *Miafra,* a tribal name.

Bibala. *Village, southwestern Angola.* The indigenous name derives from a word describing the mountainous country here, crossed by large valleys. The village had the former colonial name of *Vila Arriaga,* possibly for Manuel José de *Arriaga* (1842–1917), first president of Portugal (from 1911 to 1915), or else for Dr. Guilherme de Oliveira *Arriaga,* a Portuguese colonial official active in Mozambique.

Bié. *Town, central Angola.* The name of the town, plateau, and province is a corrupt form of the name of the chief *Vié,* who held power here before the arrival of the Portuguese in the late 15th century. In the late 19th century the town was renamed *Silva Porto,* for the Portuguese explorer António Francisco Ferreira da *Silva Porto,* who died here in 1890. After Angola gained independence in 1975, the name reverted to *Bié.* The more usual current name of the town is **Kuito.**

Big Bend. *Town, eastern Swaziland.* The town takes its name from its location in a broad bend of the Usutu River.

Biggarsberg. *Mountain range, northwestern Natal, South Africa.* The mountains, a northern extension of the Drakensberg, took their name from the English colonist Alexander *Biggar* (1781–1838), who crossed them with difficulty.

Bignona. *Town, southwestern Senegal.* The name is said to represent Dyula *big-nona,* "place of meeting," referring to the location of the town at a point where many roads meet and to its busy trading activity.

Bijagós Islands. *Islands, western Guinea-Bissau.* The islands, also known as the *Bissagos,* are off the coast of Guinea-Bissau and form part of its territory. Their name is of the same origin as that of **Bissau** (q.v.) itself.

Bikita. *Village, southeastern Zimbabwe.* The name, also that of a district, is an indigenous one meaning "ant bear," "anteater," an animal widely found here at one time.

Bindura. *Town, northeastern Zimbabwe.* The name of the town and district is said to derive from the hill here, and to mean "place of trapping." The reference would be to the fleeing of game animals in the spring when the grass of the valley is burned off, so that the Korekore hunted them on this hill.

Binga, Mount. *Mountain, western Mozambique.* The mountain, on the border with Zimbabwe, has a local name that is said to mean "dense forestland."

Bingerville. *Town and port, southern Côte d'Ivoire.* The town preserves the name of the French naval officer and explorer, Captain Louis-Gustave *Binger* (1856–1936), first governor of the Ivory Coast Colony (from 1893 to 1895). The name has a French-style pronunciation, akin to *lingerie* rather than *singer.*

Bioko. *Island, Equatorial Guinea.* The island, in the Gulf of Guinea, off the coast of Cameroon, takes its name from *Bioko,* one of the two sons of the former king Moka, his other son giving the name of **Malabo.** The island's name until 1973 was **Fernando Po,** but from 1973 to 1979 it was *Macías Nguema Bijogo,* for Francisco Macías Nguema *Biyogo* Negue Ndong (1922–1979), president of Equatorial Guinea from 1968 until his execution on charges of treason, embezzlement, and genocide.

Birchenough Bridge. *Village, southeastern Zimbabe.* The bridge, over the Sabi River, was completed in 1935 and named for its funder, Sir Henry *Birchenough* (1853–1937), president of the British South Africa Company. The ashes of Sir Henry and his wife, Mabel, are contained in one of the pillars of the bridge.

Bir Hacheim. *Village and oasis, northeastern Libya.* The village, scene of much fighting in World War II, has a name representing Arabic *bi'r ḥak*īm, "well of the sage," from *bi'r,* "well," and *ḥakīm,* "sage," "wise man."

Birni n'Konni. *Town, southern Niger.* The name means "fortress of the Konni," from Tamashek (Berber) *birni,* "fortified village," and *Konni,* a Hausa tribe whose region this once was.

Bir Ounane. *Waterhole, central Mali.* The vital desert water source has a name that represents Arabic *bi'r,* "well," and Tamashek (Berber) *ounān,* plural of *anou,* "well." The sense is thus "well of wells," a form of intensive.

Bisho. *Capital of Ciskei, South Africa.* The name of the town is the Xhosa word for "buffalo," referring to the **Buffalo** River on which the town stands.

Biskra. *Town, northeastern Algeria.* The town arose on the site of the Roman fortified frontier post of *Vescera,* and takes its name from it. The meaning of this is obscure. It almost certainly represents an even earlier name.

Bissagos Islands. See **Bijagós Islands.**

Bissandougou. *Village, eastern Guinea.* The name is a Mande one meaning "place of the rod," from *bisa,* "rod," "wand," and *dugu,* "place." The reference is to beating as a punishment.

Bissau. *Town and port, western Guinea-Bissau.* The name is a Portuguese form of the name of the *Bissagos* or *Bijuga* tribe. Their own name is of uncertain meaning, but may derive from that of an early chief or leader. See also **Bijagós Islands, Guinea-Bissau.**

Bisskirima. *Village, central Guinea.* The Mande name means "[place] by the curved branches," from *bisi,* "branch of dry wood," *kiri,* "round," "curved," and *ma,* "by," "near." The reference is either to local brushwood or to a structure of some kind.

Bitter Lakes. *Lakes, northeastern Egypt.* The two lakes of the name are actually a single sheet of water traversed by the Suez Canal. They are so called for their once marshy water, and are respectively known as the Great Bitter Lake (Arabic *al-buḥayrah al-murrah al-kubrā*) and Little Bitter Lake (Arabic *al-buḥayrah al-murrah as-sughrā*). The lakes have been identified with the biblical *Marah* ("bitter"): "And when [the Israelites] came to Marah, they could not drink of the waters of Marah, for they were bitter; therefore the name of it was called Marah" (Exodus 15:23). (Hebrew and Arabic are related Semitic languages, so that the Hebrew name *Marah* and Arabic *murr*, "bitter," are akin.)

Bizana. *Village, eastern Cape Province, South Africa.* The name is a corruption of the Xhosa word *mbizana,* meaning "small pot." The reference is to the hollow in which the village is located.

Bizerta. *Town and port, northern Tunisia.* The name represents Arabic *binzart,* a corruption of Low Latin *Hippo Zarytus,* in turn a corruption of Classical Latin *Hippo Diarrhytus,* a form of the original Greek name, *Hippōn Diarrutos,* from *hippōn,* "stable," and *diarrutos,* "flowing through" (from a verb that gave modern English *diarrhea*). The port arose at a site where horses' stables were crossed by a running stream, supplying water for drinking and washing. See also **Annaba**.

Black Volta. See **Volta.**

[1]**Blanc, Cape.** *Headland, northern Tunisia.* The name is a French translation of Arabic *raʿs al-abyaḍ,* "the white head," from *raʿs,* "head," *al,* "the," and *abyaḍ,* "white." The Arabic name is itself probably a translation of the Roman name, *Candidum promontorium,* although according to some sources the original name was given by the Portuguese, who are said to have discovered it in the mid-15th century and named it by way of contrast with Cape **Vert**, the westernmost peninsula in Africa (see **Cape Verde**). Either way, the cape, Africa's northernmost point, is so called for its light-colored sandy soil.

[2]**Blanc, Cape.** *Headland, western Mauritania/Western Sahara.* The cape, named for its light-colored soil, is the narrow peninsula on which stands the Mauritanian seaport of Nouadhibou.

Blanco. *Village, southern Cape Province, South Africa.* The village, just west of George, takes its name from the nickname of Henry Fancourt *White,* who came here from Australia in the mid-19th century to establish a mission station.

Blantyre. *City, southern Malawi.* The city, which united with neighboring Limbe in 1956 to form *Blantyre-Limbe,* takes its name from the birthplace of the Scottish explorer David Livingstone. It was founded in 1876, three years after Livingstone's death. The Scottish *Blantyre* is a town southeast of Glasgow. Its own name is said to mean "top land" or "end land," from words related to Welsh *blaen,* "end," "top," and *tir,* "land," "country." If so, whoever gave the name to the African town may have intended this additional aptness, since Blantyre is in the Shire Highlands at the southern end of the country.

Blida. *Town, northern Algeria.* The town was founded sometime in the 16th century and has a name that evolved from *boleida,* a diminutive of Arabic *balad,* "city."

Bliéron. *Coastal village, southwestern Côte d'Ivoire.* The village, close to the Liberian frontier, has a local dialect name meaning "village of oxen," from *bli,* "oxen," and *ouro,* "village."

Bloemfontein. *Capital of Orange Free State, South Africa.* The city, the judicial capital of South Africa as a whole, was founded in 1846 on a farm of the same name. The name literally means "flower fountain," from Dutch *bloem,* "flower" and *fontein,* "fountain," perhaps denoting a spring surrounded by flowers. The name is said by some, however, to relate to a landowner here, one Jan *Bloem.*

Bloemhof. *Town, southwestern Transvaal, South Africa.* The town, founded in 1864, appears to have been given a name denoting a propitious site for development, from Afrikaans *bloemhof,* "flower garden."

Blouberg. *Mountain, northern Transvaal, South Africa.* The name is Afrikaans for "blue mountain," referring to its color as viewed from below.

Blue Nile. *River, East Africa.* The Blue Nile rises in central Ethiopia and flows first southeast then northwest to join the White Nile at Khartoum. Its name translates Arabic *al-baḥr al-azraq,* from *al,* "the," *baḥr,* "sea," "river," "Nile," and *azraq,* "blue." When the river is running relatively low its waters reflect the blue of the sky. Hence its name, which also serves to contrast it with the **White Nile**. The precise source of the Blue Nile is said to be a small spring above Lake Tana, and the stream that flows into the lake is the *Abbai*, the Blue Nile's Amharic name (see **Nile**).

Blyvooruitsig. *Town, southern Transvaal, South Africa.* The goldmining town, southwest of Johannesburg, takes its name from the *Blyvvooruitzicht* Gold Mining Company that started operations here in 1937. The propitious company name is Dutch for "joyous prospect" (or, as a closer English equivalent, "blissful outlook"). The town's name is the Afrikaans form of this.

Boa Vista. *Island, eastern Cape Verde Islands.* The island has a Portuguese name meaning "good view," said to refer to the welcome sight seen by Portuguese ships when seeking shelter in a storm off the African coast here in 1486.

Bobo-Dioulasso. *City, western Burkina Faso.* The name was given by the French in 1897, and refers to the two peoples who inhabited the district, the *Bobo* and the *Dyula*, with the final *so* meaning "village" as for **Burkina Faso** itself. The original settlement here was founded in the 15th century with the name of *Sya*, meaning "island," referring to the forest clearing by a stream where it arose.

Bobonong. *Village, eastern Botswana.* The name means "place of *Sebono*," a local chief.

Bodiam. *Village, Ciskei, South Africa.* The village, near the coast, was originally named *Mandy's Farm* for a member of the farmowner's family. Its present name was adopted from that of *Bodiam* Castle, Sussex, England, perhaps through some personal association.

Boesmans. *River, southeastern Cape Province, South Africa.* The river takes its Afrikaans name from the San or *Bushmen*, who lived in the region. At its mouth is the coastal village of *Boesmansriviermond*, "Bushman river mouth."

Boetsap. *Village, northern Cape Province, South Africa.* The name is based on the Tswana word *bucwa*, meaning "fat," "sleek," referring to the cattle in the region. See also **Reivilo**.

Bogué. *Town, southwestern Mauritania.* The name is a form of Fulani (Peul) *bokké*, the old plural of *bokki*, "baobab" (the modern plural is *boude*). The reference is thus to a forest of these trees. There are none here now. Cf. **Boki**.

Bojador, Cape. See **Boujdour**.

Boki. *Village, northern Cameroon.* The village takes its name from the *Boki* River to the south. The river's own name represents the Fulani (Peul) word for "baobab." Cf. **Bogué**.

Bokkeveld Berg. *Mountain, southwestern Cape Province, South Africa.* The mountain rises over the *veld* that at one time was inhabited by a large quantity of buck (Afrikaans, *bok*).

Boksburg. *Town, southern Transvaal, South Africa.* The town, an eastern suburb of Johannesburg, arose on the gold diggings here in the 1880s and was named for Willem Eduard *Bok* (1846–1904), Dutch-born state secretary of South Africa from 1884 to 1888.

Boma. *Town, western Zaïre.* The town, an important commercial center founded as a slave market on the Congo River in the 16th century, has a local name probably meaning "palisade." The British explorer Sir Henry Morton Stanley, recounting his momentous journey down the Congo in *Darkest Africa* (1878), gives a different (though not incompatible) explanation of the name: "To-day, for the first time, I heard . . . from a man whom has visited Embomma [Boma], which I believe to mean 'place of the king' in the language of Babwendé, and to be synonymous with Kwikuru [now Seke] in Unyamwezi [Nyamwezi, western Tanzania], and Kibuga [Kiboga] in Uganda."

Bon, Cape. *Peninsula, northeastern Tunisia.* The peninsula is said to have a name of Spanish origin meaning "good cape." Its Arabic name is *jazīrat sharīk,* "eastern peninsula."

Bondoukou. *Town, eastern Côte d'Ivoire.* The name is believed to be a corruption of *Gottogo* (or some similar form), probably itself a local word meaning simply "encampment."

Bône. See **Annaba.**

Bonnievale. *Town, southwestern Cape Province, South Africa.* The name, originally that of a railroad siding here, was given in a generally propitious way for the location of the place. The village was established in 1922.

Bontberg. *Mountain, southwestern Cape Province, South Africa.* The mountain, at the western end of the Great Karoo, has an Afrikaans name meaning "speckled mountain." The reference is to red patches of terrain that contrast with a mainly black background.

Bonwapitse. *Village, eastern Botswana.* The name is that of the river here, a tributary of the Limpopo. It is of Tswana origin and is said to mean "[place] where zebras drink."

Bopa. *Village, southwestern Benin.* The village takes its name from the nearby forest of *Agbokpa,* whose own name means "near the buffalo," from local words *agbo,* "buffalo," and *kpa,* "near." The region was part of a larger forest where these animals were hunted.

Bophuthatswana. *Bantustan, northern South Africa.* The Bantu homeland is that of the *Tswana,* as the name indicates, from Tswana *bo-*, a prefix for abstract nouns, *phutha,* "to gather," and *tswana,* "Tswana," the people's ethnic name. Overall the meaning is thus "gathering of the Tswanas." See also **Botswana.**

Bordj Omar Driss. *Town, eastern Algeria.* The town has an Arabic name meaning "fort of Omar Driss," the latter being a local Muslim leader. Under French colonial rule the town was known as *Fort Flatters,* for Paul *Flatters* (1832–1881), a French officer who led two expeditions to plot the best route for a Transsaharan railway. During the second of these he was murdered by the Tuaregs. (There is still no Transsaharan railroad, or even a Transalgerian one.)

Borj Bourguiba. *Village, south central Tunisia.* The village, centered on a military prison, has a name meaning "fort of Bourguiba," with reference to Habin ben Ali *Bourguiba* (born 1903), president of Tunisia from 1957 to 1987, who was interned here under the French protectorate. (The prison later held a number of Bourguiba's own political enemies.) Many Tunisian towns and cities have a main street named *Avenue Bourguiba.* Cf. **Menzel Bourguiba.**

Bornu. *State, northeastern Nigeria.* The name of the state, first recorded in the late 13th century, is of uncertain origin. It has been traditionally explained as meaning "land of Berbers" or as representing Arabic *barr nūḥ,* "land of Noah," from *barr,* "land," and *nūḥ,* "Noah." The latter relates to a legend that Noah's ark came to rest here after the Flood. But Bornu is far from Ararat, where the ark is more usually said to have grounded, and this etymology was doubtless devised by a romantically inclined Arabist.

Bosberg. *Mountain, central Orange Free State, South Africa.* The Afrikaans name means "bush mountain," referring to the bush (woodland) on the mountain slopes.

Boshof. *Town, western Orange Free State, South Africa.* The town was founded in 1856 and named for Jacobus Nicolaas *Boshof* (1808–1881), president of the Orange Free State from 1855 to 1859.

Bothaville. *Town, northern Orange Free State, South Africa.* The town arose on part of a farm bought in approximately 1889 by Theunis Louis *Botha* and originally named by him as *Botharnia.* In 1893 the settlement that had developed was renamed *Bothaville.*

Botswana. *Republic, southern Africa.* The name of the republic, official from 1966, relates to that of its indigenous inhabitants, the Tswana, from *bo-*, a prefix for abstract nouns, and *tswana,* "Tswana," with the ethnic name itself perhaps meaning "like," "similar," referring to the people who stayed behind after most had emigrated. (This seems improbable, however, since most ethnic names emphasize a distinction, not a similarity.) The country was formerly known as *Bechuanaland,* a name introduced in 1885 when the British established a protectorate here. In this, English *land* has been suffixed to *Bechuana,* a corruption of *Botswana.*

Bouaflé. *Town, south central Côte d'Ivoire.* The name is probably a contraction of *Bouavéréfla,* "place of the Bouavéré," from a tribal name with the suffix *fla* or *flé,* "place," "village."

Bouaké. *Town, central Côte d'Ivoire.* The name represents that of *Gbweke* (died 1897), king of the Baule people, who founded the town in 1865.

Bouba Njida National Park. *National park, northwestern Cameroon.* The official French name of the park is *Parc National de Bouba Njida,* "national park of Bouba Njida." It was created as a game reserve in 1968 and named for *Bouba Njida* (died 1864), a local religious fanatic who wielded authority here. In 1804 he founded the village of *Rey Bouba* on the banks of the Mayo *Rey* River.

Boucle du Baoulé National Park. *National park, southwestern Mali.* The official French name of the national park (which includes three distinct game reserves) is *Parc National du Boucle du Baoulé,* "national park of the loop of the Baoulé," referring to the great bend in the Baoulé River here.

Boujdour. *Coastal village, western Western Sahara.* The village takes its name from the cape here, still frequently known by its formerly familiar name of *Bojador.* This is said to derive from Portuguese *bojar,* "to jut out," describing its profile.

Boulal. *Village, western Mali.* The village has a name representing Soninke *boula,* a nickname given to the local people, itself meaning "truthful." The villagers claim that they never lie. They never eat the varan, or monitor lizard, since this reptile has a "forked tongue," representing a falsehood.

Boundiali. *Town, northern Côte d'Ivoire.* The town, founded by a hunter named Nambaga Ganon some time in the 12th century, has a local name said to mean "drum dried in the sun."

Bou Rjeima. *Village, western Mauritania.* The name means "little cairns," referring to the rocky mounds here at the western end of the Inchiri desert.

Bou Saâda. *Town, northern Algeria.* The ancient town and resort arose round an oasis and has a name of Arabic origin meaning "place of happiness."

Boussoura. *Village, northwestern Guinea.* The village has a name borrowed from *Bussora,* better known as *Basra,* the port in southeastern Iraq. The name was adopted as a tribute to Islam.

Boutilimit. *Town, western Mauritania.* The local name means "place of *tilimit,*" a grass of the *Pennisetum* genus.

Brakpan. *Town, southern Transvaal, South Africa.* The town, essentially an eastern district of Johannesburg, was founded in 1886 and takes its Afrikaans name from the pan of brackish water here. The settlement owes its growth to the gold-mining shafts opened in 1905.

Brandberg. *Mountain, northwestern Namibia.* The mountain, the highest in Namibia, has a Dutch name meaning "fire mountain," referring to the glow that is sometimes observed on its heights in certain lights. This is probably a translation of its Herero name *Omukuruwaro,* with the same meaning. Its Nama name is similar, as *Daunas,* "burnt mountain."

Brandfort. *Town, central Orange Free State, South Africa.* The town, founded in 1866, has a name that is perhaps a combination of the name of Johannes (Jan) Hendricus *Brand* (1823–1888), president of the Orange Free State from 1863 to 1872 and 1873 to 1888, and *fort,* referring to an old fortification here. However, the first part of the name could also represent Afrikaans *brand,* "burning," possibly referring to the burning down of a fort. As if by way of compromise, the town's coat of arms shows a statue of Brand and a fort. See also **Zastron**.

Brandt. *Village, southern Tanzania.* The village was founded in 1908 and named for a German missionary working with the Berlin Mission here at that time.

Brandvlei. *Village, southwestern Cape Province, South Africa.* The Afrikaans name means "burning marsh," referring to South Africa's largest single thermal spring, east of Cape Town.

Brass. *Town and port, southern Nigeria.* The town lies at the mouth of the river of the same name, a channel of the Niger Delta, and takes its name from it. The name is a local one (formerly *Barasin*), said to mean "to release." As an important trading center in the 19th century, the port was called *Brasstown* by Europeans, who combined the name of the river with that of the former settlement of *Tuwon* (or *Twon*), where Brass now is. This was then corrupted to English *town.*

Brasstown. See **Brass.**

Braunschweig. *Village, Ciskei, South Africa.* The village was founded by members of the British-German Legion in 1856 and named for the German town of *Braunschweig* (Brunswick).

Brava. *Island, southwestern Cape Verde Islands.* The smallest inhabited island in the group has a Portuguese name meaning "wild." The reference is presumably to the coastline, since inland the island is neatly cultivated.

Brazzaville. *Capital of the Congo.* The city takes its name from that of the French explorer Pierre Savorgnan de *Brazza* (1852–1905), who founded it in 1883 (by "purchasing" the existing village of Ntamo). De Brazza was born an Italian count, but took French citizenship on coming of age in 1874. (His original surname was Savorgnan; the aristocratic suffix derives from the Adriatic island of *Brazza,* now *Brač,* Croatia.) De Brazza also founded **Franceville**.

Bredasdorp. *Town, southwestern Cape Province, South Africa.* The town was founded in 1838 by Michiel van *Breda* of the Cape Legislative Council, and named for him.

Bremersdorp. See **Manzini.**

Breyton. *Town, eastern Transvaal, South Africa.* The town arose in the 19th century on a farm sold to Nicolaas *Breytenbach,* and was officially named for him in 1901.

British Kaffraria. See **Kaffraria.**

Brits. *Town, southern Transvaal, South Africa.* The town, northwest of Pretoria, arose in 1924 on a farm owned by Gert *Brits,* and was named for him.

Britstown. *Town, central Cape Province, South Africa.* The town was founded in 1877 soon after the discovery of diamonds at Kimberley, and was named for Hans *Brits,* owner of the farm where it was laid out.

Broken Hill. See **Kabwe.**

Bronkhorstspruit. *Town, southern Transvaal, South Africa.* The town, east of Pretoria, was founded in 1904 and was originally named *Erasmus* for C. J. G. *Erasmus,* owner of the farm where it was laid out. In 1935 it was given its present name, Afrikaans for "watercress stream," to restore a former alternate name for the site. This referred to the watercress found here by early settlers.

Brukkaros. *Mountain, southern Namibia.* The mountain, an extinct volcano, has a name that appears to be a German adaptation of Afrikaans *broek,* "trousers," together with a local word meaning literally "apron." This translates its original Khoikhoin (Hottentot) name of *Geitsigubeb,* "large hindskirt," referring to an antiquated women's garment that the mountain was said to resemble.

Bubastis. *Ancient city, northern Egypt.* The historic site was the chief seat of worship of the goddess Bastet, usually represented with the head of a lion or cat. Its name indicates its origin, and represents Egyptian *Per-Bāstet,* "house of Bastet," from *per,* "house," and *Bāstet,* "Bastet." The name occurs in the Bible as *Pi-beseth* (Ezekiel 30:17). Some claim, on highly dubious grounds, that it was Bastet, the cat-goddess, who gave the name *Puss* for a cat.

Bubye. *River, Zimbabwe.* The river, a tributary of the Limpopo in the south of the country, has a name that is said to derive from a local word meaning "pebbles."

Buchanan. *Town and port, western Liberia.* The town was founded in 1835 by black American Quakers of the Young Men's Colonization Society of Pennsylvania. They named it *Grand Bassa,* for the *Bassa* people among whom Norman merchants had made the original settlement here in about 1365 (under the name *Petit Dieppe,* "little Dieppe," for the French port). Subsequent communities on the site were named respectively *Upper Buchanan* and *Lower Buchanan* for the first governor of Liberia (from 1839 to 1841), Thomas *Buchanan,* a relative of James Buchanan, 15th president of the United States. See also **Edina**.

Buffalo. *River, South Africa.* There are several rivers of the name in South Africa. That in central Natal is recorded as having been named in 1685 by the party of Simon van der Stel (see **Simonstown,**

Stellenbosch) when they sighted buffalo grazing on its banks. The Khoikhoin (Hottentot) name of the river is *Kanka,* representing *cgaob,* "buffalo," and *ab,* "river." All the rivers are equally known by the Afrikaans name of *Buffels.* See also **Bisho**.

Buganda. *Region, southeastern Uganda.* The former native kingdom arose in the 13th or 14th century as a union of tribes and takes its name from the *Ganda* people (also known as *Buganda*), as does **Uganda** itself.

Buhera. *Village, eastern Zimbabwe.* The name, also that of a district here, derives from that of the local *vaHera* people.

Bulawayo. *City, southwestern Zimbabwe.* The name represents Ndebele *bulawa,* "to massacre," with the locative suffix *-yo.* The meaning is thus "place of the massacre," and refers to a fort burned down by a Matabele (Ndebele) chief in 1868. The city was founded on its site in 1893.

Bulembu. *Village, northwestern Swaziland.* The village, famous for its asbestos mine, was founded in 1886 and originally named *Havelock,* for Sir Arthur Elibank *Havelock* (1844–1908), governor of Natal from 1885 to 1889. Its present indigenous name means "spider's web," presumably for some topographical allusion.

Bulwer. *Village, southern Natal, South Africa.* The village was founded in 1890 and named for Sir Henry Ernest Gascoyne *Bulwer* (1836–1914), English-born governor of Natal from 1882 to 1886.

Burgersdorp. *Town, northeastern Cape Province, South Africa.* The town was founded in 1844 and originally given the Afrikaans name *Klipdrift* ("rocky ford"). After a visit to the area in 1845 by Sir Peregrine Maitland, governor of the Cape, several residents wished to name the place "Maitland" in his honor. He declined their proposal, however, so the settlement was instead named *Burgersdorp* ("citizens' town"), since the inhabitants had initiated the name themselves.

Burkina Faso. *Republic, West Africa.* The name of the country is a hybrid meaning "fatherland of the worthy men," from Moré *burkina,* "worthy," and Dyula *faso,* "country," "native land." The latter is a compound word, comprising *fa,* "father," and *so,* "village." Before 1984 the country was known as *Upper Volta,* from the Black Volta, Red Volta, and White Volta Rivers, which all rise in it. See also **Volta.**

Burundi. *Republic, Central Africa.* The country takes its name from its indigenous people, the *Rundi,* with *Ba-* the prefix for the people, and *Bu-* that for the country. German and Belgian colonists called the country *Urundi,* from the Swahili form of its name, with the prefix *U-* denoting a country, as for **Uganda.** The language spoken by the Rundi is known as either *Rundi* or *Kirundi,* with *Ki-* the prefix denoting a language.

Busiris. *Ancient city, northern Egypt.* The name ultimately represents Egyptian *Per-Ūsīr,* "house of Osiris," from *per,* "house," and *Ūsīr,* "Osiris." Osiris was the Egyptian god who ruled the underworld and judged the dead. His name has been interpreted by some as being of Berber origin, meaning "the old one." Others claim it means "he who occupies the throne" or "he who copulates with Isis."

Butha Buthe. *Town, northern Lesotho.* The town arose round the fortress that was the home of Moshoeshoe, founder of the Basotho nation, in the 1820s. Its name means "lair," "place of lying down," referring either to the occasion when Moshoeshoe reconciled warring tribes and they rested here, or to three hills nearby that resemble lying lions.

Buto. *Ancient city, northern Egypt.* The historic town, in the Nile Delta, has a name that ultimately derives from Egyptian *Per-Wadjet,* "house of [the goddess] Wadjet," from *per,* "house," and *Wadjet,* literaly "green one." Wadjet, the cobra-goddess, was the tutelary goddess of Lower Egypt. Her greenness refers both to the color of a serpent and to the papyrus swamps here which she is said to have created.

Butterworth. *Town, Transkei, South Africa.* The town arose from the missionary station of the Wesleyan Missionary Society set up in 1827 and named for the society's former treasurer, Joseph *Butterworth.* The town was officially founded in 1880.

Buzi. *River, Mozambique.* The river, flowing east to enter the Indian Ocean south of Beira, has a local name meaning "kid," referring to the game (young antelopes) formerly found here. A village of the same name is near the mouth of the river.

Byzacium. *Historic province, North Africa.* The name is that of the Roman province which in AD 297, together with **Tripolitania** and **Africa,** was formed out of the much larger existing province of *Africa.* In area it corresponded to modern southern Tunisia. Its name is of uncertain meaning, but is probably Phoenician in origin. (It is unrelated to the name of *Byzantium.*)

Caála. *Town, west central Angola.* The town is one of the earliest European settlements in the country, and is named for a chief who had his base nearby. In 1930 it was renamed *Vila Robert Williams,* for Sir *Robert Williams* (1860–1938), the Scottish engineer and railway pioneer. The original name was readopted soon after Angola gained independence in 1975.

Cabinda. *Enclave, northwestern Angola.* The enclave and its capital take their name from the *Cabinda* people who are its indigenous inhabitants. Their own name is said to mean "gourd."

Cabo Delgado. *Province, northeastern Mozambique.* The province takes its name from that of the peninsula here, in the northeasternmost part of the country. Ostensibly the name is Portuguese for "slender cape" (cf. **Ponta Delgada**), but the second word of the name may actually have originated as that of a local chief.

Cabo Yubi. See **Tarfaya.**

Cacine. *River, Guinea-Bissau.* The river, entering the Atlantic by the border with Guinea, had its name recorded in a document of 1857 as *Rio Cassini.* This in turn represents the name of a village (now also *Cacine*) near its mouth. The meaning is uncertain, although the initial *ca-* is almost certainly a locative prefix, meaning "place."

Cacolo. *Town, central Angola.* The name is a local one meaning "to hide," perhaps referring to some tribal custom or event.

Caconda. *Town, west central Angola.* The town was established as a military post in 1682. Its name derives from the Mbundo word *okukondu,* "to go round," "to enclose," perhaps referring to an encampment of some kind.

Caene. See **Qena.**

Caesarea. See **Cherchell.**

Caia. *Town, central Mozambique.* The name represents the Ronga word for "house." In 1954 the town was renamed *Vila Fontes,* in honor of the Portuguese aristocrat Pereira de Melo, Marquis of *Fontes,* one of the founders of the Mozambique Company and its chief administrator. The old name was readopted in 1981.

Cairo. *Capital of Egypt.* The seed from which modern Cairo grew was the ancient Egyptian settlement of *Khere-ohe* or *Kheri-aha,* a name that meant "place of combat," referring to the battle between the sky god Horus and the god Seth, representing Lower and Upper Egypt respectively, which is said to have taken place here. The town was captured in 641 by forces of the calif Omar I, bringer of Islam to Egypt, and he founded a new town called *Fostat* or *Fustat,* in its Arabic form *fusṭāṭ,* meaning "military camp," from Latin *fossatum,* "that which has been dug," "trench." In AD 969 Egypt was invaded by the Fatimids, adherents of a dissident Islamic sect, and their general, Jawhar, established a new walled city on the site. It was originally given the Arabic name *al-manṣūrīyah,* "the victory" (cf. **El Mansura**), but in 974 was renamed as now. The meaning of the name is similar, since it represents Arabic *al-qāhira,* "the strong," "the victorious," "the Martian," from *al-qāhir,* "the victorious one," but in this case the reference was to the Arabic name of the planet Mars, which was in the ascendant at the precise time when construction of the new city began, on Tuesday ("Marsday"), July 6, 969. An alternate Arabic name for Cairo is *miṣr* (see **Egypt**).

Calabar. *Town and port, southeastern Nigeria.* The town, settled in the early 18th century, has a name that was originally that of a kingdom here, itself named for *Kalabari,* its founder and leader, who held power here in the mid-16th century. The town and territory came to be known as *Old Calabar,* to be distinguished from the kingdom of *New Calabar,* some 150 miles (240 km) to the west, at the mouth of what is still known as the *New Calabar* River. The name *Old Calabar* reverted to *Calabar* in 1904.

[1]**Caledon.** *Town, southwestern Cape Province, South Africa.* The original settlement, arising round hot springs in 1810, was given the Afrikaans name *Zwartberg* ("black mountain"), for the mountain (today the *Swartberg*) at the foot of which it lay. In 1813 it was renamed in honor of the Earl of *Caledon,* governor of the Cape from 1807 to 1811. The name happens to be descriptively appropriate, in that it suggests Latin *calidus,* "hot," referring to the springs. Cf. [2]**Caledon.** See also **Bethulie.**

[2]**Caledon.** *River, southeastern Africa.* The river rises in the Drakensberg Mountains, South Africa, and flows generally southwest, forming the border between South Africa and Lesotho before emptying into the Orange River. It was discovered by the Dutch-born Scottish explorer Robert Jacob Gordon in 1777 and originally named *Prinses Wilhelminarivier,* in honor of *Princess Wilhelmina* of Prussia and Orange (1751–1820). In 1809 it was renamed for the Earl of *Caledon,* governor of the Cape from 1807 to 1811. Cf. [1]**Caledon.** The river's Basuto name is *Mogokare,* meaning "river of willow trees."

Calitzdorp. *Town, southern Cape Province, South Africa.* The town, between the Little and Great Karoo, was originally established as a Dutch Reformed Church settlement on land given by Frederick *Calitz* in 1821, and was named for him.

Calvinia. *Town, western Cape Province, South Africa.* The town was founded in 1851 and at the request of the local Dutch Reformed Church minister named in honor of the Protestant theologian and reformer John *Calvin* (1509–1564).

Camacupa. *Town, central Angola.* The local name derives from the nickname of a local chief and means "one who likes to wear shorts." For some years to 1891 the town was renamed *Vila General Machado,* for the Portuguese military leader, Joaquim José *Machado* (1847–1925), governor-general of Mozambique from 1890 to 1891.

Cameron Bay. *Bay, Lake Tanganyika, northern Zambia.* The bay, in the southwestern corner of the lake, is named for Verney Lovett *Cameron* (1844–1894), English naval officer and writer of books for boys, who explored the southern half of Lake Tanganyika in 1874. The name was given by the British explorer Sir Henry Morton Stanley: "Between Kasawa and Kipimpi capes there are deep bays, which I have taken the liberty of calling the Cameron Bays" (*Through the Dark Continent,* 1878).

Cameroon. *Republic, West Africa.* The present form of the name represents Portuguese *Rio dos Camarões,* "river of prawns," the name given in the 16th century by Portuguese explorers to the Wouri River estuary, on which the country's chief port and largest city, Douala, now stands. The colonists were surprised by the abundance of these crustaceans in the river. The name was extended to the country's highest mountain, *Mount Cameroon,* northwest of Douala, and eventually to the whole territory. In colonial times the English name of the country was regularly "the *Cameroons,*" a legacy of the Portuguese plural river name.

Campbell. *Village, northern Cape Province, South Africa.* The village arose as a station of the London Missionary Society named *Knoffel Valley.* It was subsequently renamed for the Rev. John *Campbell* (1766–1840), director of the Society, who was responsible for the Society's stations in the Cape from 1812 to 1814.

Camperdown. *Village, southeastern Natal, South Africa.* The village, west of Durban, was established on the farm of the same name in 1865. The farm's own name commemorated the victory of the British fleet over the Dutch off *Camperdown,* northwestern Holland, in 1797.

Camps Bay. *Coastal town, southwestern Cape Province, South Africa.* The resort, southwest of Cape Town, takes its name from the bay here, in turn named for Ernst Friedrich von *Camptz,* a Dutch East India Company official who came to the Cape in 1778.

Canary Islands. *Island group, off northwest coast of Africa.* The Romans learned of the islands through Juba II, king of Mauretania, whose account of an expedition made in about 40 BC to *Canaria,* the central island of the group (now **Gran Canaria**), was preserved by Pliny the Elder. The island, writes Pliny, was so named "*multitudine canum ingentis magnitudinis,*" "for the large number of dogs of great size" (*Naturalis Historia,* VI, 202). The Romans therefore named the group as a whole *Canariae Insulae,* "islands of dogs," from Latin *canis,* "dog." Pliny also refers to the islands as *Fortunatae Insulae,* "fortunate islands" (see **Fuerteventura**). The local (Guanche) name for the islands is *Tamaran,* "land of the strong." The islands in turn gave the name of the *canary,* a bird native to them. See also the individual islands: **Gomera, Hierro, Lanzarote, La Palma, Tenerife.**

Cango Caves. *Caves, southern Cape Province, South Africa.* The caves, a national monument in the Groot-Swartberge, take their name from the river here. Its own name is probably a corruption of Khoikhoin (Hottentot) *!a-!kanub,* "valley in the hills." (The unusual characters represent clicks.) In 1762 the farm on which the caves are located was recorded as *De Camboys aan de Cango,* "the kitchen on the Cango."

Canopus. *Ancient town and port, northern Egypt.* The town is said to take its name from *Canopus,* pilot of the ship of King Menelaus of Sparta in Greek mythology, who brought Menelaus and his wife Helen to Egypt and who died here.

Cape Coast. *Town and former port, southern Ghana.* The town, on the Gulf of Guinea, takes its name from *Cape Coast* Castle, built by the Swedes in 1652 and passing to the British in 1664. The cape concerned is the low promontory that juts into the sea here. See also **Anécho.**

Cape Province. *Province, southern South Africa.* The province, with full formal name *Cape of Good Hope Province,* takes its name from the Cape of **Good Hope,** around which it lies. Before 1910, under British administration, the province was known as *Cape Colony.* See also **Cape Town.**

Cape Town. *Legislative capital of South Africa.* South Africa's second largest city, the capital of **Cape Province,** developed from a settlement established by the Dutch navigator Jan van Riebeeck in 1652. Its original Dutch name was simply *Cabo de Goede Hoop,* "Cape of Good Hope," a straightforward transfer from the Cape of **Good Hope** near which it had arisen. The English name *Cape Town* and Dutch (Afrikaans) name *Kaapstad* first became current in the mid-18th century. The indigenous Khoikhoin (Hottentot) name of the city is *Huigais,* meaning "stony place." This was originally applied to the castle, but was later extended to the whole town.

Cape Verde. *Island republic, off west coast of Africa.* The name is a part-translation of Portuguese *Cabo Verde,* "green cape," the name of the mainland cape (now in Senegal) to the west of which it lies. The cape was itself so named by Portuguese explorers in the 15th century with reference to the greenness of the palm trees here by contrast with the barren, sandy coast to the north: "*é assim chamado porque os primeiros que o descobriram ... encontraram-no todo verde com grandes árvores que conservam as folhas todo o ano*" ("it was so called because the first people to discover it ... found it quite green with big trees that keep their leaves all year") (João de Barros, *Dos feitos que os Portugueses fizeram no descobrimento e conquista dos mares e terras de Oriente,* 1552). For individual islands, see **Boa Vista, Brava, Fogo, Maio, Rombo, Sal, Santa Luzia, Santo Antão, São Nicolau, São Tiago, São Vicente.**

Caprivi Strip. *Region, northeastern Namibia.* The narrow strip of land, extended eastward between Angola and Zambia to the north and Botswana to the south, is a territory obtained from the British in 1893 by the German chancellor Graf Leo von *Caprivi* (1831–1899), for whom it is named. The aim of the acquisition was to link what was then German South-West Africa to Germany's possessions in East Africa.

Careysburg. *Town, western Liberia.* The town was settled in 1859 by freed black American slaves and is named for the Rev. Lott *Carey,* an American black minister who arrived in 1821 and settled in Monrovia. The town is still mainly inhabited by Carey's descendants.

Carletonville. *Town, southern Transvaal, South Africa.* The town, west of Johannesburg, takes its name from Guy *Carleton* Jones, the mining engineer and geologist who was a director of Consolidated Gold Fields here for 35 years.

Carnarvon. *Town, central Cape Province, South Africa.* The town was founded in 1860 and was at first given the Afrikaans name *Harmsfontein* ("fountain of sorrow"). It was given its present name in 1874 in honor of Henry Howard Molyneux Herbert, 4th Earl of *Carnarvon* (1841–1890), British colonial secretary from 1866 to 1867 and 1874 to 1888. The earls take their title from the historic Welsh town of *Caernarfon.*

Carnot. *Town, southwestern Central African Republic.* The town arose in the late 19th century in what was then the young French colony of Ubangi-Shari and was named for the recently assassinated French president, Sadi *Carnot* (1837–1894). Cf. **Carnotville**.

Carnotville. *Town, central Benin.* The settlement was founded on September 16, 1894, and named for Sadi *Carnot* (1837–1894), 4th president of France, assassinated a few months earlier. Cf. **Carnot**.

Carolina. *Town, eastern Transvaal, South Africa.* The town was founded in 1886 and named for *Caroline* Coetzee, née Smit, wife of its founder and an aunt of General Nicolas Jacobus Smit, vice-president of the South African Republic from 1886 to 1896.

Carthage. *Ancient city state, North Africa.* The historic city and state, on the Mediterranean coast to the northeast of modern Tunis, was founded by Phoenician colonists in the late 8th century BC. Its name is a form of Phoenician *qart ĥadaŝ,* "new town," from *qart,* "town," and ĥadaŝ, "new." It was "new" by comparison either with the Phoenician mother city of Tyre or perhaps, according to some, with **Utica**, whose name may mean "old." (Utica, some 15 miles northwest of Carthage, was founded several years earlier.) The fame of Carthage as an empire dominating North Africa and the Mediterranean led to the adoption of its name for several American towns and cities, especially during the vogue for classical names in the early 19th century. Carthage also gave the name of the Spanish port of *Cartagena* (from Latin *Carthago nova,* "new Carthage," in effect "new new town") and, in turn, the Colombian port of the same name.

Casablanca. *City and port, northwestern Morocco.* The Spanish name is a translation of Portuguese *casa branca,* "white house," from *casa,* "house," and *branca,* "white." This was the name given by the Portuguese in 1515 to the town that they founded on the site of the former village of Anfa. The reference is to the city's still predominately white buildings. The modern Arabic name is a similar translation, as *ad-dār al-bayḍāʿ,* from *al* (*ad-* before *d*), "the," *dār,* "house" (compare **Dar es Salaam**), and *bayḍāʿ,* feminine of *abyaḍ,* "white," *Anfa,* now a district of the city, has a name representing a Berber word meaning "little hill."

Casamance. *River, Senegal.* The name is both that of a river in southern Senegal and of a region here, between Gambia and Guinea-Bissau. It means "king Casa," from the name of a local chief, *Casa,* and *mansa,* "king." The name was given to the river by the Portuguese in the 15th century.

Cashel. *Village, eastern Zimbabwe.* The village, near the border with Mozambique, takes its name from Colonel E. *Cashel,* a pioneer settler who retired here after service with the British South Africa Police.

Catandica. *Village, western Mozambique.* The village, near the border with Zimbabwe, takes its name from the son of a local chief who had served in the army of the Portuguese commander Manuel

António de Sousa. Sousa was nicknamed *Gouveia* with reference to *Goa,* the Portuguese state on the west coast of India that was his birthplace, and this gave the village's colonial name of *Vila Gouveia* from 1915 to 1980. Sousa was killed in battle in 1892 in a war with the Macombi tribe.

Catembe. *Village, southern Mozambique.* The village, south of the capital, Maputo, derives its name from Ronga *ka-*, the possessive prefix, and the *Tembe* River here. Its own name is probably a tribal one.

Cathcart. *Town, southeastern Cape Province, South Africa.* The town arose in 1858 out of a military post set up in 1850. It was named for Sir George *Cathcart* (1794–1854), governor of the Cape from 1852 to his death. See also **Reivilo.**

Catherine, Mount. *Mountain, northeastern Egypt.* Egypt's highest peak, south of Mount Sinai on the Sinai Peninsula, is so named because priests are traditionally said to have found the remains of St. *Catherine* here in the 9th or 10th century. Believers claim that she was born in Alexandria in the late 3d century and that her body was transported here by "angels" after her torture (on a Catherine wheel) and martyrdom. But she has no ancient cult, and she may not even have existed. The Arabic name of the peak is *jabal katrīnah.*

Cato Ridge. *Village, southern Natal, South Africa.* The village, midway between Pietermaritzburg and Durban, derives its name from the pioneer settler George Christopher *Cato,* who had given property here for British interests. The village grew up around the ferromanganese factory on the ridge here.

Catuane. *Village, southern Mozambique.* The village, on the border with Natal, South Africa, takes its name from that of a former ruler here.

Caungula. *Town, northern Angola.* The town, originally the seat of a military captaincy, has a local name meaning "leader of the people," a chief's title.

Cavally. *River, West Africa.* The river, which forms the border between Liberia and Côte d'Ivoire, appears to have a name derived from Portuguese *cavalo* or Italian *cavallo,* "horse," although the true origin may lie in some indigenous name.

Cazombo. *Town, eastern Angola.* The town has a local name meaning literally "boy garment," from *ca,* "boy," and *zombo,* "garment worn at circumcision." The area was one where boys aged 8 to 14 were ritually circumcised wearing a special garment.

Cedarberg. *Mountain range, southwestern Cape Province, South Africa.* The range derives its name from the cedar trees that are prominent on its heights.

Centenary. *Village, northern Zimbabwe.* The village, north of the capital, Harare, was so named in 1953 to commemorate the centenary of the birth of Cecil Rhodes (1853–1902), the British colonial financier and statesman for whom **Rhodesia** was named.

Central African Empire. See **Central African Republic.**

Central African Republic. *Republic, Central Africa.* The country is obviously named for its location in the virtual center of the African continent. For three years from 1976 the country was renamed as the *Central African Empire.* Before 1958 it was known as *Ubangi-Shari,* for the names of two of its principal rivers, the **Ubangi** and the **Shari.** It is curious that this indigenous name was exchanged for a European one. Most colonial placenames have done the reverse, progressing from a European name to an African.

Ceres. *Town, southwestern Cape Province, South Africa.* The town was established on a farm in 1854 and was named for *Ceres,* Roman goddess of agriculture, as a reference to the fertility of the area.

Ceuta. *Town and port, northern Morocco.* The town, a Spanish possession opposite Gibraltar, is a historic settlement that was successively colonized by the Carthaginians, Greeks, and Romans. Its Roman name was *Septem Fratres,* "seven brothers," a borrowing of the Latin name for the group of seven hills nearby. The present name is a form of *Septem,* influenced by Arabic *sabʿa,* "seven."

Chad. *Republic, north Central Africa.* The country takes its name from Lake *Chad,* itself from a local word meaning "large expanse of water," in other words simply "lake."

Chai-Chai. See **Xai-Xai.**

Chambeshi. *River, Zambia.* The river rises in northern Zambia, then flows southwest to cross swampland south of Lake Bangweulu and become the Luapula, under which name it follows the border with Zaïre to join the Lualaba and form the Congo. Its name, also spelled *Chambezi,* has the same origin as that of the **Zambezi**, so in effect means "great river."

Changane. *River, Mozambique.* The river flows north through central Mozambique to empty into the Save. To the west of its upper reaches lie marshes. Hence its name, meaning "reed."

Changara. *Village, western Mozambique.* The village, near the border with Zimbabwe, has a name that means "place of dance and merriment," referring to an assembly site here for celebratory rituals.

Chaouèn. *Town, northern Morocco.* The town's name is a French-influenced form of Berber *iššawen,* plural of *išš,* "horn," "peak." The town is in the hilly coastal district of Er Rif.

Charl Cilliers. *Village, southeastern Transvaal, South Africa.* The village, southeast of Johannesburg, was originally named *Van Tondershoek,* for a church leader. In 1917 the name was changed in honor of the Voortrekker leader *Sarel Cilliers* (1801–1871), whose first name came to be spelled "*Charl.*"

Charlestown. *Town, northern Natal, South Africa.* The town was founded in 1889 and named for Sir *Charles* Mitchell (died 1899), governor of Natal from 1889 to 1893.

Chela, Serra da. *Mountain range, southwestern Angola.* The name may derive from the Otyela language and mean "big precipice."

Chemba. *Town, central Mozambique.* The town, on the Zambezi River near the border with Malawi, takes its name from the river that flows into the Zambezi here. Its meaning is "trench," "ditch."

Cheops. See **Giza.**

Chephren. See **Giza.**

Cherchell. *Town and port, northern Algeria.* The modern name of the port is a corruption of its Roman name, *Caesarea.* It was just one of a number of places in the Roman Empire so named for a Roman emperor bearing the title *Caesar.* Cherchell was the capital of ancient Mauretania.

Chew Bahir. See Lake **Turkana.**

Chibia. *Town, southwestern Angola.* The town originated with the

Portuguese colonial form of the name, *São Pedro da Chibia,* "St. Peter of Chibia." The last word of this is the local name, deriving from Nhaneca *tviviya,* meaning either "to present" or "to touch," probably with reference to some incident. From 1955 to 1980 the town was known as *João de Almeida,* for the Portuguese explorer of this name.

Chibuto. *Town, southern Mozambique.* The town, north of Xai-Xai, has a difficult name that may derive from a local word *butuma,* meaning "rock."

Chicapa. *River, Southern Africa.* The river rises in central Angola and flows north into Zaïre to join the Kasai. Its local name means "bark," "skin," perhaps referring to the bark craft used on it.

Chicualacuala. *Town, western Mozambique.* The town, on the border with Zimbabwe, derives its name from the local word *xi-quadja,* "quail," from the abundance of these birds here. For some years until 1981 the town was called *Malvérnia,* a name commemorating Sir Godfrey Huggins, Viscount *Malvern* (1883–1971), prime minister of Southern Rhodesia (now Zimbabwe) from 1933 to 1953 and of the Central African Federation (present-day Malawi, Zimbabwe, and Zambia) from 1953 to 1956.

Chikwawa. *Town, southern Malawi.* The town, a port on the Shire River, was established in 1892 and given a local name meaning "low river carved into a cliff."

Chililabombwe. *Town, northern Zambia.* The name of the town is a local one meaning "croaking frog," from the prevalence of these creatures here. The town was founded in 1955 under the name of *Bancroft,* for the Canadian-born geologist Dr. Joseph *Bancroft* (1882–1957), who worked in Zambia on behalf of the Anglo-American Corporation and who opened a copper mine here. The name changed to its present form in the late 1960s.

Chilimanzi. *Village, east central Zimbabwe.* The village takes its name from that of chief *Chirumanzu,* of the Govera branch of the Shona people. It is said to mean "one in a long shirt." The name is also that of a district here.

Chilumba. *Town, northern Malawi.* The town, a port on Lake Malawi, was originally known as *Deep Bay,* referring to the depth of water here. When Malawi gained independence in 1966 the name was changed to its present form. This is a Nyanja word meaning "island," again referring to the town's lakeside location.

Chimanimani. *Town, eastern Zimbabwe.* The name is not only that of the town here but of mountains and the local national park. It is a form of *Tshimanimani,* the name used by the Ndau people for the narrow pass here, and meaning "to be squeezed together," referring to the restricted defile through which the Musapa River runs. Another local name for the mountains is *Mawenje,* "rocky mountains." The town was founded in 1893 and was originally called *Melsetter,* taking this name from the Orkney estate of its two founders, the Scottish trekkers Thomas and Dunbar Moodie. When Zimbabwe gained independence in 1980, the name was changed to *Mandidzuzure,* a term for people who are native to the area. In 1982 the present name was adopted. See also **Chipinge**.

Chinguetti. *Village, west central Mauritania.* The name is of uncertain origin, but has been popularly interpreted as "springs of the horse."

Chinhoyi. *Town, north central Zimbabwe.* The name is traditionally said to be that of the Zezuru chief *Tshinoyi* who settled hear the caves here in the 19th century. The local name for the caves, now the Chinhoyi Caves National Park, is *Tshrodziva,* "fallen pool." The name was spelled *Sinoya* until 1980.

Chipata. *Town, eastern Zambia.* The town, near the border with Malawi, was founded in 1899 as the capital of North Eastern Rhodesia and was originally named *Fort James,* for the South African and Rhodesian statesman, Sir Leander Starr *Jameson* (1853–1917), who led the "Jameson Raid," or armed invasion of the Transvaal, in 1895. When Zambia gained independence in 1964, the name was changed to its present form, meaning "gateway," referring to the town's border location.

Chipinga. See **Chipinge.**

Chipinge. *Town, southeastern Zimbabwe.* The town arose in the 19th century and was originally named *Melsetter.* This name was then transferred to another settlement to the north. (See **Chimanimani** for the origin.) The present name is a local one meaning "hindrance," referring to a buttress in the eastern mountains that originally blocked the through route. The name was spelled *Chipinga* until 1980.

Chire. See **Shire.**

Chiromo. *Town, southern Malawi.* The town was the official place of entry into the country from 1892 and became a government station. Its Nyanja name means "lip of land," referring to its location between two rivers.

Chirundu. *Village, northern Zimbabwe.* The village, on the border with Zambia, takes its name from that of the hill to the northwest. It in turn is named for *Tshirundu,* a Tonka chief who once lived here, reportedly in order to escape the heat of the valley.

Chitembo. *Town, south central Angola.* The name of the town is that of a chief who once lived in the region.

Chitipa. *Town, northwestern Malawi.* The town was established as a fortified settlement in 1896 to guard the road to Tanganyika (now Tanzania). It was originally named *Fort Hill,* for Sir Clement Lloyd *Hill* (1845–1913) of the British Foreign Office. After Malawi gained independence in 1966, the name was changed to its present form, that of a chief who once lived in the district.

Chiuta, Lake. *Lake, northwestern Mozambique.* The lake, on the border with Malawi, has a Nyanja name meaning "god," perhaps referring either to the breadth of the lake or to the rainbows that frequently appear over it.

Chivhu. *Town, east central Zimbabwe.* The town was founded as a farm in 1891 and was originally known as *Enkeldoorn,* an Afrikaans name meaning "single thorn." This referred to the tree *Acacia robusta,* and implied that a single such tree grew here. When Zimbabwe gained independence in 1980, the name was changed to its present form, a local word said to mean "anthill."

Chivirira Falls. *Waterfall, Sabi River, southeastern Zimbabwe.* The falls, over which the Sabi drops before crossing the border into Mozambique, have a local name said to mean "place of boiling."

Choma. *Town, southeastern Zambia.* The town was established in about 1905 and has a Lala name meaning "large drum," apparently with reference to a ceremony regularly performed here.

Chott ech-Chergui. *Lake, northwestern Algeria.* The name is a French form of Arabic *shaṭṭ ash-sharqī,* "eastern shott," from *shaṭṭ,* "shott" (shallow salt lake) and *sharqī,* "eastern," from *sharq,* "east." Cf. **Chott el-Jerid.**

Chott el-Jerid. *Lake, west central Tunisia.* The name is a French form of Arabic *shaṭṭ al-jarīd,* "shott of the palm-trees," from *shaṭṭ,* "shott" (shallow salt lake) and *jarīd,* "palm-trees," plural of *jarīda.* Cf. **Chott ech-Chergui.**

Chrissie, Lake. *Lake, southeastern Transvaal, South Africa.* The lake is named for *Christina,* daughter of the Voortrekker leader Marthinus Wessel Pretorius (1819–1901), founder of **Pretoria** and first president of the South African Republic. The name has passed from the lake to that of the nearby village of *Lake Chrissie* (Afrikaans, *Chrissiesmeer*). The Swazi name for the site was *Kachibibi,* from *lichibi,* "lake," and *khulu,* "big." The Boers named the region *Matotoland,* a corruption of *maxoxo,* "frogs," referring to the abundance of these creatures here after rainfall.

Christiana. *Town, southwestern Transvaal, South Africa.* The town was established on a farm in 1870 and according to some is said to have been named for the owner of the farm, *Christiaan* Hattingh. It seems more likely, however, that the name was given for *Christina,* daughter of Marthinus Wessel Pretorius (1819–1901), first president of the South African Republic.

Cidade Velha. *Town and port, São Tiago, Cape Verde Islands.* The name is Portuguese for "old city." The town, now not much more than a fishing village, is the former capital of the Cape Verde Islands, and arose on the site where the Portuguese made their first base in 1461. Its original name was *Ribeira Grande,* Portuguese for "great river." (Cf. **Ribeira Grande** on Santo Antão.) It gained its present name after it was abandoned in 1712 following a French attack and the capital was moved along the coast to Praia (in 1769).

Cinnamon Coast. *Coast, East Africa.* The name was popularly given to the coastline of what is now northern Somalia, west of Cape Guardafui (Ras Asir). The reference is to the spices with which this part of Africa is associated. Somalia is still noted for its fragrant shrubs and trees, such as gum trees and the *Boswellia,* which yield frankincense. (A map of Arabia dated about 1815 labels the coast *Myrrh and Incense Country.*) Cape Guardafui itself was also known as the *Cape of Perfumes.* For a similar name the other side of Africa, see **Grain Coast.**

Cirta. See **Constantine.**

Ciskei. *Bantustan, southern Cape Province, South Africa.* The Bantu homeland has a name derived from Latin *cis,* "this side of," and **Kei** (in full, *Great Kei*), the river to the west of which it lies. Its name contrasts with that of its near (but not contiguous) neighbor, **Transkei,** which lies to the east of the Kei.

Cité de Cansado. *Residential area, western Mauritania.* The residential area, effectively a southern suburb of Nouadhibou, takes its name from *Pointe de Cansado,* one of the spurs on Cape Blanc here. This French name represents a Portuguese original, *Cabo Cansado,* literally "tiresome cape," implying one associated with navigational difficulties or some particular misfortune.

Clanwilliam. *Town, southwestern Cape Province, South Africa.* The town was originally known as *Jan Disselsvlei,* "Jan Dissel's vlei," for the owner of the farm on which it arose in the early years of the 19th century. (A *vlei* is an area of low-lying marshy ground.) In 1814 the settlement adopted its present name. It was given by Sir John Cradock, governor of the Cape, in honor of his father-in-law, the Earl of *Clanwilliam*. See also **Cradock**.

Claremont. *Southern district of Cape Town, Cape Province, South Africa.* The district arose as a village in 1850 and was named for *Claremont* House, Surrey, England, residence of Sir John Molteno, first prime minister of the Cape (in 1872). Claremont House is itself named for the Earl of *Clare,* who bought it in 1714.

Clarens. *Village, eastern Orange Free State, South Africa.* The village was founded in 1912 and named for *Clarens,* Switzerland, where President Kruger died in 1904. (He was buried in Pretoria.)

Clocolan. *Town, eastern Orange Free State, South Africa.* There appears to have been a settlement here since at least 1860, although the name is first recorded only in 1906. It perhaps represents a Sotho name *Thlothlonaneng,* meaning "there we were stabbed," or else a Zulu name *Hlohlawani,* "to push," "to press into." Either of these could refer to an incident where a group of local people were taken into a cave and massacred. The nearby mountain is named *Klokolani,* which seems to be a corruption of the Zulu name.

Cofimvaba. *Village, Transkei, South Africa.* The name has the sense "to squeeze a milk bag," from Xhosa *nku cofa,* "to press," "to work," and *im vaba,* "the milk sack." When milk in a bag turns sour and partly solidifies, it is pressed and kneaded to break it up into lumps. The reference is thus probably to the nearby stream, which after heavy rain froths like milk being kneaded in a bag.

Colenso. *Town, western Natal, South Africa.* The town, at first simply a wagon halt, was laid out in 1855 and named for Bishop John Williams *Colenso* (1814–1883), the first Anglican bishop of Natal.

Colesberg. *Town, northern Cape Province, South Africa.* The town was founded in 1830 and was at first given the Afrikaans name *Toverberg,* "magic mountain," referring to the mountain here that appears to recede as one approaches it. The present name represents that of Sir Galbraith Lowry *Cole* (1772–1842), governor of the Cape from 1828 to 1833. *Berg* was retained from the earlier name.

Coligny. *Town, southwestern Transvaal, South Africa.* The town arose from the railroad station on the main line from Kimberley to Johannesburg, and was at first named *Treurfontein,* "fountain of sorrows," for a nearby farm. In about 1918 the town was renamed at the request of the inhabitants for Gaspard de *Coligny* (1519–1572), the French Huguenot leader.

Colleen Bawn. *Village, southern Zimbabwe.* The village arose round the limestone mine opened here in 1895 by the prospector John Daly, who gave it an Irish name meaning "fair girl," perhaps as a direct adoption from Dion Boucicault's popular play *The Colleen Bawn* (1860). The placename possibly refers to the limestone here, which was light-colored and attractive. (Note: *The Times Atlas of the World,* in its 8th edition of 1990, has the name misprinted *Colleen Dawn* both on the map and in the gazetteer.)

Comoros. *Island republic, off east coast of Africa.* The island group, a former French territory in the Indian Ocean off the northwest coast of Madagascar, has a name that represents Arabic *qamar,* "moon." This was the Arabs' name for the

Magellanic Clouds which indicated the south, and which they transferred to all the islands in the southern latitudes here, including Madagascar. Some scholars also link the name with that of the mythical "Mountains of the Moon," which were said to be situated somewhere in equatorial Africa. (See **Ruwenzori.**) The local name of *Grande Comore* (or *Great Comoro*), the largest island in the group, is *Ngazidja* or *Angaziya,* of uncertain meaning. The three others are *Ndzouani, Mohéli,* and *Mayotte.*

Compassberg. *Mountain, central Cape Province, South Africa.* The name is an English alteration of Afrikaans *Kompasberg,* "compass mountain." This was the name given the mountain in 1778 by the Dutch-born Scottish explorer and soldier Robert Jacob Gordon, since the surrounding country appears as a panorama from the summit and streams descend on all sides like the points of a compass. The mountain's central location in the country gives the name added significance.

Conakry. *Capital of Guinea.* The city, on a peninsula on Tombo Island, was founded in 1884 on the site of a Susu settlement of the same name. This represents a local word *konakri,* "beyond the waters," "the other shore," referring to the location, rendering the town equally visible from north or south.

Conception Bay. *Bay, western Namibia.* The bay, south of Walvis Bay, has a name that is an English translation of Portuguese *Bahia do Conçeicão.* The reference is almost certainly to the Immaculate Conception of the Virgin Mary. The Germans translated the name as *Empfängnisbucht.*

Concession. *Village, northern Zimbabwe.* The village, north of the capital, Harare, has a name that alludes to the concession to establish a gold mine here granted by Lobengula, the Matabele (Ndebele) king, to the American Henry Clay Moore. The concession was taken over by Cecil Rhodes in 1893, and in exchange Moore was given rights to stake claims in Mashonaland.

Congo. *Republic, Central Africa.* The country takes its name from the river that today forms its eastern border. The river's name itself represents Bantu *kongo,* "mountain," referring originally to the *Bakongo* people for whom the historic kingdom of *Kongo* was named. This was an extensive region in the lower reaches of the river, ruled from the 14th to 19th century by a powerful monarch known as the *manikongo,* "lord Kongo." (His royal power was inherited by matrilinear succession, that is, by his brothers in order of seniority or by his eldest sister's sons. From the 16th century he was actually styled "king" in official correspondence with the Portuguese court and papal curia. Hence, perhaps, the name of *King Kong,* the giant ape of the famous movie. Edgar Wallace, who wrote the screenplay, lived and worked in South Africa and wrote stories set in West Africa, such as *Sanders of the River,* the river in this actually being the Congo.) Names based on *Congo* were also formerly used for present-day **Zaïre,** itself now named for its own name for the river, which forms its western border. From 1960 to 1970 Congo was obliged to be known as *Congo (Brazzaville),* for its capital, in order to be distinguished from *Congo (Léopoldville)* and (from 1965) *Congo (Kinshasa).* The Congo River was renamed *Livingstone* by the British explorer Sir Henry Morton Stanley when he made his momentous descent of it in 1876–77 (see **Lualaba**).

Congo (Brazzaville). See **Congo.**

Congo (Kinshasa). See **Zaïre.**

Congo (Léopoldville). See **Zaïre.**

Congo Free State. See **Zaïre.**

Constantiaberg. *Mountain, southwestern Cape Province, South Africa.* The mountain, south of Cape Town, takes its name from the famous estate of *Groot Constantia* here, the source of *Constantia* wine. The estate is said to have been named by Simon van der Stel, governor of the Cape from 1691 to 1699, for his wife, *Constantia.* Some authorities, however, claim he named it for another Constantia, daughter of Commissioner Rijkloff van Goens.

Constantine. *City, northeastern Algeria.* The city takes its name from the Roman emperor *Constantine* the Great, who rebuilt it in AD 311. The historic Carthaginian name of the town was *Sarim Batim.* In the 2d century BC it then became the capital of the Numidian kings under the Latin name of *Cirta,* from Punic *qart,* "town" (see **Carthage**). The present Arabic form of the name is *qasanṭīna.*

Cookhouse. *Village, southern Cape Province, South Africa.* The village, north of Port Elizabeth, has a name referring either to an actual military cookhouse here, where troops could rest and eat, or else metaphorically to the baking climate of the region.

Copperbelt. *Province, northern Zambia.* The name of the province before 1969 was *Western,* not entirely accurate for this northern region of the country. It was changed to denote the rich copper deposits here; *Western* was relocated more precisely.

Coppolani. *Coastal village, western Mauritania.* The village, north of the capital, Nouakchott, is one of the few places in Mauritania to have a colonial name. It is that of Xavier *Coppolani,* French commandant of Mauritania Civil Territory for just seven months from 1904 to 1905, when he was assassinated by religious fanatics from the Adrar region.

Coquilhatville. See **Mbandaka.**

Cornelia. *Village, northeastern Orange Free State, South Africa.* The village was founded in 1917 and named for the second wife, *Cornelia,* née Mulder, of Francis William Reitz (1844–1934), president of the Orange Free State from 1889 to 1895. See also **Reitz.**

Corvo. *Island, northwestern Azores.* The northwesternmost and smallest island of the group has a Portuguese name meaning "raven," presumably because these birds were sighted here. Compare the name of the **Azores** themselves.

Côte d'Ivoire. *Republic, West Africa.* The country's present French name was officially adopted in 1986, following the republic's request that this form of the name be utilized as the protocol version in all languages. Previous to this, countries had simply translated the name into the vernacular, giving English *Ivory Coast,* German *Elfenbeinküste,* Spanish *Costa de Marfil,* Italian *Costa d'Avorio,* Russian *Bereg Slonovoy Kosti,* and so on. The name originated as that of the coastal region here where ivory was traded from the late 15th century. The first European settlers here were French missionaries in 1637. The country became a formal French protectorate in 1889 and a colony in 1893.

Cotonou. *Town and port, southern Benin.* The name of the former *de facto* capital of Dahomey represents the local name *Ko Tonu,* from *ku,* "dead," and *tonu,* "lake." A legend tells how the souls of the dead were carried down the Ouémé River to the sea. The trees at the river mouth are reddish in color, and it was believed that this was caused by traces of blood from the dead bodies when they became entangled in the sharp branches. The former name of the town was *Donukpa,* from Aizo *donu* or *tonu,* "lake," and *kpa,* "near."

Coyah. *Village, western Guinea.* The village, northeast of Conakry, the capital, has a Mandenyi name meaning "place of the snake," from *ko,* "snake," "serpent," and *ya,* "place."

Cradock. *Town, southeastern Cape Province, South Africa.* The town, founded in 1813 as a frontier outpost, was named in honor of Sir John Francis *Cradock* (1762–1839), governor of the Cape from 1811 to 1814. See also *Clanwilliam.*

Creighton. *Village, southern Natal, South Africa.* The village was established in 1865 and was originally known as *Dronkvlei,* "drunken marsh," since the local water seemed to make the cattle reel drunkenly. When Sir Henry McCallum became governor of Natal in 1901, the name was changed to *Creighton,* for the maiden name of his wife, Maud.

Crocodilopolis. See **El Faiyûm.**

Cross, Cape. *Cape, northwestern Namibia.* The cape gets its name from the stone cross erected here by the Portuguese navigator Diogo Cão in 1484.

Crystal Mountains. *Mountain range, Central Africa.* The low mountains extend south from northwestern Gabon and eastern Equatorial Guinea to northwestern Angola, and are named for their precambrian crystalline rock.

Cuando. *River, Southern Africa.* The river, a tributary of the Zambezi, rises in south central Angola and flows generally southeast along the border between Angola and Zambia, then along that between Namibia and Botswana, to become the Linyanti in its lower reaches. Its name is a Portuguese form of *Kwando,* the name of a powerful chief in the region.

Cuango. *River, Central Africa.* The river rises in central Angola and flows generally north along the border between Angola and Zaïre to empty into the Kasai, itself a tributary of the Congo, in western Zaïre. Its name is a Portuguese spelling of *Kwango,* a Bantu name meaning simply "great river."

Cuanza. *River, Angola.* The river rises in south central Angola and flows generally southwest to enter the Atlantic near Luanda. Its name is a Portuguese form of *Kwanza,* a Bantu word meaning "prime," "most important," a description still valid today for Angola's main river. The name was adopted for the two provinces of *Cuanza Norte* ("North Cuanza") and *Cuanza Sul* ("South Cuanza") and also became that of Angola's basic monetary unit, the *kwanza.*

Cubal. *Town, western Angola.* The name, also that of a river here, is of Okuvala origin, meaning "to start where no one has arrived." The reference is to a settlement in virgin territory.

Cullinan. *Town, south central Transvaal, South Africa.* The mining town was laid out in 1902 and was named for the South African industrialist Sir Thomas Major *Cullinan* (1862–1836), discoverer of the Premier Diamond Mine nearby. The famous *Cullinan* diamond, the world's largest, was found in this mine in 1905.

Cunene. See **Kunene.**

Cuvette. *Region, north central Congo.* The region takes its name from French *cuvette,* "basin," "depression," referring to the western section of the Congo River basin that extends here from the western mountains and plateaus to the Congo itself in the east.

Cwebeni. See **Richards Bay.**

Cydamus. See **Gadamès.**

Cyrenaica. *Historic region, eastern Libya.* The region takes its name from Latin *Cyrenaica,* "of **Cyrene,**" referring to the ancient colony that had this town as its capital. In modern times the name was revived for a province here (1951–1963). See also **Pentapolis.**

Cyrene. *Ancient city, eastern Libya.* The historic city, founded by the Greeks in about 630 BC, takes its name from the mythological nymph *Cyrene.* It gave its name to **Cyrenaica,** the territory of which it became the capital.

Dahab. *Town and resort, northeastern Egypt.* The town, on the Gulf of Aqaba, has a name representing Arabic *dahab,* "gold." Reference is to the golden sand of the beaches here.

Dahomey. *Former name of Benin.* The country that was renamed **Benin** in 1975 took its old name from the former kingdom of *Dan Homé,* said to mean "[built] on the stomach of Dan." The reference is to the palace of King Wegbaya, which was built on the site where his old enemy Dan was buried. However, the name may equally be related to that of **Abomey,** a town in the south of the country.

Dakar. *Capital of Senegal.* The name is believed to represent Wolof *n'dakar,* "tamarind tree." The story goes that when the first explorers asked local people the name of their settlement, they thought they were being asked to identify a prominent tamarind tree on the coast here, and so gave its name. It is possible, however, that the actual origin may be in a Wolof word meaning either "waterless" or "refuge." The present city was founded in 1857.

Dakhla. See **Ad Dakhla.**

Dakhla Oasis. *Oasis, central Egypt.* The name represents Arabic *ad-dakhla,* "the inner," and refers to the location of this oasis by comparison with that further east at *El-Kharga.*

Daloa. *Town, west central Côte d'Ivoire.* The original settlement here was founded by two Africans and named for one of them, *Dalo,* of the Guro tribe. The present town, retaining the name, developed from the French military post set up in 1903.

Dalton. *Village, east central Natal, South Africa.* The village arose at the turn of the 20th century and was named as a tribute to Henry Boast of North *Dalton,* Yorkshire, England, who organized the emigration of Yorkshire people to Natal in about 1850.

Damanhūr. *City, northern Egypt.* The city's present name has evolved from its ancient Egyptian name of *Timinhor,* "city of Horus," with reference to the solar god of Egyptian mythology, who was worshipped here. In Hellenistic times its name was *Hermopolis Parva,* "little Hermopolis," as distinct from *Hermopolis Magna,* "great Hermopolis," modern **El-Ashmunein.** See also **Damietta.**

Damaraland. *Region, central Namibia.* The region, a plateau, takes its name from the *Damara,* a Khoikhoin (Hottentot) people, to which English *land* has been added. *Damara* is said to be the dual feminine form of the insulting name *Daman,* used by the British to designate the inhabitants. This could itself come from a San (Bushman) word *dama,* "child," or possibly mean "riches," as in the local expression *gamocha-dama,* "riches of oxen." The theory has also been proposed that *Damara* derives from Malay *damar,* the name of a coniferous tree of southeastern Asia that yields a dark resin. (The word is itself Malay for "resin.") The suggestion is that Dutch colonists in Africa would have been familiar with the Malay word and therefore used it to describe the skin color of the

Namibian people. The name is certainly unlikely to have originated in that of the biblical character *Damaris* (Acts 17:34), as some have conjectured, on the grounds that Damaris was a female convert to Christianity, and that the Africans were similarly converted. The Damara people call themselves *Herero* (see **Herero**), *Nu-Khoin,* "black men," or *Hau-Khoin,* "upright men."

Damba. *Town, northern Angola.* The name derives from that of a local chief, Fumuachi *Mandamba,* nicknamed "king of the world."

Dambam. *Village, east central Nigeria.* The name is said to mean "full of water," referring to a local well.

Damietta. *City and port, northern Egypt.* The name is an Italian alteration of Arabic *dumyāṭ,* itself a corruption of the town's original Coptic name of *Tamiati.* The precise sense of this is uncertain, but the initial *Tam-* almost certainly means "city," as for **Damanhūr.**

Danakil. *Region, northeastern Africa.* The desert region, in northeastern Ethiopia, southern Eritrea, and northern Djibouti, takes its name from its indigenous people, the *Danakil,* whose name derives from an Ethiopian root meaning "sea." Danakil is not far inland from the Red Sea. The Danakil are also known as the Afars (see **Djibouti**).

Dande. *River, Angola.* The river rises in central Angola and flows west to enter the Atlantic north of Luanda. Its name has been recorded on old maps as *Madalena,* suggesting that it may have been sighted and named by Portuguese colonists on July 22, St. Mary *Magdalene*'s day. If so, the present name would be a corruption of this.

Danger Point. *Headland, southwestern Cape Province, South Africa.* The promontory, south of Walker Bay, is so named because its reefs and rocks present a serious hazard to shipping. It has claimed many ships in the past, including notoriously the *Birkenhead* troopship in 1852, with the loss of 454 lives. The Portuguese navigator Bartholomeu Dias arrived here in 1488 and named the headland *Ponta da São Brandão,* "St. Brendan's Point," presumably because he reached it on this saint's feastday, May 16.

Danielskuil. *Village, northern Cape Province, South Africa.* The village, west of Kimberley, has an Afrikaans name meaning "Daniel's pit," with reference to a conical depression in the limestone here, formerly serving as a prison. The allusion is biblical, to the story of Daniel in the lion's den.

Dannhauser. *Village, northwestern Natal, South Africa.* The village is believed to take its name from the owner of the farm on which it was established in 1937, Thomas Richard *Dannhauser,* a member of the Voortrekker Volksraad (legislative assembly).

Daren. See **Atlas Mountains.**

Dar es Salaam. *City and port, eastern Tanzania.* The economic and administrative center of Tanzania (but not its capital, which since 1985 has been **Dodoma**) has a Swahili name representing Arabic *dār as-salām,* "house of peace," from *dār,* "house," *as,* "the" (the form of *al* before *s*), and *salām,* "peace." This name may have originally applied to the palace of Sayyid Majid, Sultan of Zanzibar, who founded the town in 1862. Alternately, it could relate to the town as a place where merchants could trade freely. The name is sometimes interpreted as if from Hindi *bandar,* "harbor," "port," although no early records have the name in this form, and it is unlikely that *Bandar,* stressed on the first syllable, would have been reduced to *Dar.* The village on which the city was founded had the Swahili name of *Mzizima,* "whole place," implying that the different parts of the village belonged to a single administrative unit.

Darfur. *State, western Sudan.* The name of the state is Arabic in origin, from *dār,* "house" (Cf. **Dar es Salaam**) and the name of the *Fur* people who are indigenous inhabitants of the region.

Darketon. *Village, northwestern Swaziland.* The village takes its name from Grosvenor *Darke,* a pioneer trader in Swaziland.

Darling. *Town, southwestern Cape Province, South Africa.* The town was founded in 1853 and was originally given the Afrikaans name *Groene Kloof* ("green ravine"). It was soon renamed, however, for Sir Charles Henry *Darling* (1809–1870), lieutenant-governor of the Cape from 1851 to 1854. (His uncle, Sir Ralph Darling, gave the name of the *Darling* River, Australia.)

Dassen Island. *Island, off southwestern Cape Province, South Africa.* The island, northwest of Table Bay, takes its name from Dutch *dassen,* plural of *das,* "badger" (cf. German *Dachs*), here applied to the rock rabbit or Cape badger (*Hyrex capensis*). Early Portuguese explorers named the island *Ilha Branca,* "white island." The official Afrikaans form of the name is *Dasseneisland.*

Daura. *Town, northern Nigeria.* The name, historically that of a kingdom here from the early 8th century to 1805, is of Tuareg origin meaning "blacksmith."

Davel. *Village, southeastern Transvaal, South Africa.* The village was established in about 1908 and named for a local farmer, J. *Davel.*

Daveyton. *Township, southern Transvaal, South Africa.* The township, east of Johannesburg, was laid out in 1956 and named for Mrs. M. *Davey,* the town councillor who helped establish it.

De Aar. *Town, central Cape Province, South Africa.* The town bears the name of the farm on which it arose. It represents Afrikaans *de aar,* literally "the bloodvessel" (related to English *artery*), a term used for an underground watercourse. A small settlement developed round the station when the railroad reached here in 1881.

Dealesville. *Town, western Orange Free State, South Africa.* The town takes its name from the owner of the farm on which it arose in the late 19th century, John Henry *Deale.*

Débo, Lake. *Lake, central Mali.* The name represents Songhai *debe,* "mat." The lake is located on a section of the Niger River that here spreads out flat, like a mat.

De Doorns. *Town, southwestern Cape Province, South Africa.* The name is Afrikaans for "the thorns," referring to the many thorn trees that once grew in the area. The town arose on the farm that was recorded here as early as 1725.

Deep Bay. See **Chilumba.**

Deir al-Bahri. *Temple site, east central Egypt.* The historic site, on the west bank of the Nile near Thebes (modern Luxor), has a name representing Arabic *dayr al-baḥrī,* "monastery of the river," from *dayr,* "monastery," *al,* "the," and *baḥrī,* the adjectival form of *baḥr,* "sea," "river," in this case the Nile. The monastery referred to was built in the 7th century AD.

Deir al-Medineh. *Temple site, east central Egypt.* The site, on the west bank of the Nile at Thebes (modern Luxor), has a name that represents Arabic *dayr al-madīna,* "monastery of the town," from *dayr,* "monastery," *al,* "the," and *madīna,* "town" (as for *Medina* in Saudi Arabia). The temple was occupied by monks early in the Christian era.

Dèitagui. *Village, southwestern Niger.* The village, north of Niamey, the capital, has a Djerma name meaning "new well."

Deka. *Village, western Zimbabwe.* The village takes its name from the river on which it lies. The river's own name derives from the local word *kuteka,* "to draw water," implying that the river is constant, not intermittent.

Delagoa Bay. See **Maputo.**

Delareyville. *Town, southwestern Transvaal, South Africa.* The town was established in 1914 and named in the year of his death for the Boer leader, General Jacobus Hercules *de la Rey* (1847–1914), shot and killed by police when the automobile in which he was traveling failed to stop at a road block.

Delgado, Cabo. See **Cabo Delgado.**

Delmas. *Town, southern Transvaal, South Africa.* The town, east of Johannesburg, was laid out in 1907 by Frank Campbell Dumat. He named it for the French dialectal word for a small farm, since his grandfather owned such a farm in France.

Delportshoop. *Village, northern Cape Province, South Africa.* The village arose round a diamond diggers' camp in the 1870s and is said to have been named for the first person *(Delport)* to discover diamonds here. The name as a whole thus means "Delport's hope." The Tswana name for the village is *Dekgathlong,* meaning "meeting place," referring to a river confluence here.

Dendera. *Ancient city, east central Egypt.* The name of the historic site, on the west bank of the Nile, has evolved through Coptic and Greek from *Iunit Tentōre,* itself a corrupt form of the original name *Iunit ta Netert,* "Iunit of the goddess." *Iunit* is based on Egyptian *iun,* "column," while *ta Netet,* from Egyptian *netert,* "goddess," was added to distinguish this place from another of the same name, now usually known as *On* or **Heliopolis**, and mentioned in the Bible as *Beth-Shemesh,* "temple of the sun" (Jeremiah 43:13).

Dendi. *Region, West Africa.* The region extends from southwestern Niger across the border into northern Benin. The meaning is "downstream," referring to the area's location, on the Niger River below Gao (and Niamey).

Deneysville. *Village, northern Orange Free State, South Africa.* The village, on the border with Transvaal, was established in 1936 and named for Colonel *Deneys* Reitz, minister of lands at the time.

Derby. *Village, southern Transvaal, South Africa.* The village, northwest of Johannesburg, was established in the 1880s and named for Edward Henry Smith Stanley, 15th Earl of *Derby* (1826–1893), colonial secretary from 1882 to 1885.

Despatch. *Town, southern Cape Province, South Africa.* The name refers to the "despatch" of bricks from here when brickmaking was the original industry, some time before 1924.

Dete. *Village, western Zimbabwe.* The village takes its name from the river here. Its own name means "reedy."

Devil's Peak. See **Table Mountain.**

Devon. *Village, southern Transvaal, South Africa.* The village, east of Johannesburg, takes its name from that of the native county of the English surveyor who laid it out.

Devure. *River, Zimbabwe.* The river, a tributary of the Sabi in the southeast of the country, has a local name meaning "spiller," "pourer," from its habit of flooding its banks.

Dewetsdorp. *Town, southeastern Orange Free State, South Africa.* The town was founded in 1880 on the initiative of Field-Cornet Jacobus Ignatius *de Wet*, father of the Boer leader, General C. R. de Wet.

Dia. *Village, south central Mali.* The village, on the river of the same name (also known as the *Diaka*), a tributary of the Niger, takes its name from *Dia*-Founé, ancester of the Soninke people. Many placenames in the region also contain his name, such as **Diafarabé** and **Djenne**. Dia-Founé's own name means "founder of Dia."

Diafarabé. *Village, south central Mali.* The village is situated south of **Dia** at the confluence of the **Dia** (or Diaka) and the Niger, and has a name that indicates this, meaning "meeting-place of the sharing of Dia."

Dialafara. *Village, western Mali.* The village has a Mande name meaning "crack by the cailcedra," from *dyala,* "cailcedra" (an African mahogany tree), and *fara,* "crack," "fissure."

Dialakoro. *Village, western Mali.* The village, south of Bamako, the capital, has a Mande name meaning "at the foot of the cailcedra," from *dyala,* "cailcedra" (an African mahogany tree), and *koro,* "foot." Cf. **Dialafara**.

Diandioumé. *Village, western Mali.* The village, on the border witih Mauritania, has a Soninke name meaning "field of fonio" (a type of crabgrass with seeds used as cereal).

Dias Point. *Cape, southwestern Namibia.* The cape, southwest of Lüderitz, is named for the famous Portuguese navigator Bartholomeu *Dias,* who erected a stone cross here on July 25, 1488, dedicating it to St. James, whose feastday it was.

Dibete. *Village, eastern Botswana.* The name is Tswana for "livers," and is that of a hill here whose contours are said to resemble this organ of the body.

Diégo-Suarez. See **Antseranana.**

Dilolo, Lake. *Lake, eastern Angola.* The lake, near the border with Zaïre, is named for a local chief. Stories about him are associated with the lake.

Dimbokro. *Town, south central Côte d'Ivoire.* The name means "Dimbo's village," referring to a local chief. Final *-kro* means "village." Compare the name of the country's capital, **Yamoussoukro,**

Dinokwe. *Village, eastern Botswana.* The name is Tswana in origin and means "place of porcupines."

Diospolis. See **Thebes.**

Dire Dawa. *City, eastern Ethiopia.* The city arose on the edge of dry fields that yield little cultivation. Hence its name, from local words meaning "empty plain."

Djenné. *Town, south central Mali.* The name probably represents an earlier form *Diané,* meaning "little Dia," referring to **Dia,** to the northwest. The town is an ancient one, said to have been founded by Soninke merchants in the 8th century, and was their capital for a time. Some authorities, on dubious grounds, have related the name to that of **Guinea**. Local Muslim influence seems to have brought about the present form of the name, associating it with Arabic *janni,* "paradise."

Djibouti. *Republic, East Africa.* The country takes its name from its capital, whose own name is said to derive from an Afar word *gabouri,* meaning "plate." The reference is to a plate woven from doum palm fibers and raised on a pedestal for ceremonial purposes. As the town took its name from that of the cape on which it was founded in the 1880s, the original "plate" was presumably the cape's rocky or irregular surface. Djibouti was formerly a French possession, known as *French Somaliland* (see **Somaliland**) from 1896 to 1967, and as (the Territory of the) *Afars and Issas* from 1967 until gaining independence in 1977. The latter name is that of the two peoples who inhabit the country: the *Afars* (or **Danakil**) in the north and west, and the Somali *Issas* in the south.

Dodoma. *Capital of Tanzania.* The capital city (since 1985) takes its Swahili name from that of a nearby mountain. The meaning of the name itself is uncertain.

Dohne. *Village, southeastern Cape Province, South Africa.* The village was founded in 1857 and named for the Rev. Jacob Ludwig *Döhne* (1811–1879) of the Berlin Missionary Society.

Dona Ana. *Village, central Mozambique.* The village, on the Zambezi River, takes its name ("Lady Anne") from the original landowner here, *Ana* Cativa, described by the Portuguese officer João de Azevedo Coutinho in *Memories of an Old Sailor and Soldier in Africa* (1941) as "a very beautiful and rich white woman from the Zambezi district who was said to have possessed in her prime a backpack inlaid with gold."

Dondo. *Village, eastern Mozambique.* The village, northwest of Beira, takes its name from the fruit-bearing *dondo* tree *(Cordyla africana Lour)* that grows abundantly here.

Dongola. *Town, northern Sudan.* The small town was built on the site of Old Dongola, capital of the Christian kingdom of Nubia from the 6th to the 14th century. The name is ethnic in origin, from the *Dongola,* a Nubian people. The meaning of their name, also spelled *Dunqulah,* is uncertain.

Donnybrook. *Village, central Natal, South Africa.* The village was named for *Donnybrook,* a suburb of Dublin, Ireland, by the owner of the farm on which it was laid out, one Robert Comrie.

Dordabis. *Village, central Namibia.* The village, southeast of the capital, Windhoek, has a name of Khoikhoin (Hottentot) origin perhaps meaning "arid place."

Dordrecht. *Town, eastern Cape Province, South Africa.* The town was established in 1856 by a minister of the Dutch Reformed Church and named for the town in the Netherlands where the historic synod of the Reformed Churches was held in 1618.

Dori. *Town, northwestern Burkina Faso.* The name is said to represent a local word meaning either "warthog" or "river bank," or else, in another language, a sense "bad," referring to "bad magic" or actual difficulties experienced by the Songhai here.

Douala. *City and port, western Cameroon.* The name of the city comes from that of the *Douala,* a Bantu people who have lived here from the 18th century. Their own name derives from Douala *Diwálá,* "place of Ewále," from their eponymous ancestor. The city, which evolved in the second half of the 19th century, has been so named only since 1907. Earlier it was *Kamerun,* a German form of *Cameroon,* a name set aside that year to apply solely to the country.

Douglas. *Town, eastern Cape Province, South Africa.* The town was established in 1838 as a mission station and was originally named *Backhouse,* for the English Quaker missionary and botanist, James *Backhouse* (1794–1869). In 1867 it was renamed in honor of Sir Percy *Douglas,* lieutenant-governor of the British Cape Colony.

Doukkala. *Plain, western Morocco.* The plain, extending along the Atlantic seaboard between Azemmour and Safi, has a name that is also that of a tribe which inhabited the region. It derives from Berber *ddou,* "under," and *akàl,* "land," so can be generally understood as simply "lowland," "plain."

Drakensberg. *Mountain range, Southern Africa.* The name of the range, in eastern South Africa, Lesotho, and Swaziland, is Afrikaans for "dragon mountain," alluding to the mountains' formidable peaks and dangerous rocks. Their Sotho name is *Quathlamba* (the spelling varies), meaning "barrier of pointed spears," also referring to the peaks. See also **Khahlamba** (as one such variant).

Drummond. *Village, eastern Natal, South Africa.* The village, west of Durban, was named for F. C. *Drummond,* a former director of the Natal Land and Colonisation Company.

Duiwelskloof. *Village, northern Transvaal, South Africa.* The Afrikaans name means "devil's ravine," probably referring to the difficulty experienced by trekkers when passing through the ravine in the rainy season. The original name of the railroad halt here was *Modjadje,* for a local rain queen.

Dullstroom. *Town, eastern Transvaal, South Africa.* The town was established in 1882 and named for its Dutch founder, Wolterus *Dull.* The *stroom* ("stream") is the Crocodile River nearby.

Dundee. *Town, western Natal, South Africa.* The town was founded in 1882 by Thomas Patterson Smith, who named it for his birthplace in Scotland.

Durban. *City and port, eastern Natal, South Africa.* White settlement of the region here began in 1824, with the site known as *Port Natal* (see **Natal**). The present city was founded in 1835 and named for Sir Benjamin *D'Urban* (1777–1849), governor of the Cape from 1834 to 1838. The name was spelled thus until 1854, when it was simplified to its present form. The name happens to be appropriate for a major *urban* development. See also **Durbanville**.

Durbanville. *Town, southwestern Cape Province, South Africa.* The town, northeast of Cape Town, was founded in 1824 as an outspan (rest area for travelers and their animals) originally named *Pampoenkraal* ("pumpkin kraal"). In 1836 it was renamed *D'Urban* for Sir Benjamin *D'Urban* (1777–1849), governor of the Cape from 1834 to 1838. Since confusion arose with *D'Urban* (modern **Durban**), Natal, the name was modified to its present form in 1886.

Dwars Berg. *Mountain range, western Transvaal, South Africa.* The Afrikaans name means literally "across mountain," referring to the location of the range to west and east of the Marico River, which flows through it from south to north.

Dwyka. *Village, southwestern Cape Province, South Africa.* The village takes its name from the river here, a tributary of the Gamka at the western end of the Great Karoo. The river's own name represents the Khoikhoin (Hottentot) word for "brackish."

Eastern Desert. *Desert region, eastern Egypt.* The conventional English name translates Arabic *aṣ-ṣaḥrā' ash-sharqīyah,* literally "the desert the east." (Arabic adjectives follow the noun and repeat the article.) The region lies to the east of the Nile and is considerably smaller in extent than the corresponding **Western Desert**.

East London. *City and port, southeastern Cape Province, South Africa.* The port was so named in 1848 for the British capital, with *East* apparently referring either to its longitudinal location in relation to that city or to the fact that it lies east of Cape Town or some other southern port such as **Port Elizabeth**. (It also lies at a river mouth in the southeast of the country, as London does in England.) At first it was known as *Port Rex,* probably after John *Rex* who took surveys and soundings, here, although popularly said to refer to George *Rex,* an illegitimate son of George III (Latin *rex* meaning "king").

Edenburg. *Town, southern Orange Free State, South Africa.* The town was established in 1862 as a church village and apparently given a name intended to suggest the biblical Garden of *Eden*. Some claim, however, that the name is a corruption of *Edinburgh,* a reference to the Scottish birthplace of the Rev. Andrew Murray, for long the only minister in the state.

Edendale. *Residental area, central Natal, South Africa.* The settlement, a housing estate just west of Pietermaritzburg, was established as a Wesleyan Methodist Mission in 1855 and named for the biblical Garden of *Eden*.

Edenvale. *Town, southern Transvaal, South Africa.* The town was established in 1903 on a farm owned by John *Eden,* and the name almost certainly derives from his. At the same time it propitiously suggests a "Garden of Eden."

Edenville. *Village, northern Orange Free State, South Africa.* The village was established in 1912 and given a name that was probably intended to evoke the biblical Garden of *Eden*. See **Edenburg, Edendale**.

Edfu. *Ancient city, southeastern Egypt.* The name, of uncertain meaning, represents Egyptian *Edba* or *Djeba* as well as Coptic *Atbo*. The Roman name of the town was *Apollinaris Magna,* showing earlier worship of the Greek god Apollo.

Edina. *Town and port, western Liberia.* The coastal town, now part of **Buchanan,** was settled at the mouth of the St. John River in 1832 as a colony for freed American black slaves by the New York and Pennsylvania Colonization Societies. Its name suggests a connection with *Edinburgh,* Scotland, as does *Edina* in Minnesota and Missouri. Presumably the namer had Scottish connections.

Edward, Lake. *Lake, Central Africa.* The lake, between Uganda and Zaïre, was discovered by the British explorer Sir Henry Morton Stanley in 1888 and originally named by him *Albert Edward Nyanza,* for the Prince of Wales, *Albert Edward* (1841–1910), later King Edward VII. (*Nyanza* is the Bantu word for "lake.") In 1908 the king himself approved the alteration of the name to *Lake Edward*. For five years from 1973 the lake was renamed *Lake Idi Amin Dada* (or simply *Lake Amin*) for the Ugandan head of state, *Idi Amin* (born 1925). After his overthrow in 1979, however, it reverted to its earlier name.

Egwembeni. See **Zambezi**.

Egypt. *Republic, northeastern Africa.* The name goes back through Latin and Greek to Egyptian *ḥūt-kā-ptaḥ,* "temple of the soul of Ptah," from *ḥūt,* "temple," *kā,* "soul," and *Ptaḥ,* the name of the god Ptah. The name was originally one of those applied to Memphis, where Ptah was worshipped, but was extended by the Greeks to the whole country. The modern Egyptian name of Egypt is *kemet,* meaning "dark land," either for the contrast of the dark soil with the light sands of the desert, or more likely for the dark skins of the ancient Egyptians (proven by scientific tests). The name has itself been associated with that of the biblical *Ham,* son of Noah, although its own meaning is probably "warm." Hence *Hamitic* as the name of the north African languages related to Semitic, one of them being Egyptian. The Arabic name of Egypt is *miṣr,* from an Assyrian word meaning "strong." This name in turn has been associated with the biblical *Mizraim,* one of the sons of Ham. Hence the name for Egypt in various modern languages, such as Turkish *Mısır* or Hindi *misr,* and even for its capital, **Cairo**, in modern Greek (*Misiri*). Through the classical Greek form of the name *(Aiguptos)* a false interpretation was made to mean "land of vultures," as if from *aia,* "land," and *gups,* genitive *gupos,* "vulture," or direct from *aigupios,* "vulture." (Egypt's national emblem has in fact always been a bird of prey: currently a golden eagle, and formerly a falcon.)

Eikams. See **Windhoek.**

El Aaiún. *Capital of Western Sahara.* The town's name represents Arabic *al-ᶜayūn,* "the springs," from *al,* "the," and *ᶜayūn,* plural of *ᶜayn,* "spring." The reference is to the oases here that furnish the town's water supply. An alternate form of the name is *Laayoune.*

El Alamein. *Coastal village, northern Egypt.* The village, famous as the scene of the Allied victory over the Axis forces in World War II, has a coincidentally apt Arabic name meaning "the two flags," from *al,* "the," and *ᶜalamayn,* the dual form of *ᶜalam,* "flag."

Elandsberg. *Mountain, eastern Cape Province, South Africa.* The Afrikaans name means "eland's mountain," referring to the large spiral-horned antelopes *Taurotragus oryx* that inhabit the region.

Elandslaagte. *Town, northwestern Natal, South Africa.* The town, a farming and coalmining center, has an Afrikaans descriptive name meaning "eland's valley." See **Elandsberg.**

El-Arish. *Coastal town, northeastern Egypt.* The town, the largest settlement of the Sinai Peninsula, lies on the Mediterranean near the mouth of the river of the same name. Its name represents Arabic *al-ᶜarīsh,* "the hut," referring to a biblical legend that Jacob stayed here in a hut that he built for himself on his journey from Canaan into Egypt. (This was one factor that caused El-Arish to be selected in the early 20th century as the possible nucleus for a new Jewish state near, but not in, Palestine. The project was vetoed by the British, however.) As a Roman garrison town it was known as *Rhinocorura* or *Rhinocolura,* "severed nose," from Greek *rhis,* genitive *rhinos,* "nose," and *koloyein,* "to cut short," apparently because prisoners were branded by having their noses cut off. The river here, with the Arabic name of *wādī al-ᶜarīsh,* is traditionally identified with the biblical "river of Egypt" (Genesis 15:18), as the southwest frontier of the Promised Land.

El-Ashmunein. *Village, north central Egypt.* The village, near the west bank of the Nile, stands on the site of the ancient Greek town of *Hermopolis,* later known as *Hermopolis Magna,* "great Hermopolis," as distinct from *Hermopolis Parva,* "little Hermopolis" (see **Damanhūr**). This was named for *Hermes,* the god whom the Greeks had identified with the Egyptian god Thoth, who was worshipped here, as were the eight gods of the so-called Ogdoad (group of eight). It is in reference to them that the Egyptians came to call the town *Khmunu,* from *ĥemen,* "eight." The Coptic form of this name was *Ŝmoun,* which in turn evolved to the present name of the village, in Arabic *al-ashmūnayn.*

El Djouf. *Desert region, West Africa.* The region, at the western end of the Sahara, extends across eastern Mauritania and western Mali. Its Arabic name means "the hollow [place]."

Eldoret. *Town, west central Kenya.* The town takes its name from the *Eldare* River on which it lies. It arose in 1912 on a backwoods post office called *Farm 64,* so named for its distance in miles from Londiani, to the southeast.

Elephantine. *Island, Nile River, northern Egypt.* The island, opposite Aswan, has a name of Greek origin, from *elephantinos,* "of ivory," from *elephas,* "elephant," "ivory," itself translating the island's Egyptian name, *Ābū,* "elephant." The island was the border point between ancient Egypt and Cush, and a center for the trade of ivory (among other things) between the two countries. Hence the name. However, some sources refer the name to the huge black rocks at the southern end of the island, which resemble the backs of a herd of elephants bathing in the river. The final part of the name is pronounced either as *tiny* or as *teeny.* The modern Arabic name of the island is simply *gazīra,* "island."

El Faiyûm. *City and governorate, northern Egypt.* The name represents Arabic *al-fayyūm,* from Coptic *Fiom,* a word comprising the article *f-,* another form of *p-,* and *iom,* "sea," "lake." Ancient Egyptian corresponded to this with the name as *pā-yom,* from *pā,* the article, and *yom,* "sea," "lake," a word borrowed from Hebrew *yam.* The Egyptian name itself translated the Greek name, *Limnē,* "lake," "sea," which the Greeks had themselves translated from the original Egyptian *Tāŝā,* "land of the lake," or "land of the sea." All these names were originally that of the region (the modern governorate), so that there were different names for the city. Its Egyptian name was *Ŝedit,* its Latin name *Arsinoë,* for the wife of Ptolemy II Philadelphus, and its Greek name *Krokodeilōs polis* (rendered in Latin as *Crocodilopolis*), in honor of the crocodile god Sebek. The ancient site of this last name today lies near the modern city. An alternate name of the city is *Medinet el-Faiyûm,* where the first word represents Arabic *madīnat,* from *madīna,* "town" (also giving the name of the holy Muslim city of *Medina,* Saudi Arabia).

El Fasher. See **Al-Fashir.**

El Gezira. *Region, east central Sudan.* The name of the region between the Blue Nile and White Nile rivers represents Arabic *al-jazā'ir,* "the islands," referring to the well irrigated areas of agricultural land here. The name is sometimes found in the form *The Gezira.* In origin it is exactly the same as that of **Algiers.**

El-Gîza. See **Giza.**

El Golea. *Town, central Algeria.* The town, in the largest oasis in the Sahara, has an Arabic name meaning "the citadel," from *el,* "the," and *ḳal'a,* "fortress," "castle." The reference is to the 9th century tribal stronghold that dominates the region to the east, with a view over the whole oasis.

Elgon, Mount. *Mountain, eastern Uganda.* The mountain, an extinct volcano on the border with Kenya, takes its name from Maasai *ilgoon,* "breast," with reference to its low outline and gentle slopes.

Elim. *Village, southwestern Cape Province, South Africa.* The village was founded in 1824 as a Moravian mission station and named for the biblical place where the Israelites rested (Exodus 15:27).

Elisabethville. See **Lubumbashi.**

El Jadida. *Town and port, western Morocco.* The town was founded in 1502 by the Portuguese and originally named *Mazagan,* for the *Mazg'anna* tribe which inhabited this region in medieval times. It was resettled by Moroccan Jews in 1821 and then given its present Arabic name, in full *al-brija al-jadīda,* "the new little port." The latter half of this, representing "the new," serves as the name today.

El-Kharga. *Town, central Egypt.* The town takes its name from the region here in the governorate of New Valley (of which it is the capital). The Arabic name of this is *al-wāḥāt al-khārijah,* "the outer oases," from *wāḥāt,* plural of *wāḥ,* "oasis," and *khārijah,* plural of *khārij,* "outer." The reference is to the two groups of oases here in the Libyan Desert, which are "outer" by comparison with the **Dakhla Oasis**, to the west. The Romans knew both groups by the single name *Oasis Magna,* "great oasis" ("great" also by comparison with that at Dakhla, which is smaller), and the English name *The Great Oasis* is still found on some maps. The name of the town is also spelled *Al-Kharga* or *Kharga* or, closer to the Arabic, *Al-Kharijah.*

El-Lahun. *Village, northern Egypt.* The village, a historic site midway between El Faiyûm and Beni Suef, lies just north of the junction of the Bahr Yusuf canal and the Nile River. Its name relates to this location, and represents Coptic *Lehone,* "mouth of the canal."

Elliot. *Town, eastern Cape Province, South Africa.* The town was founded in 1885 and named for Sir Henry George *Elliot* (1826–1912), chief magistrate of Tembuland and later (from 1891 to 1902) of the Transkeian Territories. Cf. **Elliotdale.**

Elliotdale. *Town, Transkei, South Africa.* The town takes its name from Sir Henry George *Eliot* (1826–1912), chief magistrate of Transkei from 1891 to 1902. The indigenous name of the town is *Xhora,* possibly representing *i Xora,* "to pick out," alluding to a favored place or a chosen leader. Cf. **Elliot.**

El Mahallah el Kubra. *City, northern Egypt.* Egypt's fourth biggest city dates from before the 10th century and has a name representing Arabic *al-maḥallah al-kubrā,* "the great place," implying an important trading center.

El Mansura. *City, northeastern Egypt.* The name represents Arabic *al-manṣūra,* "the victorious," from *al,* "the," and *manṣūr,* "victorious," ultimately from *naṣr,* "victory." The reference is apparently to the battle of February 8, 1250, in which Crusaders under Louis IX of France were decimated by Muslim forces and Louis himself was captured. The city originated in 1219 as a camp set up by Al-Malik Al-Kamill, nephew of Saladin, the Muslim sultan and hero.

Elmina. *Town and port, southern Ghana.* The town was founded by Portuguese traders in 1482, and the fort built here then was originally called *São Jorge da Mina,* "St. George of the mine." The name was given by King John II of Portugal, who thought that this was where the gold of Guinea was mined. (It was actually not mined at all, but panned from alluvial deposits.) The present name subsequently evolved from the earlier form.

El Oued. *Town, northeastern Algeria.* The town takes its name from the river (Arabic *al-wādī*) that at one time flowed to the east here, but that was swallowed up by the encroaching sands.

El Qantara. *Town, northeastern Egypt.* The town, also known as *Al-Qantara* or simply *Qantara,* is situated on the east bank of the Suez Canal between Port Said and Ismailia. Its name represents Arabic *al-qanṭara,* "the bridge." Before the canal was built, it was here that armies and pilgrims usually crossed the Isthmus of Suez. (Compare *Alcántara,* the town in western Spain, named for its Roman bridge.)

Elsburg. *Town, southern Transvaal, South Africa.* The town, southeast of Johannesburg, was established on a farm in 1887 and named for the farmowner, F. C. *Els.*

El Tell el-Kebir. *Village, northern Egypt.* The village, midway between Zagazig and Ismailia, is famous as the scene of the British victory over the Egyptians in 1882. Its Arabic name means "the great mound," indicating that it arose on the site of a much larger place.

El Tell el-Maskhutah. *Ancient city, northern Egypt.* The present site of the name, west of Ismailia, is that of the ancient city of *Pithom,* mentioned in the Bible (Exodus 1:11) as one of the treasure cities built for Pharaoh by the Hebrews. This biblical name represents ancient Egyptian *per-Atum,* "house of Atum," referring to a sun god. The modern name represents Arabic *tell al-maskhūṭah,* "mound of the image." The reference is to the statue of Rameses II that formerly stood here, and that is now in the Garden of the Stelae at Ismailia. The stela of Rameses has a relief of him offering an "image" of Maat, goddess of truth, to the falcon-headed god Ra-Harakhty. Rameses was the Egyptian king who built Pithom in about 1260 BC, and the Exodus may have taken place in his reign.

Emin Pasha Gulf. *Gulf, Lake Victoria, northwestern Tanzania.* The gulf, in the southwestern corner of the lake, is named for the German explorer Mehmed Emin Pasha, original name Eduard Schnitzer (1840–1892), who visited the region here with the British explorer Sir Henry Morton Stanley in 1889 and who was murdered by Arab slave-traders near Stanley Falls. His assumed name testifies to the Turkish way of life that he adopted. (From 1878 to 1889 he was governor of the Sudanese province of Equatoria, succeeding other "Pashas" and "Beys.")

Emlembe. *Mountain, northwestern Swaziland.* The name of Swaziland's highest mountain, more accurately spelled *mLembe,* means "place of the spider."

Empangeni. *Town, eastern Natal, South Africa.* The town, founded in 1885, has a Zulu name meaning "to seize." The reference is to the fertile soil here, which the Zulus had to "seize" in order to prevent disputes of ownership.

Engcobo. *Town, Transkei, South Africa.* The town, which arose in 1876, has a self-descriptive Xhosa name meaning "place of long grass."

Enkeldoorn. See **Chivhu.**

Entebbe. *City, southern Uganda.* The former Ugandan capital (to 1962) is said to take its name from the phrase *entebe za mugula,* "headquarters of *Mugula,*" referring to a local chief who held authority here before the founding of a garrison post by the British in 1893.

Entre-Rios. See **Malema.**

Enugu. *City, southern Nigeria.* The former capital of Biafra was founded in 1917 and has a name representing the local words *enu* *ugwu,* "at the top of the hill." This itself was a borrowing of the name of the traditional Ibo village of *Enugu* Ngwo, just west of the city. Enugu lies at the foot of the Udi Plateau here, but Enugu Ngwo is actually on the plateau.

Enugu Gwo. See **Enugu.**

Epukiro. *Village, eastern Namibia.* The name is of Herero origin and is said to mean "country where people are lost." The village was founded as a Roman Catholic mission station in 1903.

Équateur. *Province, northwestern Zaïre.* The French name of the province refers to the fact that the *Equator* passes almost through its center.

Equatorial Guinea. *Republic, West Africa.* The country takes its name from its location close to the Equator, between latitudes 1°N and 2°N. It is well inside the extensive territory of historical **Guinea** (and also historical **Ghana**). The country is the only independent Spanish-speaking state in Africa, a legacy from its colonial period, latterly as *Spanish Guinea* from 1926 to 1963, and earlier as the Spanish possessions of Fernando Po and Annobon from 1778 to 1926 (apart from a 28-year period of British administration in Fernando Po from 1827). Cf. **Guinea-Bissau.**

Erasmus. See **Bronkhorstspruit.**

Eritrea. *Independent state, northeastern Africa.* The country, which became Africa's newest independent state in 1993, was created as an Italian colony on January 1, 1890, and named by the Italians for the Latin name, *Mare Erythraeum,* of the Red Sea, along which it lies.

Ermelo. *Town, southeastern Transvaal, South Africa.* The town was founded in 1872 and named by one of the first Dutch Reformed Church ministers here for the Netherlands town of *Ermelo,* near Amersfoort.

Erongo Mountains. *Mountains, northwestern Namibia.* The mountain mass, southwest of Omaruru, has a Herero name said to mean "large home." Its Nama name is *Oegab,* "wooden vat," referring to its shape.

Er Rashidia. *Town, southeastern Morocco.* The town takes its name from Moulay *Ar-Rashid,* founder of the Muslim Alawite dynasty that has ruled in Morocco since 1666, when he captured Fès. The French established the modern town as a regional capital in World War I, and under them it was known as *Ksar es Souk,* "enclosure of the market," with reference to the French Foreign Legion fort here. The name is still found on some maps. (For the origin of Ar-Rashid's own name, see **Rosetta.**)

Errego. *Village, north central Mozambique.* The name is traditionally said to derive from that of a Captain *Rego,* commander of a military detachment here.

Er Rif. *Mountainous region, northern Morocco.* The region, also known simply as *Rif,* derives its name from Arabic *ar-rīf,* "the coastland," referring to its location by the Mediterranean.

Erundu. *Village, northern Namibia.* The village takes its name from the watercourse here. Its own name is of Herero origin and probably means "big river."

Eshowe. *Town, northeastern Natal, South Africa.* The town, capital of the former Zululand, was founded in about 1880. Its Zulu name probably means "windy place," suggested by the noise of high winds in the pine trees here.

Espungabera. *Village, western Mozambique.* The village, near the border with Zimbabwe, has a name meaning "wood of the rock rabbits" (see **Dassen Island**).

Essaouira. *City and port, western Morocco.* Under French colonial rule the city was long familiar as *Mogador.* This represents a Berber name recorded in the 11th century as *Amogdoul,* itself deriving from *Magdoul,* a Muslim holy man buried here. The present name is a French-influenced form of Arabic *as-sawīra,* "the little wall," from a diminutive form of *sūr,* "wall" (not *ṣūra,* "picture," as sometimes stated).

Es Souk. *Village, northeastern Mali.* The village, in the valley of the Tilemsi River, has a name representing Arabic *es-sūḳ,* "the market." This was the name given by the Arabs to the former town of *Tadmekket* here, founded by the Berbers in pre-Christian times. The Arabs named it thus because the town was the sole trading center in the central Sahara and the point where caravans called on their route from Tripolitania to Nigerian lands. As lovers of learned etymologies, the Arabs interpreted the name *Tadmekket* to mean "like Mecca," explaining that the place was located between two hills, as Mecca itself was. Whatever its true meaning, the name almost certainly predates Islam.

Estcourt. *Town, western Natal, South Africa.* The original name of the settlement here was *Bushman's Drift* or *Bushman's River Post,* with reference to its location on the *Bushman's* River. In 1863 it was renamed for Thomas Henry Sutton Sotheron *Estcourt* (1801–1876), the British politician who sponsored the immigration of settlers here.

Estuaire. *Province, western Gabon.* The province, bordering the Atlantic, has a French name meaning "estuary," referring to that of the Ogooué River, whose basin covers most of the country.

Ethiopia. *State, northeastern Africa.* The name derives from the Greek word for the indigenous people of the region. This was *aithiops,* literally "burnt appearance," from *aithō,* "I burn," and *opsis,* "aspect," "appearance." The reference is to their dark skin color. (Although ostensibly Greek, the name may actually be a translation, or even corruption, of some earlier name.) The country was long also familiar under its alternate name of **Abyssinia**. The ancient Egyptian name for Ethiopia was *Kāš,* and the biblical (Hebrew) name *kūš,* or in English terms, *Cush.* This was also the name of one of the sons of Ham. (For another, see **Egypt**).

Etosha Pan. *Salt basin, northern Namibia.* The large salt basin was discovered in 1851 and has a local name meaning "place of mirages," since these are frequently experienced here in the dry season. The name is now also that of the *Etosha* National Park, established in 1907 as a game park and since extended.

Euhesperides. See **Benghazi.**

Excelsior. *Village, eastern Orange Free State, South Africa.* The village was established on two farms, *Sunlight* and *Excelsior,* and adopted the name of the latter.

Fada Ngurma. *Town, eastern Burkina Faso.* The town was originally named *Bingo,* a word denoting a slave settlement. Its present Hausa name is said to mean "place where no tax is paid."

Faial. *Island, western Azores.* The island has a Portuguese name meaning "beech tree" (modern *faia*).

Faiyûm. See **El Faiyûm.**

False Bay. *Bay, southwestern Cape Province, South Africa.* The bay appears on a Portuguese map of 1489 as *Golfo dentro las serras,* "Gulf between the mountains." The present name is an English translation of a later Portuguese name, *Cabo Falso.* It arose since early navigators returning from the east mistook Cape Hangklip for Cape Point, so sailed into False Bay instead of Table Bay, their intended destination.

Fassangouni. *Village, southern Guinea.* The village has a local name meaning "by the rock."

Fauresmith. *Town, southern Orange Free State, South Africa.* A church settlement was established here in 1849. The town was subsequently named for the Rev. Philip Eduard *Faure,* moderator of the Dutch Reformed Church, and Sir Harry *Smith* (1787–1860), governor of the Cape from 1847 to 1852.

Fayum. See **El Faiyûm.**

Fdérik. *Town, north central Mauritania.* The name is a Zenaga (Berber) one for a local well, abstracted from a poetic legend about the Kediat region: "O Kediat, there is much water in thy breast, but it is in thy neck *(fi-de-rik)* that there is more." The reference is to a narrow pass in the hills here. The colonial name of the town until the 1960s was *Fort-Gouraud,* for the French army officer Henri-Joseph-Eugène *Gouraud* (1867–1946), head of the French colonial army in World War I.

Feira. See **Luangwa.**

Felixton. *Village, northeastern Natal, South Africa.* The village, near the coast south of Empangeni, is said to take its name from that of *Felix* Piccione, an early pioneer here.

Fernando Po. *Former name of* **Bioko.** The island west of Cameroon, in the Gulf of Guinea, where it is now part of Equatorial Guinea, takes its old name from the Portuguese navigator *Fernaõ do Pó,* who discovered it probably in 1472. (The *do* of his name, meaning "of," became the final *-do* of *Fernando; Fernando* and *Fernão* are one and the same Portuguese name, more familiar in English as *Ferdinand.*) The explorer himself called the island *Formosa,* "beautiful," a name that was in use until 1494, when it was replaced by his own. It was renamed **Bioko** in 1979.

Fernão Veloso, Baía de. *Bay, northeastern Mozambique.* The bay, north of Moçambique, is named for its discoverer in about 1506, the Portuguese explorer *Fernão Veloso,* a companion of Vasco da Gama.

Ferro. See **Hierro.**

Ferryville. See **Menzel Bourguiba.**

Fès. *City, north central Morocco.* The present form of the name represents Arabic *fās.* This is an altered form of Berber *sàf,* itself an abbreviation of *isaffen,* the plural of *asif,* meaning "river." (Cf. **Ifni** and **Safi.**) A folk etymology derives the name from Arabic *fās,* "hatchet," supposedly referring to the implement with which Idris I, the town's founder in AD 790, marked out the site of the city walls. This was the town that gave the name of the *fez,* the Turkish red cap, which was originally manufactured here.

Fez. See **Fès.**

Fezzan. *Region, southwestern Libya.* The region, a former province, takes its name from the *Phazāni,* the people native to this part of the Sahara. The meaning of their name is uncertain.

Fianarantsoa. *Town, southeastern Madagascar.* The name represents Malagasy *fianàrana,* "school," "study," and *sòa,* "good." The overall sense is thus "place where one learns what is good."

Ficksburg. *Town, eastern Orange Free State, South Africa.* The town was founded in 1867 and named for Commandant-General Johan Izak Jacobus *Fick* (1816–1892), leader of Orange Free State forces against the Basuto in the wars of 1865–1868.

Figtree. *Village, southwestern Zimbabwe.* The name relates to that of an old fig tree and landmark here, still in existence.

Fika. *Town, east central Nigeria.* The town takes its name from the Bolewa or *Fika* people who are said to have settled in the region in the 1440s. The present town was not built until about 1805, however, and received its name soon afterwards.

Filabusi. *Village, southern Zimbabwe.* The village, southeast of Bulawayo, takes its name from the local word *emfelabuso,* literally "death in the face." The reference is probably to a particular hostile encounter or incident here.

Fingoe. *Village, northwestern Mozambique.* The village has a name that is a European corruption of the original tribal (Abambo) name, *amafengu,* "people who starve in their search for work." The name is also that of a mountain here, north of the Zambezi River.

Firestone Plantation. *Village, western Liberia.* The village, east of the capital, Monrovia, takes its name from the *Firestone* Company of the United States, which in 1926 granted a concession of 1 million acres (400,000 ha) for a rubber plantation in Liberia. There is another settlement of the same name in the southeast of the country.

Fish. *River, Namibia.* The river rises in the south central region of the country and flows south to enter the Orange. Its name, a translation of Nama *//aub* or *//oub*, is self-descriptive, referring to the river's abundance of fish. (The initial character in the Nama name denotes a click.) The name was formerly also current as *Great Fish.*

Fish Hoek. *Town, southwestern Cape Province, South Africa.* The town and resort, south of Cape Town, arose as a fishing and whaling station, and originally had the Afrikaans name *Vishoek,* "fish corner." The current name is a blend of English and Afrikaans.

Flores. *Island, northwestern Azores.* The island has a Portuguese name meaning "flowers." The reference is to its lush flora. (The name was popularized by the opening line of Tennyson's poem *The Revenge*: "At Flores in the Azores Sir Richard Grenville lay.")

Florida. *Town, southern Transvaal, South Africa.* The town, now a western district of Johannesburg, was established in 1889 on a farm owned by Hendrik van der Hoven. Its name appears to have only secondary reference to the American state, since according to family archives it was given in memory of *Florrie,* van der Hoven's young niece, who died at age 4 just before the settlement was established.

Florisbad. *Village, central Orange Free State, South Africa.* The village is a health resort, and takes its name, meaning "Floris's springs," from one *Floris* Venter who opened the mineral springs here in about 1910.

Fochville. *Town, southern Transvaal, South Africa.* The town, southwest of Johannesburg, was established in World War I and named for Marshal Ferdinand *Foch* (1851–1929), French commander-in-chief of the Allied Forces in France.

Fogo. *Island, southern Cape Verde Islands.* The island is centered on an active volcano, the highest point in the group, and accordingly has a name that is the Portuguese word for "fire." The volcano last erupted in 1951.

Forbes Reef. *Village, northwestern Swaziland.* Now a "ghost town," the village arose as a settlement round a gold-bearing reef discovered here in 1884 by Alex *Forbes* and C. J. Swears.

Formigas. *Island group, eastern Azores.* The islands, a cluster of dark rocks northeast of Santa Maria, have a Portuguese descriptive name meaning "ants."

Formosa Peak. *Mountain, southern Cape Province, South Africa.* The peak, in the Tsitsikamma Mountains not far from the coast, has a Portuguese name meaning "beautiful." It was adopted from the earlier name of what is now Plettenberg Bay here.

Fort Beaufort. *Town, southeastern Cape Province, South Africa.* The town was founded as a fortress in 1822 and named for the Duke of *Beaufort,* father of Lord Charles Somerset, governor of the Cape from 1814 to 1826.

Fort Flatters. See **Bordj Omar Driss.**

Fort-Gouraud. See **Fdérik.**

Fort Hill. See **Chitipa.**

Fort Jameson. See **Chipata.**

Fort Johnston. See **Mangoche.**

Fort Lamy. See **N'Djamena.**

Fort Manning. See **Mchinji.**

Fort Portal. *Town, western Uganda.* The town takes its name from the British diplomat Sir Gerald *Portal* (1858–1894), sent to Uganda by the government in 1893 to report whether the British should retain this part of Africa or leave it. (They kept it.) The town was founded that year and was originally known as *Fort Gerry.*

Fort Rixon. *Village, south central Zimbabwe.* The village takes its name from the former farm owner here, Theodore *Rixon.* The fort, now in ruins, was built in 1893 during the war with the Matabele (Ndenbele).

Fort Rosebery. See **Mansa.**

Fort Victoria. See **Masvingo.**

Fostat. See **Cairo.**

Fouriesburg. *Town, eastern Orange Free State, South Africa.* The town was founded on a farm in 1892 and is named for the owner, Christoffel *Fourie.*

Fourteen Streams. *Village, northern Cape Province, South Africa.* The village, on the Vaal River near the Transvaal border, has a descriptive name referring to the many streams and rivulets into which the Vaal divides here. The local Tswana name is *Melacaneng,* "at the streams."

Fouta. *Plain, northern Senegal.* The plain, a semidesert region to the south of the Senegal River, has a Mande name meaning "plain." Cf. **Fouta Djalon.**

Fouta Djalon. *Mountainous district, western Guinea.* The district takes its name from Mande *fouta,* "plain," and *dyalon,* "slope." The latter word gave the name of the *Dialonke* people, early inhabitants of the region. Compare **Fouta.**

Franceville. *Town, southeastern Gabon.* The town was founded by the French explorer Pierre Savorgnan de Brazza (see **Brazzaville**) in 1880, when he named it for his native *France.*

Francistown. *Town, northern Botswana.* The town is named for Daniel *Francis* (1840–1920), goldminer and prospector here in 1869, to whom the Matabele (Ndebele) chief Lobengula subsequently granted land. The precolonial name of the town, to which it may one day revert, was *Nyangabgwe,* which in the Kalanga dialect of Shona means "approach the rock." The reference is to a hunter who is said to have mistaken a rock for an antelope.

Frankfort. *Town, northeastern Orange Free State, South Africa.* The town was founded in 1869 and named for *Frankfurt,* Germany.

Franschhoek. *Town, southwestern Cape Province, South Africa.* The town, east of Cape Town, has an Afrikaans name meaning "French corner," referring to the settlement of Huguenot refugees from France here in 1688.

Fraserburg. *Town, southern Cape Province, South Africa.* The town was established in 1850 and named either for the Rev. Colin Mackenzie *Fraser,* father-in-law of Marthinus Steyn, president of the Orange Free State from 1896 to 1900, or Fraser's father John, a minister from Beaufort West. The final *-burg* means "town" here as elsewhere, but also refers to the local elder, Gerrit Jacobus *Meyburgh.*

Freetown. *Capital of Sierra Leone.* The city was founded by the British in 1787 for freed or rescued African slaves, then destitute in England, who had been granted land here by a local chieftain. Hence the name. The site was selected by the English abolitionist Granville Sharp (1735–1813), and for five years to 1792 the settlement was known as *Granvillestown.*

French Somaliland. See **Djibouti.**

Fresco. *Coastal village, southern Côte d'Ivoire.* The name is that of a river here, called by the Portuguese *Rio Fresco,* "fresh river," that is, one with fresh water. Cf. **Rufisque.**

Fuerteventura. *Island, eastern Canaries.* The second largest island in the group, and one of the closest to the African mainland, was settled by the French in the 15th century and named by them *Forte Aventure,* "great fortune." This may have been a deliberate echo of the Latin name *Fortunatae Insulae,* "Fortunate Islands," by which the Canaries were collectively known in ancient times and for which they were named by medieval mapmakers. The name was later superseded by the Spanish equivalent. The Canaries were the "Islands of the Blessed" of Greek mythology, that is, the islands west of the Pillars of Hercules where after their death favored mortals spent a blissful afterlife.

Funchal. *Capital of Madeira.* The city and port was founded in 1421 by the Portuguese explorer João Gonçalves Zarco, who the previous year had discovered Madeira itself. He named the settlement for the abundance of fennel (Portuguese *fenolh*) growing here. Zarco is buried in Funchal.

Furancungo. *Village, northwestern Mozambique.* The name is that of the mountain here, near the border with Malawi. The origin may be in *afura* or *fura,* "mountains of the interior," although some sources seek a link with the name of the biblical *Ophir,* whatever its own origin may be.

Fustat. See **Cairo.**

Gaberones. See **Gaborone.**

Gabès. *Port and gulf, eastern Tunisia.* The name, in Arabic *qābis,* goes back ultimately to Punic *Takape.* The sense of this is uncertain, but has been explained as denoting a wet or irrigated place. The Roman name of the gulf was *Syrtis Minor.*

Gabon. *Republic, Central Africa.* The country takes its name from the bay or estuary here on the west coast. This had been discovered at the end of the 15th century by the Portuguese, who named it *Gabão,* from *gabão,* "cloak," presumably either from its shape or from the fact that rivers flowed into it from under a dense "cloak" of undergrowth or foliage.

Gaborone. *Capital of Botswana.* The town was founded in the 1890s and took the name of *Gaborone* from a Batlokwa chief who held power here from 1880 to 1931 and who died in 1932 at the reputed age of 106. His own name is said to mean "it is not unbecoming," referring to his office of chief. Until 1969, the name was spelled *Gaberones.*

Gadamès. *Town and oasis, northwestern Libya.* The name evolved from that of the Roman stronghold of *Cydamus,* although the meaning of this is uncertain. Alternate forms of the modern name are *Ghadamès* or *Rhadamès.*

Gafsa. *Town, west central Tunisia.* The town takes its name from that of the Roman settlement of *Capsa* on which it arose. The Roman name appears to represent Latin *capsa,* "holder," perhaps referring to the oasis here, which is "held" at a transitional point between mountains to the north and desert to the south. This location has long made the town an important place.

Gago Coutinho. See **Lumbala.**

Galana. *River, Kenya.* The river rises in the south of the country, then flows southeast to enter the Indian Ocean just north of Malindi. Its name means simply "river."

Galekaland. *Region, Transkei, South Africa.* The historic region, along the coast between the Great Kei and Umtata rivers, takes its name from the Xhosa chief *Gcaleka,* who held power here from 1750 to 1792. The name was official for the territory from 1750 to 1835.

Gamawa. *Village, northeastern Nigeria.* The name derives from the local word *gamu* meaning "to meet," presumably because the village became an important local trading center.

Gambia. *Republic, West Africa.* The country lies along both banks of the *Gambia* River, and takes its name from it. The river was so named by Portuguese explorers in the mid-15th century. For once, they did not bestow a European name, but adopted the native name *Ba-Dimma,* meaning simply "river." The country is officially styled *The Gambia,* a reminder that the name originated from the river.

Gamka. *River, Cape Province, South Africa.* The river, a tributary of the Gourits, has a Khoikhoin (Hottentot) name meaning "lions," referring to the abundance of these animals here. Cf. **Gamtoos.**

Gamtoos. *River, southern Cape Province, South Africa.* The river, which flows eastward to the Indian Ocean, has a Khoikhoin (Hottentot) name that is probably tribal in origin and that means "wily as a lion." This could refer not so much to the tribe itself but to the unexpected and frequent flooding of the river. Cf. **Gamka.**

Ganda. *Town, western Angola.* The town itself has a local name meaning "payment," referring to payment made to a witch doctor, and originally applied to a nearby rock where such payments were made. Until 1980 the town bore the Portuguese colonial name of *Mariano Machado.*

Gansbaai. *Village and port, southwestern Cape Province, South Africa.* The Afrikaans name means "goose bay," referring to the wild geese that abound here, a short distance inland from Danger Point.

Ganvié. *Town, southern Benin.* The town, on the northwest side of Lake Nokoué, opposite Cotonou, has a name that is said to derive from the Tofinu words *gan,* "we are saved," and *vié,* "community." The reference is to the safe haven found here by the Tofinu people when pursued by the Dan-Homey, since the latter people were prevented by their religion from crossing the water.

Gao. *Town, eastern Mali.* The town, a port on the Niger River, has a name representing Fulani (Peul) *kunku,* "island," referring to its location. The name was corrupted by the Arabs into *kawkaw,* which became *Gaogao,* and finally just *Gao.*

Garies. *Town, western Cape Province, South Africa.* The town takes its name from the river here. Its own name is a Khoikhoin (Hottentot) one meaning "couchgrass." The original name of the town was *Genisdal,* "Genis' valley," for a local schoolteacher, Evert *Genis.*

Garoua. *Town, northern Cameroon.* The name is that of the Bata chief who founded the town before the arrival of the Peul (Fulani) here. The meaning of his own name is uncertain.

Garub. *Village, southwestern Namibia.* The village, east of Lüderitz, takes its name from the mountain here. Its own name represents Khoikhoin (Hottentot) */garub,* "tiger mountain," presumably for its shape or the striped appearance of its rocks. (The unusual character that begins the name represents a click.)

Gatooma. See **Kadoma.**

Gatsrand. *Hill ridge, southern Transvaal, South Africa.* The range of hills, southwest of Johannesberg, has an Afrikaans name meaning literally "hole range," from *gat,* "hole," and *rand,* "ridge" (see also **Witwatersrand**). The reference is to the many sinkholes and caves in the foothills here.

Gayaza. *Village, southwestern Uganda.* The name is said to derive from a local word *okugayala,* "to be lazy," perhaps implying that the land here was so fertile and bountiful that it made its inhabitants indolent.

Gaza. *Province, southwestern Mozambique.* The name is that of the tribe of the local chief's grandfather, Soshangane, who himself created a large empire in the region in the 1830s. The Gazas said of themselves: "*Singu gaza owajwa-intava,*" "We are the Gazas who roam from one direction to another."

GazaNkulu. *Bantustan, northeastern Transvaal, South Africa.* The Bantu homeland, which gained self-governing status in 1973, has a name meaning "*Gaza* independence," from the tribe that gave the name of the former *Gaza* Empire in this part of Africa (see **Gaza**). An alternate but now outmoded name for the territory is *Machanganaland,* referring to the *Shangaan* people for whom it is set aside.

Gemsbok National Park. See **Kalahari.**

Genadendal. *Town, southwestern Cape Province, South Africa.* The town arose in 1737 as the oldest mission in South Africa. When originally founded it was given the Afrikaans name *Baviaanskloof,* "baboons' ravine." This was changed in 1806 to a name more appropriate for a Moravian mission station, meaning "vale of mercy."

George. *Town, southern Cape Province, South Africa.* The town was originally named *Georgetown,* for King *George* III of England (1738–1820), who donated a Bible to the church here. The present name was adopted in 1811.

George, Lake. *Lake, southwestern Uganda.* The small lake was visited in 1875 by the British explorer Sir Henry Morton Stanley, who named it *Beatrice Gulf* in the belief that it was part of Lake **Albert** (Lake **Mobutu Sese Seko**), to the north—"The arm of the lake named by me 'Beatrice Gulf'" (*Through the Dark Continent,* 1878). It is, however, connected to Lake **Edward**, to the southwest. The name paid tribute to Princess *Beatrice* (1857–1944), fifth daughter and youngest child of Queen Victoria and Prince Albert. The lake was renamed in 1908 for the Prince of Wales, later King *George* V (1865–1936).

Georgetown. *Town, central Gambia.* The town, a port on the Gambia River, was founded in 1823 as a settlement for freed slaves and named for *George* IV, king of England (1762–1830).

Germiston. *City, southern Transvaal, South Africa.* The city, southeast of Johannesburg, arose on a farm here in 1886 bought by two gold prospectors, August Simmer and John Jack. The town that developed was named for Jack's Scottish birthplace, *Germiston,* a former northeastern district of Glasgow.

Geysdorp. *Town, southwestern Transvaal, South Africa.* The town, southwest of Johannesburg, was laid out in 1895 and is probably named for Commandant N. C. *Gey* van Pittius (1837–1893), administrator of the Boer republic of Goshen from 1882 to 1883.

Gezira. *Region, east central Sudan.* The region lies between the Blue Nile and the White Nile. Hence its name, representing Arabic *al-gazīra,* "the island" (compare **Algiers**).

Ghadamès. See **Gadamès.**

Ghana. *Republic, West Africa.* The name, in Arabic *ghānā,* is a local word meaning "king." This was the title of the ruler of the vast trading empire that existed until the 13th century and that was itself called *Aoukâr,* with a territory greater than that of modern Ghana. Before 1957 the country was called *Gold Coast,* an English translation of Portuguese *Costa do Ouro.* This was the name given by Portuguese explorers who arrived here in the 15th century, found gold, and began shipping out both gold and slaves. There have been plausible attempts to link the name of Ghana with that of **Guinea** (q.v. for the evidence).

Ghanzi. *District, west central Botswana.* The name of the district, and also that of a town here, is said to derive from Tswana *gantshi,* meaning "place of flies." However, it may originally have derived from a San (Bushman) word for a one-stringed instrument.

Ghardaïa. *Town, north central Algeria.* The town was founded in the 11th century around a cave and is said to take its name from Arabic *dhār,* "cave," and the name of the woman saint, *Daïa,* who reputedly inhabited it. The cave is still venerated by local women.

Ghar el Melh. *Coastal town, northern Tunisia.* The former port, east of Bizerta, has a name meaning "cave of salt," from Arabic *dhār,* "cave," and *milh,* "salt." The reference may be to the lagoon round the town, created by the Medjerda River.

Giant's Castle. *Peak, Drakensberg Mountains, southeastern Africa.* The peak, on the border between Lesotho and the South African state of Natal, was so named in 1835 for its great size and for its resemblance to Edinburgh Castle, Scotland, when seen from certain angles.

Gibeon. *Town, south central Namibia.* Missionary records tell how the local Nama chief, Kido Witbooi, said that the place where the gospel was preached should have a beautiful name. He thus proposed the biblical name *Gibeon,* famous as the high place where Solomon offered sacrifices.

Gilé. *Village, southern Mozambique.* The name represents *gilé-gilé* (*egile egile* in Chichuabo, *egile* in Makua), meaning "epilepsy." Occurrences of this were formerly frequent here.

Gingidlovu. *Village, eastern Natal, South Africa.* The village, a short distance from the coast, has a Zulu name meaning "swallower of the elephant." The reference is probably to the victory of the Zulu chief Cetshwayo over his brother Mbulazi here in 1856.

Girga. *Town, east central Egypt.* The town, on the west bank of the Nile, is said to take its name from the ancient Coptic monastery of Mar *Girgis* here, this itself so called as it was dedicated to St. *George.* The name is also spelled *Jirja.*

Giza. *City, northern Egypt.* The ancient city, near the Great Pyramid of Cheops and the Sphinx, has the Arabic name of *al-gīza,* representing Egyptian *Er-ges-ḥer,* "beside the high," that is, beside the Great Pyramid, from *ges,* "beside," and *ḥer,* "high." The name is now sometimes officially rendered *El-Gîza. Cheops* itself is the Greek form of Egyptian *Khūfū,* the name of the king of the 4th dynasty (c. 2613–c. 2494 BC) who built the pyramid. The nearby pyramid of *Chephren* bears the name of his son, *Kheʿfreʿ.*

Glencoe. *Town, northwestern Natal, South Africa.* The town was laid out in 1921 and was originally called *Biggarsberg Junction,* for the range of hills here, themselves named for an early pioneer in Natal, Robert *Biggar.* The present name was adopted from the valley in western Scotland.

Gluckstadt. *Village, northern Natal, South Africa.* The village arose in 1906 as a center for farming families. Its name was probably adopted from the town of *Glückstadt,* Germany, bearing in mind that this literally means "town of fortune."

Goageb. *Village, southern Namibia.* The village, east of Lüderitz, has a Nama name meaning "twin rivers." The village lies at the confluence of two rivers, the larger of which is the **Konkib** (q.v.).

Goas. *Village, northwestern Namibia.* The village arose as a Roman Catholic mission station and has a Khoikhoin (Hottentot) name meaning "place of bullfrogs."

Gobabis. *Town, eastern Namibia.* The name of the town is of Khoikhoin (Hottentot) origin, meaning "place of discussion" (not "place of elephants," as often stated). The town arose from a mission station established in 1856.

Gochas. *Village, eastern Namibia.* The village has a Khoikhoin (Hottentot) name meaning "abundance of *!go* bushes" *(Acacia hebeclada).* (The initial *!* represents a click.)

Goedgegun. See **Nhlangano.**

Gokwe. *Village, northwestern Zimbabwe.* The name is that of a small river here, more accurately rendered *Gogwe.* This is probably the name of a chief who had a kraal here.

Gold Coast. See **Ghana.**

Golden Gate Highlands National Park. *National park, Orange Free State, South Africa.* The park, which opened in 1963, takes its name from the twin peaks of colored sandstone that form a feature at its entrance and that have a golden appearance at sunset.

[1]**Golden Valley.** *Village, southeastern Cape Province, South Africa.* The name refers to the golden color of ripe fruit in the valley here, southeast of Somerset East. The region was one of the world's largest producers of apricots in the 1920s.

[2]**Golden Valley.** *Village, central Zimbabwe.* The village, just northwest of Kadoma, has a name referring to the former gold mines here, the first of which opened in 1899.

Golela. *Town, southeastern Transvaal, South Africa.* The town, on the border with Swaziland, has a Swazi name meaning "animals' gathering place," referring to the region where Nyawo chiefs used to hunt. The portion of the town across the border in Swaziland was renamed **Lavumisa**. A former spelling for the South African name was *Gollel.*

Gollel. See **Golela.**

Gombe. *Town, northeastern Nigeria.* The name is that of a former emirate here, said to have been founded in 1804 by the Fulani (Peul) chief, Buba Yero (died 1841). In 1824 he founded the present town as the emirate capital, and on his death it was named *Gombe Aba,* "old Gombe," in his honor. It was renamed *Gombe* in 1919. The meaning of the basic name itself is uncertain.

Gomera. *Island, western Canaries.* The island has a Spanish name meaning "gum-tree," referring to the eucalyptus that grow here.

Gona-Re-Zhou National Park. *National park, southeastern Zimbabwe.* The park was established as a game reserve in 1967 on the site of a former hunting ground. Its Shona name means "refuge of the elephants."

Gonubie Mouth. *Coastal town, southeastern Cape Province, South Africa.* The seaside resort takes its name from the river at the mouth of which it stands. The river's own name is believed to represent the Xhosa word *qunube,* meaning "wild brambles."

Good Hope, Cape of. *Cape, southwestern South Africa.* The cape was first rounded in 1488 by the Portuguese navigator Bartholomeu Dias, who named it *Cabo Tormentoso,* "cape of storms," with reference to the rough seas here, where the waters of the Indian Ocean meet those of the Atlantic. King John II of Portugal is said to have then renamed it more propitiously *Cabo da Boa Esperança,* "cape of good hope," since it promised hope of a sea route to India. (Some authorities, however, attribute the present name to Dias himself.) The cape gave the name of South Africa's **Cape Province** and **Cape Town.**

Goodwood. *District of Cape Town, Cape Province, South Africa.* The northeastern district of Cape Town was established as a settlement in 1905 and named for the well-known racecourse in Sussex, England, since originally its owners planned a racecourse here. This was built, but was abandoned after only one race.

Gordons Bay. *Town and resort, southwestern Cape Province, South Africa.* The town, on the eastern side of Valsbaai, opposite **Fish Hoek,** was itself originally known as *Visch Hoek,* with the same meaning, when it was a fishing harbor in the 17th century. Because of confusion with its namesake, it was subsequently renamed for the traveler and soldier, Colonel Robert Jacob *Gordon* (1743–1795), who explored the coastline here in 1778 for the Dutch East India Company.

Gorée. *Island and town, western Senegal.* The small island lies east of Dakar in the harbor formed by Cape Vert peninsula. The town on it was the first capital of French West Africa. Dutch adventurers occupied the island in 1588, and referred to the harbor as a *goede reede,* "good roadstead." This is believed to have given the present name, which may, however, have been equally suggested by the island of *Goeree,* in the Netherlands.

Gorgoram. *Village, northeastern Nigeria.* The name is said to mean "deep" or "high," perhaps with some reference to the river here.

Gorongosa National Park. *National park, central Mozambique.* The name, also that of a mountain and settlement here, is that of an indigenous tribe, but is itself of uncertain meaning. The settlement was originally known by the Portuguese name of *Vila Paiva de Andrada,* for Colonel *Paiva de Andrada,* who in 1888 made application to develop some of the territory to the south of the Zambezi River.

Goshen. *Historic territory, western Transvaal, South Africa.* The territory was established as a Boer republic in 1882 and was given the name of the biblical "land of Goshen" (Genesis 45:10), itself a district of ancient Egypt east of the Nile Delta. The meaning of the original name is uncertain, but the Boers may have taken it to mean "pasturage." In 1883 the republic merged with *Stellaland* (see **Vryburg**) to form a united state, but this was annulled in 1885 and the territory went to Bechuanaland (now Botswana).

Gouda. *Town, southwestern Cape Province, South Africa.* The town, northeast of Cape Town, was originally known as *Porterville Road,* from its location on the road from Wellington to Porterville. The present name is not a borrowing from the Dutch town of Gouda, as might be supposed, but represents a Khoikhoin (Hottentot) name perhaps meaning "honey path." Cf. **Goudini.**

Goudini. *Village, southwestern Cape Province, South Africa.* The village, a health resort northeast of Cape Town, has a name that is believed to be of Khoikhoin (Hottentot) origin, meaning "bitter honey valley." Cf. **Gouda.**

Gourits. *River, Cape Province, South Africa.* The river, formed by the confluence of the Groot and Olifant, flows south to enter the Indian Ocean near Mossel Bay. Its name appears to refer to the Khoikhoin (Hottentot) tribe of the *Gouriquas,* whose own name means "dirty." This tribe was encountered by the Portuguese in 1667, and they probably transferred the name to the river. An earlier Portuguese name for the river, however, was *Rio dos vaqueiros,* "river of cowboys," since previous explorers had seen cows being herded on the banks here.

Graaff-Reinet. *Town, southern Cape Province, South Africa.* The town was founded in 1786 and named for Cornelis van de *Graaff,* governor of the Cape from 1785 to 1791, and his wife Cornelia, née *Reinet.*

Grabouw. *Town, southwestern Cape Province, South Africa.* The town, east of Cape Town, was laid out on a farm owned by a German immigrant, who named it for *Grabow,* his birthplace in Germany. The first plots were sold in 1858 and the name subsequently became corrupted to its present form.

Graciosa. *Island, northern Azores.* The island has a Spanish name meaning "gracious," "attractive." The island is less mountainous than the others in the group. The same name was given by the Spanish to a small island in the eastern Canaries, north of Lanzarote.

Grahamstown. *Town, southeastern Cape Province, South Africa.* The town was founded in 1811 and at first named *Graham's Town* by the governor of the Cape, Sir John Cradock, for Colonel John *Graham,* whose troops had cleared the Zuurfeld of Xhosas. The community became the center of the British Settlers of 1820 and its name was subsequently simplified.

Grain Coast. *Coast, West Africa.* The name was applied by the Portuguese to that part of the coast, now in Liberia, which lies between Cape Mesurado in the north and Cape Palmas, on the border with Sierra Leone, in the south. It refers not to cereals but to the former trade in grains of Paradise or Guinea pepper *(Amomum melegueta)*, a kind of pepper used as a spice and in medicine. On the other side of Africa, compare **Cinnamon Coast.**

Gran Canaria. *Island, central Canary Islands.* The name, meaning "great Canary," is that of the most important (but not largest) island in the group. The name is frequently anglicized as *Grand Canary.*

Grand Bassam. *Town and port, southeastern Côte d'Ivoire.* The town was founded in the early 19th century by local people, and was originally simply known as *bassam,* a term for a coastal village. French *Grand* was added when the growing town became capital of the Ivory Coast Colony in 1893. See also **Port-Bouët.**

Grand Canary. See **Gran Canaria.**

Grande Comore. See **Comoros.**

Grand Erg Occidental. *Desert region, north central Algeria.* The name is part French, part Arabic. It translates as "Great Western Erg," where *erg* represents Arabic *ʿirj,* a word of Berber origin used for a large expanse of sand dunes. Cf. **Grand Erg Oriental.**

Grand Erg Oriental. *Desert region, eastern Algeria.* The part French, part Arabic name translates as "Great Eastern Erg." See **Grand Erg Occidental.**

Grand Popo. *Town and port, southwestern Benin.* The second part of the name probably represents a Portuguese Creole word meaning "fisherman," with reference to the importance of the place as a fishing port. For the corresponding *Petit Popo,* see **Aného.**

Great Comoro. See **Comoros.**

Great Escarpment. *Mountain chain, South Africa.* The name, rarely found on maps or even in gazetteers, is that of the great sweep of mountains in South Africa that extends from the Drakensberg in the northeast to the Bokkeveld and Kamiesberg mountains in the west. It does *not* include the mountain chains in the south that run parallel to the Atlantic coast south of the Great Karoo, such as the Hottentots Holland, Drakenstein, Langeberg, and Cedarberg ranges. (These were collectively named the *Mountains of Africa* by the 17th century Dutch pioneer Jan Van Riebeeck—see **Riebeek East.**) The name is geographically nonspecific, and a better name would be something like *South African Ranges.* Russian geographers use the name *Kapskiye gory,* "Cape mountains," for the two groups that comprise the ranges running parallel to the Little Karoo, such as the Swartberge (to the north) and Langeberg and Outeniqua Mountains (to the south), and the coastal chains in the southwest, such as the Cedarberg and Olifants River Berge.

Great Fish. See **Fish.**

Great Kei. See **Kei.**

Great Oasis, The. See **El-Kharga.**

Great Rift Valley. *Rift Valley, East Africa.* The rift is the most extensive on the earth's surface, extending southward from the Jordan valley in Syria to Mozambique. Its name is generally descriptive of its size and geological nature, a *rift valley* being a long, narrow valley resulting from the subsidence of land between two parallel faults. See also **Rift Valley.**

Green Mountain. *Mountain, Ascension Island.* Ascension is of volcanic origin, and the mountain is the extinct volcano's crater. The island is rocky and barren and almost without vegetation except for a small area atop Green Mountain; hence its name.

Greenville. *Town and port, southern Liberia.* The port was settled in 1838 at the mouth of the Sinoe River by a group of freed American black slaves, sponsored by the Mississippi Colonization society. It was at first named *Sinoe* (or *Sino*), for the river, a name still in alternate use today. Its colonial name was given soon after for James *Green,* an American colonization advocate.

Greylingstad. *Town, southern Transvaal, South Africa.* The town, southeast of Johannesburg, was founded as a church settlement in 1909 and named for P. J. *Greyling,* a local pioneer and stepson of the Voortrekker leader Piet Retief. In 1913 another town was laid out nearby and named *Willemsdal* for the owner of the site, *Willem* Bezuidenhout. The original Greylingstad was vacated the following year and transferred to Willemstad, together with its name.

Greyton. *Village, southwestern Cape Province, South Africa.* The village takes its name from Sir George *Grey* (1812–1898), governor of the Cape from 1854 to 1859 and again from 1860 to 1861. See also **Lady Grey.**

Greytown. *Town, central Natal, South Africa.* The town was laid out in 1850 and named for Sir George *Grey* (1812–1898), governor of the Cape from 1854 to 1859 and again from 1860 to 1861. See also **Lady Grey.**

Griqualand East. *Region, eastern Cape Province, South Africa.* The region was originally known as *No-Man's-Land.* In 1861 Sir George Grey, governor of the Cape, offered it to the Khoikhoin (Hottentot) *Griqua* tribes, who trekked from **Griquatown** through the Orange Free State then southward to the region. See also **Griqualand West, Griquatown,** and **Kokstad.**

Griqualand West. *Region, northern Cape Province, South Africa.* The region was settled by *Griqua* tribes from **Griquatown,** as in **Griqualand East,** and was originally simply named *Griqualand.* In 1871 the territory, with its diamond mines, passed to the British, and was given the suffix *West* to distinguish it from Griqualand East.

Griquatown. *Town, north central Cape Province, South Africa.* The town was founded as a mission station in 1802 and was at first given the Afrikaans name of *Klaarwater,* "clear water," with reference to the local spring. The name was changed to its present form in 1813, for the Khoikhoin (Hottentot) *Griqua* tribes here. Their own history began in the 17th century as the *Grigriquas,* a name probably based on that of one of their chiefs. See also **Griqualand East** and **Griqualand West.**

Groblersdal. *Town, southern Transvaal, South Africa.* The Afrikaans name means "Grobler's valley," referring to Willem Jacobus *Grobler,* the farmowner on whose land the town arose in the 1930s.

Grootfontein. *Town, northern Namibia.* The town was originally known by the Herero name *Otjivandatatjonque,* meaning “hill of the leopard.” The San (Bushmen) called it *Gei≠/ous,* meaning “big fountain,” however, and the Afrikaans equivalent of this was adopted by the first white settlers here. (In the San name, the unusual characters represent clicks.)

Groot Laagte. *Watercourse, Southern Africa.* The intermittent river rises in central Namibia and flows east across the border with Botswana. Its name is Dutch for “great valley.”

Groot Vloer. *Region, western Cape Province, South Africa.* The region east of the Katkop Hills is essentially a salt lake formed by the standing floodwater of the Sak River. Its descriptive Afrikaans name means “great floor.”

Grünau. *Village, southern Namibia.* The village has a German name meaning “green meadow,” presumably referring to the green vegetation that appears here after a rainfall. The Khoikhoin (Hottentot) name of the place is *Ameis,* “green face.”

Guardafui, Cape. See Ras **Asir.**

Guban. *Coastal region, northwestern Somalia.* The region, a barren plain, has a local name meaning “burned.”

Guinea. *Republic, West Africa.* The name was originally applied to the coastal region bordering the North Atlantic here, extending from southern Senegal to as far south as Gabon. It is thought to be Berber in origin, and to represent either *akal-n-iguinaouen,* “land of blacks” (cf. **Sudan,** and comment on *Azania* under **South Africa**) or *iguawen,* “blind ones.” The latter name is said to have been given by the Berbers to their southern neighbors because these could not understand the Berber language. At the same time there are good grounds for linking the name of Guinea with that of **Ghana.** The names are not only similar but the two countries are near neighbors (separated only by the Côte d’Ivoire), with modern Guinea occupying territory that was part of the former ancient kingdom of Ghana. (On most 17th century maps, *Genehoa* is the name of the region of West Africa north of the Senegal, corresponding to modern Mauritania and Mali, while *Guinea* is the region south of the Niger, corresponding to modern Côte d’Ivoire, Ghana, Togo, Benin, and Nigeria.) There is another association: the former English gold coin, the *guinea,* was made from gold brought from this region, and *Gold Coast* was the former name of Ghana. Guinea itself gave the name of *New Guinea,* now Papua New Guinea, in the southwestern Pacific, an island whose inhabitants were thought by early European explorers to resemble those of West Africa. (Cf. **Equatorial Guinea.**)

Guinea-Bissau. *Republic, West Africa.* The country, known as *Portuguese Guinea* until 1973, takes its modern name from **Guinea,** which borders it to the south and southeast, and **Bissau**, its capital. Its name thus refers to its location in the much larger territory that Guinea historically once was. (The addition of “Bissau” distinguishes this Guinea from Guinea proper, which for the same reason is sometimes known as *Guinea-Conakry,* for its capital.) Cf. **Equatorial Guinea.**

Gumel. *Town, northern Nigeria.* The name is that of the former emirate here from 1749 to 1903, of which the town was the capital from 1845. The name represents the Fulani (Peul) word *gubele,* a term for a short-horned cow.

Guruè. *Town, central Mozambique.* The origin of the name is uncertain. It may derive from the phrase *curui-curui,* representing the cry of a partridge and serving as the nickname of a local hunter. Alternately, it may come from *gulué* (or *eculuè* or *ngulué*), meaning "wild boar," an animal common here and regarded by local tribes as totemic. The town's earlier Portuguese colonial name was *Vila Junqueiro,* for Manuel Saraira *Junqueiro,* a Portuguese tea planter. The original plan was to name the place for the administrator Vaz de Sá, who was the true pioneer of tea planting in Mozambique, especially in the Guruè area. However, the name went to Junqueiro, primarily because he was killed in an air crash when returning home to Lisbon, and the disaster prompted the selection of his name as a commemoration. This name was in use for the town from 1947 to 1981.

Gutu. *Village, east central Zimbabwe.* The name means "sling for carrying arrows," and probably derives from that of a chief once here, or relates to an incident of some kind. The name is also that of a district.

Gwanda. *Town, southern Zimbabwe.* The town, founded in 1900, was given the name of a local chief, *Gwanda* or *Jawunda.* The name is also that of a district.

Gwandu. *Town, northwestern Nigeria.* The name was that of the former emirate here from 1808 to 1903. It represents the surrounding *gandu,* the royal farmlands.

Gwebi. *Village, northern Zimbabwe.* The village, northwest of the capital, Harare, takes its name from the river here. The river's name (more accurately *Gwivi*) meaning "hairless," referring to the scant grass on its banks.

Gwelo. See **Gweru.**

Gweru. *City, central Zimbabwe.* The name was adopted from the river here, and is probably from the local word *kwela,* "to climb," with reference to the river's steep banks. The origin may, however, be in a Shona word meaning "dry," since the river flows intermittently. The town was founded in 1894, and the name was spelled *Gwelo* until 1982.

Gweta. *Village, northeastern Botswana.* The name is of San (Bushman) origin and is said to mean "[place] where big frogs meet."

Haarlem. *Village, southern Cape Province, South Africa.* The village was laid out in 1856 and named for the city in the Netherlands.

Hadrumetum. See **Sousse.**

Haenertsburg. *Village, northern Transvaal, South Africa.* The village was named in 1894 for the discoverer of gold here in 1886, C. F. *Haenert.*

Hafun, Ras. *Cape, northeastern Somalia.* The easternmost point of Africa has a name meaning "edge headland," from Arabic *ra's,* "head," and *ḥaffi,* "edge," "border." Cf. Ras **Asir.**

Haga-Haga. *Coastal village, southeastern Cape Province, South Africa.* The name of the seaside resort is said to be imitative, evoking the sound of waves breaking on the shore here.

Halfway House. *Town, southern Transvaal, South Africa.* The town was laid out in 1890 and given a name indicating its location on a coach route midway between Johannesburg and Pretoria.

Halq el Oued. *Town and port, northern Tunisia.* The town, an outport for Tunis, has a name representing Arabic *ḥalq al-wādī,* literally "gullet of the watercourse," referring to the harbor narrows here, now linked to the country's capital by a canal. The town's French name, *La Goulette,* "the gully," "the narrows," is still alternately in use.

Hamada el Homra. See **Al-Ḥammadah al-Ḥamrā'.**

Hamburg. *Village, Ciskei, South Africa.* The village was founded in 1857 by German settlers of the British-German Legion, who named it for *Hamburg,* Germany.

Hamman Salahine. *Village, northeastern Algeria.* The village grew up round hot sulfur springs a short distance west of Biskra. Its name means "bath of the righteous," from Arabic *ḥammān,* "[hot] bath," and a word related to *ṣalāḥ,* "righteousness." (Compare *Saladin,* "righteousness of the faith," as the name of the 12th century sultan of Egypt who opposed the Crusaders.)

Hammanskraal. *Town, central Transvaal, South Africa.* The town, north of Pretoria, arose only in the 1950s and was probably named for a Mr. *Hamman,* a nature commissioner here. Some sources, however, derive the name from a cattleman called *Hamman* who built a *kraal* (stockade) here to protect his stock.

Hangklip. *Cape, southwestern Cape Province, South Africa.* The cape, east of False Bay, has a self-descriptive Afrikaans name meaning "hanging rock." This is a corruption of the original name of *Hanglip,* referring to its shape, given by the English explorer William Burchell in 1822. Early Portuguese explorers called the cape *Cabo Falso,* "false cape," or *Ponta Espinosa,* "thorny point."

Hankey. *Town, southern Cape Province, South Africa.* A station of the London Missionary Society was established here, west of Port Elizabeth, in 1825 and named for the Society's treasurer, William Alers *Hankey.*

Hanover. *Town, central Cape Province, South Africa.* The town was established on a farm in 1854 and named for *Hanover,* German hometown of the farmowner's parents.

Harar. *City, eastern Ethiopia.* The name, also occurring as *Harer* or *Harerge,* is an Amharic corruption of a word meaning "trading post." The city lies midway between the capital, Addis Ababa, and the Red Sea coast. The name is also that of the region here, now administratively divided into the provinces of Eastern Harerge and Western Harerge.

Harare. *Capital of Zimbabwe.* The name represents that of *Neharawa,* a tribal chief buried on the hillock where the British raised their flag on September 13, 1890. (The site is that of the present African Unity Square, until 1988 called Cecil Square.) They named the new settlement *Fort Salisbury,* in honor of the British statesman Robert Cecil, 3d Marquess of *Salisbury* (1830–1903), three times prime minister. (The marquess was the lineal descendant of Robert Cecil, 1st Earl of Salisbury, who took his title from *Salisbury,* Wiltshire.) The original colonial name became simply *Salisbury* in 1897 and remained in use until 1982, two years after Zimbabwe gained independence.

Hararge. See **Harar.**

Hardap Dam. *Dam Fish River, central Namibia.* The name, adopted from that of a round hill nearby, is Khoikhoin (Hottentot) in origin and means "nipple," referring to the hill's contour. The name is also that of a game reserve and holiday resort here.

Harding. *Town, southern Natal, South Africa.* The town was founded as a military station in 1877 and named for Sir Walter *Harding* (1812–1874), Natal's first chief justice.

Haribonga, Lake. *Lake, central Mali.* The lake is linked with the Niger River, as its Songhai name indicates, meaning "head of the water."

Harper. *Town and port, southeastern Liberia.* The settlement was founded on Cape Palmas in 1834 by a group of freed black American slaves sponsored by the Maryland Colonization Society (see also **Maryland**), and was originally itself named *Cape Palmas.* In 1857 the colony passed to Liberia, and the port was renamed for the American politician Robert Goodloe *Harper* (1766–1825), a member of the American Colonization Society, who himself named **Liberia** and its capital, **Monrovia.**

Harrismith. *Town, northeastern Orange Free State, South Africa.* A settlement was founded here in 1849 and at first given the Afrikaans name *Vrededorp,* "peace village." It was subsequently found that there was insufficient water for the needs of the community, so the village was moved to *Gemsbokhoek,* "gemsbok corner," on the Wilge River. (A gemsbok is an oryx, or large antelope.) Sir *Harry Smith* (1787–1860), governor of the Cape, was asked if the place should remain *Vrededorp* or if it could now be named for him. Although Sir Harry preferred the name to remain unchanged, it was nevertheless altered to its present form as a tribute to the man who was governor from 1847 to 1852.

Hartebeesfontein. *Town, southwestern Transvaal, South Africa.* The name, Afrikaans for "hartebeest spring," is first recorded in 1843. It is said to derive from an incident in which two Voortrekkers, pursuing a wounded hartebeest (antelope), found it dead by a spring here.

Hartenbos. *Coastal town, southern Cape Province, South Africa.* The seaside resort, northwest of Mossel Bay, takes its name from the farm on which it was established. The Afrikaans name means "hart thicket," referring to antelopes here in former times.

Hartswater. *Town, northern Cape Province, South Africa.* The town was laid out in 1948 to provide a northern base for the irrigation scheme based on the Vaal and *Harts* rivers here. The second part of the name refers generally to this scheme.

Hausaland. *Region, northern Nigeria.* The name is sometimes found for the region of Nigeria lying north of the Niger and Benue rivers. It relates to the largest ethnic group in the area, the *Hausa.* Their own name is said to derive from Arabic *al-lisān,* "the language," referring to people who spoke a common tongue.

Hawston. *Village and port, southwestern Cape Province, South Africa.* The fishing village takes its name from that of a Mr. *Haw,* a local civil commissioner.

Healdtown. *Village, Ciskei, South Africa.* The village arose as a mission station in 1853 and takes its name from James *Heald,* treasurer of the Wesleyan Missionary Society, which partly financed the venture.

Heany Junction. *Village, southern Zimbabwe.* The village, a railroad junction, is named for the American-born Rhodesian pioneer, Captain Maurice *Heany* (died 1927).

Heatonville. *Village, northeastern Natal, South Africa.* The village is named for Senator the Rt. Hon. George *Heaton* Nicholls (1876–1959), member of parliament for Zululand from 1920 and high commissioner for South Africa in London from 1944 to 1947.

[1]**Heidelberg.** *Town, southwestern Cape Province, South Africa.* The town was established in 1855 by members of the Dutch Reformed Church, and was named for *Heidelberg,* Germany, the city where the

Heidelberg Catechism was drawn up in 1562. The name was thus a tribute to this confession of faith. See also **Bethulie.**

[2]**Heidelberg.** *Town, southern Transvaal, South Africa.* In 1860 a German trader, Heinrich Veckermann, settled in this area. A town was laid out, and in 1866 was named for the university town in Germany where Veckermann had received his training. See also **Bethulie.**

Heilbron. *Town, northern Orange Free State, South Africa.* The town was founded in 1872 and named for the German city of *Heilbronn.* Its own name means "holy spring," and this was considered appropriate for the new settlement with its nearby spring.

Heliopolis. *Ancient city, northern Egypt.* This is the Greek name of the ancient city of *Iunu,* immediately northeast of modern Cairo. It means "sun city," from Greek *hēlios,* "sun," and *polis,* "city," referring to the sun god Ra (or Re), who was worshipped here. The Egyptian name means "pillar," with reference to the sacred obelisks here. (Two of them, each known as Cleopatra's Needle, were later shipped west and set up respectively on the Thames Embankment, London, and in Central Park, New York City.) The Egyptian name appears in the Hebrew form *On* in the Bible (Genesis 41:45).

Hell-Ville. *Capital of Nossi-Bé, northwestern Madagascar.* The town arose in 1840 when the island was ceded to the French. The name was given by Pierre Passot, captain of the warship *Colibri,* which arrived here that year, in honor of his commander-in-chief, Admiral Louis de *Hell,* governor of Réunion (then known as Bourbon) from 1838 to 1841.

Helmeringhausen. *Village, south central Namibia.* The village, a farmers' meeting place, was so named by European settlers for the village of the same name in Westphalia, Germany.

Helpmekaar. *Village, central Natal, South Africa.* The Afrikaans name means literally "help each other," and refers to the mutual assistance needed among transport riders when they built a road over a hill here.

Hendrik Verwoerd Dam. *Dam, Orange River, Orange Free State, South Africa.* The dam was officially opened in 1972 and named for *Hendrik Verwoerd* (1901–1966), prime minister of South Africa from 1958 to his assassination.

Hendrina. *Town, southeastern Transvaal, South Africa.* The town was founded in 1914 on a farm and named for the owner's wife, *Hendrina* Beukes.

Hennenman. *Town, north central Orange Free State, South Africa.* The original site here was a railroad station known as *Venterburg Road.* In 1927 the settlement was given its present name in honor of Petrus F. *Hennenman* (1844–1932), a prominent local farmer.

Herero. *Homeland, northeastern Namibia.* The name is that of the Bantu-speaking *Herero* people who inhabit this part of Africa. Their own name is said to be onomatopoeic, representing the sound of a spear in flight.

Hermanus. *Town, southwestern Cape Province, South Africa.* The town was established as a fishing village in 1855 and was at first known as *Hermanuspietersfontein,* for a local herdsman, *Hermanus Pieters,* who watered his stock at a nearby spring (Afrikaans *fontein*). The name was shortened to its present form in 1904.

Hermon. *Village, southwestern Cape Province, South Africa.* The name is of biblical origin, and was adopted from Mount *Hermon,* no doubt alluding to the original meaning of the name as "sacred place."

Hermopolis Magna. See **El-Ashmunein.**

Hermopolis Parva. See **Damanhūr.**

Herschel. *Village, Transkei, South Africa.* The village was founded in 1879 and named for the English astronomer Sir John *Herschel* (1792–1871), who worked at the Cape in the 1830s.

Hertzogville. *Town, northwestern Orange Free State, South Africa.* The town was established in 1915 and named for General James Barry Munnik *Hertzog* (1866–1942), prime minister of South Africa from 1924 to 1939 and founder of the National Party.

Hesperides. See **Benghazi.**

Hibberdene. *Coastal village, southeastern Natal, South Africa.* The holiday resort is named for C. Maxwell-*Hibberd,* a former postmaster of Natal.

Hierakonpolis. See **Kom el-Ahmar.**

Hierro. *Island, western Canaries.* The westernmost island of the group, formerly known as *Ferro,* has a name that would appear to mean "iron," from Spanish *hierro* (Portuguese *ferro*). This apparently relates to the fact that ancient geographers, such as Ptolemy, regarded the island as the limit of the Western World and so reckoned longitude from it. The reference would thus be to the deviation, or lack of it, of a compass needle. But the name is almost certainly of Guanche origin, meaning "wells." (By coincidence, the island's main town, *Valverde,* has a name meaning "green valley," and *Greenwich,* England, the place from which longitude is now recorded, means "green harbor.")

Hillcrest. *Village, southeastern Natal, South Africa.* The village, between Durban and Pietermaritzburg, has a self-descriptive name, referring to its location on the crest of a hill.

Himeville. *Village, southwestern Natal, South Africa.* The village takes its name from Sir Albert Henry *Hime* (1842–1919), Irish-born prime minister of Natal from 1899 to his resignation in 1903.

Hippo. See **Annaba.**

Hlabisa. *Village, northeastern Natal, South Africa.* The village, established in 1892, takes its name from that of a Zulu tribe. Their own name may mean "to slaughter," referring to the presenting of an animal for ritual sacrifice.

Hlatikulu. *Town, southwestern Swaziland.* The name is a compound of Swazi *ihlatsi,* "bush," and *ikhulu,* "large object." The overall sense is thus "big bush," otherwise "large forest."

Hlobane. *Village, northern Natal, South Africa.* The village arose round a colliery founded in 1904 and was originally known simply as *Kraal,* "tribal village." The present name is of Zulu origin, perhaps meaning "beautiful place."

Hluhluwe Game Reserve. *Game reserve, eastern Natal, South Africa.* The reserve, established in 1897, has a name that is a Zulu word for the thorny monkey rope *(Dalbergia armata),* a species of creeping plant that grows profusely on the banks of the identically named river here. The name is pronounced "Shlooshloo-way."

Hluti. *Village, southern Swaziland.* The name is that of a nearby hill, whose summit resembles a *hluti,* the bushy hairstyle of Swazi women.

Hobhouse. *Town, eastern Orange Free State, South Africa.* The town, near the border with Lesotho, was established in 1912 and named for Emily *Hobhouse* (1860–1926), the English social worker who did much to reform conditions in the concentration camps of the Boer War.

Hochfeld. *Village, north central Namibia.* The name, German for "high veld," is descriptive of the site.

Hodh. *Region, southern Mauritania.* The name means "basin," "depression," describing the low-lying desert terrain in the southeastern quarter of the country.

Hofmeyr. *Town, southeastern Cape Province, South Africa.* The town was laid out in 1873 and originally named *Maraisburg,* for Daniel *Marais,* who played an important role in its founding. In order to avoid confusion with the Transvaal town of the same name, it was renamed in 1911 to honor Jan Hendrik *Hofmeyr* (1845–1909), known as "Onze Jan" ("our Jan"), the South African statesman and historian who gained recognition of Dutch as an official language of South Africa.

Hoggar. See **Ahaggar.**

Hombori. *Mountains, southern Mali.* The name, also that of a village here, is a Fulani (Peul) form of the Mande and Hausa name *Tombola,* from the *Tombo* people who inhabit the region. Their own name means "ruins," "debris," referring to the tumbledown, craggy nature of the rocks. The Arabic name of the area is *al-ḥajar,* "the stone."

Hondeklip Bay. *Bay, southwestern Cape Province, South Africa.* The bay has an Afrikaans name meaning "dog rock," referring to a rock formerly here that resembled a seated dog. When lightning struck the rock, however, the dog lost its head, so the resemblance is no longer obvious. There is a fishing village here of the same name.

Hoopstad. *Town, northwestern Orange Free State, South Africa.* The town was founded in 1876 and was originally named *Hauptstad,* for the site surveyor, A. P. *Haupt.* It was realized, however, that this could be interpreted as "chief town," "capital" (German *Hauptstadt*), so the name was modified to one that would instead literally mean "hope town."

Hopetown. *Town, northeastern Cape Province, South Africa.* The town was founded in 1854 and named for Major William *Hope,* auditor-general of the Cape.

Hore Bay. *Bay, Lake Tanganyika, northern Zambia.* The southernmost bay of the lake is named for Edward Goode *Hore,* the English naval officer who charted it and who launched the Church Missionary Society's steamboat *Good News* on it in 1884.

Horn of Africa. *Promontory, East Africa.* The name is traditionally given to the most easterly projection of the African continent, territorially occupied by Somalia or, more broadly, by Somalia, Ethiopia, Eritrea, and Djibouti. *Horn* here is the standard word in the sense "pointed projection." The word (or its equivalent) was used thus by ancient geographers, and Ptolemy, in the 2d century AD, named this part of Africa *Southern Horn.* (Cape Horn, the southern extremity of South America, is also such a "horn" but is actually named for *Hoorn* in Holland, the home town of the Dutch navigator W. C. Schouten, who rounded it in 1616.) The northeastern extremity of the Horn of Africa is Cape Guardafui (see Ras **Asir**); the easternmost point is Ras **Hafun.**

Horta. *Town and port, central Azores.* The town, on the southeastern coast of the island of Faial, has a Portuguese name meaning "garden," "orchard." Horta is noted for its exports of wine, oranges, and grain.

Hotazel. *Village, northern Cape Province, South Africa.* The name is that of the farm on which the village arose, and is said to be a fanciful corruption of "hot as hell," describing the weather at the time when the farm was surveyed.

Hottentot Bay. *Bay, southwestern Namibia.* The bay, north of Lüderitz, is named for the indigenous people of Southern Africa who are now more usually known as the Khoikhoin. The origin of the name is disputed, but it may derive from an unknown Dutch word meaning "stutterer," alluding to the characteristic clicks in their speech. Just south of the bay is *Hottentot Point.*

Hout Bay. *Town, southwestern Cape Province, South Africa.* The town, just south of Cape Town, was so named in 1653 from the bay here. The meaning is "wood bay," referring to the wealth of timber found here by settlers. The official Afrikaans form of the name is *Houtbaai.*

Howick. *Town, central Natal, South Africa.* The town was founded in 1850 and named for Sir Henry George Grey, Viscount *Howick* (1802–1894), British secretary of state for the colonies from 1846 to 1852. Sir Henry, later Earl Grey, took his title from the family home at *Howick,* Northumberland.

Huab. *River, Namibia.* The seasonal watercourse, in the northwest of the country, has a Khoikhoin (Hottentot) name probably meaning "crooked bends."

Huambo. *Town and province, west central Angola.* The name is a Portuguese corruption of the local name for the region, *Ouimbundu.* The meaning of this is uncertain. The present town was founded in 1912 by Portuguese settlers and in 1928 was renamed *Nova Lisboa,* "New Lisbon," to emphasize colonial ties, since it was intended to be the capital of Angola. It reverted to its original name in 1975.

Huigais. See **Cape Town.**

Huila. *Province, southwestern Angola.* The name is that of the *Mwila* tribe who formerly lived on the plateau here. Their own name derives from *hila,* "grass," referring to the rich pastures that they found when settling here.

Hukuntsi. *Village, southwestern Botswana.* The name is said to be of Ngologa origin and to mean "many corners."

Humansdorp. *Town, southern Cape Province, South Africa.* The town was laid out in 1849 on a farm owned by Matthys Gerhardus *Human,* and is named for him.

Hunericopolis. See **Sousse.**

Huns Mountains. *Mountains, southern Namibia.* The name derives from a Khoikhoin (Hottentot) word meaning "to turn back," presumably referring to a difficult route through the mountains here.

Hunters Road. *Village, central Zimbabwe.* The name refers to the road between Gweru and Kwekwe that was formerly used by European and South African hunters visiting Matabeleland from the southwest.

Hunyani Range. *Mountain range, northern Zimbabwe.* The name, more accurately *Mhanyami,* simply means "high land," and is also that of the river here.

Hutchinson. *Village, southern Cape Province, South Africa.* A railroad junction was established here in 1885, originally with the name of *Victoria West Road,* for its proximity to **Victoria West.** In 1901 the village that developed was renamed in honor of Sir Walter Francis Hely-*Hutchinson* (1847–1913), governor of Natal from 1893 to 1901 and of the Cape Colony from 1901 to 1910.

Hwange. *Town, western Zimbabwe.* The name is that of a chief, *Hwange* Rusumbami, head of the Nambiya section of the Rozvi tribe who lived in the area. The town arose in 1903 around a coal mine opened in 1899. The name is now also that of the district here and of the *Hwange* National Park. Until 1982 the name was spelled *Wankie.*

Ibadan. *City, southwestern Nigeria.* The city's origins are obscure, and its modern history begins only in 1829. Its name has been explained as evolving from its Yoruba name, *Eba Odan,* meaning "near the savanna." However, it could equally represent Arabic *ʿibāda,* "worship," from *ʿabd,* "servant (of God)" (as in the personal name *Abdullah*), plural *ʿibād.* The city has long been a center of Islam.

Icosium. See **Algiers.**

Idi Amin Dada, Lake. See Lake **Edward.**

Idutywa. *Town, Transkei, South Africa.* The name, also that of a river here, is derived from Xhosa *ukuduba,* "to disturb," in the passive, *ukudutywa,* "the disturbed one." The reference is to some shooting or hunting incident, or an invasion by a warring tribe. The town was laid out in 1884 on the site of a military post set up in 1858.

Ife. *Town, west central Nigeria.* The Greeks knew the ancient settlement here as *Ouphas.* The similarity of the two names and the fact that Ife has gold mines has led to a popular association with the biblical *Ophir,* renowned for its gold and precious stones. It remains uncertain to what extent such a linguistic or historical link is genuinely tenable. (Ophir has also had its name associated with that of *Africa* itself.) The Yoruba hold Ife to be a sacred city, and for that reason its name has equally been associated with *Ifa,* the god of divination.

Ifni. *Territory, southern Morocco.* The former province of Spain, on the Atlantic coast, derives its name from Berber *ifni,* from *isaffen,* plural of *asif,* "river," "water," referring to its maritime location. (Cf. **Fès** and **Safi**). The territory was ceded to Morocco in 1969.

Ifrane. *Town, northern Morocco.* The town, a resort in the Middle Atlas Mountain, derives its name from the plural form of Berber *ifri,* "cave."

Ijebu-Ode. *Town, southwestern Nigeria.* The town was established by the 16th century as the central settlement of the *Ijebu* people, a subdivision of the Yoruba, and is named for them.

Ilebo. *Town, south central Zaïre.* The town, which received its present local name in 1972, was known until that year as *Port-Francqui.* Its name, referring to its location as a port on the Kasai River, is a compliment to the Belgian politician and banker, Émile *Francqui* (1863–1935), who explored Katanga in the 1890s.

Îles de Los. See **Los Islands.**

Ilesha. *Town, southwestern Nigeria.* The town takes its name from the *Ilesha* people, a branch of the Yoruba.

Illovo. *Village, southeastern Natal, South Africa.* The name is that of the river here, itself representing the Zulu name *Lovu,* said to mean "welcome." *Ilovo Beach* is a nearby seaside resort.

Ilorin. *City, southwestern Nigeria.* The city was founded in about 1785 by the Yoruba people and has a local name said to mean "town of the elephant."

Impendle. *Town, southern Natal, South Africa.* The town was founded in 1894 and named for a prominent hill here, east of the Drakensberg. The name is Zulu, and means "uncovered," "exposed."

I-n-Abalene. *Watersource, northeastern Mali.* The Tuareg name means "the one of the young camels," referring to a valley here in the mountains of the Adrar des Iforas, on the border with Algeria. There are dozens of such names for each valley and source, such as *I-n-Akinbeou,* "the one [i.e., place] of the calf's nose," *I-n-ebser,* "the one of the razor," *I-n-oul,* "the one of the heart," and the like. The names are descriptive, mostly referring to the physical appearance, nature, or vegetation of the place.

Inchiri. *Region, western Mauritania.* The name of the formerly fertile region is of Zenaga origin and is said to represent either *in-ch iri,* "tent by the camel herds," or *in-charan,* "the one [i.e., place] of the trees."

Indwe. *Town, eastern Cape Province, South Africa.* The town was established in 1896 on the site of a coal mine opened in 1867. It takes its name from the river here, in turn deriving from the Xhosa name for the blue crane *(Tetrapteryx paradisea),* once common locally.

Ingwavuma. *Village, northern Natal, South Africa.* The village, near the border with Swaziland, takes its name from the river here. The first part of the name apparently represents the Zulu word for "tiger." There are no tigers in Africa, however, so the reference may be either to the leopard, or figuratively to a river that "roars" or "growls" like a tiger. Another local Zulu name for the area is *Mthombeni,* "place of the wild fig tree."

Inhaca. *Island and peninsula, southeastern Mozambique.* The local name of the island, opposite the capital, Maputo, means "marsh," "low-lying land."

Inhambane. *City and port, southeastern Mozambique.* There are various explanations to account for the name, including the following: (1) It is a corruption of *ambane,* "goodbye," allegedly said to the Portuguese colonists on their departure by the indigenous people; (2) It represents the words *ina bano*, "We [are] people," the reply given by chiefs to the Portuguese sailors who asked them who they were by means of gestures; (3) It represents the words *gu bela nhumbane,* "Go into the hut," addressed to the Portuguese navigator Vasco da Gama, who was waiting to note the name in writing, by the people here; (4) It is a tribal name, perhaps meaning "land of good people." Of these, the last is the most likely. The name is also that of the province here.

Inhaminga. *Village, central Mozambique.* The name seems to be a combination of the local words *nhama,* "flesh," and *minga,* "points," perhaps with reference to some prickly plant that grew here.

Inharrime. *Village, southeastern Mozambique.* The village takes its name from the river on which it stands. This itself may mean "cultivator," "tiller," and so refer to the fertility of the surrounding land.

In Salah. *Town, central Algeria.* The town and oasis, a former important trade link between northern and southern Africa, has a name representing Arabic *ʿayn salah,* "good well."

Inyanga. *Village, eastern Zimbabwe.* The name is that of a village, a district, a national park, and a mountain *(Inyangani),* all close to the border with Mozambique. The source of the name lies with a witch doctor, *Sanyanga,* who had authority here in the first part of the 19th century. His own name may be a Nyanga one meaning "elephant tusk." The national park was established as such in 1950. It was originally the *Rhodes Inyanga National Park,* the first word of this honoring the statesman Cecil John *Rhodes* (see **Rhodesia**), who grew fruit crops here on an estate that he opened to the public.

Inyantue. *Village, western Zimbabwe.* The name is that of the local river, whose own name, more accurately rendered *Nyantuwe,* means "stopping place." The reference would be to a place where travelers could rest and animals drink.

Inyati. *Village, west central Zimbabwe.* The village has a name that is either a missionary corruption of *nyathi,* "buffalo," or an alteration of an original name *Emhlangeni,* meaning "bed of reeds," with reference to the river here.

Irene. *Town, southern Transvaal, South Africa.* The town, to the south of Pretoria, was founded in 1889 by Alois Hugo Nellmapius, who named it for his daughter, *Irene* Violet, bearing in mind that her name means "peace." (This was just after the first Boer War.) Irene was incorporated into Lyttelton in 1964.

Irharhar. *Watercourse, eastern Algeria.* There are several intermittent rivers of the name, or of some similar name, in North Africa. The origin is ultimately in Berber *irhzer,* "watercourse," "river."

Isando. *Township, southern Transvaal, South Africa.* The industrial township, an eastern extension of Johannesburg, was laid out in 1949. It has a Bantu (Nguni) name said to represent the beating of a hammer.

Isipingo. *Coastal village, southeastern Natal, South Africa.* The seaside resort, which with *Isipingo Beach* is a virtual southern suburb of Durban, takes its name from the *Sipingo* River here. The river's own name may derive from a local word for a type of wild fruit *(Scutia commersonii)* that grows (or grew) along its banks.

Ismailia. *City, northeastern Egypt.* The name is Arabic in origin, and represents *ismaʿīl,* "Ismael," the name of *Ismael* Pasha (1830–1895), viceroy, then khedive, of Egypt from 1863 to 1879. The town was founded in 1863 as a halfway station on the Suez Canal, construction of which had been actively encouraged by Ismail. Ismail's sons gave the names of **Port Fuad** and **Port Taufiq**, while his uncle gave that of **Port Said**.

Isoka. *Village, northern Zambia.* The name derives from Lala *nsoka,* "snake," and more exactly represents *leta isoka,* "to make poisonous remarks." The reference is apparently to some hostile encounter. The village was founded in 1894 and was originally named *Fife,* for the Duke of *Fife,* a director of the British South Africa Company.

Iunu. See **Heliopolis.**

Ivory Coast. See **Côte d'Ivoire.**

Ixopo. *Town, south central Natal, South Africa.* The town, southwest of Pietermaritzburg, was founded in 1878 and was originally named *Stuartstown,* for Martinhus *Stuart,* the district magistrate. The local name prevailed, however, and derives from the Zulu word *exobo,* meaning "marsh," itself representing the squelching sound of a foot or hoof withdrawn from mud.

Jacobsdal. *Town, western Orange Free State, South Africa.* The town was laid out on a farm in 1859 and takes its name from the farm owner, Christoffel Johannes *Jacobs.*

Jacqueville. *Coastal town, southern Côte d'Ivoire.* The name is a French rendering of English *Half-Jack,* a nickname of the village that arose near a settlement already named by the English as *Big Jack* (rendered by the French as *Grand Jack*). The story goes that this was itself an English perversion of its native name *Bodo-Ladja* (stressed on the final syllable), in turn deriving from the question asked of its founder, one Boya Bodo: "*Bodo maa eladja*?", literally "Bodo what question?", that is, "What does Bodo mean by that?" Boyo Bodo, the youngest of three sons, had asked his brothers what name the village should have.

Jadotville. See **Likasi.**

Jagersfontein. *Town, southwestern Orange Free State, South Africa.* The name is that of the Griqua farm-owner, Evert *Jagers,* on whose land the mining town was established in 1878. Jagers lived at the spring (Afrikaans *fontein*) above the present site of the mine.

[1]**Jamestown.** *Capital of St. Helena.* The town was founded in 1659, when the British East India Company built a fort and named it for the Duke of York, from 1685 King *James* II of Great Britain (1633–1701).

[2]**Jamestown.** *Town, east central Cape Province, South Africa.* The town is named for *James* Wagenaar, the original owner of the farm on which the town was laid out in 1874. Wagenaar's actual first names were Johannes Jacobus, but his English-speaking friends knew him as "James."

Jan Kemp. *Town, northern Cape Province, South Africa.* The town was founded in 1938 and was originally named *Andalusia,* for the farm where it was laid out. (The name itself is that of a historic kingdom of Spain.) In 1953 it received its present name, given for General Johannes ("*Jan*") C. J. *Kemp*, a former minister of lands.

Jansenville. *Town, southern Cape Province, South Africa.* The town was laid out by members of the Dutch Reformed Church in 1854 and named for the last Dutch governor of the Cape, Lieutenant-General Jan Willem *Janssens* (1762–1838).

Jeffreys Bay. *Town and resort, southern Cape Province, South Africa.* The former fishing village, west of Port Elizabeth, was named for a Mr. *Jeffreys,* a trader or whaler who owned a commercial business in the area. By 1849 the firm of Jeffreys & Glendenning was trading with Port Elizabeth.

Jinja. *Town, southern Uganda.* The town, at the effluence of the Victoria Nile from Lake Victoria, was founded in 1901 as a British administrative center and given the local (Luganda) name of the site here, meaning "stones."

Jirja. See **Girga.**

João Belo. See **Xai-Xai.**

João de Almeida. See **Chibia.**

Johannesburg. *City, Transvaal, South Africa.* South Africa's largest city was founded in 1886 by gold miners working in the Witwatersrand. It is generally said to take its name from two men: *Johann* Rissik (1857–1925), principal clerk of the office of the surveyor-general of the Transvaal republic, and Christiaan *Johannes* Joubert (1834–1911), chief of mining and member of the Volksraad (legislative assembly). However, there were other men named *Johannes* who played their part in the establishment of the town, and the intention may have been to commemorate them also. They include another member of the Volksraad, Field Cornet *Johannes* Petrus Meyer (see **Meyerton**), and the man appointed to lay out the town, *Johannes* Lindeque.

Joubertina. *Town, southern Cape Province, South Africa.* The town was founded in 1907 and named for the Rev. W. A. *Joubert,* Dutch Reformed Church minister in nearby Uniondale from 1878 to 1893.

Juan de Nova. *Island, Mozambique Channel.* The small island, a French possession west of Madagascar, bears the name of the Portuguese navigator *João da Nova,* who discovered it (also Ascension and St. Helena) in the 15th century. Although in the service of Portugal, da Nova was born in Spain, so the Spanish form of the name is faithful to his country of origin.

Jumba la Mtwana. *Lost city, southeastern Kenya.* The historic site, one of Kenya's national monuments, lies by the coast north of Mombasa. It is that of a city abandoned some time in the 14th or 15th century, but rediscovered in the late 1960s and cleared of jungle growth in the early 1970s. Its Swahili name means "house of slaves."

Justinianopolis. See **Sousse.**

Kaapmuiden. *Village, eastern Transvaal, South Africa.* The Afrikaans name of the village east of Nelspruit means "mouth of the *Kaap,*" since it is here that the Kaap River joins the Crocodile.

Kaapsehoop. *Village, eastern Transvaal, South Africa.* The Afrikaans name of the village southwest of Nelspruit means "hope of the Cape," with reference to an irregular rock formation here that (fancifully) suggests the *Cape of Good Hope* (Afrikaans, *Kaap die Goeie Hoop*). The *hoop* of the name both alludes to the Cape and means "hope" in its own right: gold was discovered here in 1882 and a camp set up soon after.

Kaapstad. See **Cape Town.**

Kaarta. *Region, southwestern Mali.* The region, lying mainly in the valley of the Baoulé River, has a name with two possible origins. One explains it as "land of the *Karo,*" referring to a local people. The other sees it as representing Mande *kangara-ta,* based on *kanga,* "foam," "boiling," with reference to the turbulent waters of the Baoulé or some other river here, perhaps even the Niger, to the south.

Kabalega Falls. *Waterfall, Victoria Nile River, Uganda.* The waterfall, upriver from Lake Mobutu, was discovered in 1863 by the British explorer Sir Samuel White Baker and named by him *Murchison Falls,* for the Scottish geologist and explorer Sir Roderick *Murchison* (1792–1871). In 1972 the falls were renamed for the Bunyoro leader Cwa II *Kabalega* (died 1923), national hero of the Bunyoro and of Uganda generally. See also **Kabalega National Park.**

Kabalega National Park. *National park, western Uganda.* The park was founded in 1952 with the aim of conserving the natural environment in the region of the **Kabalega Falls**, which form its central feature. It originally bore the old name of the falls as the *Murchison Falls National Park* but was renamed when the falls were.

Kaberamaido. *Village, central Uganda.* The name is said to mean "place where there are good groundnuts," from the Lango placename prefix *ka-* (corresponding to Bantu *wa-*), Lango *ber,* "good," and Lusoga *amaido,* "groundnuts."

Kabwe. *Town, central Zambia.* The town has a Lala name meaning "small stone," "pebble." The original name of the town was *Broken Hill,* given in 1904 by an Australian mining engineer, Thomas G. Davey, who discovered the site with its precious minerals and who adopted the name of *Broken Hill,* Australia, an already famous mining center. The Zambian mine was opened in 1906, and the town was renamed in 1965, a year after the country gained its independence.

Kabylie. *Mountain range, northern Algeria.* There are two main sections of the rugged mountain range along the coastal region between Algiers and Skikda: the *Grande Kabylie,* to the west, and the *Petite Kabylie,* to the east. Their basic name represents that of the *Kabyle,* the Berber people who are the region's indigenous inhabitants. Their own name represents Arabic *qabā'il,* the plural of *qabīla,* "tribe," implying a tribe of Bedouins, a nomadic people. (The Arabic word is related to the Hebrew word that gave English *cabal* as a group of plotters.)

Ka Dake. *Village, northwestern Swaziland.* The name is a local corruption of that of Grosvenor *Darke,* a trader from Zululand who set up a store and inn here in the 1880s. He also gave his name to **Darketon.**

Kadoma. *Town, central Zimbabwe.* The town was founded in 1906 and takes its name from that of a local Tonka chief. Until 1980 the name was spelled *Gatooma.*

Kaduna. *Town, central Nigeria.* The town was established in 1913 and takes its name from the river on which it lies. The river's own name represents the Hausa word for "crocodiles."

Kaffraria. *Former region, Cape Province, South Africa.* The historic region extended from the (Great) Kei River, in the south of the province, to Natal in the north. It took its name from the *Kaffirs,* a word formerly used for all black peoples of southern Africa other than the Khoikhoin (Hottentots) and San (Bushmen), and itself deriving from Arabic *kāfir,* "infidel." The term is now regarded as derogatory. *British Kaffraria* was the territory in the southwest of the region, between the Kei and Fish (Great Fish) rivers. A map of 1713 shows the southern portion of southeastern Africa as *Caffraria Lusitanis,* "Portuguese Kaffraria," and the northern portion as *Costa de Caffres,* "Kaffir Coast."

Kafr el Sheik. *Town, northern Egypt.* The town has an Arabic name, more accurately spelled *Kafr ash-Shaykh,* that means literally "village of the chief." It contains the former royal palace of King Farouk, who ruled Egypt from 1936 to 1952. The name has now passed to the governorate here.

Kafue. *Town, southeastern Zambia.* The town was established in about 1905 and took the name of the river on which it stands. The river name is an Ila word meaning "hippopotamus river." The name is also that of a dam, gorge, and national park here.

Kahawa. *Village, southern Kenya.* The village, just northeast of the capital, Nairobi, has a name derived from the Swahili word for "coffee."

Kakamas. *Town, western Cape Province, South Africa.* The small town has a name that is said to be a corruption of the Khoikhoin (Hottentot) name *Gamagas,* meaning either "brown," with reference to the red clay that the local women apply to their faces, or "place of drinking." The town arose in the 1880s when the

Dutch Reformed Church founded the settlement to provide work for impoverished families.

Kalaat es Senam. *Village, northwestern Tunisia.* The name means "fort of Senam," from Arabic *ḳaˁla,* "castle," "fort," and *Senam,* the name of a local bandit who made his base on the nearby mountain ("Jugurtha's Table").

Kalahari. *Plateau and desert, Southern Africa.* The arid plateau, mainly in Botswana but extending into parts of Namibia and South Africa, has a name that probably originates from a Tswana word *kgalagadi,* meaning simply "desert," "large arid plateau." According to some authorities, however, the name represents *karri-karri,* literally "sufferings," "torments," with the final *-ri* a Tswana alteration of Khoikhoin (Hottentot) *-di.* If so, the name has the same origin as that of the *Makgadikgadi* or (earlier) *Makarikari* salt pans in northeastern Botswana, which represent the lowest part of the Kalahari. The Boers called the desert by the Dutch name *Bosjeveld,* "wooded plain." The first half of this relates directly to the word that gave English *Bushmen,* the former name for the San people whose main place of habitation is the Kalahari. *Kgalagadi* is now a district of southwestern Botswana. In northwestern Cape Province, South Africa, is the *Kalahari Gemsbok National Park,* named for the animal, a type of antelope, that it was specifically created to protect. Its counterpart, the *Gemsbok National Park,* lies east across the border in Botswana.

Kalk Bay. *Coastal village, southwestern Cape Province, South Africa.* The seaside resort, south of Cape Town, has an Afrikaans name (officially *Kalkbaai*) meaning "chalk bay," referring to lime kilns in use by the bay here in the 17th century. The nearby hill *Kalkbaaiberg* is also named for the bay.

Kalkfeld. *Village, north central Namibia.* The name is German for "chalk field," referring to the white limestone found locally. The original Herero name of the village was *Okovakuatjivi,* meaning literally "place where people are," in other words "village." The German name was adopted in 1909. Cf. **Kalkrand.**

Kalkrand. *Village, central Namibia.* The village has a German name meaning "chalk ridge," referring to its location near the escarpment known as *Die Kalk,* "the limestone." Cf. **Kalkfeld.**

Kamanjab. *Village, northwestern Namibia.* The name is of Herero origin and probably means "big rocks," with reference to the large granite boulders here.

Kamerun. See **Cameroon.**

Kamieskroon. *Village, western Cape Province, South Africa.* The village was laid out on a farm in 1864 and was originally called *Bowesville* (later *Bowesdorp*), for the district surgeon, Dr. Henry *Bowe.* The first part of the present name is probably of Khoikhoin (Hottentot) origin, representing either *kam,* "two," or *xami,* "lion." If the former, the reference would be to the double-headed mountain here. The second part is Dutch *kroon,* "crown," denoting a huge rock atop a nearby peak.

Kammanassieberge. *Mountain range, southern Cape Province, South Africa.* The mountains, east of the Little Karoo, take their name from the river here, itself of Khoikhoin (Hottentot) origin and probably meaning "washing water."

Kampala. *Capital of Uganda.* The city arose as a fort built in 1890 by the British colonial administrator Frederick Lugard on a hill bearing a local (Luganda) name. This is believed to represent *akasozi ka mpala,* "hill of the impala," referring to the antelope that some local kabaka (king) grazed in herds on its slopes.

KaNgwane. *Bantustan, Southern Africa.* The Bantu homeland, on the border between Transvaal, South Africa, and Swaziland, was formed in 1981 and has a Swazi name meaning "land of the Ngwane," from *ka-*, placename prefix, and *Ngwane,* the people from whom the Swazis came. See also **Swaziland.**

Kano. *City and state, northern Nigeria.* The state and former kingdom is named for the city, itself founded some time before the 9th century and said to be named for *Kano,* a blacksmith of the Gaya tribe who came here in search of iron.

Kanye. *Town, southeastern Botswana.* The town, the capital of the Ngwaketse people, has a Tswana name said to mean "hill of the chief." It was founded in the mid-18th century, when the chief in question was Makaba I.

Kaoko Otavi. *Village, northwestern Namibia.* The village lies in the *Kaoko* homeland, and has a name representing Herero *okaoko,* "the left arm," and *otavi,* "flowing spring." The first word of the name relates to the **Kaokoveld**, which lies to the west of the village.

Kaokoveld. *Mountain range, northwestern Namibia.* The range, parallel to the coast and just east of the Namib Desert, has a name representing Herero *okaoko,* "the left arm." (Cf. **Kunene.**) The reference is to the location of the range, which runs south from the left bank of the Kunene River on the border with Angola. The second part of the name is Afrikaans *veld,* the term for an open or partly forested plain. See also **Kaoko Otavi.**

Kaoma. *Town, west central Zambia.* The name is a Lala one meaning "small drum," with some local reference, perhaps alluding to some drum-shaped feature here. To about 1970 the town's earlier name was *Mankoya,* deriving from the *Nkoya* tribe who live here.

Karakoro. *Watercourse, southern Mauritania.* The watercourse, a tributary of the Senegal, forms part of the border with Mali. Its Sarakole name means "big valley," from *kare,* "valley," and *khoro,* "big."

Karasburg. *Town, southern Namibia.* The original name of the town was *Kalkfontein-Suid,* "southern limestone spring." This was confused with the village of *Kalkfontein* to the north, however, just over the border in Botswana, so was changed in 1939 to its present form. The first part of the name derives from that of the *Karas* Mountains north of the town, themselves distinguished as the *Great Karas Berg* and *Little Karas Berg.* Their name represents Khoikhoin (Hottentot) *!a-as,* meaning "sharp stone," "rock." (The unusual character denotes a click.) The former Nama name for the location was *Nomsoros,* meaning "chalky place with springs," so relating to the original Afrikaans name.

Karas Mountains. See **Karasburg.**

Kareedouw. *Town, southern Cape Province, South Africa.* The town was established in 1905 and has a name of Khoikhoin (Hottentot) origin meaning either "white kloof," referring to the quartzite rock in the kloof (mountain pass) here or deriving from the word *!karegadaob,* meaning "path rich in karree trees" *(Rhus viminalis).* (The initial character of the name represents a click.)

Kariba Dam. *Dam, Zambezi River, Southern Africa.* The well-known dam was built across the

Zambezi in 1958 in order to provide hydroelectric power. Its name properly refers to the gorge in which it is located, between southeastern Zambia and northern Zimbabwe. It is a Tonka word, meaning "little trap," alluding to the gorge seen as a small stone trap set for birds, mice, and other small animals. Lake *Kariba* here was created by the construction of the dam, and the name is also that of a village and district.

Karibib. *Town, west central Namibia.* The name comes from the Nama word *ga-ei-beb,* meaning "place with a plain," alluding to the terrain here. The town was established soon after 1864, when a trader named Otto Hälbich arrived in Walvis Bay.

Kariega. *River, southern Cape Province, South Africa.* The river, a tributary of the Sundays, has a name of Khoikhoin (Hottentot) origin, representing *!aris-a,* "steenbok" (a small antelope), with the suffix either indicating abundance or else representing *!ab,* "river." (The unusual characters here represent clicks.)

Karnak. *Ancient village, southern Egypt.* The historic settlement today forms the northern part of the modern town of **Luxor**, the southern part of which stands on the ancient city of Thebes. The Arabic name of the village is *al-karnak,* apparently based on an Indoeuropean root word *kar* meaning "stone," "rock," to which modern Celtic *carn* and *cairn* are probably related. The reference could well be to the stones of the great (now ruined) temple of Amon here, built in prehistoric times. If this etymology is correct, the name of Karnak could be related to that of the Breton village of *Carnac,* northwestern France, famous for its ancient alignments of stone menhirs.

Karoi. *Village, northern Zimbabwe.* The name is that of the river here. It is traditionally derived from *muroyi,* "witch," referring to the drowning of a witch in it at some time in the past.

Karonga. *Town, northern Malawi.* The town, south of the border with Tanzania, was established in the 1880s as an outpost and mission station on the northwestern shore of Lake Malawi. Its Nyanja name is the title of a prince of chief, and may relate to a particular person who was involved with the mission station or who helped abolish the slave trade here.

Karoo. *Plateau, South Africa.* The name is used of more than one plateau, but is particularly associated with the Great Karoo and Little Karoo in southern Cape Province. The High Veldt, north of the Great Karoo, is also sometimes called the Northern Karoo. The name represents Khoikhoin (Hottentot) *harrô,* "dry," "arid." The name is also spelled *Karroo.*

Karroo. See **Karoo.**

Kasai. *River, Southern Africa.* The river, a main tributary of the Congo, rises in central Angola, then flows east and north to form the border between Angola and Zaïre before continuing north to empty into the Congo on the border with Congo. Its name is from the *Kasai* people who inhabit the region north of it in Zaïre. Two administrative regions are named for the tribe in the latter country: *Kasai Occidental* and *Kasai Oriental.*

Kasane. *Town, northern Botswana.* The town, at the junction of the borders of Botswana, Zambia, Zimbabwe, and Namibia (Caprivi Strip), has a name that is a local word for the tree *Syzygium guineense.*

Kasba Tadla. *Town, north central Morocco.* The town, an important economic center of the Middle Atlas region, has a name that is part Arabic, part Berber. The first word is Arabic dialect *kasba,* "citadel." The second represents a Berber word meaning "sheaf of cereals."

Kasserine. *Town, north central Tunisia.* The town, near the site of the Roman settlement of Cillium, has a name that represents Arabic *al-ḳaṣrayn,* "the two palaces." The reference is to two Roman mausoleums here.

Kasungu. *Town, central Malawi.* The town has a Chichewa name meaning either "hero" or "mountain." The name is also that of a national park here.

Kasupi. *Village, southern Malawi.* The name is a Chichewa one, meaning "fountain," "spring." The village arose round such a watersource.

Katanga. See **Shaba.**

Katsina. *Town, northern Nigeria.* The town, capital of the historic kingdom of the same name, was founded about 1100. It is itself said to be named for *Katsina,* wife of a local king and a princess of Daura, the legendary home of the Hausa people.

Katunga. See **Oyo.**

Kaura Namoda. *Town, northern Nigeria.* The town takes its name from a Fulani (Peul) warrior, *Kaura Namoda,* who was installed as king of the local state of Zamfara in the early 19th century. *Kaura* is a title equivalent to "warlord."

Kavango. *Region, northeastern Namibia.* The region is a homeland for various tribes, and takes its name from a chief of one of them, *Kavango,* said to have been the first to settle here.

Kavimba. *Village, northern Botswana.* The village, near the border with Namibia, has a name that is a Subia one for a type of tropical tree found here, *Combreta imberbe.*

Kayes. *Town, southwestern Mali.* The town, near the border with Senegal, has a Wolof name meaning "cailcedra," the African mahogany *(Khaya senegalensis).* The wood of the tall tree is suitable for joinery and its bark for preparing a bitter tonic medicine.

Kazaure. *Town, northern Nigeria.* The town takes its name from the former emirate here, itself founded in 1807 and named for a local hunter. The town was the capital of the emirate from 1824 until 1906, when it was captured by the British and the emirate itself became part of the Northern Nigeria Protectorate.

Kazungula. *Village, southern Zambia.* The name refers to a large *masungula* tree *(Kigelia africana)* here by the Zambezi River (marking the border with Botswana and Zimbabwe).

Kearsney. *Village, eastern Natal, South Africa.* The village arose round the house of Sir James Liege Hulett (1838–1928), English-born South African parliamentarian and tea grower, who built it in the 1880s and named it for his birthplace near Dover, Kent, England.

Keetmanshoop. *Town, southern Namibia.* The original Afrikaans name of the settlement here in 1810 was *Swartmodder,* "black mud," a translation of the Khoikhoin (Hottentot) name *NuGoeis.* In 1866 the Rhenish Missionary Society founded a station for the Nama people and named it for their chairman, Johann *Keetman,* who financed the foundation. The last part of the name is Afrikaans *hoop,* "hope," a word found in the names of various places originating as mission stations (or gold mines).

Keffi. *Town, central Nigeria.* The town, capital of a kingdom (later, state) of the same name in existence from about 1750 to 1902, is said to take its name from a local word meaning "stockade."

Kei. *River, eastern Cape Province, South Africa.* The river, also known as the *Great Kei,* is formed near Queenstown by the junction of the White Kei *(Wit-Kei)* and Black Kei *(Swart-Kei)* and flows generally southeast along the border with **Transkei** (named for it) to enter the Indian Ocean. Its basic name is a Khoikhoin (Hottentot) word meaning "sandy," "white." See also **Ciskei.**

Keimoes. *Town, west central Cape Province, South Africa.* The town, on the Orange River, has a Khoikhoin (Hottentot) name representing *gei,* "great," and *müs,* "fountain." The name is thus the equivalent of Afrikaans *Grootfontein.*

Keishammahoek. *Town, Ciskei, South Africa.* The first part of the name is a Khoikhoin (Hottentot) word said to mean "puff adder," with reference to the abundance of these snakes by the *Keiskamma* River, also named for them. The last part of the name is Afrikaans *hoek,* "corner," referring to the location where the settlement arose in 1853 from a frontier post.

Kellé. *Village, western Senegal.* The village, northeast of Dakar, the capital, derives its name from *kel,* the Wolof word for a shrub with birchlike leaves bearing berries and nuts. Its bark yields a tough fiber used for cordmaking.

Kempton Park. *Town, southern Transvaal, South Africa.* The town, now a northeastern district of Johannesburg, was established in 1903 by a Bavarian farmer who named the settlement *Kempten* from his native town in Germany. The name was later anglicized to its present form, perhaps under the influence of *Kempton Park,* the well-known racecourse near London, England.

Kenhardt. *Town, west central Cape Province, South Africa.* The town was founded in 1876 on the site of a border police settlement established eight years previously. The precise origin of the name is uncertain although it may represent the surname of a trader here.

Kenitra. *City and port, northwestern Morocco.* The town was founded in 1913 by the French and was originally named *Port-Lyautey,* for Marshal of France Louis Hubert *Lyautey* (1854–1934), who ordered it to be built. There was already a fort here with the local name of *Kenitra,* however, and this was reverted to soon after 1956 when Morocco gained independence. It represents a diminutive form of Arabic *al-ḳanṭara,* "the bridge."

Kenya. *Republic, East Africa.* The country takes its name from Mount *Kenya,* the lofty extinct volcano in its center. Its own name probably arose as a shortening of its Kikuyu name, *Kirinyaga,* representing *kere nyaga,* "white mountain," referring to its permanent snows and glaciers. The former European pronunciation of the country's name with a long *e* (as "Keenya") thus reflects the original name.

Kerewan. *Village, western Gambia.* The village, on the northern bank of the Gambia River, has a name transferred from the Tunisian city of *Kairouan.* The transfer is the result of local Islamic influence: Kerouan is a holy city of the Muslims. The same city gave the name of *Hérouané,* a village in southern Guinea.

Kerkennah Islands. *Island group, off east coast of Tunisia.* The islands, opposite Sfax, derived the present form of their name from their Roman name of *Cercina.* This is traditionally linked with *Circe,* the goddess of classical legend who turned Odysseus' men into swine on the fabulous island of Aeaea. But Aeaea is more usually identified (albeit in popular etymology) with the promontory of *Circeii* in Italy, south of Rome, not the African islands.

Kérouané. See **Kerewan.**

Kestell. *Town, northeastern Orange Free State, South Africa.* The town was founded in 1905 and named for the Rev. John Daniel *Kestell* (1854–1941), a leader of the Dutch Reformed Church in the Orange Free State.

Kgalagadi. See **Kalahari.**

Kgatleng. *District, southeastern Botswana.* The name is a tribal one, that of the *Kgatla* people.

Khahlamba. *Mountain range, eastern Natal, South Africa.* The range, a southern spur of the Drakensberg, runs along the western border of Swaziland. Its name is of Zulu origin and means "barrier."

Kharaes. See **Upington.**

Kharga. See **El-Kharga.**

Khartoum. *Capital of Sudan.* The name represents Arabic *al-khurṭūm,* an abbreviated form of *ra's al-khurṭūm,* "elephant's trunk," from *ra's,* "head," "end," *al,* "the" and *khurṭūm,* "elephant's trunk." The name is descriptive of the narrow strip of land between the White Nile and Blue Nile on which the town was founded in 1825.

Khomas Highland. *Mountains, west central Namibia.* The name is that of the plateau west of the capital, Windhoek. The first word of the name is of Khoikhoin (Hottentot) origin and means simply "mountain," "hilly terrain." The second word is alternately found as German *Hochland.*

Khorixas. *Town, northwestern Namibia.* The name of the town is of Khoikhoin (Hottentot) origin and denotes a type of tree with edible berries, perhaps *Salvadore persica.* When the town was laid out in 1954 it was originally named *Welwitschia,* for the desert plant *Welwitschia bainesii,* which grew in profusion here.

Kibo. See **Kilimanjaro.**

Kiboko. *Village, southern Kenya.* The village has a Swahili name meaning "whip," perhaps referring to some battle or incident here, or some punishment administered.

Kigali. *Capital of Rwanda.* The city takes its name from Mount *Kigali,* near which it arose in the closing years of the 19th century in the German East Africa Protectorate. The name represents the Bantu prefix *ki-* and Rwanda *gali,* "broad," "wide," a reference to the mountain's extensive area.

Kilimanjaro. *Volcano, northeastern Tanzania.* The volcanic massif has a Swahili name derived from the two words *kilima,* "mountain," and *njaro,* probably "god of cold" but perhaps meaning simply "white," "sparkling." The massif is famous for the glaciers on its heights. The name is not used by local pepole, who instead talk of the massif's two main peaks: *Kibo,* the highest point in Africa, and *Mawenzi,* the next highest. *Kibo* means "speckled," referring to the dark color of the mountain's rocks and the whiteness of its snow. *Mawenzi* means "toothed," "indented," with reference to the peak's jagged contour. See also **Quelimane.**

Kilosa. *Town, east central Tanzania.* The town has a name representing the local word *kirosa,* meaning "crossing place," referring to the bridge over the river here. There are other places of the same name.

Kimberley. *City, northern Cape Province, South Africa.* The city arose in the 1870s from a diamond-mining camp and was named for the British colonial secretary, John Wodehouse, 1st Earl of *Kimberley* (1826–1902), who had effected the annexation of the diamond fields on behalf of Britain. The earl's own title comes from the village of *Kimberley,* Norfolk. The personal name Kimberley or Kimberly (now often abbreviated to Kim) arose from the association with the South African town, which was in the news in 1900 when under siege during the second Boer War. (It was originally a boys' name, but later passed to the girls.)

Kimbiji. *Coastal village, northeastern Tanzania.* The village, southeast of Dar es Salaam, has a name representing the local word *jikimbia,* "lost." The village is in a remote locality and not readily visible.

King William's Town. *Town, southeastern Cape Province, South Africa.* The town was laid out in 1835 on the site of an earlier mission station and was named for the reigning British monarch, *King William* IV of England (1765–1837). The spellings *King Williams Town* and *Kingwilliamstown* are also found, while the town is locally known simply as *King.*

Kinross. *Town, southern Transvaal, South Africa.* The town takes its name from *Kinross,* Scotland, the home of the engineers who constructed the railroad from Springs to Breyten which runs through the town, itself founded in 1910.

Kinshasa. *Capital of Zaïre.* The name is that of one of the original settlements from which the present city arose in 1881, when the British explorer Sir Henry Morton Stanley built a fort here. Until 1965, however, it was known as *Léopoldville,* and was capital of the Belgian Congo (now Zaïre) from 1923 to that year. Stanley gave the name in honor of his patron, the Belgian king *Léopold* II (1835–1909). The meaning of the present Bantu name is uncertain.

Kirkwood. *Town, southern Cape Province, South Africa.* The town was originally known as *Bayville* in 1885, presumably for its relative proximity to either St. Francis Bay or Algoa Bay. The town then appears to have fallen into disuse, and was reestablished in 1913 under its present name. This was given in honor of James Somers *Kirkwood,* a local pioneer of the irrigation development here.

Kisangani. *City, northeastern Zaïre.* The city, on the Congo River, was founded in 1883 by Europeans and was at first known as *Falls Station,* for the nearby Stanley Falls (now usually known as the Boyoma Falls), before being named *Stanleyville,* for the British explorer Sir Henry Morton *Stanley* (1841–1904), who opened up the Congo region in the early 1880s. In 1966 the city took its present (but not new) Swahili name, meaning "in the sand," with reference to the fine, sandy soil here. See also **Pool.**

Kisangire. *Village, eastern Tanzania.* The village, southwest of Dar es Salaam, has a local (Kisaramo) name meaning "copal," referring to the fossil resin found locally.

Kissidougou. *Town, southwestern Guinea.* The name means "town of the *Kissi,*" from a tribal name that itself represents Mande *kisi,* "help," "aid."

Klaarstroom. *Village, southern Cape Province, South Africa.* The

Afrikaans name means "clear stream," referring to the many streams that flow through the mountainous area here, in the Groot-Swartberge. The original name of the village was *Pietersburg,* presumably for the Voortrekker leader, *Piet* Retief (see **Piet Retief**).

Klawer. *Village, western Cape Province, South Africa.* The village has an Afrikaans name meaning "clover," referring to the wild variety that grows in the valley here.

Kleinmond. *Coastal village, southwestern Cape Province, South Africa.* The Afrikaans name means "small mouth," referring to the mouth of the Bot River where the seaside resort is located. The original full name of the place was *Kleinmondstrand,* "small mouth beach." This was shortened as now in 1960.

Klerksdorp. *Town, southern Transvaal, South Africa.* The town was established in 1837 and was at first known simply by the Afrikaans name of *Oude Dorp,* "old town." Subsequently, Jacob de *Clercq* became the first landdrost (chief district magistrate) and the place was named for him. The name appears to have been first applied in 1853.

Klipplaat. *Town, southern Cape Province, South Africa.* The Afrikaans name means literally "rocky flats," and refers to the large stone slabs on the surface of the ground here.

Klokolani. See **Clocolan.**

Kloof. *Town, southeastern Natal, South Africa.* The town, west of Durban, was originally known as *Kranskloof,* literally "precipice gorge," a descriptive Afrikaans name for its location by a deep gorge with high precipice on both sides. The name was later shortened.

Knysna. *Town, southern Cape Province, South Africa.* The town was founded in 1862 as a union of two existing settlements. The name is that of the river here, and itself probably represents Khoikhoin (Hottentot) *!gao-//na,* meaning "straight down," and so referring to the steep *kranses* (precipices) that fall down to the sea. Other authorities derive the name from a local word meaning "fern leaf," or from a Xhosa expression meaning "large sheet of water," with reference to the lagoon here. (The unusual characters in the Khoikhoin name represent clicks.)

Koës. *Village, southeastern Namibia.* The village derives its name from the Nama word *khois,* meaning "women's place," perhaps because men found no work here.

Koffiefontein. *Town, western Orange Free State, South Africa.* The Afrikaans name is that of the farm where diamonds were found in 1870 and where the town arose as a result. It means "coffee spring," although the sense of this is uncertain. Perhaps coffee beans were found in or near the spring, or possibly coffee-trading was carried on by it.

Kokong. *Village, southern Botswana.* The local name is said to mean "place where the sick were nursed," with reference to some particular incident such as an epidemic or battle.

Kokstad. *Town, northeastern Cape Province, South Africa.* The town was founded in 1871 and named for the Griqua chief Adam *Kok* III (1811–1875) who trekked here in 1862. The town was the capital of **Griqualand East** until 1874, when it was annexed to the Cape.

Kola. *Village, eastern Tanzania.* The village, west of Dar es Salaam, has a local name meaning "snail." The reference is to the many different kinds of the mollusc found locally.

Kolmanskop. *Village, southwestern Namibia.* The village, east of

Lüderitz, is a "ghost town," resulting from the thriving settlement that arose in 1908 after the discovery of diamonds here. The Afrikaans name means "Kolman's hill," apparently for a person (presumably a prospector) surnamed *Kolman* or *Coleman*.

Komatipoort. *Town, eastern Transvaal, South Africa.* The town is close to the *poort* (Afrikaans, "gorge") where the *Komati* River flows through the Lebombo Mountains. The river itself has a local name meaning "cow," presumably referring to hippopotami in its waters.

Kom el-Ahmar. *Village, east central Egypt.* The village, on the west bank of the Nile, is famous for the remains and cemeteries of the ancient town of *Hierakonpolis*. The Greek name means "falcon city," referring to the bird that was the sacred animal of the town's protective god, Horus. This arose on the even older Egyptian settlement of *Nekhen*. The modern Arabic name of the site means "the red hill," from *kōm*, "mound," *al*, "the," and *aḥmar*, "red."

Komga. *Town, southeastern Cape Province, South Africa.* The original name of the town, laid out in 1877, was *Komgha*, from a Khoikhoin (Hottentot) word probably not meaning "brown," as often stated, but more likely "full of clay," with reference to the soil here.

Kom Ombo. *Town, southeastern Egypt.* The town has an Arabic name meaning "mound of Ombos," preserving the name of the ancient city of *Ombos* on this site, a strategic location commanding both the Nile and the routes from Nubia to the Nile Valley.

Kompasberg. See **Compassberg.**

Konkib. *River, Namibia.* The seasonal watercourse, a tributary of the Great Fish River in the south of the country, has a name that is a form of its Khoikhoin (Hottentot) name, *Goageb*, meaning "twin river." Cf. **Goageb.**

Kontagora. *Town, western Nigeria.* The town, capital of the historic emirate of the same name, was founded in 1864 and has a name said to represent the local words *kwanta gora*, "lay down your gourds."

Koonap. *Village, southeastern Cape Province, South Africa.* The village takes its name from the local river. Its own name probably represents Khoikhoin (Hottentot) *!onab*, "crooked," referring to its winding course. (The *!* denotes a click, to which the initial *K-* corresponds.)

Koppies. *Town, northern Orange Free State, South Africa.* The town takes its Afrikaans name from that of the farm on which it was founded in 1910. This was *Honingkopjes*, "honey hills."

Kordofan. *Region, central Sudan.* The name, of uncertain meaning, is that of a hill in the region.

Korhogo. *Town, north central Côte d'Ivoire.* The town is said to have been founded by a 14th century patriarch, Nangui or Nengué. The present town has a name that appears to refer to this, since it derives from a local word meaning "heritage."

Koringberg. *Village, southwestern Cape Province, South Africa.* The Afrikaans name means "wheat mountain," referring to the location of the village in a wheat-growing area.

Kosi Lake. *Lake, northern Natal, South Africa.* The lake takes its name from that of the short river that flows from it into the Indian Ocean at *Kosi Bay*. It represents Zulu *ukozi*, a word for the tawny eagle *(Aquila rapax)*. Portuguese colonists knew the river as *Rio dos Medões de Ouro,* "river of golden dunes."

Kosmos. *Village, southern Transvaal, South Africa.* The pleasure resort, west of the capital, Pretoria, has a name of Greek origin meaning "universe." It is said to have been suggested by a fine view of the night sky at the time the resort was established.

Kosséoua. *Village, northern Cameroon.* The name is of Peul (Fulani) origin and means "big hill."

Koster. *Town, southern Transvaal, South Africa.* The town, west of the capital, Pretoria, was founded on a farm in 1913 and takes its name from that of the farmowner, Bastiaan Hendricus *Koster.*

Koulikoro. *Town, southwestern Mali.* The town, on the Niger River northeast of Bamako, the capital, has a Mande name meaning "near the rock," from *kulu,* "rock," and *koro,* "near."

Kouroussa. *Town, east central Guinea.* The town, on the Niger River, has a Mande name meaning "death of the canoes," from *kuru,* "canoe," and *sa,* "funeral," "mourning." The town lies at the limit of navigation on the river.

Koutiala. *Town, southwestern Mali.* The town, southeast of Ségou, has a name representing Mande *ku-t'ya-la,* "yams are abundant," based on *ku,* "yam."

Kraai. *River, South Africa.* The river, a tributary of the Orange in northeastern Cape Province, appears to have a name meaning "crow" (Afrikaans, *kraai*). Records show, however, that it is actually a corruption of the name of General Henry George *Grey,* troop commander at the time the name was given in 1809.

Kraaifontein. *Town, southwestern Cape Province, South Africa.* The town, northeast of Cape Town, has an Afrikaans name meaning "crow spring," presumably with reference to the presence of these birds here.

Kranskop. *Town, central Natal, South Africa.* The town was laid out in 1894 and originally named *Hopetown.* This was confused with **Hopetown** in Cape Province, however, so the settlement was given its present Afrikaans name, meaning "cliff top," and referring to a nearby peak. (The name is found elsewhere for individual mountains, such as that in eastern Orange Free State.) The Zulu name for the town is *Ntunjambili,* meaning "the two holes," and referring to the two gaps near the summit of the peak.

Kribi. *Town and port, southwestern Cameroon.* The name is said to derive from the local word *kiridi,* meaning approximately "short people." As such, it is a reminder that the southern forests of Cameroon are pygmy country.

Krokodil River. See **Limpopo.**

Kromdraii. *Village, south central Transvaal, South Africa.* The village, east of the capital, Pretoria, has an Afrikaans name meaning "crooked bend," referring to the topography of the location.

Kroonstad. *Town, northern Orange Free State, South Africa.* The town takes its name from the *Kroonspruit,* the stream by which it was laid out in 1854. The stream's name literally means "crown stream," although the sense of "crown" here is uncertain. According to local legend, *Kroon* was the name of a horse that broke its leg here when trying to cross.

Kroufa. *Village, western Mauritania.* The village, south of Nouakchott, the capital, has a Zenaga name meaning "ewe lamb" or "little cloud." The derivation appears to lie in a nickname.

Kruger National Park. *National park, eastern Transvaal, South Africa.* The wildlife sanctuary, the world's largest game reserve, on the frontier with Mozambique, was opened in 1898 as the *Sabi Game Reserve,* taking its name from the river that now flows through its southern part. In its present form, the Kruger National Park came into existence in 1926, when it was named for Stephanus Johannes Paulus *Kruger* (1825–1904), president of the Transvaal from 1883 to 1900. See also **Krugersdorp.**

Krugersdorp. *City, southern Transvaal, South Africa.* The city, west of Johannesburg, was laid out in 1887 as a public gold-digging settlement and was named in honor of Stephanus Johannes Paulus *Kruger* (1825–1904), president of the Transvaal from 1883 to 1900. See also **Kruger National Park.**

Ksar el Kebir. See **Alcazarquivir.**

Ksar es Souk. See **Er Rashidia.**

Ksour, Monts des. *Mountain ranges, North Africa.* There are two noted ranges of the name, one in northwestern Algeria, the other in eastern Tunisia. The name represents the plural of Arabic *ksār,* a term for a fortified enclosure of some kind. In Tunisia the *ksour* are fortified communal granaries, enclosing mountain villages.

Kuilsrivier. *Town, southwestern Cape Province, South Africa.* The town, east of Cape Town, was originally named *De Cuylen,* from Dutch *de kuylen,* "the pools," referring to the intermittent river here, which dries up in summer leaving only pools. This then evolved into the present name, which is also that of the river itself.

Kuiseb. *River, Namibia.* The seasonal river, flowing generally west to lose itself in the sand near Walvis Bay, has a Khoikhoin (Hottentot) name perhaps meaning "root river," referring to the edible roots that grow along its course.

Kuito. *Town, central Angola.* The name is a local one meaning "place of meat," from *ko,* "place," and *osito,* "meat." The reference is to the large number of animals here. The name is thus the same as that of the *Cuito* River, in the south of the country. The town was formerly known by the Portuguese colonial name of *Silva Porto,* for the Portuguese explorer António Francisco Ferreira da *Silva Porto,* who died here in 1890. The name changed to its present form after Angola gained independence in 1975. An alternate name for the town still sometimes encountered, and today that of the province of which it is the capital, is **Bié.**

Kukawa. *Town, northeastern Nigeria.* The town, not far from the western shore of Lake Chad, takes its name from the *kuka,* a local word for the baobab tree *(Adansonia digitata).* Kukawa was the capital of the Bornu Empire from 1814 to 1907.

Kule. *Village, western Botswana.* The village, close to the border with Namibia, has a name of Khoikhoin (Hottentot) origin denoting a type of root plant like a potato, commonly found here.

Kumasi. *City, southern Ghana.* The city was founded in the late 17th century by Osei Tutu, the first great Ashanti chief, on the advice of the powerful fetish priest, Okomfo Ankoye. Okomfo planted the seeds of two *kum* trees in different places, and one sprouted showing where the Ashanti capital was to be. Hence the name, representing *kum asi,* "under the *kum.*"

Kunene. *River, southwestern Africa.* The river rises in southwestern

Angola and flows westward along the border between Angola and Namibia to the Atlantic. Its local name represents *okunene,* meaning "on the right side," with reference to Angola, which lies on its right bank as it flows to the sea. In Angola itself, the name is often spelled *Cunene.* Cf. **Kaokoveld.**

Kuruman. *Town, northern Cape Province, South Africa.* The town was laid out on the river of the same name in 1887. The river's own local name may mean either "calabash" or "tortoise," depending on its precise language of origin. If it is a Khoikhoin (Hottentot) name, it could mean "place where wild tobacco stands."

KwaMbonambi. *Village, northern Natal, South Africa.* The name means "home of the *Mbonambi* people," their own name meaning "place of ill omen."

KwaNdebele. *Bantustan, central Transvaal, South Africa.* The Bantu homeland, which gained self-governing status in 1981, has a name meaning "home of the *Ndebele,*" that is, of the people formerly known as the *Matabele.* (See **Matabeleland.**)

Kwango. See **Cuango.**

Kwanza. See **Cuanza.**

KwaZulu. *Bantustan, eastern Natal, South Africa.* The name is that of the Bantu homeland established here in 1972 in place of the former *Zululand.* The new name has basically the same meaning as the old, "place of the Zulus," with *kwa-* the Zulu locative formative denoting "in" or "at." The original territory here was annexed by the British in 1887 and in 1897 became part of Natal. The Zulu people's own name derives from that of their ancestor who founded the royal line in the 16th century, and itself means "sky."

Kwekwe. *Town, central Zimbabwe.* The name of the town is that of the river on which it lies, itself almost certainly imitative of the sound of frogs in its waters at night. The town was founded in 1900, and until 1980 its name was spelled *Que Que.*

Kweneng. *District, south central Botswana.* The name is that of the *Kwena* people who inhabit the region.

Kyle, Lake. *Lake, southwestern Zimbabwe.* The lake was formed in 1961, when the *Kyle Dam* was built here near the Zimbabwe National Monument. It took the name of the farm that was submerged when the lake was created. It is a Scottish name, meaning appropriately "channel of water."

Laayoune. See **El Aaiún.**

Labdah. *Ruined site, northwestern Libya.* The ruins on the coastal site are those of the Roman city of *Leptis Magna,* one of the three cities of Tripolis (see **Tripoli**). The name is believed to be of Punic origin and to mean "anchorage," "harbor." It was *Magna* ("Great") by comparison with *Leptis Minor,* modern *Lamta,* southeast of Sousse, Tunisia.

Labé. *Town, west central Guinea.* The town was founded in the 1720s by the Dialonke people and named for their chief, Mange *Labé.*

Lacerdónia. *Village, eastern Mozambique.* The village, on the Zambezi River downstream from Dona Ana, was established in 1893 and named in honor of the Portuguese astronomer and mathematician Dr. Francisco de *Lacerda* e Almeida (1750–1798), who in 1797 attempted to cross Africa from Mozambique to Angola, but only got as far as Lake Mweru (modern Zaïre/Zambia), where he died of fever.

Ladismith. *Town, southwestern Cape Province, South Africa.* The town was established in 1852 and named for *Lady* Juana *Smith,* Spanish wife of Sir Harry Smith, governor of the Cape from 1847 to 1852. At first the name was spelled simply *Lady Smith.* This was confused with **Ladysmith,** Natal, however, so a proposal was made to change the name to *Juanasmith.* This failed, so the name was finally altered to its present form. See also **Harrismith.**

Ladybrand. *Town, eastern Orange Free State, South Africa.* The town was laid out by the Boers in 1867 and named in honor of *Lady* Catharina Frederica *Brand,* wife of Sir Christoffel Brand (1797–1875), speaker of the Cape legislative assembly and father of Sir Johannes Hendricus Brand (1823–1888), president of the Orange Free State.

Lady Frere. *Town, Transkei, South Africa.* The town was established in 1879 and named for *Lady* Catherine *Frere,* wife of Sir Henry Bartle Edward *Frere* (1815–1884), governor of the Cape from 1877 to 1880.

Lady Grey. *Town, eastern Cape Province, South Africa.* The town, at the foot of the Witberge, was founded in 1858 and named for *Lady* Harriet *Grey,* wife of Sir George Grey (1812–1898), governor of the Cape from 1854 to 1859 and again from 1860 to 1861. See also **Greyton, Greytown.**

Ladysmith. *Town, western Natal, South Africa.* The town was established in 1847, when it was originally known as *Windsor,* for a local trader, George *Windsor.* It was later renamed for *Lady* Juana *Smith,* the (Spanish) wife of Sir Harry Smith (1787–1860), governor of the Cape from 1847 to 1852.

Lafia. *Town, central Nigeria.* The town capital (from 1804 to 1900) of the former emirate of the same name, has a local name said to mean "comfortably settled."

Lafiagi. *Town, west central Nigeria.* The town was founded in 1810 by a Fulani (Peul) chief and from then to 1900 was the capital of the former emirate of the same name. Its own name represents a Nupe word meaning "small hill."

Laghouat. *Town, northern Algeria.* The name represents Arabic *al-wāḥāt,* "the oases." The town is located in an oasis on the Mzi River in what was formerly the Oasis province (and is now, though smaller, that of Laghouat). It has many fertile gardens and groves of date palms, figs, oranges, and pomegranates.

Lagos. *City and port, southwestern Nigeria.* The former Nigerian capital (to 1992, when it was transferred to **Abuja**) takes its name from a shortening of *Rio de Lagos,* "river of lakes," the name given by Portuguese explorers in the 15th century to this part of the coast, which has numerous lagoons and lakes. The city itself is at the western end of one such large lake. At the same time the name also relates to *Lagos,* the town and port in southern Portugal. The original settlement on the site of present Lagos was known to the Bini people as *Eko,* said to mean "war camp." The city in turn gave its name to the present state here.

La Goulette. See **Halq el Oued.**

Laingsburg. *Town, southwestern Cape Province, South Africa.* The town was founded in 1881 and named for the Hon. John *Laing,* commissioner of crown lands.

Lake Chrissie. See Lake **Chrissie.**

La Laguna. *Town, northern Tenerife, Canary Islands.* The former capital of Tenerife was founded in the late 15th century and named for the now extinct lagoon here.

Lalibela. *Town, northern Ethiopia.* The town arose in the 12th and 13th centuries when the Zagwe dynasty took possession of Ethiopia. It was named for the emperor who founded it (and hewed churches out of the solid rock here), Gebra Maskal *Lalibela,* in power from 1172 to 1212.

Lamberts Bay. *Coastal village, southwestern Cape Province, South Africa.* The village, established in 1913, takes its name from the inlet here, itself named for Rear-Admiral Sir Robert *Lambert,* commander of the naval station at the Cape from 1820 to 1821.

Lamta. See **Labdah.**

Langebaan. *Coastal village, southwestern Cape Province, South Africa.* The village, founded in about 1870, has a Dutch name meaning "long course," referring to the long stretch of beach here.

Langeberg. *Mountain range, southwestern Cape Province, South Africa.* The range has a Dutch descriptive name simply meaning "long mountain." The mountains run for about 125 miles (200 km) from Worcester in the west to a point near George in the east.

Lanzarote. *Island, eastern Canary Islands.* The easternmost island of the group is named after *Lanciloto* Malocello, an Italian navigator in Portuguese service, who built a castle on it in the 14th century. His first name, the Italian form of *Lancelot,* was later altered to the Spanish form of the name, to conform to other Spanish names in the islands.

La Palma. *Island, northwestern Canary Islands.* The northwesternmost island of the group has a Spanish name meaning simply "the palm-tree." This is the short form of the original full name, *San Miguel de la Palma,* "St. Michael of the palm." Cf. **Las Palmas.**

Larache. *Town and port, northern Morocco.* The present town has developed from an ancient city that was important both under the Phoenicians and as a Roman colony (when it was known as *Lixus*). Its name is a Spanish corruption of Arabic *al-ʿarāʾish,* "the huts," from *al,* "the," and *ʿarāʾish,* plural of *ʿarīsh,* "hut."

Las Palmas. *City and port, Canary Islands.* The city, on northeastern Grand Canary, was founded by the Spanish in 1478. They named the settlement *Las Palmas,* "the palms," for the abundance of such trees here. Cf. **La Palma.**

Lavumisa. *Town, southeastern Swaziland.* The town is bisected by the border between Swaziland and Transvaal, South Africa. *Lavumisa* is the name of the northern, Swaziland part. It is that of the daughter of the 19th century Ndwandwe chief, Zwide. She had settled here with her son, Tsekwane, a refugee like herself from Natal, as a result of military action ordered by the Swazi king Mswati II against his half-brother, Malambule, when the latter stole some royal cattle. The name of the southern, South African part of the town is **Golela** (q.v.).

Lawley. *Village, southern Transvaal, South Africa.* The village, southwest of Johannesburg, is named for Sir Arthur *Lawley* (1860–1932), lieutenant-governor of Transvaal from 1902 to 1906.

Lebombo Mountains. *Mountain range, Southern Africa.* The range runs from north to south mainly along the border between South Africa and Mozambique and Swaziland and Mozambique. The name represents Zulu *ubombo,* meaning "big ridge." The southernmost section of the chain, in northern Natal, is known as the **Ubombo,** with the same meaning.

Lebowa. *Bantustan, central Transvaal, South Africa.* The Bantu homeland was established in 1972 for the Northern Sotho people and was given a name that indicates this, meaning "northern."

Leeudoringstad. *Town, southwestern Transvaal, South Africa.* The town was founded in 1918 and took its name from the railroad station of *Leeudorns* already there. This was itself named by pioneers for the locally prolific lionthorn *(Haragophytum procumbens),* a species of acacia so called because it can conceal a lion.

Leeugamka. *Town, southern Cape Province, South Africa.* The town stands at the confluence of two rivers, the *Leeu* and the *Gamka,* and is named for them. Both their names mean "lion," respectively from Afrikaans and Khoikhoin (Hottentot). An earlier name of the town was *Fraserburg Road,* from its location at the point where the road to *Fraserburg* branches off to the northwest.

Lehututu. *Village, southwestern Botswana.* The name is a Ngola one for the ground hornbill *(Bucorvus),* a bird commonly found here.

Le Kef. *Town, northwestern Tunisia.* The name of the town is a half-French form of Arabic *al-kāf,* "the rock," referring to the steep rock on which the town stands. The site is that of an ancient Carthaginian town and later of the Roman colony *Sicca Veneria,* a name relating to the cult of the goddess Venus.

Leonardville. *Village, eastern Namibia.* The village arose on a farm called *Pretorius* and originally also had this name. It was later renamed for the Rev. E. J. *Leonard,* a pioneer minister of the Dutch Reformed Church.

Leopold, Lake. See Lake **Mai-Ndombe.**

Léopoldville. See **Kinshasa.**

Lephepe. *Village, southeastern Botswana.* The Tswana name is said to mean "clear water," referring to a stream here.

Leptis Magna. See **Labdah.**

Leptis Minor. See **Labdah.**

Leraba. *Village, northern Côte d'Ivoire.* The village takes its name from the river here, a tributary of the Comoé. Its own name means "river of *Lera,*" with the *-ba* ("river") suffix found in many river names.

Leribe. *Town and district, northwestern Lesotho.* The original name of the town, on the border with South Africa, was *Hlotse Heights* or *Thlotse Heights,* for the *Hlotse* river here. Its own name means "dead meat," referring to the habit travelers had of throwing pieces of dead meat to crocodiles here in order to distract them while crossing. The present name probably means "undulating," with reference to the surrounding terrain. Alternately, it could derive from a word *leriba,* meaning "forehead," referring to a high rock here resembling a baboon's forehead.

Leslie. *Village, southern Transvaal, South Africa.* The village, east of Johannesburg, is probably named for *Leslie,* Fife, Scotland, presumably for some local Scottish connection.

Lesotho. *Kingdom, Southern Africa.* The country's name represents Sesotho *le-*, a prefix indicating the singular, and *sotho,* "Sotho," the name of the indigenous people here. The plural of *sotho* is *basotho,* with the plural prefix, *ba-*, which gave the name of *Basutoland,* the former name of Lesotho (from 1884, when it became a British protectorate, to 1966, when it gained its independence). The name of the people itself perhaps means "brown," "dark," referring to their skin color. Some authorities, however, apply this description to the waters of the **Usutu** River, Swaziland, on the banks of which the Basuto lived.

Letaba. *River, South Africa.* The river, a tributary of the Limpopo in northeastern Transvaal, has a name that probably derives from North Sotho *le hlaba,* "sandy river," with the *hl* of this corrupted to *t* by local people.

Letlhakane. *Village, east central Botswana.* The Tswana name, which is also that of a valley here, means "place of reeds." Cf. **Letlhakeng.**

Letlhakeng. *Village, southeastern Botswana.* The Tswana name means "place of reeds." Cf. **Letlhakane.**

Lévrier, Baie du. *Bay, northwestern Mauritania.* The bay, east of Nouadhibou on Cape Blanc, has a French name meaning "bay of the greyhound," perhaps for a ship that once called here.

Leydsdorp. *Village, northern Transvaal, South Africa.* The village is a "ghost town" on the site of a gold mining camp established in 1880 and named *French Bob's Camp,* for one of the prospectors. The town itself was founded in 1890 and named for Dr. Willem Johannes *Leyds* (1859–1940), state secretary of South Africa from 1888 to 1897. When the main gold rush of the Murchison Range here abated, most prospectors moved to the Witwatersrand.

Liberia. *Republic, West Africa.* The present country arose out of the project for the settlement of freed black American slaves begun by the American Colonization Society (ACS) in 1816. Land for this purpose was acquired in 1821 on the site of modern *Monrovia,* and the first group of emigrants arrived in early 1822, when Monrovia itself was founded. On February 20, 1924, Robert Goodloe Harper, an original member of the ACS, named the colony *Liberia,* basing this on Latin *liber,* "free." (He had earlier named **Monrovia,** the Liberian capital, and is himself commemorated in **Harper.**) The settlers' original motto, now part of the Liberian coat of arms, was "The love of liberty brought us here," and the Liberian flag is based on that of the United States. Compare the names **Freetown, Libreville.**

Libode. *Town, Transkei, South Africa.* The town takes its name from that of a Pondo chief who was killed here in an intertribal dispute.

Libreville. *Capital of Gabon.* The city has its origins in *Fort d'Aumale,* a fortified post set up by French traders in 1843 on the estuary of the Gabon River here. This was named for Henri d'Orléans, Duc *d'Aumale* (1822–1897), fourth son of the French king Louis-Philippe, who that same year captured the retinue of the Algerian leader Abdelkader and who became governor-general of Algeria in 1847. In 1849 a settlement of freed black slaves from the Portuguese slave ship *Elizia* was established, and given the city's present French name, meaning "free town." Cf. **Freetown** (its English counterpart) and **Liberia.**

Libya. *Republic, North Africa.* The name of the country is believed to come from the *Libu,* a local nomadic tribe. For the Greeks, *Libuē* was the name of the whole of Africa, or that part of it that they knew. The Romans also used *Libya* generally for the African part of the Roman Empire. The name of people and country is thus very ancient, and is known in Egyptian hieroglyphics of 2000 BC. Some biblical scholars regard the Old Testament mention of *Lebahim* (Genesis 10:13), one of the descendants of the sons of Noah, as a reference to the people, and "the Lubims" (2 Chronicles 12:3) as another such reference.

Lichinga. *Town, northwestern Mozambique.* The Ajaua name means either "cattle pen" or "wall." The latter could refer to the two streams of the Amaramba River here which flow by the mountain face (the "wall"). The town was established in 1931 and until 1982 was known as *Vila Cabral,* for the Portuguese governor-general, Colonel José Ricardo Pereira *Cabral* (1879–1956).

Lichtenburg. *Town, southwestern Transvaal, South Africa.* The town, founded in 1866, has a name of uncertain origin. It seems to be based on Dutch *lichten,* "lights," and may refer to the town's high altitude, so that it stands out like a beacon. Alternately, it could be that of a local farm. The town has also been known as *Wilgedorp,* "willow town," since its streets are lined with these trees.

Ligonha. *River, Mozambique.* The river, in the northern part of the country, flows south to enter the Mozambique Channel below Moma. Its name represents the local word *igonha,* "crocodile," from the abundance of these reptiles in its waters.

Likasi. *Town, southeastern Zaïre.* The town arose in 1892 when Belgian explorers discovered copper nearby. The urban area of *Likasi-Panda* that developed was in 1931 named *Jadotville* for the Belgian mining and railway engineer Jean *Jadot* (1862–1932), first president of the Union Minière du Haut-Katanga, established here in 1910. The town reverted to its original name in 1966.

Lilongwe. *Capital of Malawi.* The city takes its name from the river on which it was founded in 1902. The river's own name probably means simply "river," "water."

Limpopo. *River, Southern Africa.* The long river rises in Transvaal, South Africa, and for some distance of its course forms the border between South Africa and Zimbabwe before flowing through Mozambique to the Indian Ocean. Its name arose as a Portuguese corruption of its local name *Lebepe* or *Lebempe.* The meaning of this is uncertain, but it may represent Ndebele *ilimphopho,* "river of the waterfall," referring to such a feature on its upper course. The Boers knew it as *Krokodil Rivier,* "crocodile river." This same name in its Afrikaans or English form *(Krokodilrivier, Crocodile River)* is still in use for its headstream. Various names, at various times, have been recorded for different sections of the river. Its local name in its middle reaches, for example, is *Nqulukudela,* "river that floods," while in Mozambique its lower reaches are known as *Megombene Mete,* "swallower" or (a Zulu name) *ukuPopoza,* "fast-flowing." Further names recorded by other explorers and cartographers (in parentheses, with dates) include, in their Portuguese forms: *Rio do Cobre,* "river of copper" (Álvare Velho, 1497), *Rio dos Reis,* "river of the kings") (Vasco da Gama, 1498), *Rio da Aguada,* "river of great water" (Waldseemüller, 1507), *Rio dos Fetos,* "river of the ferns" (Lopo Homem, 1519), *Rio dos Reis,* "river of the kings" (João de Barros, 1552), *Baroi,* "sandbar" (Lázaro Luís, 1563), *Rio do Ouro,* "river of gold" (Perestrelo, 1565), *Rio da Misericórdia,* "river of mercy" (Gaspar Correia, mid-16th century), *Rio do Baro,* "river of the sandbar" (Felipe Pigafetta, 1578), *Aroe,* presumably a corruption of this last (Guillaume Delisle, 1708).

Linchwe. *Village, southeastern Botswana.* The name is said to derive from that of a Tswana chief. Its meaning is uncertain.

Lindi. *Town and port, southeastern Tanzania.* The Swahili name means "swampy place." The description no longer applies, and the swamps shown on old British colonial maps of the area have now all dried up.

Lindley. *Town, northeastern Orange Free State, South Africa.* The town was established in 1875 and named for the American Presbyterian missionary, the Rev. Daniel *Lindley* (1801–1881), who ministered to the Voortrekkers.

Linguère. *Town, north central Senegal.* The name represents Fulani (Peul) or Mande *lingèr,* the title formerly given to the mother of the king of Kayor, now a province of Senegal.

Lioma. *Village, northern Mozambique.* The name derives from the local word *ohoma,* "assegais," referring to the use of these spears for hunting, instead of traps and nets, by indigenous tribesmen.

Littoral. *Province, western Cameroon.* The province, bordering the Atlantic, has a French name meaning "coastal." Of Cameroon's ten provinces, nine have French "locational" names. The others are *Centre, Est, Extrême-Nord, Nord, Nord-Ouest, Ouest, Sud,* and *Sud-Ouest.* The only indigenous name is that of *Adamoua,* from the plateau in the southwest of the country (see **Adamawa**).

Livingstone. *Town, southern Zambia.* The town, on the Zambezi River near the Victoria Falls, was founded in 1905 and named in honor of the British explorer David *Livingstone* (1813–1873), who discovered the falls in 1855. Its alternate name is *Maramba,* a local word for the plantain, a type of banana tree. There have been plans in recent years to rename Livingstone *Mosi-oa-Tunya,* the indigenous name of the falls (see **Victoria Falls**). The name *Livingstone* had earlier been given by Stanley to the *Congo.*

Livingstone Falls. *Rapids, Congo River, Zaïre.* The various rapids on the Congo between Kinshasa and Matadi were named in honor of the British explorer David *Livingstone* (1813–1873). The Congo was itself named the *Livingstone* by Stanley (see **Congo**).

Livingstone Mountains. *Mountain range, southern Tanzania.* The range, along the border with Malawi (which here is the eastern shore of Lake Malawi), is named for the British explorer David *Livingstone* (1813–1873), who discovered it during his second African expedition (1858–1863).

Livingstonia. *Town, northern Malawi.* The first memorial mission to the British explorer David *Livingstone* (1813–1873) was established in 1875, under the name *Livingstonia,* at Cape Maclear, at the southern end of Lake Malawi (Lake Nyasa). Because the climate was unduly hot and humid, however, the mission was moved north to Bandawe, on the western shore of the lake. It was later moved to its present site, further north again and some distance inland from the lake.

Lobatse. *Town, southeastern Botswana.* The town, established in the early 20th century, has a name that is said to be that of a former chief here, *Molebatse.* Some authorities, however, derive the name from a Tswana word meaning "lumps of wood," referring to the great number of kopjes (small hills) in the vicinity.

Lobito. *City and port, western Angola.* The city, founded by the Portuguese in 1843, has a name representing the local word *lupito,* "passage," implying that the Atlantic port is reached only with difficulty.

Loeriesfontein. *Village, western Cape Province, South Africa.* The name derives from the large number of loeries (a type of parrot, *Turacus corythaix*) formerly found here.

Lolodorf. *Town, southwestern Cameroon.* The name, meaning "Lolo's village," for a local chief, is one of the few in the country that remain as a reminder of the German presence in Cameroon from 1885 to 1922 (German *Dorf* is "village"). Most of the towns and villages in the country with German names were renamed by the French.

Lomé. *Capital of Togo.* The city, founded in the late 18th century on the site of an Ewe settlement, has a name derived from a local word meaning "little market."

Longonot. *Mountain, south central Kenya.* The mountain, famous for its huge crater, has a name that is a corruption of Maasai *oloonong'ot,* "mountain of many spurs," referring to the deep gulches and narrow ridges formed through the erosion of volcanic deposits.

Los Islands. *Island group off west coast of Guinea.* The islands, off Conakry, Guinea's capital, were originally named by the Portuguese as *Idolos,* for the idol-worshipping Guineans here in the 15th century. This name was then corrupted by the French into *Îles de Los,* as which they are commonly still known today.

Loskop Dam. *Dam, Olifants River, central Transvaal, South Africa.* The dam was built from 1934 to 1946 in order to permit largescale irrigation in the region. Its name, Afrikaans for "loose hill," is that of the farm on which the original dam wall was built.

Louis Trichardt. *Town, northern Transvaal, South Africa.* The town was founded in 1898 and named commemoratively for the Voortrekker leader of Swedish ancestry, *Louis Trichardt* (1783–1838). The name was given at the request of his grandson, Colonel S. Trichardt.

Lourenço Marques. See **Maputo.**

Louwsburg. *Village, northern Natal, South Africa.* The village is named for a local pioneer, David *Louw.*

Lower Egypt. *Region, northern Egypt.* The name traditionally applies to the Nile Delta, north of Cairo, where the terrain is generally lower than in the southern region of the country. Compare **Upper Egypt.**

Loxton. *Town, south central Cape Province, South Africa.* The town is named for A. E. *Loxton,* owner of the farm on which it was laid out in 1899.

Lualaba. *River, Zaïre.* The river, in the southeast of the country, joins the Luapala to form the Congo. Its name means simply "big river." The element *lu-*, meaning "river," is found in other river names and names derived from rivers, such as **Luangwa,** Luapula itself (see **Chambeshi**), and **Lubumbashi**. Although the Lualaba is now generally defined as the headstream of the Congo, or that part of it above the Boyoma Falls, the British explorer Sir Henry Morton Stanley delimited it to a much shorter stretch when he renamed the Congo as the *Livingstone*: "On the 19th [November, 1876] a march . . . brought us to the Lualaba, in south latitude 3° 35′, just forty-one geographical miles north of the Arab depot Nyangwé. . . . The name Lualaba terminates here. I mean to speak of it henceforth as THE LIVINGSTONE" (*Through the Dark Continent,* 1878).

Luanda. *Capital of Angola.* The name of the city derives from the local word *luanda,* meaning "tax," "duty." The reference is to the cowrie shells on the Atlantic coast here, which were at one time used by the local people to pay their dues to the king of the Congo. The present town was founded in 1575 by the Portuguese governor of Angola colony

Paulo Dias de Novais, who had been granted a stretch of land here the previous year by the Portuguese government. He named the settlement *São Paulo de Loanda,* "St. Paul of Luanda," for his personal patron saint.

Luangwa. *Town, southeastern Zambia.* The town takes its name from the river here, a tributary of the Zambezi. Its earlier, colonial name was *Feira,* Portuguese for "fair," "market." See also **Lualaba.**

Lubango. *Town, southwestern Angola.* The town was established by Portuguese colonists in 1885 and was originally named *Sá da Bandeira,* for Bernardo de *Sá da Bandeira* (1795–1876), premier of Portugal, who attempted to extend Portuguese colonial control in the region. The name was in use until Angola gained independence in 1975, when it was changed to its present form. This is a local name probably representing *ombango,* "passage through the mountains." The reference is to the town's location at the entrance to a larger area in the mountains.

Lubumbashi. *City, southeastern Zaïre.* The city was founded by the Belgians in 1910 as a copper-mining settlement and named *Elisabethville,* for Queen *Elisabeth,* wife of Albert I, king of the Belgians, whom he had married in 1900. In 1966 the city adopted its present name, for the small stream on which it stands.

Luckhoff. *Town, southwestern Orange Free State, South Africa.* The town was established in 1892 and apparently named for the Rev. Heinrich Jacob *Luckhoff* (1842–1943), minister of the Dutch Reformed Church at nearby Fauresmith at that time.

Lüderitz. *Town and port, southern Namibia.* The Portuguese navigator Barthlomeu Dias landed on the Atlantic coast here in 1487 and named the bay *Angra das Voltas,* "bay of turns." A year later he renamed it *Golfo de São Cristovão,* "St. Christopher's gulf." A subsequent name for the bay was simply *Angra Pequena,* "little bay." The first proper shore settlement was set up only 300 years later, when in 1883 a German merchant, Franz Adolf Eduard *Lüderitz* (1834–1886), persuaded the German government to place the region under German protection. He renamed the bay for himself as *Lüderitzbucht.* This name then passed to the settlement that he founded, but was subsequently shortened to *Lüderitz.*

Lugela. *Town, northern Mozambique.* The name derives from the local word *ologela,* "to greet," from the obligation imposed on travelers here to greet the district chief.

Lumbala. *Town, southeastern Angola.* The name means "settlement between two rivers," so is self-descriptive for the town. Before 1975, when Angola gained independence, the town was named *Gago Coutinho,* for the Portuguese scholar and naval officer Carlos Viegas *Gago Coutinho* (1879–1959), one of the first men to fly from Portugal to Brazil.

Lumbo. *Village, northeastern Mozambique.* The village, west of Moçambique, has a name said to derive from Zulu *ilumbo,* "to tell lies," referring to the stories told by slaves here when the settlement was an important trading center.

Lupa Market. *Village, southern Tanzania.* The village, formerly famous for its market, takes its name from the *Lupa* River on which it lies.

Lusaka. *Capital of Zambia.* The city took its name from that of *Lusaakas,* chief of the village near the original railroad siding in 1905, when it served the Broken Hill mine (now the city of Kabwe). The city became the capital of Northern Rhodesia in 1935.

Lusikisiki. *Village, Transkei, South Africa.* The name is imitative, for the sound of the wind blowing through the reeds here. The village grew from a military camp established in 1894.

Lutzville. *Village, southwestern Cape Province, South Africa.* The village was established in 1923 and named for its founder, Johan J. *Lutz.*

Luxor. *Town, east central Egypt.* The name is a corruption of Arabic *al-uqṣur* or *al-quṣūr,* "the camps," from *al,* "the," and *quṣūr,* plural of *qaṣr,* "military camp," itself adopted from Latin *castrum* with the same meaning. The reference is to the Roman encampment here. The southern part of the town stands on the site of the ancient Greek city of **Thebes,** which was joined to the equally ancient **Karnak,** to the north, by an avenue of sphinxes.

Lycopolis. See **Asyut.**

Lydenburg. *Town, east central Transvaal, South Africa.* The Afrikaans name means "town of suffering," and refers to the troubles experienced by the Voortrekkers in the region here. They had attempted to settle further north, but were stricken with malaria and forced to move to higher ground, eventually founding the present town in 1850. The local name of the town is *Masising,* "place of long grass."

Mabalane. *Village, southern Mozambique.* The name is said to be a corruption of the verb *gu balekabala,* "to relate," referring to the interpreters here who were keen to advertise their services to travelers. The colonial name of the village was *Vila Pinto Teixeira,* for the Portuguese railway engineer, Major Francisco dos Santos *Pinto Teixeira,* who came to Mozambique in 1928 and did much to improve the country's public transport system. Mabalane is itself on a railroad and trunk road midway between Chicualacuala and Guija.

Mabuasehube Game Reserve. *Game reserve, southern Botswana.* The reserve, an eastward extension of the Gemsbok National Park, has a Tswana name meaning "red sands." The reference is to the oxidized pan in the northern part of the reserve.

Mabutsane. *Village, southern Botswana.* The Tswana name means "soft sand."

MacCarthy Island. *Island, west central Gambia.* The island, in the Gambia River, was originally known as *Lemain Island.* It was renamed for Sir Charles *MacCarthy* (1770–1824), governor of Sierra Leone from 1821 to his death (from a fatal wound in a dispute with the Ashanti, who then took his head as a war trophy). Gambia Territory was under the rule of Sierra Leone at this time. The name is also that of one of Gambia's administrative divisions, with a capital at **Georgetown.**

Macenta. *Town, southern Guinea.* The town, near the Liberian border, takes its name from the *Massada* River here. The river's own name means "tributary of the chief," from Toma *masa,* "chief," and *da,* "stream."

McGregor. *Village, southwestern Cape Province, South Africa.* The village takes its name from a local minister of the Dutch Reformed Church, the Rev. Andrew *McGregor* (1829–1918).

Machadodorp. *Town, eastern Transvaal, South Africa.* The small town originated as an outspan (halting-place) in the days of horse transport and developed in 1895 after the opening of the railroad the previous year. It was named for the Portuguese general Joaquim José *Machado* (1847–1925), governor-general of Mozambique, who had played an active part in the promotion of railroad routes.

Machakos. *Town, south central Kenya.* The town was founded in 1889 and takes its name from a local chief, *Masaku,* with the final *-s* probably an English possessive (as if *Masaku's*).

Machanganaland. See **Gazan-Kulu.**

Macheke. *Village, eastern Zimbabwe.* The village, southeast of the capital, Harare, takes its name from the river on which its lies. This in turn has a name meaning "boundary," as it here marks the border between Mashonaland and Manicaland.

Macia. *Village, southern Mozambique.* The name appears to be a tribal one, although an interpretation "orphan" is possible, perhaps referring to a cemetery here, west of Xai-Xai.

Macías Nguema Bijogo. See **Bioko.**

McIlwaine, Lake. *Lake, east central Zimbabwe.* The lake, west of Harare, is named for Sir Robert *McIlwaine* (1871–1943), Irish-born civil servant and holder of many local government offices in Rhodesia, including that of first chairman of the Natural Resources Board (from 1941).

Macleantown. *Village, southeastern Cape Province, South Africa.* The village was so named in 1881 for Colonel John *Maclean* (1810–1874), lieutenant-governor of British Kaffraria from 1860.

Maclear. *Town, eastern Cape Province, South Africa.* The town arose in 1876 as a settlement a round an army camp. It is named for Sir Thomas *MacLear* (1794–1879), the astronomer who pioneered a trigonometrical survey of the Cape.

Macuze. *Coastal village, eastern Mozambique.* The village east of Quelimane is said to derive its name from the local word *macode,* "snail," as these molluscs are abundant here.

Madagascar. *Island republic, off southeastern coast of Africa.* The current form of the name represents Malagasy *Madagasikara,* itself from Old French *Madeigascar.* This name is mentioned by Marco Polo in the 13th century, although he used it for the eastern coast of Somalia and for the town of *Mogadishu* there. The error came about because he had translated as "island" the Arabic word *jazīra,* which can have not only this meaning, but also that of "peninsula." In 1492 the German navigator and geographer Martin Behaim constructed his famous terrestrial globe showing false geographical conceptions prior to the discovery of America. "Madagascar" on this appears as an island east of Zanzibar and of similar size. When the Portuguese navigator Diego Dias discovered Madagascar on August 10, 1500, the feastday of St. Lawrence, he named the island *São Laurenço,* "St. Lawrence." As a result, contemporary maps of the island named it as either *St. Laurence* (or its equivalent) or *Madagascar:* the former from Dias' name, the latter from Marco Polo's, as if there were two distinct islands. The error was discovered in 1531 by the French mathematician Oronce Fine, and the name *Madagascar* was preferred. (Even so, the alternate name continued in use until at least the 18th century.) The name thus derives from that of **Mogadishu,** now the Somali capital. There has never been a single original Malagasy name for the island as a whole, only different names for different parts of it. When Madagascar gained its independence from France in 1960, it changed its name to the *Malagasy Republic,* with reference to its indigenous people and their language. It reverted to *Madagascar* in 1975. In view of the known origin of the country's language and culture in Indonesia, rather than the African continent, it is tempting to link the name *Malagasy* with that of *Malaya.* But it is probably an altered form, through the medium of some other language, of *Madagascar* itself. (The alternate spelling *Malagash* was also formerly in use for the people or their language. The French for *Malagasy* is *Malegache* similarly.)

Madeira. *Island group, North Atlantic.* The group, west of Morocco, takes its name from that of its chief island. This was discovered by the Portuguese navigator João Gonçalves Zarco in 1420 and named for its many trees (Portuguese *madeira,* "wood," "timber," a word related to English *material,* implying building material). Zarco was the founder of the island's capital, **Funchal**. The Roman name of the islands was *Insulae Purpurariae,* "islands of purple" for the purple dye extracted from the trees here. This was itself almost certainly a translation of an earlier Punic name.

Mafeking. See **Mafikeng.**

Mafeteng. *Town, western Lesotho.* The town, established in 1874, has a name of uncertain origin. Some relate it to *Lefeta,* a Basuto nickname meaning "the man who passes by" given to the town's first magistrate, Emile Rolland. The name could thus mean "place of Lefeta's people." Other sources, however, interpret the name as either "a place of crossing," referring to the original site of the town at a crossing over the Caledon River, or as "place of unmarried women," with reference to the unmarried daughters of a chief.

Mafikeng. *Town, Bophuthatswana, South Africa.* The town has a Tswana name meaning "place of rocks," from *mafika,* the plural of *lefika,* "rock," with the locative suffix *-ng.* It was established in 1885 after British annexation of the territory here, and for many years was familiar as *Mafeking,* perhaps by association with English *king,* especially during the second Boer War (1899–1902), when it was besieged by the Boers for 217 days. (This was a time of British patriotic fervor, especially since *King* Edward VII of England, popular eldest son of Queen Victoria, succeeded to the throne actually during the war.) In 1980 the name was adjusted to its present, more correct form.

Magaliesberg. *Mountain range, southern Transvaal, South Africa.* The range, west of the capital, Pretoria, is named for the chief that the Voortrekkers met here in the 1830s, *Mohale* or *Magali.*

Magaliesburg. *Village, southern Transvaal, South Africa.* The village, southwest of the capital, Pretoria, takes its name from the *Magaliesberg* mountains, to the north.

Maghama. *Village, southern Mauritania.* The village, near the Senegal border just north of the Senegal River, was given its name in 1866 by Tierno Brahima, Islamic scholar and saint of the Mohi Nalla people. The Arabic name means "place of rest," and is a reference to Brahima's holy namesake, Abraham, who according to the Koran "raised the foundations" of the Kaaba, the holiest Muslim shrine, in Mecca. The Koran further specifies: "The first sanctuary created for men is that of Mecca, which is blessed and which is the guide of the universe. There are clear signs that it is Abraham's *place* *of rest,* and whoever enters it is assured of safe conduct...."

Maghreb. *Region, northwestern Africa.* The extensive region has a name used to include Morocco, Algeria, Tunisia, and sometimes Libya. It derives from Arabic *ǧarb,* "west." (Compare Portugal's *Algarve,* representing Arabic *al-gharb,* "the west.")

Magude. *Village, southern Mozambique.* The village takes its name from *Magudzo* (died 1874), son of the local Cossa chief Pucuana.

Magudu. *Village, northern Natal, South Africa.* The village takes its name from that of a local Zulu chief. The name itself is said to mean "enchanted."

Mahajanga. *City and port, northwestern Madagascar.* The name is Malagasy, and perhaps means "healing one," referring to the curative waters of the Betsiboka River here. Some sources, however, trace the name to an original form *Mji-angaia,* meaning "village of *angaia,*" from the local name of a type of flowering shrub. Until 1977 the name was more familiar as *Majunga.*

Mahalapye. *Village, eastern Botswana.* The present name of the village is a corrupt form of *Mhalatswe,* referring to the impala antelope that once frequented the region. Compare **Palapye.**

Mahamba. *Village, southeastern Transvaal, South Africa.* The village, on the border with Swaziland, has a name meaning "the runaways," referring to the flight to Natal of Wesleyan missionaries and refugees after a battle among the Swazis in the 1830s.

Mahavavy. *River, Madagascar.* The river, in the northwest of the island, has a Malagasy name meaning "making a woman," from *màha,* "able to," "capable of," and *vàvy,* "woman." The reference is to men who fear to venture in or on the river because of its crocodiles.

Mahé. *Island, Seychelles.* The chief island of the Seychelles was so named in 1742 by Captain Lazare Picault in honor of Bertrand-François *Mahé,* Comte de la Bourdonnais (1699–1753), then governor of the Île de France (modern Mauritius). His title gave the original name of the **Seychelles** as a whole. See also **Mahébourg.**

Mahébourg. *Town and port, southeastern Mauritius.* The town takes its name from Bertrand-François *Mahé,* French governor of the island in the 18th century. See also **Mahé.**

Mahlabatini. *Village, northern Natal, South Africa.* The Zulu name of the village is said to mean "country of white sandy soil."

Maiko. See **Mai-Ndombe.**

Mai-Ndombe, Lake. *Lake, western Zaïre.* The lake took its present name in 1973 from the *Mundombe* or *Ndombe* people. It was discovered by the British explorer Sir Henry Morton Stanley in 1882, during his third expedition, and named by him *Lake Leopold,* for the Belgian king *Leopold* II (1865–1909), who financed Stanley's expedition and gained control of what was then the Congo as his private empire. (See also **Kinshasa.**) In 1876, during his second expedition, Stanley had similarly named the river now known as the *Maiko,* a tributary of the Congo in the east of the country: "At 4 p.m. we came opposite a river about 200 yards wide, which I have called the Leopold River, in honour of his Majesty Leopold II., King of the Belgians, and which the natives called either the Kankora, Mikonju, or Munduku. Perhaps the natives were misleading me, or perhaps they really possessed a superfluity of names, but I think that whatever name they give it should be mentioned in connection with each stream" (*Through the Dark Continent,* 1878).

Maintirano. *Town and port, western Madagascar.* The Malagasy name means "black water," referring to the river here.

Maio. *Island, southeastern Cape Verde Islands.* The island was first sighted by the Portuguese on May 1, 1460. Hence its name, from Portuguese *maio,* "May."

Majunga. See **Mahajanga.**

Makalamabedi. *Village, north central Botswana.* The name of the village means "*makala* with two branches," referring to a conspicuous tree of this type here. Alternate names for the village are Herero *Tjoruuma,* "dry place," and Yei *Kungxuru,* "at the palm tree."

Makgadikgadi. See **Kalahari.**

Makopong. *Village, southern Botswana.* The name is of Tswana origin and is said to mean either "place of the sound of running water" or "place where hungry people should go."

Makwiro. *Village, north central Zimbabwe.* The village, southwest of the capital, Harare, takes its name from a local river. Its own name means "to climb," referring to the hilly terrain here.

Malabo. *Capital of Equatorial Guinea.* The name of the town and port derives from that of *Malabo,* king of the Bubi, who died in 1937. He was one of the two sons of Moka, whose other son, Bioko, gave the name of **Bioko,** the island on which Malabo is located. The town was founded in 1827 by the English vice-admiral William F. Owen, who named it *Port Clarence,* for the Duke of *Clarence* (1765–1837), the future King William IV of England. In 1843 the island, then known as Fernando Po, passed to the Spanish, who renamed the town *Santa Isabel,* "St. Elizabeth," for Queen *Isabella* II of Spain (1830–1904). In 1973 the capital was given its present name.

Malagasy Republic. See **Madagascar.**

Malanje. *Town, north central Angola.* The town, established in 1857, has a name of uncertain origin. It was formerly spelled *Malange,* and may derive from the name of a river here, and perhaps mean "stones," referring to the river bed. An alternate origin may lie in the local words *landjo,* "big," and *oli,* "house," with reference to some local dwelling or building. The name is also that of a province.

Malanville. *Town, northeastern Benin.* The town, on the Niger River, is named for Henri *Malan* (died 1912), French lieutenant-governor of Dahomey (now Benin) in 1909 and again in 1911.

Malawi. *Republic, Central Africa.* The name represents that of the *Maravi,* a local people known here since the 14th century. Their name is said to mean "flames," possibly referring to the rays of the rising sun on Lake Malawi. When under British control, the country's former name was *Nyasaland,* from the old name of Lake Malawi, Lake **Nyasa.** Since this itself represents the Swahili word for "lake," the country's name effectively meant "Lakeland" (and that of Lake Nyasa, "Lake Lake"). The same name gave that of the *Nyanja* people and their language. The republic acquired its present name on gaining independence in 1964. See also **Niassa.**

Malelane. *Village, eastern Transvaal, South Africa.* The village takes its name from that of the farm on which it arose. This is said either to represent the local word *emlalani,* "place of *lala* palms," or to derive from the name of a Swazi people meaning "guardians," referring to their control of a ford across the Crocodile River here.

Malema. *Town, northern Mozambique.* The town takes its name from the river here, a tributary of the Lúrio. It is the plural form of *ilema,* the local word for a type of conical basket used for river fishing. *Ilema* is also the name of a nearby hill, itself shaped like such a basket. The town is still sometimes known by its old Portuguese colonial name of *Entre-Rios,* "between the rivers," with reference to its location between the Malema and Mutivari rivers.

Mali. *Republic, West Africa.* The former French Sudan (prior to 1958) and Sudanese Republic (from 1958 to 1960), acquired its present name on September 22, 1960, on gaining independence. The name is a very old one, mentioned (in the form *Mallal*) by the Arab historian Al-Yakubi in the late 9th century, and is that of an empire that effectively disappeared in the 17th century. It probably derives from that of the *Malinke* people who are indigenous to Mali, although some accounts trace the name from a Malinke word meaning either "place where the king resides" or "hippopotamus." The Malinke (or Mandinka) themselves are said to take their name from Malinke *ma,* "mother," and *dink* or *denk,* "child," alluding to the matrilinear descent that they traditionally follow. See also **Sudan.**

Malmesbury. *Town, southwestern Cape Province.* The town, north of Cape Town, was founded in 1829 and originally bore the Afrikaans name of *Swartlandskerk,* "black country church," for the district here popularly known as the *Zwartland,* perhaps with reference to the color of the soil or to the dense weed called renosterbos (literally "rhinoceros bush," *Elytropappus rhinocerotis*), which frequently turns black. It subsequently received its present name, given by the Cape governor, Sir Lowry Cole, in honor of his father-in-law, Sir James Harris, 1st Earl of *Malmesbury* (1746–1820), whose second daughter Frances he had married in 1815. The earl's own title comes from the town of *Malmesbury,* Wiltshire.

Maltahöhe. *Town, central Namibia.* The town, laid out in 1900, takes its name from Frau *Malta* von Burgsdorff, wife of the garrison commander at Gibeon, with *Höhe* the German word for "height."

Malvérnia. See **Chicualacuala.**

Mamfe. *Town, western Cameroon.* The name is a corruption of *Mansfeld,* the surname of the town's first German district officer, following the Germans' acquisition of what is now Cameroon in 1884.

Mamre. *Village, southwestern Cape Province, South Africa.* The village north of Cape Town arose from a military post established in 1701. This was abandoned in 1791, and a Moravian mission station was set up on the site in 1808. It was given a biblical name (Genesis 13:18) believed to mean "fatness" and so to be propitious.

Mandidzudzure. See **Chimanimani.**

Mandini. *Village, eastern Natal, South Africa.* The village, northeast of Durban, has a Zulu name meaning "place of the spurge trees" *(Euphorbia tiruculli).*

Mangoche. *Town, southern Malawi.* The town arose in 1891 as a military post on Lake Malawi named *Fort Johnston,* for Sir Harry Hamilton

Johnston (1858–1927), the first commissioner of Nyasaland (present Malawi). When Malawi gained independence in 1964, the present name was adopted. It derives from that of the chief, *Mangoche,* who held authority here when the settlement was founded.

Manica. *Province, west central Mozambique.* The name, also that of a town here, derives from the *Nica* people, the region's original indigenous inhabitants. The same people gave the name of the province of *Manicaland,* eastern Zimbabwe.

Manicaland. See **Manica.**

Manjakaze. *Village, southern Mozambique.* The name means "power of blood," and was the title of the kraal where the local chief had his residence.

Mankayane. *Town, southwestern Swaziland.* The Tswana name of the town means "little steps," either alluding to the hilly topography of the place, which compels those walking to take short steps, or else borrowed direct from the name of a chief, and given to him in the first place as a descriptive nickname.

Mansa. *Town, northern Zambia.* The town was founded in the 1890s as an outpost named *Fort Rosebery,* for Archibald Philip Primrose, 5th Earl *Rosebery* (1847–1929), British foreign secretary in 1886 and from 1892 to 1894. Rosebery was a noted imperialist, and a friend of both Cecil Rhodes (see **Rhodesia**) and Sir Leander Starr Jameson (see **Chipata**). The present name, probably that of a local chief, was adopted after 1964 when Zambia gained independence.

Mansura. See **El Mansura.**

Manuel, Cape. *Promontory, Cape Vert peninsula, western Senegal.* The cape is the southernmost point of the peninsula on which Dakar, Senegal's capital, is situated. It was probably named for *Manuel* the Fortunate (1469–1521), king of Portugal from 1495 to 1521. (His byname refers to the fact that his reign was the golden age of Portuguese discovery and colonization.)

Manzini. *City, central Swaziland.* The town was founded in 1890 and until 1902 was the capital of Swaziland. Its original Afrikaans name was *Bremersdorp,* for Albert *Bremer,* a trader who helped establish it. The present name was adopted in 1960 as a form of the historic local name of the place, *KwaManzini,* "place of Manzini," referring to *Manzini* Motsa, the local chief who held authority here.

Mapulanguene. *Village, southwestern Mozambique.* The village, near the border with South Africa, takes its name from the local word *mapulango,* plural of *pulango,* "plank" (a borrowing of English *plank*). The reference is to timber building materials here.

Mapumulo. *Village, eastern Natal, South Africa.* The village was established in 1894 and has a local name meaning "place of rest." The reference is said to be to a Zulu people who sought refuge here after being driven from their homeland by the Zulu leader Shaka.

Maputo. *Capital of Mozambique.* The city, in the south of the country, takes its name from that of the river which flows into the bay on which it stands. The river was itself named for one of the sons of the local chief Nuagobe, who lived in the 18th century. Until 1976 the capital was called *Lourenço Marques,* from the name of the Portuguese trader who first explored the region in 1544. This name was given to the settlement which developed round a Portuguese fort built in 1787. The original name of the site, however, was *Baía da*

Lagoa. This is the Portuguese name of the bay here today known in English as *Delagoa Bay*. The name itself simply means "bay of the lagoon." Cf. **Algoa Bay**.

Maquelo do Zombo. *Town, northern Angola*. The name combines those of a local chief, *Maquelo*, and his tribe, *Zombo*. The fact that the two names are joined by Portuguese *do*, "of," suggests that the overall name was devised by a Portuguese colonial official.

Marabadiassa. *Village, central Côte d'Ivoire*. The village was founded in the late 19th century by Mory-Touré, a Hausa warrior, who named it "fort of the Hausa," from *maraba*, "fort," and *dyassa*, "Hausa."

Maradi. *Town, southern Niger*. The name was a title, of uncertain meaning, of a local landholder, who "bequeathed" it to the village that belonged to him and that provided him with his income by way of taxes.

Maraisburg. *Town, southern Transvaal, south Africa*. The town, now a western district of Johannesburg, takes its name from that of an early mining agent, Piet *Marais*, one of the first to be active here in the 1880s. See also **Nigel**.

Maralalang. *Village, southern Botswana*. The name means "place often visited," presumably for some popular or essential local amenities.

Marandellas. See **Marondera**.

Marble Hall. *Village, central Transvaal, South Africa*. The village was laid out in 1942 and has a name that is said to be a corruption of *marble hole*, referring to the Marble Lime Mine here from which the present township arose.

Marchand. See **Rommani**.

Margate. *Town and resort, southeastern Natal, South Africa*. The original seaside site here was bought in 1919 with the aim of creating a town to be called *Inkongweni*, for the nearby *Kongweni* River. (The latter name means "place of entreaty," since travelers were apparently obliged to beg for hospitality here.) When the settlement was declared a township in 1941, however, it was named *Margate*, for the English seaside resort in Kent, also in the southeast. See also **Ramsgate**.

Margherita, Mount. *Mountain, central Africa*. The mountain is the highest summit of the Ruwenzori range on the border between Uganda and Zaïre. It was first climbed in 1906 by the Italian mountaineer, Luigi Amedeo, duca d'Abruzzi, and named for Queen *Margherita* of Italy (1851–1926), wife of King Umberto I and mother of King Vittorio Emanuele I.

Mariannhill. *Village, southeastern Natal, South Africa*. The village, west of Durban, is the largest Roman Catholic mission in Southern Africa, founded in 1882 as a Trappist monastery. Hence its name, honoring the Virgin *Mary* and her mother, St. *Anne*.

Mariano Machado. See **Ganda**.

Mariental. *Town, south central Namibia*. The town was established in 1912 by the German administration. Roman Catholic missionaries gave it a name that means "Mary's valley," for the Virgin *Mary*.

Marion Island. See **Prince Edward Islands**.

Marondera. *Town, east central Zimbabwe*. The town arose in 1890 under British colonial administration and took its name from *Marondera*, a local chief of the Baroswi tribe. The earlier form of the name was *Marandellas*, corrected in 1982.

Maroua. *Town, northern Cameroon*. The name derives from that of a 19th century (Fulani) Peul chief in what was then known as Mandara.

Marquard. *Town, east central Orange Free State, South Africa.* The town was established in 1905 and named for the Rev. J. J. T. *Marquard,* minister of the Dutch Reformed Church in nearby Winburg, who had advocated the setting up of a town here.

Marracuene. *Town, southern Mozambique.* The town, north of the capital, Maputo, has a name that seems to be based on *marro,* "lowland," "mudflat," which would certainly be appropriate for its location on marshland near the mouth of the Incomati River. Its colonial name, before Mozambique gained independence in 1975, was *Vila Luísa,* for the daughter of António Enes, governor-general of Mozambique Colony (see **Angoche**) in 1895, the year of Marracuene's foundation. Cf. **Marromeu.**

Marrakech. *City, west central Morocco.* The former Moroccan capital has a name that represents Arabic *marrākuŝ,* originally *marūkus,* a Berber word meaning "fortified." The city was founded in 1092 as African capital of the Almoravides dynasty. It was Marrakech that gave the name of **Morocco** itself.

Marromeu. *Town, eastern Mozambique.* The town has a name based on *marro,* "lowland," "mudflat," referring to its location on the right bank of the Zambezi River. Cf. **Marracuene.**

Marrupa. *Village, northern Mozambique.* The name derives from *marupe,* the term for a type of grain similar to the cereal known as *meixoeira.*

Marsabit. *Town, northern Kenya.* The town, a hill oasis above the desert, has a local name meaning "place of cold." At night the temperatures here can drop very low.

Marula. *Village, southwestern Zimbabwe.* The village, southwest of Bulawayo, takes its name from that of the *marula* tree *(Sclerocarya caffra).* The plumlike fruit of the tree, with a taste similar to that of the mango, is used for making an alcoholic drink. See also **Plumtree.**

Marydale. *Village, west central Cape Province, South Africa.* The village, northwest of Prieska, was founded on a farm in 1902 and named for the farm owner's wife, *Mary* Snyman.

Maryland. *County, southeastern Liberia.* The county takes its name from the colony founded in 1834 for freed black American slaves by James Hall of the *Maryland* Colonization Society. See also its capital, **Harper.**

Mascara. *Town, northwestern Algeria.* The town was founded in 1701 as a Turkish military garrison and from 1832 to 1847 was capital of the emirate of the same name. Its own name is Arabic in origin and means literally "mother of soldiers," from *umm,* "mother," and *ʿasker,* "army," "soldiers." (The name has nothing to do with English *mascara.*)

Mascarene Islands. *Island group, Indian Ocean.* The islands, lying east of Madagascar, comprise Réunion, Mauritius, and Rodriguez. They take their name from the Portuguese explorer Pedro de *Mascarenhas,* who discovered **Réunion** (q.v. also) in about 1513.

Maseru. *Capital of Lesotho.* The name represents Sotho *maseru,* plural of *leseru,* "red sandstone." The reference is to the rocky height where Commandant J. H. Bowker, high commissioner for South Africa, built his headquarters in 1869 when the former Basutoland (present Lesotho) was placed under his authority.

Mashava. *Village, south central Zimbabwe.* The village, west of

Masvingo, takes its name from that of the hills here. Their own name means "red," describing their prevailing color.

Mashonaland. *Region, northeastern Zimbabwe.* The region, now divided into the provinces of *Mashonaland Central, Mashonaland East,* and *Mashonaland West,* takes its name from the *Mashona* or *Shona* people who inhabit this part of Africa. Their own name is of uncertain origin, but according to one theory represents Zulu *tshona langa,* "sunset," that is, "people of the east."

Masimo. See **Bethulie.**

Masising. See **Lydenburg.**

Massangano. *Village, western Angola.* The town, southeast of the capital, Luanda, has a name with an anecdotal origin, said to represent the phrase *massa negano,* "mealies, sir," the reply given to the Portuguese by the local people when the colonists saw a mealie field here and asked what the crop was.

Massénya. *Town, southwestern Chad.* The town is said to take its name from the local word *mass,* "tamarind," with reference to a tree of this kind that grew in the market place.

Massinga. *Town, southeastern Mozambique.* The small town, near the coast, appears to take its name from that of the *Singo* tribe, a Venda people who came here from northern Transvaal.

Massingir. *Village, southwestern Mozambique.* The name is said to derive from the local verb *ku txindja* or *ku txindjira,* meaning "to cut timber for building forts."

Masvingo. *Town, southeastern Zimbabwe.* The present name of the town is the third in its history. It was founded in 1890 as a military post named *Fort Victoria,* from Queen *Victoria* of England (1819–1901). When Zimbabwe gained independence in 1980, the name was changed to *Nyanda,* said to be that of a witch, and the second wife of the legendary African leader Monomotapa. In 1982 the name was changed again to its present form, meaning "caves."

Matabeleland. *Region, western Zimbabwe.* The region is named for the *Matabele,* the formerly warlike people of Southern Africa, who came here in 1837 when they were driven north over the Limpopo from the Transvaal, South Africa, by the Boers. (In the Transvaal itself they are more commonly known as the *Ndebele.* This form of the name has the singular *n-* prefix, while *Matabele,* more common in Zimbabwe, has the plural *ma-* prefix.) *Matabele* represents the Zulu word *amandebele,* "the disappearing ones," referring either to this eviction or, according to another theory, to the fact that the people "disappeared," or ducked down out of sight, when challenged in armed conflict. The regional name is now in use for the two provinces of *Matabeleland North* and *Matabeleland South.*

Matadi. *City, western Zaïre.* The city, on the Congo (Zaïre) River, takes its name from a Kikongo word meaning "stone." The name has been associated with the Bantu nickname, *Bula Matari,* meaning "break stones," that was conferred on the British explorer Sir Henry Morton Stanley, from his ordering the Africans to crush rocks on the river bank with a sledgehammer when setting up a trading station here in 1879. (The name appears on the rough stone erected over Stanley's grave in the village churchyard at Pirbright, Surrey, England.) However, this name may equally well have been an attempt to translate his English surname, which literally means "stone clearing."

Matala. *Town, southwestern Angola.* The original name of the settlement here was *Capelongo,* from the local word *ulongo,* a term for a forked stick used to carry loads on the back. During Portuguese colonial administration, the name was changed to *Artur de Paiva,* for an army lieutenant. The present name came into use when Angola gained independence in 1975. It is a local word for an outdoor shelf used for drying and storing vegetables.

Matam. *Town, northeastern Senegal.* The town, on the Senegal River, is said to derive its name from the Tukulor word *matama,* "to pay cash." Slaves sold by the Fulani (Peul) on credit often ran away or died of exhaustion. The purchaser would then refuse to pay, saying the goods were defective. As a result, the slave owners refused to sell on credit and instead insisted on a cash payment.

Matatiele. *Town, Transkei, South Africa.* The name is said to represent Sotho *mada-i-yila,* meaning "the ducks have flown," referring to the drying up of the vlei (marshland) here and the consequent departure of waterfowl.

Matjiesfontein. *Village, southwestern Cape Province, South Africa.* The name is derived from the rush *Cyperus textilis,* known in Afrikaans as the *matjiesgoed,* literally "little mat material," for its use to make small mats. The village arose by a spring *(fontein)* where such rushes grew.

Matopo Hills National Park. *National park, southwestern Zimbabwe.* The park takes its name from the hills. According to tradition, they were themselves named by Mzilikazi, the Ndebele king, with reference to their granite domes, which resembled the bald heads of the elders of his tribe. Hence the origin of the name in Ndebele *amaTobo,* "the bald heads."

Matroosberg. *Mountain, southwestern Cape Province, South Africa.* The name of the mountain is either derived from that of Klaas *Matroos,* a shepherd who lived here, or else can be translated from the Afrikaans as "sailor mountain," perhaps referring to a rock suggesting the figure of a sailor standing on the prow of a ship.

Matsapha. *Town, west central Swaziland.* The town, west of Manzini, has a name of uncertain origin, claimed by some to refer to the gathering of something (such as fruit) free of charge.

Matsieng. *Village, western Lesotho.* The name means "people of *Letsie,*" referring to a local chief. His own name means "locust," as he was born during a plague of these insects.

Maun. *Town, northern Botswana.* The name, more accurately *Maung,* is a Yei word meaning "place of short reeds." The town lies on the *Thamalakane* River, whose own name means "river that goes straight."

Mauretania. See **Mauritania.**

Mauritania. *Republic, northwestern Africa.* The republic was established as a French protectorate in 1903 and took the Roman name *(Mauretania)* of the ancient region here, corresponding to the northern parts of modern Algeria and Morocco. This derives from Latin *Maurus,* "Moor," with the same Latin suffix as in regional names such as *Aquitania* (modern French *Aquitaine*), meaning "land of." The Moors were the Muslim people, of mixed Arabic and Berber descent, who were the indigenous inhabitants of this part of Africa. Their own name is said to derive either from Greek *amauros,* "dark," referring to their skin color, or Punic *mahurīm,* "western," a word probably related to the name of the **Maghreb.**

Mauritius. *Island republic, east of Madagascar.* The island has had a number of names over the centuries. It was uninhabited until the early 16th century, though known to Arab explorers in the 8th century, who marked it on their maps as *Dina Arobi,* said to mean "silver island." The first Europeans to discover the island were the Portuguese, in 1507. They called it *Ilha do Cerne,* "tree-ring island," after one of their ships. It then remained unclaimed until 1598, when the Dutch renamed it with its present name, giving this in honor of *Maurice* of Nassau, the future Prince of Orange (1567–1625), stadholder (chief executive) of the Dutch Republic from 1584. (The name is the Latin form of his personal name.) The Dutch left the island in 1710, and in 1715 a group of French sailors arrived. French colonists from Réunion came in 1721 and renamed it *Île de France,* "island of France," a name not only territorially descriptive but already in use for the region surrounding Paris, the French capital. In 1810 the island was taken by the British. It was ceded to them four years later, and the former name *Mauritius* was restored.

Mavinga. *Town, southeastern Angola.* The name is the plural form of the local word *vinga,* "horn," said to refer to the large number of animal horns found here at one time.

Mavuradonha Mountains. *Mountains, northeastern Zimbabwe.* The propitious name means "the rains fall," referring to the rains that it is hoped the mountains will bring.

Mawenzi. See **Kilimanjaro.**

Mayotte. *Island, southeastern Comoros Islands.* The island was the only one of the group to remain French when the others became independent in 1976. Its name is thus a French form of its indigenous name, *Mawutu* or *Mahori,* of unknown meaning.

Mazagan. See **El Jadida.**

Mazeppa Bay. *Coastal village, Transkei, South Africa.* The seaside resort is named for the bay to which in 1839 the schooner *Mazeppa* brought a party of Voortrekkers.

Mazowe. *Village, northern Zimbabwe.* The village, north of the capital, Harare, takes its name from the river here. Its own name is a Karanga word meaning "place of elephants."

Mbabane. *Capital of Swaziland.* The town arose in the late 19th century near a royal cattle kraal established by chief Mbandzeni. It was named for *Mbabane* Kunene, the chief who lived here before the arrival of European settlers.

Mbahiakro. *Village, east central Côte d'Ivoire.* The name means "village of *M'Bahia,*" for a local chief.

Mbala. *Town, northeastern Zambia.* The town was established in 1893 as *Abercorn,* so named for James Hamilton, 2d Duke of *Abercorn* (1838–1913), a friend of Cecil Rhodes, founder of Rhodesia, and first chairman of the British South Africa Company. The town was renamed in 1968, with its new name a Lala one meaning "bullet," "burn mark," referring to some local incident or topographical feature.

Mbalabala. *Town, southern Zimbabwe.* The name is the Ndebele word for the greater kudu, and refers to the granite dome here, fawn with white stripes, the coloring of this animal.

Mbandaka. *Town, western Zaïre.* The town, on the Congo River, probably takes its name from that of a local chief who held authority here before its founding as a colonial center in 1886. Until 1966, in the former Congo Free State (later the Belgian Congo), it was known as *Coquilhatville,* for Camille-Aimé *Coquilhat* (1853–1892), Belgian governor of Congo Free State from 1891 to 1892.

Mbanza Kongo. *Town, northern Angola.* The town, capital of the Congo (or Kongo) kingdom from the 16th to 18th centuries, has a name that relates to this status, meaning "city of the Congo." Its name was recorded as *Ambassa Congo* in 1490 by Portuguese missionaries who built a cathedral and fort here. In about 1530 the town was given the Portuguese name of *São Salvador do Congo,* "St. Savior of the Congo," usually shortened to *São Salvador.* The present name dates from 1980. Cf. **Mbanza-Ngungu.**

Mbanza-Ngungu. *Town, western Zaïre.* The town has a name of exactly the same origin as that of **Mbanza Kongo** (q.v.) in Angola, some 100 miles (160 km) to the southwest. The meaning is therefore "town of the Congo," though in this case more for the Bakongo people than the kingdom to which they gave their name. The town is about 50 miles (80 km) south of the Congo River. The former colonial name of the town was *Thysville,* for Albert *Thys,* Belgian founder of the Compagnie du Congo, a company set up in 1886 to plan a railroad route and explore the commercial possibilities of what was then the Moyen-Congo. The present name was adopted in 1966.

Mberengwa. *Village, southern Zimbabwe.* The name is that of the mountain here, with its own Shona name meaning "the notable one."

Mbini. *Town and port, western continental Equatorial Guinea.* The name is a local form of that of the *Río Benito,* the river at the mouth of which the port stands. The river's own name is Spanish for "Benedictine river" (or "blessed river"), a survival of the years of Spanish rule. The river's name is still found occasionally in use for the port itself.

Mbour. *Coastal town, western Senegal.* The town, south of the capital, Dakar, has a Serer name meaning "royal residence," based on *bur,* "king."

Mbuji-Mayi. *City, southern Zaïre.* The city, a diamond-mining center, has a Swahili name meaning literally "water goat," alluding to a local legend. Until 1966 the name of the city was *Bakwanga,* an ethnic name derived from that of the *Kwango* River.

Mchinji. *Town, western Malawi.* The town, west of the capital, Lilongwe, arose from the fort built here in 1897 by the Chartered Company of Northern Rhodesia to keep the peace on the border between Rhodesia (present Zambia) and French Sudan (now Malawi). It was named *Fort Manning,* for Captain (later Brigadier-General) Sir William *Manning* (1863–1932), appointed deputy commissioner and consul for British Central Africa that year. The present local name means "mountain," "group of hills."

Mecufi. *Coastal village, northeastern Mozambique.* The name may derive from *mkufu* or *mkufe,* "metal necklace," referring to the ornaments made here by local craftsmen.

Médéa. *Town, northern Algeria.* The town is said to take its name from a Roman settlement here called *Mediae* or *Ad Medias,* from Latin *medius,* "middle," supposedly because it lay between two other towns. But the Roman name was actually *Lamida,* and the name evolved from this.

Medina. *Village, west central Senegal.* The village, on the border with Gambia, is one of a number of the names bestowed by Muslim Arabs as a tribute to *Medina,* Saudi Arabia, the second most important holy city of Islam.

Medinet el-Faiyûm. See **El Faiyûm.**

Mediterranean. *Sea bordering coast of North Africa.* The sea forms the entire North African seaboard, and extends along the coasts of Morocco, Algeria, Tunisia, Libya, and Egypt, linking at its western end with the Atlantic by the Strait of Gibraltar, and at its eastern end with the Red Sea by the Suez Canal. It derives its name from Latin *Mediterraneum mare,* "sea in the middle of the land," referring to its geographical location, virtually enclosed by Europe in the west and north, Asia in the east, and Africa in the south. Two other Roman names for it were *Mare internum,* "inner sea," and *Mare nostrum,* "our sea," as it lay at the heart of the Roman Empire. Many European languages translate the name literally, such as German *Mittelmeer,* modern Greek *Mesogeios,* and Russian *Sredizemnoye more.* Arabic names for the sea are *al-baḥr al-mutawassiṭ,* "the middle sea," *al-baḥr ar-rūm,* "the sea of Rome," and *al-baḥr al-abyaḍ,* "the white sea."

Meknès. *City, north central Morocco.* The town, a former capital of Morocco, was founded in the 10th century by the Zanatah tribe of *Miknassa* Berbers, from whom it takes its name. The ethnic name represents Arabic *miknās,* from the root word *kanasa,* "to sweep," "to carry off." Its original fulll Arabic name was *miknās ez-zaitūn,* "Meknes of the olives." The Berbers had founded the town on being attracted to the forests of olive trees here.

Melilla. *Town, northeastern Morocco.* The town, built on a huge rock overlooking the Mediterranean, has been a Spanish possession since 1497. It was colonized by Phoenicians, Greeks, and Romans successively and was originally known as *Russ Adir,* meaning "cape of the cliff." Its present name is based on the Berber root word *mell,* meaning "white," presumably with reference to the color of the rock. Cf. **Beni-Mellal.**

Melkbosstrand. *Coastal village, southwestern Cape Province, South Africa.* The seaside resort, north of Cape Town, has an Afrikaans name meaning "milkbush beach," referring to the plant *Sideroxylon inerme,* which grows abundantly here. The plant has a milky sap.

Melmoth. *Town, east central Natal, South Africa.* The town was founded in 1879 and named for Sir *Melmoth* Osborn (1833–1899), commissioner and chief magistrate of Zululand from 1880 to his death.

Melsetter. See **Chimanimani.**

Memba. *Coastal village, northeastern Mozambique.* The name is said to represent *mbuepa,* "tamarind," although in Chinianja *memba* means "very rich," and the reference could be to some wealthy slavetrader formerly here.

Memel. *Town, northeastern Orange Free State, South Africa.* The town was established in 1911 and given the name of the Prussian town of Memel, now Klaipeda, Lithuania, in the belief that this meant "surrounded by water." The new settlement lay between two streams with marshland to the north. (The European name is actually derived from that of the Neman River, on which the town stands.)

Memphis. *Ruined city, northern Egypt.* The capital of ancient Egypt, renowned as a center of worship to the god Ptah, has a name that is a Greek form of its Egyptian name, *Mennefer,* meaning "his beauty," from *men,* "his," and *nefer,* "beauty" (as for the Egyptian queen *Nefertiti,* famed for *her* beauty). The reference is to the handsomeness of the Pharoah Pepi I, who reigned in the 24th century BC. The city is mentioned several times in the Bible, either as *Noph* (Jeremiah 46:19) or under its more familiar name (Hosea 9:6). It was this ancient city that gave the name of *Memphis,* Tennessee, so named in 1826, either to evoke a place of grandeur or because its location on the Mississippi suggested that of its historic namesake on the Nile.

Menongue. *Town, southern Angola.* The name of the town is that of a former chief here. It was also the name of the town to the 1930s, when it was renamed *Serpa Pinto,* for the Portuguese explorer and colonial administrator Alexandre Alberto da Rocha *Serpa Pinto* (1846–1900), who crossed Africa from west to east in 1877–1879 and became governor of Mozambique in 1889. The old name was readopted in 1980.

Menzel Bourguiba. *Town, northern Tunisia.* The town was founded by the French in the 1880s and named *Ferryville* for the French premier Jules François Camille *Ferry* (1832–1893), who actively encouraged French colonial expansion in Africa. The French evacuated the town's important naval installations on Lake Bizerta in 1963, and it was renamed for Tunisia's first president, Habib ben Ali *Bourguiba* (born 1903). The first word of the name represents Arabic *manzil,* "halting-place," from *nizil,* "to descend," "to alight." Cf. **Borj Bourguiba.**

Meob Bay. *Bay, western Namibia.* The bay, south of Walvis Bay, is said to take its name from that of a prospector here in the early 20th century. However, the actual personal name is disputed, as the placename has also been recorded in the forms *Mitchell's Bay* and *Mutzel Bay.*

Merrivale. *Village, south central Natal, South Africa.* The village is named for Herman *Merrivale,* assistant secretary of state for the colonies in 1848, when the settlement was founded.

Mers el-Kebir. *Town and port, northwestern Algeria.* The name represents Arabic *al-marsā al-kabīr,* "the great port," from *al,* "the," *marsā,* "port," and *kabīr,* "great," "big." It is possible the town was the site of the Roman *Portus Magnus,* in which case the Arabic name translates the Latin. **Oran,** however, immediately to the east, also claims this title, as does Arzew, further east again. The port has long been associated with sea power.

Merweville. *Village, southern Cape Province, South Africa.* The village was established in 1904 and named for a local minister of the Dutch Reformed Church, the Rev. P. van der *Merwe* (1860–1940).

Messina. *Town, northern Transvaal, South Africa.* The copper-mining town was founded in 1904 and has a local name said to represent Venda *musina,* "the spoiler," referring to copper that softened the iron mined here.

Metangula. *Village, northwestern Mozambique.* The village, on Lake Malawi (Lake Nyasa), has a name that is said to be a corruption of *Matangoni,* although the meaning of this is uncertain. From 1938 to 1980, under Portuguese administration, the village was known as *Augusto Cardoso,* for Commandant *Augusto* de Melo Pinto *Cardoso* (1859–1930), the Portuguese naval officer and explorer who crossed Africa with Serpa Pinto (see **Menongue**).

Metil. *Village, northeastern Mozambique.* The village takes its name from the metil tree *(Sterculia quinquelobia)*, of the gum tragacanth genus, which grows locally. The same tree gave the name of **Nametil,** to the north of the village.

Meyerton. *Town, southern Transvaal, South Africa.* The town, south of Johannesburg, was established in 1891 and was probably named for Field Cornet J. P. *Meyer,* a member of the Transvaal Volksraad (administrative assembly).

Mhangura. *Village, northern Zimbabwe.* The name is a Shona word meaning "copper," with reference to the copper mine here.

Mhlambanyati. *Town, western Swaziland.* The town has a Swazi name meaning "buffalo crossing," or "buffaloes' bathing place."

Mhlume. *Town, northeastern Swaziland.* The Swazi name of the town means "good growth," referring to the lush crops cultivated in this low veldt area of the country.

[1]**Middelburg.** *Town, central Cape Province, South Africa.* The town was established in 1852 and was given an Afrikaans name ("middle town") that not only described its location at the center of other settlements (it is almost equidistant from Cradock, Colesberg, Steynsburg, and Richmond) but also commemorated the historic Dutch town of *Middelburg.*

[2]**Middelburg.** *Town, south central Transvaal, South Africa.* The town was founded in 1866 and originally named *Nazareth* for the biblical town associated with the early life of Jesus. In 1874 it was renamed for the historic Dutch town of *Middelburg.*

Middledrift. *Village, Ciskei, Cape Province, South Africa.* The village was founded in 1853 and originally named *Beaconsfield,* apparently for Benjamin Disraeli, 1st Earl of *Beaconsfield* (1804–1881), the British politician (and later prime minister), although he did not assume his title until 1876. The name was confused with that of **Beaconsfield** in the Cape, however, so was changed to its present form, referring to the location of the town at the middle *drift* (ford) over the Keiskamma River.

Midlands. *Province, central Zimbabwe.* The name is descriptive of the location of the province in the center of the country.

Mifraz Shlomo. See **Sharm el-Sheikh.**

Mikindani. *Coastal town, southeastern Tanzania.* The name means literally "[place] by the dances." The town arose on a site where local women regularly danced.

Milo. *Village, southern Tanzania.* The settlement arose in 1902 as a German mission station and was named for *Milow,* Germany, the birthplace of a friend and sponsor of the mission named Bolle.

Mindelo. *City and port, northwestern Cape Verde Islands.* The city, on the northwestern coast of the island of São Vicente, is the largest port in the islands and is named for the port of *Mindelo* in Portugal, north of Oporto. A former alternate name for the Cape Verde port was *Porto Grande,* "big harbor."

Missira. *Village, eastern Senegal.* There are at least two villages of the name in eastern Senegal, as well as *Missirah* near the western coast. The name was given under Islamic influence, and is a borrowing of *miṣr,* the Arabic name of Egypt.

Mlilwane Game Reserve. *Game reserve, western Swaziland.* The Swazi name is that of a mountain here and means "little fire." The reference is to the mountain's iron content, which attracts lightning during summer rainstorms.

Mmabatho. *Capital of Bophuthatswana, South Africa.* The bantustan's capital city has a Tswana name meaning "mother of the people," referring to the dominance of the Tswana here. It was built in 1977, when the black state gained independence.

Mmadinare. *Village, eastern Botswana.* The Tswana name means "mother of buffaloes."

Mobaye. *Town, southern Central African Republic.* The town, by the Ubangi River, which here forms the border with Zaïre, has a local name meaning "place by the river," "port." Across the river in Zaïre, with a name of identical meaning, is **Mobayi-Mbongo.**

Mobayi-Mbongo. *Town, northern Zaïre.* The town, by the Ubangi River, which here forms the border with the Central African Republic, takes the first part of its name from local words meaning "place by the river," "port." The second half of the name, added to distinguish this place from **Mobaye,** which lies across the river in the Central African Republic, derives from the *Bongo* people who inhabit this part of Zaïre. The former name of the town to 1972 was *Banzyville.* This, meaning "town of the Banzys," was given to the settlement founded here in 1889 by the Belgian explorer A. van Gele, who established that the Uele was a headstream of the Ubangi. The *Banzy* people, who also inhabit this northern part of Zaïre, have a name related to that of the *Bangi.* See **Bangui, Ubangi.**

Mobutu Sese Seko, Lake. *Lake, Central Africa.* The lake, divided between Uganda and Zaïre, was so named in 1973 by the Zaïrean president *Mobutu Sese Seko* (born 1930) for himself. Its former name, still found on most maps, was *Lake Albert,* given by the British explorer Samuel Baker, who discovered it in 1864, for Prince *Albert* (1819–1891), consort of Queen Victoria. A local (Lunyoro) name for the lake is *Ruitanzige,* "killer of locusts," presumably because swarms of these insects perish in its waters. (The same name is also found for other lakes.)

Moçambique. See **Mozambique.**

Moçâmedes. See **Namibe.**

Mochudi. *Town, southeastern Botswana.* The town was founded in 1871 by the chief Kgamanyane and takes its name from *Motshodi,* an individual who pioneered the site. The present name evolved as a corrupt form of this.

Mocuba. *Town, north central Mozambique.* The name derives from the local word *nicuba,* "gruel," "porridge." A tradition says that travelers used to eat porridge before crossing the Licungo River here so as not to catch any disease.

Modderfontein. *Town, southern Transvaal, South Africa.* The industrial settlement, northeast of Johannesburg, was established in 1896 and has an Afrikaans name meaning "muddy spring."

Modderpoort. *Village, eastern Orange Free State, South Africa.* The village arose as a mission station in 1868 and has a name meaning "muddy mountain pass," referring to the *poort* (pass) nearby.

Moeris, Lake. *Ancient lake, northern Egypt.* The name goes back through Latin and Greek to Egyptian *mer-ur,* "big lake," from *mer,* "lake," "canal," and *ur,* "big."

Mogadiscio. See **Mogadishu.**

Mogadishu. *Capital of Somalia.* The name represents Arabic *maqdashū* or *muqdishū,* from the root element *qds,* "holy." (Compare *Al-Quds,* "the holy," the Arabic name of Jerusalem, Israel.) The city is one of the oldest settlements on the East African coast, dating from at least the 12th century, and founded by Arab and Persian traders. Until the 17th century the name was also that of a city-state here. It was Mogadishu that, through error, gave the name of **Madagascar.** The name of the capital is sometimes spelled *Mogadiscio,* its Italian form.

Mogador. See **Essaouira.**

Mogokare. See **²Caledor.**

Mohales Hoek. *Town, southwestern Lesotho.* The name derives from that of *Mohale,* half-brother of Moshesh, paramount chief and founder of the Basuto nation in the 1820s. Mohale thus had his *hoek* or "corner" here as his own territory.

Mohammedia. *Town and port, northwestern Morocco.* The coastal town, originally named *Fedala,* was given its present name in the 1960s as a tribute to *Mohammed* V (1909–1961), sultan and king (from 1957) of Morocco, deported by the French in 1953 but restored to power in 1955 and playing a leading role in independent Morocco from 1956.

Mohoro. *Town, eastern Tanzania.* The name is said to mean "town of the timid." The reference is supposedly to the state of panic experienced by local people on hearing an alarm of any kind, even one that turns out to be false.

Mokhotlong. *Village, eastern Lesotho.* The village was founded as a police post in 1905 and named for the river here. Its own name represents a local word for the bald ibis, a wading bird similar to a heron here. The name is also that of the district.

Molepolole. *Town, southeastern Botswana.* The name of the town is said to be Tswana for "seat of judgment," given the settlement by a former chief, Sechele, who lived here as the representative of three tribes. However, a local legend tells how the name originated from a curse placed on the site by a wizard. When the chief decided to build his capital here, the wizard was ordered to remove his curse. Hence the name, allegedly meaning "Let him undo it."

Molteno. *Town, east central Cape Province, South Africa.* The town was founded in 1875 when coal was discovered locally. It was named for Sir John Charles *Molteno* (1814–1886), first prime minister of the Cape, from 1872 to 1878. See also **Claremont.**

Moma. *Coastal village, northeastern Mozambique.* The name of the village was originally *Macone,* apparently from the local word *maca,* meaning "man of salt," "man of the beach," probably the name of a local chief.

Mombasa. *City and port, southern Kenya.* The city was founded by the Arabs in the 11th century, who transferred to the settlement the name of a town in Oman, itself representing Arabic *mumbaṣa,* of uncertain meaning. Mombasa was actually subject to Oman in the 18th century.

Monastir. *Town and port, northeastern Tunisia.* The town has the Arabic name of *al-munastīr,* probably deriving from Latin *monasterium* or Greek *monastērion,* "monastery." If so, the implication is that there was a Christian religious house here before Islam. However, the name has also been documented as *Munāsīr* and *Manāsīr,* and local inhabitants pronounce it *Mistīr.* These suggest that there may be some other origin. The Roman name of the settlement here was *Ruspina,* of Phoenician origin and uncertain meaning.

Monomotapa Empire. *Historic kingdom, Southern Africa.* Maps of

Africa from the 15th to 17th centuries show the name MONOMOTAPA extending across a region today occupied by Zimbabwe and Mozambique. It represents the title of the rulers over this territory during this period, beginning with Nyatsimba Mutota in about 1430. The title, more correctly spelled *Mwene Mutapa,* means "ravager of the lands," and was held by the rulers down to as recently as 1917, although from the 17th century, under colonial administration, their "empire" was much reduced in size and restricted to a small kingdom in the north of what is now Zimbabwe.

Monong. *Village, western Botswana.* The Ngolagola name means "place of salt," referring to the salt pan here in the Kalahari Desert.

Monrovia. *Capital of Liberia.* The country's chief port, on the Atlantic, was founded in 1822 by the American Colonization Society as a haven for freed black slaves. It was named by Robert Goodloe Harper, an original member of the Society, for James *Monroe* (1758–1831), fifth president of the United States. Harper also named **Liberia** itself, and was in turn commemorated in **Harper.**

Montagu. *Town and health resort, southwestern Cape Province, South Africa.* The town, east of Cape Town, was founded in 1850 and named for John *Montagu* (1797–1853), colonial secretary at the Cape from 1843 to his death.

Mont aux Sources. *Peak, Drakensberg Mountains, northern Lesotho.* The peak, near the border between Orange Free State and Natal, South Africa, has a French name meaning "mountain of springs." This was given in 1836 by two French missionaries with reference to the mountain's function as the source of several rivers in southern Africa, including the important Orange, Vaal, and Tugela. The local name for the mountain is *Pofung,* "eland," since these animals were formerly hunted here.

Montserrado. *County, northwestern Liberia.* The coastal county takes its name from Cape *Mesurado,* just south of the capital, Monrovia. The cape's name is a corruption of its original name, *Montserado,* "serrated mountain" (as for the West Indian island *Montserrat*), given by the 15th-century Portuguese navigator Pedro de Sintra. (The name of neighboring **Sierra Leone** was also recorded by de Sintra.) The county has thus revived the original name.

Monze. *Village, southern Zambia.* The village was established in 1938 and is named for a local Tonga leader (not chief) who was the rainmaker at one of the main shrines here in the mid–19th century.

Moodie's Drift. *Ford and pass, Sabi River, eastern Zimbabwe.* The name of the drift (ford) is that of the *Moodie* family who led the pioneer trek through the hills here in 1892 to settle the area round Melsetter (present Chimanimani).

Mooirivier. *Town, central Natal, South Africa.* The town, also known as *Mooi River,* takes its name from the river on which it stands. The name itself means "beautiful," and is generally descriptive of the locality.

Moorreesburg. *Town, southwestern Cape Province, South Africa.* The town was founded in 1879 and named for J. C. le Febre *Moorrees* (1807–1885), minister of the Swartland congregation from 1833 to 1881.

Mopêia Velha. *Village, central Mozambique.* The Portuguese name means "old *Mopêia,*" the basic name representing a local word *peia* meaning "to place," "to rest," referring to a shady tree formerly here where travelers rested, not far from the Zambezi River.

Mopipi. *Village, east central Botswana.* The name, also that of a saltpan here, is the local word for a species of tree, *Boscia foetida.*

Mopti. *Town, south central Mali.* The name of the town is a Mande one meaning "little contact," from *mi,* "that which is touched," "contact," and *piti,* "small," "unimportant." The town is located at the confluence of the Niger and the Bani, and is the place where boat travelers would pause (but not stay) during their journey.

Mora. *Town, northern Cameroon.* The name, more exactly spelled *Moura,* is that of a Mandara chief who took refuge on the hill (also named for him) to the south of the present town.

Moremi Wildlife Reserve. *Wildlife reserve, northern Botswana.* The name commemorates that of Pulane *Moremi,* who in 1961, as the widow of chief Moremi III, founded the reserve here on her tribe's own land. This was the first foundation of a gamepark by an African tribe.

Morgan's Bay. *Coastal village, southeastern Cape Province, South Africa.* The seaside resort takes its name from A. F. *Morgan,* master of the Royal Navy ship *Barracouta* which surveyed the area in 1822.

Morgenzon. *Village, southeastern Transvaal, South Africa.* The village takes its name from that of the farm on which it arose in 1912. The name itself is Afrikaans for "morning sun."

Morija. *Town, western Lesotho.* The town was founded in 1833 by missionaries and named for the biblical Mount *Moriah* (Genesis 22:2), the place of Isaac's sacrifice, identified with the hill on which the temple of Jerusalem was built.

Morocco. *Kingdom, northwestern Africa.* Most European versions of the name, such as French *Maroc,* Spanish *Marruecos,* and German *Marokko,* reflect Arabic *marūkus,* an old form of the name of **Marrakech** (q.v.). The earliest European occurrence of the name appears to be in the *Nibelungenlied* of the late 12th century, in which it is given as *Marroch.* The current Arabic name of the country is *al-magrib al-aqṣā,* "the far west." Cf. **Maghreb.**

Morombé. *Town and port, southwestern Madagascar.* The Malagasy name means "big shore."

Morondava. *Town and port, western Madagascar.* The Malagasy name means literally "[place] which has a long sandbank."

Morrumbala. *Hills, central Mozambique.* The hills, north of the Zambezi, have a name that is said to derive from *morruba,* "animal skin," "pelt," and *uabala,* "to wear." The reference is reportedly to local people who at one time dressed in skins.

Morrumbene. *Coastal village, southeastern Mozambique.* The name represents *morrombe,* the local word for a type of tree found here.

Mosetse. *Village, northeastern Botswana.* The name is of Tswana origin and means "core of a horn." The precise application of the name is uncertain.

Mosi-oa-tunya. See [1]**Victoria Falls.**

Mosopa. *Village, southern Botswana.* The name is that of the local chief who first settled here.

Mossel Bay. *Town and port, southern Cape Province, South Africa.* When the Portuguese navigator Bartholomeu Dias landed here in an inlet of the Indian Ocean in 1488 he called the bay *Angra dos Vaqueiros,* "bay of cowherds," for the many cattle he found on the shore. In 1497 Vasco da Gama reached the area and named the bay *Angra de São Bras,* "St. Bras's bay." The present name of the bay was given in 1601 when the Dutch navigator Paulus van Caerden surveyed the coast and commented on the many mussel shells in the bay. The town of Mossel Bay (Afrikaans *Mosselbaai*) was established in 1848 and was originally called *Aliwal South,* as a commemoration of Sir Harry Smith's victory at Aliwal (see **Aliwal North**). The name was not popular, however, and the townsfolk renamed it for the bay.

Motloutse. *River, Botswana.* The river is a tributary of the Limpopo in the east of the country. Its name is Kalanga in origin, meaning "place where elephants dig holes with their trunks."

Moulay Idriss. *Town, northern Morocco.* The village, west of Fès, takes its name from its founder, *Moulay Idriss* el Akbar ("the elder") (died 792), Morocco's most venerable saint and the great-grandson of Muhammad, the founder of Islam. His tomb lies at the center of the town and is an important object of Muslim pilgrimage.

Mount Ayliff. *Town, Transkei, South Africa.* The town was established in 1878 and is named either for John *Ayliff,* a missionary active here, or William *Ayliff,* a government official, or James *Ayliff,* a local magistrate.

Mount Darwin. *Town, northeastern Zimbabwe.* The town takes its name from the mountain to the southeast. It was itself so named for the naturalist Charles *Darwin* (1809–1892) by the English-born Rhodesian hunter and explorer, Frederick Courtney Selous. The indigenous (Korekore) name for the mountain is *Pfuru,* meaning "one that surpasses."

Mount Fletcher. *Town, Transkei, South Africa.* The town was founded in 1882 and is probably named for the Rev. John *Fletcher* (1729–1785), vicar of Madeley, England, and a friend of John Wesley, founder of Methodism.

Moxico. *Province, eastern Angola.* The name of the province, established as an administrative district in 1917, represents a local word for a basket with a large handle. Such baskets were used by local people for carrying groceries, with the handle slung round the neck and the basket itself carried on the back.

Mozambique. *Republic, southeastern Africa.* The name is probably a corruption of Arabic *mūsā malik,* "Musa king," from *mūsā,* "Musa," the name of a chief (perhaps itself a form of *Moses*), and *malik,* "king." The chief, son of an Arab pirate, was the ruler of what is now the small coral island of *Mozambique,* in the Mozambique Channel, off the northeastern coast of Mozambique, when the Portuguese navigator Vasco da Gama landed there on March 2, 1498. (The historic town and port of *Moçambique* on the island has the same name. Until 1907 it was the capital of Mozambique as a whole.) The name was then transferred by the Portuguese from the island to the mainland territory. Some sources derive the name from the chief's full name, *Musa Mbiki.* Da Gama himself interpreted it as meaning "gathering of boats."

Mphoengs. *Village, southwestern Zimbabwe.* The village, on the border with Botswana, takes its name from that of a local chief. The name itself is of uncertain meaning.

Mqanduli. *Village, Transkei, South Africa.* The village takes its name from a nearby hill, itself said to be named from Xhosa *umqanduli,* "grindstone-maker," referring to a local craftsman.

Msindaji. *Coastal village, eastern Tanzania.* The village, south of Dar es Salaam, has a name that is traditionally explained as follows. Some young local men were sent into battle by their chief. They were defeated, and on their return home were greeted with the words "*mmeshindwaje*?", "What, you were beaten?" From then on their village was known by this name.

Mtakuja. *Village, western Tanzania.* The village, on the eastern shore of Lake Tanganyika, has a name that is said to derive from the local word *mtakuja,* meaning "you come back." The story behind this is as follows. When the original settlers came here, some stayed, while others made to move on further. Those who stayed said to the others, "Why go on? You'll be back!"

Mtarazi Falls. *Waterfall, eastern Zimbabwe.* The falls have a name representing *Mutazari,* "sound of falling water," with reference to their drop over a 600-foot (200-meter) cliff into the Honde River valley.

Mtilikwe. *River, Zimbabwe.* The river, in the southeast of the country, has a name meaning "gatherer," referring to its many tributaries.

Mtito Andei. *Village, southern Kenya.* The village, midway between Nairobi and Mombasa, takes its name from that of the forest here, meaning "forest of vultures."

Mtubatuba. *Town, northeastern Natal, South Africa.* The Zulu name is that of a former local chief, whose name itself is said to mean either "he who was pummeled out," referring to his difficult birth, or "creator of opportunities." The town developed when a crushing mill was built near the coast here in 1916.

Mtunzini. *Coastal village, northeastern Natal, South Africa.* The name is a Zulu word meaning "place of shade," referring to the many shady trees here.

Muembe. *Village, northwestern Mozambique.* The name is the local word for the mango tree, referring specifically to the one planted here by the first Mataka sultan, Niambi, whose subjects consulted him in its shade. When attacked by Europeans in 1912 he fled to Tanganyika.

Mufulira. *Town, north central Zambia.* The local name is that of the large copper mine here, where production began in 1933. The meaning is "place of abundance."

Mufumbiro Mountains. See **Virunga Mountains.**

Muhavura. See **Virunga Mountains.**

Muizenberg. *Town, southwestern Cape Province, South Africa.* The town, now a southern suburb of Cape Town, arose as a cattle post in 1673 and later became a military post for the Dutch East India Company in 1743. The Afrikaans name means literally "Muijs' mountain," for Wynand Willem *Muijs,* sergeant in charge of the post in 1844 and subsequently garrison commander. The name was recorded in 1744 as *Muijzenburg,* "Muijs' town," but this was later modified to *Muijzenberg* and then to the present spelling. An alternate explanation, however, derives the name from that of the *Moetjesons,* a Khoikhoin (Hottentot) group who lived here.

Mukono. *Town, southern Uganda.* The town, just east of the capital, Kampala, is said to take its name from the reply made by local people when asked how they had come by their plentiful produce: "*Mukono gumpadde,*" "From the work of my arm."

Mumias. *Town, western Kenya.* The town takes its name from a local chief, *Mumia,* who came to power in 1880 and died in 1949, allegedly aged 100. The final *-s* may represent an English possessive (as if *Mumia's*).

Mungari. *Village, western Mozambique.* The village, south of Tete, has a name that is probably a Chisema word for the tree *Sterculia appendiculata,* a fine specimen of which once grew here. Alternately, the name could be a corruption of the word *munungari,* a kind of rice *(Combretum imberbe)* known to have been grown here in about 1835.

Munyati. See **Umniati.**

Murchison Falls. See **Kabalega Falls.**

Murchison Falls National Park. See **Kabalega National Park.**

Murema. *Village, northeastern Zimbabwe.* The name means "one who is talked about," apparently referring to a local chief or leader. The name is also that of the district here.

Murraysburg. *Town, south central Cape Province, South Africa.* The town was founded in 1856 and named for two men: the Rev. Andrew *Murray,* Dutch Reformed Church minister at Graaff-Reinet, and Barend O. J. *Burger,* who played a part in the establishment of the town. The latter's name was subsequently assimilated to Dutch *burg,* "town."

Murrupula. *Village, northern Mozambique.* The name may derive from either the local words *orrupa epula,* "to rain," or else from *m'rrupula,* referring to blows made with a knife.

Murzuq. *Town, western Libya.* The name is properly that of the desert south of the town. Its meaning is "sand sea."

Mutare. *Town, eastern Zimbabwe.* The town, near the border with Mozambique, was founded in 1891 and takes its name from the Nyika form of the name of the river on which it lies. This means "river of ore." Until 1982 the town was known as *Umtali,* the Shangaan form of the name.

Mutoko. *Village, northeastern Zimbabwe.* The name is a Shona word for the bambarra nut or groundnut *(Voandzeia subterranea),* found locally. The name is also that of the district here.

Mvuma. *Town, east central Zimbabwe.* The name of the mining town, formerly spelled *Umvuma,* is that of the river on which it stands. It means "place of magic singing," with legendary reference to the sounds of singing, drumming, and cattle lowing heard at the taboo pool here.

Mwami. *Village, northern Zimbabwe.* The name, also that of the river here, is a local word for "boar," "warthog," an animal once common here.

Mwenezi. *Village, southern Zimbabwe.* The name is said to represent *Mwana wezeru,* "child of yesterday," referring to the river here, since in the dry season ("yesterday") it was like an innocent child, but is now a raging torrent.

Mweru, Lake. *Lake, Central Africa.* The lake, divided between Zaïre (on the west) and Zambia (on the east), has a Bantu name meaning "white."

Na'ama. *Town and resort, northeastern Egypt.* The town, at the southern tip of the Sinai Peninsula, has a Hebrew name meaning "pleasant," from the same word that gave the girl's name *Naomi.*

Nababiep. *Village, western Cape Province, South Africa.* The mining center has a name representing two Nama words: *naba,* "animal's neck," and *bib,* "small spring." The reference is to a local feature resembling a neck or hump.

Nabeul. *Town, northeastern Tunisia.* The coastal town originated as a Phoenician settlement. It was destroyed by the Romans in the 2nd century BC, then rebuilt as a Roman colony named *Neapolis* ("new city"). Both the present name and its Arabic equivalent, *nābul,* are a corruption of this.

Naboomspruit. *Town, north central Transvaal, South Africa.* The town, established in 1907, is named for the naboom, the cactus-like plant *Euphorbia ingens,* which grows locally, with Afrikaans *spruit* meaning "stream."

Nabusanke. *Village, south central Uganda.* The village, southwest of the capital, Kampala, has a local name meaning "place of the waxbills," from the placename prefix *na-* (corresponding to Bantu *wa-*), and *busanke,* "waxbills," small red-breasted birds that fly in dense flocks.

Nacala. *Town, northeastern Mozambique.* There are two towns of the name, either side of the Baia Fernão Veloso, an inlet of the Indian Ocean. One, on the eastern side, is simply *Nacala.* The other, to the west, is *Nacala-a-Velha,* the Portuguese suffix meaning "the old." Both take their name from that of the river that flows into the bay here. Its own name may be a Kikua word for the local people, who are Macua in origin. Alternately, the name could represent the local words *na cala,* "place of crabs," although these creatures are not numerous here. A third possibility is a source in Kikua *nacala,* "calm," referring to the calm waters of the bay. Perhaps this is the most likely origin.

Nairobi. *Capital of Kenya.* The city was founded in about 1899 as the site of railroad workshops. It took the name of the valley here, known to the Maasai people as *Enkare Nairobi,* "stream of cold water."

Naivasha. *Town, central Kenya.* The town takes its name from the lake here, whose own name is a corruption of Maasai *e-na-iposha,* "heaving waters."

Nakuru. *Town, west central Kenya.* The town takes its name from the nearby lake. This itself has a name of uncertain origin, perhaps either from a Swahili word meaning "place of the waterbuck," or Maasai in origin and meaning "swirling dust" or "little soda lake."

Nalubale. See Lake **Victoria.**

Namaacha. *Town, southwestern Mozambique.* The town is on the border with Swaziland, and in the latter country is known as *Lomahasha.* This more accurately represents the origin of the name in that of *Lomahasha* Mahlalela, the chief who played an important part in boundary demarcation negotiations here at the end of the 19th century.

Namacurra. *Village, central Mozambique.* The village was originally called *Nadobe,* for the river here. It later gained its present name, from *nama* "hunt," and *curra,* "fatness." The reference is to the abundance of game locally.

Namaqualand. *Coastal region, southwestern Africa.* The region, which extends from near Windhoek, Namibia, into Cape Province, South Africa, takes its name from the Khoikhoin (Hottentot) *Nama* people, whose name is related to, or even derived from, that of the *Namib* Desert, **Namibia.** *Namaqua* is the plural of their name, the final *-qua* meaning "men" and being the same as the *Khoi-* of *Khoikhoin* (whose name thus literally means "men of men").

Nametil. *Town, northeastern Mozambique.* The town takes its name from the metil tree found locally. Cf. **Metil.**

Namibe. *Town and port, southwestern Angola.* The port takes its name from the *Namib* Desert, which itself gave the name of **Namibia,** Angola's southern neighbor. The town was originally known as *Moçâmedes,* for the Barão de Moçâmedes (Baron of Mossâmedes), governor of Portuguese West Africa (present Angola) from 1784 to 1790, the period when the Portuguese first colonized this area. The baron took his title from *Mossâmedes,* in central Brazil, and immigrants from Brazil settled in the African coastal site in 1849. The present name, also that of the province here, was adopted in 1982.

Namibia. *Country, southwestern Africa.* The country takes its name from the *Namib* Desert here, itself said to mean "land where nothing grows" and to be related to the name of the *Nama,* the Khoikhoin (Hottentot) people who also gave the name of **Namaqualand.** The country was annexed by Germany in 1884, and mandated to South Africa in 1920, after which it was usually known as *South West Africa* until 1968. It finally gained independence in 1990.

Nampula. *Town and province, northern Mozambique.* The town, which gave the name of the province, was founded as a military post in 1907. It takes its name from that of a chief here, *Mpula,* whose own name means "rain," since his people, also called the *Mpula* (or *M'vula*), believed they were generated by rain, as fertile crops are.

Namutoni. *Fort and rest camp, northern Namibia.* the name is that of the region here, known to the Ovambo as "high place seen from afar." The fort was built in 1905 and is now part of the Etosha National Park.

Nanyuki. *Town, central Kenya.* The town takes its name from the river on which it lies, known to the Maasai as *Ngare Nanyuki,* "red river."

Napier. *Town, southwestern Cape Province, South Africa.* The town was established in 1838 and is named for Sir George Thomas *Napier* (1784–1855), governor of the Cape from 1837 to 1844.

Narubis. *Village, southern Namibia.* The name derives from *!naru,* the Khoikhoin (Hottentot) word for the tree *Euclea pseudebenus.* (The initial *!* represents a click.)

Nasser, Lake. *Lake, northeastern Africa.* The lake, in southern Egypt and northern Sudan, was formed in the 1960s as a result of the construction of the Aswan High Dam. It was named for Gamal Abdel *Nasser* (1918–1970), Egyptian president from 1956 to 1970 and builder of the Aswan High Dam.

Nata. *Village, northeastern Botswana.* The village takes its name from the river here. Its own name means "drink," referring to it as a source of water for people and animals.

Natal. *Province, eastern South Africa.* The name derives from Portuguese *Costa do Natal,* "Christmas coast," given by the navigator Vasco da Gama to the region here when he discovered it on Christmas Day, December 25, 1497. See also **Durban.**

Natron, Lake. *Lake, northeastern Tanzania.* The lake, on the border with Kenya, is named for its natron deposits. (Natron is a mineral that consists of hydrated sodium carbonate and that occurs in saline deposits and salt lakes such as this. Cf. **Wadi Natrun.**) An alternate name for Lake Natron is *Lake Soda.*

Ncheu. *Town, southwestern Malawi.* The town is an immigration post near the border with Mozambique, and the name represents a Chichewa word meaning simply "border."

N'Dande. *Village, northwestern Senegal.* The village takes its name from Wolof *dandé,* "suitable place to dig a well."

Ndioum. *Village, northern Senegal.* The village, near the border with Mauritania, derives its name from Wolof *ndyum,* "aim," "target," with reference to its location.

N'Djamena. *Capital of Chad.* The name is said to derive from a local word meaning "place of rest," perhaps alluding to a settlement where travelers could take refuge from the extreme heat. The city's name until 1973 was *Fort-Lamy,* for the French soldier and explorer François *Lamy* (1858–1900), killed by Africans at Lake Chad, to the northwest. The city was founded in the year of his death as a French military post.

Ndola. *Town, north central Zambia.* The Lala name of the town means "clear spring."

Ndwedwe. *Village, eastern Natal, South Africa.* The village, north of Durban, has a Zulu name meaning "long bare ridge," referring to the local topography.

Neapolis. See **Nabeul.**

Negomano. *Village, northern Mozambique.* The village, on the border with Tanzania, takes its name from the local word *ngomano,* "confluence," referring to the confluence of the Lugenda and Rovuma rivers here.

Negroland. See **Nigeria.**

Nelspruit. *Town, eastern Transvaal, South Africa.* The town was founded in 1889 and developed when the railroad from Delagoa Bay reached it in 1891. The railroad station was named for the brothers Gert, Andries, and Louis *Nel* who moved to the area each winter and who owned the farm on which the original settlement was laid out. The second part of the name is Afrikaans *spruit,* "watercourse."

Neno. *Village, southwestern Malawi.* The name is believed to derive from Chichewa *nneno,* meaning "large red beads." Perhaps such beads were worn locally, or were traded here.

Nérékoro. *Village, southern Mali.* The Mande or Bambara name means "near the nitta," from *néré,* "nitta" (the tropical tree *Parkia biglobosa*), and *koro,* "near."

New Calabar. See **Calabar.**

Newcastle. *Town, northwestern Natal, South Africa.* The town was founded in 1864 and named for Henry Pelham Fiennes Pelham Clinton, 5th Duke of *Newcastle* (1811–1864), secretary of state for the colonies in 1852 and 1859. The duke took his title from *Newcastle*-under-Lyme, Staffordshire.

New England. *Region, eastern Cape Province, South Africa.* The region, in the Kraai River valley near the southern end of the Drakensberg mountains, was colonized in 1860 by descendants of the British settlers of 1820 and named for their homeland.

New Guelderland. *Village, eastern Natal, South Africa.* The village, northeast of Durban, was established by a Dutch immigrant in 1859 and named for his home province, *Guelderland,* Netherlands.

New Hanover. *Town, central Natal, South Africa.* The town, northeast of Pietermaritzburg, was founded as a German immigrant settlement in 1850 and named for the German city of *Hanover.*

New Republic. See **Vryheid.**

New Valley. *District, southwestern Egypt.* The name, in Arabic *al-wādī al-jadīd,* is that of the governorate established in 1958 in place of the earlier *Southern Desert* governorate (Arabic *aṣ-ṣaḥrā' al-janūbīyah*). There are four oases here, tapping the great water sheet beneath the Libyan Desert. Work on exploiting the region began in the 1970s, but has been slow to proceed.

Ngagane. *Village, northwestern Natal, South Africa.* The name is of Zulu origin, and has been variously interpreted as "unexpected one," referring to the periodic flooding of the river here, as "thorn-tree river," for the acacias that grow on its banks, or as "skeleton river," perhaps with reference to an occasion when a skeleton was discovered.

Ngami. *Lake, northwestern Botswana.* The lake has a name that is said to be a local word meaning simply "big." The San (Bushmen) caled it *Nxhabe,* "place of giraffes," and the Yei knew it as *Ncami,* "place of reeds." The lake gave the name of the district here, *Ngamiland.* See also **Nghabe.**

Ngamiland. See **Ngami.**

Ngelewa. *Village, northeastern Nigeria.* The name means "doorkeeper," presumably itself the name or title of a local chief.

Nghabe. *River, Botswana.* The season river has a name that is probably the same as that of Lake **Ngami,** into which it flows from the east, so means either "giraffes" or "reeds."

Ngqeleni. *Village, Transkei, South Africa.* The name represents the Xhosa word *ngqele,* "frost," "cold." This apparently refers to the stream here, which is actually called the Coldstream.

Nguru. *Town, northeastern Nigeria.* The local name means "[place of] hippopotami."

Ngwane. See **Swaziland.**

Nhlangano. *Town, southwestern Swaziland.* The town was founded by South Africans in 1921, and its Swazi name means "meeting place," from the verb *ukhuhlangana,* "to get together," "to meet." Its original Afrikaans name on its foundation was *Goedgegun,* "gone well" (from *goed,* "good," and *gegun,* "gone," the past participle of *gaan,* "to go"). This appears to indicate a successful migration to Swaziland by a group of Afrikaans Boers.

Niamey. *Capital of Niger.* According to local legend, a chief said to the seven slaves that he had captured, "*oua niammané,*" "Settle here." This then became *Niamma* and eventually *Niamey.* But this account is probably apocryphal. The present city arose from a small fishing village on the Niger River here in the 19th century.

Niassa. *Province, northwestern Mozambique.* The name is the local word meaning "water," "lake," with reference to Lake **Malawi,** which the province borders to the west. See also Lake **Nyasa.**

Niekerkshoop. *Village, central Cape Province, South Africa.* The village was established on a farm in 1902 and named for the *Van Niekerk* brothers who owned it.

Nieuwoudtville. *Town, western Cape Province, South Africa.* The town was founded in 1897 by the Dutch Reformed Church on land owned by the *Nieuwoudt* brothers and was named for them.

Nigel. *Town, southern Transvaal, South Africa.* The town, now a southeastern suburb of Johannesburg, is said to take its name from

Sir Walter Scott's novel, *The Fortunes of Nigel,* which the Afrikaner mining magnate Piet Marais (see **Maraisburg**) was reading when he struck gold here in 1886. He thus named his company the *Nigel* Gold Mining Company, and the name then passed to the town, which was founded in 1909. However, some sources trace the name back to one *Nigel* MacLeish, discoverer of the original mine.

Niger. *Republic, West Africa.* The country is named for the river that flows through its western part. The first Arab travelers here called the river *nahr al-anhur,* "river of rivers," representing a translation of the Tuareg phrase of the same meaning, *egereou n-igereouen,* from *egereou,* "big river," "sea," plural *igereouen.* This implies that the Tuaregs had no actual name as such for the river. The name *Niger* thus probably comes from *n-igereouen.* However, Latin *niger* means "black," and it was probably under the influence of this association that the Arab explorer Leo Africanus recorded the river name as *Niger* in 1526, as if it meant "river of the blacks." His use of the name is the earliest documentation we have of it. In the second century AD, Ptolemy wrote of a river named *Nigeir,* with a name probably of the same origin. But this seems to have been applied to some other river. Pronunciation of the name to rhyme with English "obliger" is purely Western. Nigerians themselves pronounce the name in the French fashion, that is, similar to "Neezhair." See also **Nigeria.**

Nigeria. *Republic, West Africa.* The country takes its name from the *Niger* River, which flows through it from the republic's northern neighbor, **Niger** (q.v.). The name *Nigeria* itself, with its Latin-style suffix, dates from 1899, when under British administration the Niger Coast Protectorate became the Southern Nigeria Protectorate. An earlier general name for this region of West Africa was *Negroland* or *Nigritia,* defined in the first edition of the *Encyclopaedia Britannica* (1771) as a land "bounded by Zaara [Sahara], or the desart [*sic*], on the north, by unknown countries on the east, by Guinea on the south, and by the Atlantic ocean on the west." (This same work defines "Negroes" as "the inhabitants of Nigritia in Africa.") When the British colony of Nigeria was formed in 1914 out of the former Southern Nigeria and Northern Nigeria protectorates, the name *Nigeria* was proposed for it by the wife of the colony's governor-general, Sir Frederick Lugard. (The name seems obvious, but *Nigritia* and *Goldesia* were also contenders. The latter name was intended for Sir George *Goldie,* the British colonial administrator who created the Niger Districts Protectorate in 1885 and who was officially designated "founder of Nigeria.")

Nile. *River, northeastern Africa.* The world's longest river has a name that is one of the oldest in the world, going back to the Semitic root word *nahal,* meaning simply "river." In the Bible, the Nile is never mentioned as such by name, but is always referred to as "the river" (Hebrew *yᵉ'or*), for example: "And it came to pass at the end of two full years, that Pharaoh dreamed; and behold, he stood by the river" (Genesis 41:1). (In Isaiah 23:3 and Jeremiah 2:18, the Nile is referred to as *Sihor,* an Egyptian name meaning "pool of Horus," for the sun god.) In the *Odyssey,* Homer names the Nile as *ho Aiguptos,* with the masculine definite article, while Egypt itself is *hē Aiguptos,* with the feminine. This is because Egypt is the "wife" of the Nile. The Arabic name for the river is either *an-nil* or simply *baḥr*, "sea." Its Egyptian name was *ḥepy* or *ḥeper,* giving Amharic *abbay*, "Nile." *Abbai* (or *Abai* or *Abay*) is today the name of the headstream of the Blue Nile, as it flows from its source in the Ethiopian mountains into Lake Tana. The Nile proper has its source in Lake Victoria, Uganda, and from here northward to Lake Mobutu Sese Seko it is known as the *Victoria Nile*. The section of the river between this lake and Sudan is known as the *Albert Nile*, for the former (or alternate) name of the lake. See also **Blue Nile, White Nile.**

Nivaria. See **Tenerife.**

Nkandla. *Village, north central Natal, South Africa.* The name is believed to derive from the Zulu word *kandla*, "to tire," "to exhaust," perhaps referring to some incident such as a battle.

Nkhata Bay. *Town, north central Malawi.* The town, a port on Lake Malawi, takes its name from a Chichewa word for a grass ring for the head on which burdens can be carried. The exact reference is obscure, but possibly the grass that grew here was suitable for making such rings, or perhaps the curve of the bay suggested a ring shape.

Nkongsamba. *Town, western Cameroon.* The town has a local name meaning "seven hills," referring to its location.

Nkurenkuru. *Village, northern Namibia.* The village, on the Kavango River, which here forms the border with Angola, has a name that is said to mean "old home."

Nogareb. See **Swartberg.**

Nokaneng. *Village, northwestern Botswana.* The village, on the western edge of the Okavango Delta, has a Tswana name meaning "[place] at the small river" or "[place] towards the stream."

Nongoma. *Village, northern Natal, South Africa.* A magistracy was established here in 1887 and was called *Ndwandwe*, for the local tribe. This name was later changed to the present one, that of the chief's principal kraal. Its origin is perhaps in *KwaNongoma*, "place of the witch doctor."

Noordoewer. *Village, southern Namibia.* The village extends for some 12 miles (20 km) along the north bank of the Orange River, here forming the border with South Africa. Its Afrikaans name, meaning "north bank," indicates this location.

Noqui. *Town, northwestern Angola.* The town, on the Zaïre River (here forming the border with Zaïre), takes its name from that of a former local chief, *Nenoqui.*

Northern Rhodesia. See **Zambia.**

Norton. *Village, north central Zimbabwe.* The village, west of the capital, Harare, bears the name of Joseph *Norton*, owner of the farm here on which it arose in the late 19th century.

Norton de Matos. See **Balombo.**

Norvalspont. *Village, northeastern Cape Province, South Africa.* The village on the south bank of the Orange River, here forming the border with Orange Free State, has an Afrikaans name meaning "*Norval*'s ferry," referring to a Scotsman who set up a ferry service here in 1848.

Nossi-Bé. *Island, off northwestern coast of Madagascar.* The island, in the Mozambique Channel, has a Malagasy name meaning "big island," from *nòsy*, "island," and *be*, "big," "many." The name is also spelled *Nosy-Bé*. Cf. **Nosy Radama.**

Nossob. *River, Southern Africa.* The river rises as the two streams *White Nossob* and *Black Nossob* in central Namibia, flowing southeast as a single course to form the border with Botswana and South Africa before entering the Molopo. Its name may be of Khoikhoin (Hottentot) origin and mean "black river," referring to the color of its waters for much of the way.

Nosy-Bé. See **Nossi-Bé.**

Nosy Radama. *Island group, off northwestern coast of Madagascar.* The islands were so named in 1824 for the first king of Madagascar, *Radama* I, who reigned from 1810 to 1828. The first word of the name is Malagasy *nòsy*, "island." Cf. **Nossi-Bé.**

Notsé. *Town, southern Togo.* The name of the town is an Ashanti dialect form of what should properly be *Awodzoe.* This means "eight-town," referring to the eight different districts that make up the town, each having its own individual name.

Nottingham Road. *Village, south central Natal, South Africa.* The village, northwest of Pietermaritzburg, was founded in 1850 and named for the English *Nottinghamshire* Regiment, who were stationed here at that time, when possible conflict with the Basuto was expected.

Nouadhibou. *Town and port, northwestern Mauritania.* The present town, on the Cape Blanc peninsula, was founded by the French in 1905 as *Port-Étienne,* so named for the French colonial official Eugène *Étienne* (1844–1921). In the 1960s it reverted to the original indigenous name of the settlement here, meaning "well of jackals."

Nouakshott. *Capital of Mauritania.* The name represents Arabic *nūʿakshūṭ* or *nūʿakhshūṭ,* perhaps itself deriving from a Berber (Zenaga) dialect phrase *in wakchodh*, "having no ears," from *akchud,* "ear." This presumably described a local chief here at some time. However, some sources translate the name as "place where winds blow," while others prefer "place of floating seashells." The first of these would be appropriate for a town near the coast, in the path of the western trade winds. The city was founded soon after 1900 as a fortified settlement, and its present name dates from 1905.

Noupoort. *Town, central Cape Province, South Africa.* The town has an Afrikaans name meaning "narrow pass," referring to a pass in the Carlton Hills that lie to the northwest.

Nova Chaves. *Village, northern Mozambique.* The Portuguese name means "new *Chaves*," for the town in northern Portugal. This was the hometown not only of the army officer José Júlio Botelho de Castro e Silva, governor of the district of Moçambique at the time the railroad reached here in 1932, but also, coincidentally, of many of the railway construction workers themselves.

Nova Lisboa. See **Huambo.**

Nova Mambone. *Coastal town, eastern Mozambique.* The town, south of Beira, derives the second word of its name from *mambo,* "chief," "place where the chief lives." Portuguese *Nova,* "new," was added to this when the present town was founded in 1921 to replace the rapidly disappearing original settlement of *Mambone.*

Nova Sofala. *Town and port, eastern Mozambique.* The town, with a Portuguese name meaning "New Sofala," was established in 1894 to replace old *Sofala,* itself founded by Portuguese royal charter in 1761. It takes its basic name from Arabic *sufalah,* "lowland." The Arabs used the name for the whole region between the Limpopo and Zambezi rivers. *Sofala* is also the name of the province here.

Nqutu. *Village, north central Natal, South Africa.* The name derives from Zulu *ingqutu*, a word for a type of flat-topped vessel, with descriptive reference to the mountain nearby.

Nsanje. *Town, southern Malawi.* The town was founded here on the Shire River in 1890 and was originally known as *Port Herald*. This seems to have been simply an evocative name, designed to suggest a propitious future for a "pioneer" settlement that was located at the southern approach to the country from Mozambique. When Malawi gained independence in 1964, the name was changed to its present form, a local word for a type of grass found along the Shire.

Ntabamhlope. *Village, western Natal, South Africa.* The village, on the border with Lesotho, takes its name from the mountain here. This has a Zulu name meaning "white mountain," from *ntaba*, "mountain," and *mhlope*, "white," no doubt referring to the mountain's snow cover in winter.

Nubia. *Ancient region, northeastern Africa.* The historic territory extended along the Nile valley in what is now Egypt and Sudan, and corresponded to the biblical **Cush** and to **Ethiopia** as the Greeks understood it. Its name relates to its indigenous people, the *Nubians*, whose own name may derive from Coptic *noubti*, "to weave," referring to the important craft of basket-weaving. Some sources, however, trace the name back to Nubian *nub*, "gold," alluding to another craft, that of fashioning gold ornaments. The ancient name is preserved on the map in that of the *Nubian Desert*, in northeastern Sudan.

Nugaal. *Region, northern Somalia.* The name means "fertile land," referring to the formerly fertile lowlands here. In recent years, however, the name has become a misnomer, since the region has become severely eroded and has lost much of its rich soil and lush vegetation.

Numidia. *Ancient country, North Africa.* The historic region, corresponding roughly to present Algeria, derives its name from its indigenous people, the *Numidians*. Their name is the same as modern *nomad*, as they were a wandering tribe. *Nomad* itself is from a Greek word related to Greek *nemein*, "to pasture," since such people roamed from one pastureland to another.

Nun Entrance. *Mouth of Niger River, southern Nigeria.* The name, that of one of the many mouths of the Niger, was recorded by the Portuguese as *Cabo de Não*, "Cape Nun." The meaning of *Nun* is obscure, but Portuguese *não* means "not," "no," so that the name was popularly interpreted as "Cape Nay," as if the cape itself were a sort of *ne plus ultra*, or point that mariners were unable to pass. A punning Portuguese proverb ran: "*Quem passar o Cabo de Não ou voltarra ou não*," "Whoever passes Cape Nun will either return or not."

Nunez. *Bay, western Guinea.* The bay is named for the small river which flows into the Atlantic here. Its own name commemorates the Portuguese explorer *Nuño* Tristão (killed here in 1443), who discovered Cape Blanc. He also gave his name to the Îles **Tristão**, a short distance up the coast.

Nungo. *Village, northern Mozambique.* The name derives from the local word for "porcupine," equally used by the Makonde people as a name for God.

Nxaunhau. *Village, northwestern Botswana.* The name means "bitter water," referring to a local watercourse.

Nyahururu. *Town, central Kenya.* The town was originally known as *Thomson's Falls,* from the nearby waterfall so named for his father in 1883 by the Scottish explorer Joseph *Thomson* (1858–1895). It took its present local (Maasai) name in 1975.

Nyali. *Residential area, Mombasa, Kenya.* The private residential estate and beach, north of Mombasa Harbor, has a name that is the Swahili word for "clearing." The locality here was cleared in the early years of the 20th century as a sisal estate.

Nyamandhlovu. *Village, southwestern Zimbabwe.* The name is that of a former Matabele (Ndebele) regiment, and derives from *enyamayendhlovu,* "flesh of the elephant." The regiment were garrisoned here and acted as game wardens in the private hunting preserve of Mzilikazi, their headman. The name is also that of the district here.

Nyamwezi. *Region, west central Tanzania.* The name of the plateau here, also spelled *Unyamwezi*, is an ethnic one, for the *Nyamwezi* people who inhabit this region. Their own name means "land of the moon," from Swahili *u*, "land," *nya*, sign of the possessive, and *mwezi*, "moon." The name *Sea of Unyamwezi* (*Lake Uniamesi* on a map of 1863) was used by 19th century European explorers for the vast inland sea that they imagined was here, and of which they reckoned the three separate lakes of Victoria ("Ukerewe"), Tanganyika, and Malawi ("Nyasa") to be a part.

Nyanda. See **Masvingo.**

Nyanga. *Township, southwestern Cape Province, South Africa.* The township, now an eastern district of Cape Town, has a Xhosa name meaning "moon." It was established in 1946 and was given a name designed to match that of nearby *Langa*, whose name means "sun."

Nyangabgwe. See **Francistown.**

Nyanza. *Province, southwestern Kenya.* The province has a Bantu name meaning "lake," referring to its location on the eastern shore of Lake **Victoria** (q.v.). See also Lake **Nyasa**.

Nyasa, Lake. *Lake, Central Africa.* The lake, the third largest in Africa, is at the southern end of the Great Rift Valley, and is bounded on the west and south by Malawi (whose inhabitants call it **Lake Malawi**, as do most modern maps), on the north and northeast by Tanzania, and on the east by Mozambique. For the origin of its name, also spelled *Nyassa*, see **Malawi**. Cf. also **Niassa; Nyanza.**

Nyasaland. See **Malawi.**

Nyassa, Lake. See (1) **Malawi;** (2) Lake **Nyasa.**

Nyika National Park. *National park, northern Malawi.* The game reserve takes its name from the *Nyika* Plateau here. Its own name is a Chichewa word meaning "to steep in liquid," "to tread lightly," with some reference to the local topography.

Nylstroom. *Town, central Transvaal, South Africa.* The town was established in 1866 and named for the river here. The latter was reached by the first white explorers in the 1860s and was given the Afrikaans name meaning "Nile stream," since they apparently took it to be a stretch of the Nile (and the hill now called Kranskop to be a pyramid).

Nzeto. *Town and port, northwestern Angola.* The name appears to derive from that of *Nzeto*, a former chief here. The town was formerly known as *Ambrizete,* "little **Ambriz,**" referring to a port further down the coast. The relationship between the names of the two ports is not altogether clear.

Oasis Magna. See **El-Kharga.**

Odendaalsrus. *Town, north central Orange Free State, South Africa.* The town is named for J. J. *Odendaal*, owner of the farm on which the town was laid out in 1878. The final part of the name represents Afrikaans *rust*, "rest," in the sense "home."

Odzi. *Village, eastern Zimbabwe.* The village takes its name from the river on which it lies. Its own name derives from the local word *kuodza*, "to rot," referring to the damage done to the crops locally when the river floods.

Ogaden. *Region, southeastern Ethiopia.* The region, a desert plateau, has an Amharic name, representing *wĕgaden* or *wŭgaden*. The meaning of this is uncertain.

Ogies. *Village, southeastern Transvaal, South Africa.* The mining settlement takes its name from that of the farm on which it was laid out in 1928. This was *Oogiesfontein*, literally "eye fountain," that is, one with a number of "eyes" or springs.

Ohrigstad. *Town, eastern Transvaal, South Africa.* The town was founded in 1845 and was originally named *Andries-Ohrigstad*, for its founder, the Voortrekker leader *Andries* Hendrik Potgieter (1792–1852), and the Amsterdam merchant Georgius Gerardus *Ohrig* (1806–1852), a friend of the Voortrekkers. The name was later shortened to its present form.

Okahandja. *Town, central Namibia.* The Herero name is that of the river here and means "the small wide one." At this point, the Okahandja is wider than the Swakop River of which it is a tributary.

Okaputa. *Village, northern Namibia.* The name is Herero, and is said to mean "little round place." The reference appears to be to a local custom of building huts all round a waterhole instead of to one side of it, as was more usual.

Okaukuejo. *Village, northern Namibia.* The village, at the western end of the Etosha Pan, has a name of Herero origin perhaps meaning "place of red waters."

Okavango. *River, Southern Africa.* The river rises in central Angola, flows south and east to form a section of the border between Angola and Namibia, then crosses the Caprivi Strip to empty into the *Okavango* basin, a large marsh in northern Botswana. Its name derives from that of the first chief to settle here, *Kavango.*

Okombahe. *Village, northwestern Namibia.* The name of the village, west of Omaruru, is Herero in origin and is said to mean "place of the giraffe," referring to the shape of a nearby mountain.

Old Calabar. See **Calabar.**

Ol Doinyo Orok. *Mountain, southern Kenya.* The mountain, on the border with Tanzania, has a Maasai name meaning "the black mountain."

Ol Doinyo Sapuk. *Mountain, south central Kenya.* The mountain, east of the capital, Nairobi, has a Maasai name meaning "the big mountain." Its Kikuyu name is *Kilima Mbogo,* "buffalo mountain."

Olifants. *River, South Africa.* The name is borne by several rivers in South Africa, with the principal one a tributary of the Limpopo in the Transvaal. In each case the Afrikaans name means "elephant," referring to a region where elephants live or where they were seen on a particular occasion.

Olifantshoek. *Village, north central Cape Province, South Africa.* The Afrikaans name means "elephants' corner," referring to the discovery of elephant bones here when the village was established as a police post in about 1886.

Omaruru. *Town, west central Namibia.* The name probably represents the Herero words *oma-ere*, "sour milk," and *ruru*, "bitter." The reference is said to be to the sour milk produced by the cattle here because they grazed on unsuitable herbage.

Omatako. *Mountain, north central Namibia.* The mountain has a Herero name meaning "buttocks," referring to the shape of its twin peaks.

Ombombo. *Village, northwestern Namibia.* The name is of Herero origin and is said to refer to butterflies or moths.

Omdurman. *City, northeastern Sudan.* The city, one of the "Three Towns" (with Khartoum and Khartoum North), at the confluence of the White Nile and Blue Nile, is Sudan's largest. Its name represents that of the local Muslim saint *Um-Mariyam* (1646–1730), whose tomb is here. Omdurman became a city only after the Mahdi (Muhammad Ahmad) defeated the British in 1885 and made it his capital.

Omitara. *Village, east central Namibia.* The name is of Herero origin and is said to mean "incomplete shelters."

On. See **Heliopolis.**

Ondangwa. *Village, northern Namibia.* The name, of uncertain meaning, is that of a local Ndonga tribe.

Ondekaremba. *Village, central Namibia.* The village, east of the capital, Windhoek, has a name of Herero origin, perhaps meaning "place of reeds."

Onseepkans. *Village, western Cape Province, South Africa.* The village, on the south bank of the Orange River, which here forms the border with Namibia, has a name that is said to be a combination of Khoikhoin (Hottentot) *tconslep*, "projecting elbow," *nias*, "rocky surface," and *tcaans*, "thorn trees," referring to local natural features. At one time the place was known by the Afrikaans name of *Oranjedal*, "orange vale." This relates both to the Orange River and to the oranges grown on the fruit farms here.

Opobo. *Town and port, southern Nigeria.* The town, originally the fishing village of *Ekwanga*, takes its present name from the kingdom set up here in 1870 by a local ruler from neighboring Bonny. He named it for *Opobo*, a king of Bonny, who reigned from 1792 to 1830. The name is also that of the river here.

Opuwo. *Town, northwestern Namibia.* The name is of Herero origin and is said to mean "enough," "sufficient," implying a satisfactory situation or location.

Oran. *City and port, northwestern Algeria.* Algeria's second largest city has a name of Arabic origin. It represents *wahrān*, the name of a medieval Berber chief, itself derived from Berber *iren*, "lions." The town was founded by Arabs from Andalusia in the early 10th century. The original Roman name of the site here on the Mediterranean was *Portus Divinus*, "divine port," or *Portus Magnus*, "great port." (With regard to the latter, see also **Mers el-Kebir**.)

Orange Free State. *Province, central South Africa.* The province lies north of the *Orange* River, and is named for it. The river was so named in 1777 by the Dutch-born Scottish explorer Robert Jacob Gordon in honor of the Dutch royal house of *Orange*. This was itself so named for *Orange*, the historic principality in the south of France, which passed in 1544 to the count of Nassau, familiar as William of *Orange*, otherwise King William III of England. The *Orange Free State* received its name in 1854, when its constitution was framed by the Boers.

Oranjemund. *Coastal town, southern Namibia.* The town lies at the mouth of the Orange River, here forming the border with South Africa. The Afrikaans name thus means "Orange mouth."

Oranjeville. *Town, northern Orange Free State, South Africa.* The town takes its name from the state in which it is (just) situated, close to the border with Transvaal.

Orkney. *Town, southwestern Transvaal, South Africa.* The town, close to the Orange Free State border, arose when rich deposits of gold were discovered here in the late 19th century, and takes its name from a gold mine owned by a Scotsman from the *Orkney* Islands.

Oshakati. *Town, northern Namibia.* The name represents a Ndonga word meaning "in the middle." The town is situated at the point where three regions meet: Ondangwa, Kwanjama, and Ukwanbi.

Oshikango. *Village, northern Namibia.* The village has an Owanbo name meaning "one pan," "single depression."

Oshivelo. *Village, northern Namibia.* The village, at the eastern end of the Etosha Pan, has an Owsambo name meaning "passage," "thoroughfare," referring to its location on the road to Ovamboland.

Oshoek. *Village, southeastern Transvaal, South Africa.* The village, on the border with Swaziland, has an Afrikaans name meaning "ox corner." European gold prospectors entered South Africa at this point and would stop at an inn here while their oxen rested.

Osona. *Village, central Namibia.* The village, just south of Okahandja, has a Herero name that may mean "place of the fat ram."

Otavi. *Town, northern Namibia.* The town's name is a contraction of its original Herero name, *Okutavi,* said to mean "to seek food from an udder," as of a calf butting its mother's teats. The reference is probably to the gushing waters of the fountain nearby, resembling frothing cow's milk.

Otjikondo. *Village, northwestern Namibia.* The Herero name means "place of the *kondo* cattle," *kondo* being a word for an animal's coat that is red or black with a white stripe across the back.

Otjimbingwe. *Village, central Namibia.* The village was founded as a mission station in 1849. Its Herero name is said to mean either "place of refreshment" or "place of the tiger." The former name would refer to a spring here in the Omusema River.

Otjiwarongo. *Town, north central Namibia.* The town has a Herero name meaning "place of fat cattle."

Otjozondjou. *River, Namibia.* The seasonal watercourse, in the northeast of the country, has a Herero name meaning "place of elephants." The river is also known as the *Omuramba Otjozondjou,* the first word of which means "seasonal watercourse."

Ottoshoop. *Village, southwestern Transvaal, South Africa.* The Afrikaans name means "Otto's hope," with reference to Cornelius B. *Otto*, a local magistrate, who expected rich rewards from the gold discovered here in 1875.

Ouadane. *Village, west central Mauritania.* The village and oasis, in the Adrar, is said to take its name from Tuareg *wādān,* plural of *tadant,* the tree *Boscia senegalis.*

Ouagadougou. *Capital of Burkina Faso.* The city is said to take its name from two African languages: Moré *ouaga*, meaning "come," and Dyula *dougou,* meaning "village." But this may simply be an attempt to explain the name, of which the true origin is uncertain. The town was probably founded in the late 15th century. The spelling of the name is due to French influence. The English spelling would be *Wagadugu*, and this is still conventionally used for the Mossi kingdom that existed in this part of Africa from the founding of the town to 1896.

Ouahigouya. *Town, northwestern Burkina Faso.* The town was founded in 1757 as the capital of the former kingdom of Yatenga, now a province. It is said to take its name from the command that Yatenga's king Kango made to his chiefs to pay him homage: "*waka yuguya*," "Come and greet."

Oualata. *Town, southeastern Mauritania.* The name of the town is a Berber form of Mande *wala,* "place of makeshift shelter," from *wa*, "makeshift shelter," and *la*, "place." The reference is to a simple straw roof on poles serving as a market stall and shelter.

Oudtshoorn. *Town, southern Cape Province, South Africa.* The town was founded in 1847 and named for Baron Pieter van Rheede van *Oudtshoorn,* who came to South Africa in 1741 and was appointed governor of the Cape in 1772. He died on his voyage out to the Cape from Holland in 1773.

Ouezzane. *City, northern Morocco.* Ouezzane, one of the holy cities of Islam, founded as a *zawiya* (religious cult center) in the 18th century, has a name that ultimately derives from Arabic *waʿz,* "preaching." An alternate spelling of the name is *Wazzan.*

Ouidah. *Town, southern Benin.* The Portuguese arrived here in 1580 and named the region *da Juda,* implying "kingdom of Judah," for the biblical name. This then became *d'Adjuda,* influenced on the one hand by the name *Ajuda*, a group of hills in eastern Portugal, and on the other by the Portuguese word *ajuda,* "help," explained as referring to the assistance given the settlers in building their fort. The true source of the name, however, is in that of the local king of the Popo people, *Ouéda.* He owned a farm which gave the original African name of the place, *Gléhoué,* "house of the fields," based on *houé,* "house."

Oum el Asel. *Watersource, northwestern Mali.* The name represents Arabic *umm al ʿasel,* "mother of honey," referring to the sweet water of the springs here.

Oum er Rbia. *River, Morocco.* The river, entering the Atlantic near Azemmour, has an Arabic name meaning literally "mother of grass," from *umm*, "mother," and *rabīʿ*, "grass" (implying fresh, spring grass). "Mother" in this sense means "giver," "furnisher." Unusually, the Arabic name has superseded the original Berber one, which was *asif wànsifen,* "river of rivers." (The original Arabic name of the **Niger** has the same meaning.)

Ouossebougou-Bambara. *Village, southwestern Mali.* The village, north of the capital, Bamako, has a name meaning "Bambara place of the reaching of the hole," from Mande *wo*, "hole," "hollow," "cave," *se,* "to arrive at," *bugu,* "place," and the ethnic name. The reference is to a village populated by people who originally lived in caves but who then emerged to build proper huts.

Outeniqua Mountains. *Mountain range, southern Cape Province, South Africa.* The range, known in Afrikaans as *Outeniekwaberge,* has a Khoikhoin (Hottentot) ethnic name meaning "men laden with honey." The reference is to wild bees found locally.

Outjo. *Town, north central Namibia.* The name is said to be of Herero origin. It may be a word for the terraces here, or perhaps refer to something sweet, such as honey or water from the local fountain. The town arose from a German military post set up in 1895.

Ovamboland. *Region, northern Namibia.* The name is that of the *Ovambo* people who live here, their own name being a collective one for eight different tribes.

Oyo. *Town and state, southwestern Nigeria.* The town takes its name from the kingdom founded by a section of the Yoruba people in about 1400. The city of *Old Oyo* arose as its capital in the mid-16th century. This fell to Muslim raiders in 1820s, when the present city was founded to the south. The name itself may derive from the kingdom's first ruler, *Oranyan.* An alternate name of Old Oyo was *Katunga,* said to mean "wall," "building." The name *Yoruba* is believed by some authorities to be a corruption of *Yooba,* meaning "dialect of the *Oyo* people." Others have derived it from a word meaning "meeting-place."

Paarl. *Town, southwestern Cape Province, South Africa.* The name derives from the great domes of rock which crown the ridge overlooking the town, and which were named the *Diamandtende Peerlberg,* "diamond and pearl mountains," by Abraham Gabbema when he saw them glistening with dew in the morning sun one day in 1657. The valley was colonized and called *De Paarl* in 1687, and the present town was founded under this name in 1690.

Padrão, Ponta. *Point, northwestern Angola.* The southern cape of the Zaïre River estuary has a Portuguese name meaning "stone pillar point," from *ponta,* "point," and *padrão,* "stone pillar," "monument." The reference is to a column erected here in 1483, as on all newly discovered lands at this time, by order of King John II of Portugal.

Pagalu. See **Annobón.**

Paiva Couceiro. See **Gambos.**

Palapye. *Village, eastern Botswana.* The name of the village is a corrupt form of *Phalatswe,* referring to the impala antelope that once lived here. Compare the name of **Mahalapye,** a village 45 miles (73 km) to the south.

Palma. *Coastal village, northeastern Mozambique.* The village takes its name from José Raimundo *Palmo* Velho, the Portuguese army officer who directed operations to build a settlement here in 1889.

Palmas, Cape. *Cape, southeastern Liberia.* The cape was originally named *Cabo des Palmas,* "cape of the palmtrees," by Portuguese navigators in the 15th century. The town of Harper, on the cape, was at first itself also named *Cape Palmas.*

Panda. *Village, southern Mozambique.* The village, southwest of Inhambane, was established in 1916. Its name is a Chitsua word meaning "game," "meat," "animal to be hunted." The reference is to the large quantity of game in the region at one time.

Panopolis See **Akhmīm.**

Pansiansi. *Village, northern Tanzania.* The village, just north of Mwanza on the southern shore of Lake Victoria, has a name that is a Swahili corruption of German *Pass Eins,* "Pass No. 1."

Parc National de Bouba Njida. See **Bouba Njida National Park.**

Parc National de la Boucle du Baoulé. See **Boucle du Baoulé National Park.**

Parc National du "W" du Niger. See **"W" National Park.**

Park Rynie. *Coastal town, southeastern Natal, South Africa.* The seaside resort was founded in 1857 and named for *Rynie,* the pet name of Catherine *Renetta* Hoffman, wife of one of the developers here. The popular explanation of the name, that the original estate was damp and "rainy," is a fiction.

Parow. *Residential area, southwestern Cape Province, South Africa.* The area, a municipality east of Cape Town, is named for Johann Heinrich Ferdinand *Parow* (1833–1910), a Prussian ship's captain who was shipwrecked in the Cape in 1865 and who came to own land locally.

Parys. *Town, northern Orange Free State, South Africa.* The town, laid out in 1876, is said to have been named for *Paris,* France (Afrikaans, *Parys*) on the suggestion of a German surveyor who had been present at the siege of Paris in the Franco-Prussian War (1870–1871).

Paternoster. *Coastal village, southwestern Cape Province, South Africa.* The fishing village has a name, Latin for "Our Father," that refers either to the Lord's Prayer or to prayers in general that were offered by Roman Catholic Portuguese seamen when shipwrecked here at some time. Old maps have the name as *St. Martin's Paternoster.*

Paterson. *Village, southeastern Cape Province, South Africa.* The village, northeast of Port Elizabeth, was laid out in 1879 and named for its founder, John *Paterson* (1822–1880), politician and educationist.

Paulpietersburg. *Town, northern Natal, South Africa.* The town was named for the South African president *Paul* Kruger (1825–1904) and his fellow statesman (but political opponent), General *Pieter* Joubert (1831–1900), when it was part of the Transvaal republic in 1888. It was originally known as *Paulpietersrust,* the final part of the name being Afrikaans *rust,* "rest," that is, "home." This was then changed to *Paulpietersdorp,* with Afrikaans *dorp,* "village," and finally to its present form (with *burg,* "town") in 1896. See also **Pietersburg.**

Paul Roux. *Town, eastern Orange Free State, South Africa.* The town was established in 1910 and at first called *Duplessisville,* for Frans *Du Plessis,* a member of the influential South African *Du Plessis* family. It was later renamed for *Paul* Hendrik *Roux* (1862–1911), an Orange Free State general in the second Boer War.

Pearston. *Town, southern Cape Province, South Africa.* The town, on the road between Graaff-Reinet and Somerset East, was established in 1859 by the Dutch Reformed Church and was named for its first minister, the Rev. John *Pears.*

Peddie. *Town, Ciskei, South Africa.* The town arose around Fort *Peddie,* established in 1835 as a frontier post and itself named for Lieutenant-Colonel John *Peddie* (died 1840), who led a force against the Xhosa.

Pella. *Village, western Cape Province, South Africa.* The village, near the border with Namibia, was established as a mission station in about 1806 and given a biblical name, for *Pella*, east of the Jordan, where Christians went after the sacking of Jerusalem in AD 70.

[1]**Pemba.** *Island, eastern Tanzania.* The island, in the Indian Ocean north of Zanzibar, has a name of Bantu origin but unknown meaning. Its Arabic name is *al-jazīra al-khaḍrā',* "the green island," implying that it is more fertile than Zanzibar.

[2]**Pemba.** *Town and port, northeastern Mozambique.* The name of the town is the same as that of the mountain of *Pemba* near Tete, in the far west of the country, and represents Zulu *pemba,* meaning "to ignite," "to take action" (as in battle), referring to some natural or human activity associated with the place. Until 1976 the town was known as *Porto Amélia,* a name given it in 1899 for Queen *Amélia* of Portugal, who had entrusted the building of the settlement to the Niassa Company as a future capital of Portuguese Nyasaland. The name was approved by the queen's husband, Carlos (Charles) I, king of Portugal from 1889 to 1908.

Penhalonga. *Town, eastern Zimbabwe.* The mining town, near the border with Mozambique, takes its name from a gold mine opened in about 1890. It is named for Count *Penhalonga,* an official of the Mozambique Company of Portugal that ran the mining activities here. The name also happens to translate appropriately as "long rock," from Portuguese *penha,* "rock," and *longa,* "long."

Pentapolis. *Ancient city group, North Africa.* The name represents Greek *pente,* "five," and *polis,* "city." The "five cities," in Cyrenaica, in what is now eastern Libya, were Apollonia, Arsinoë (modern **El Faiyûm**), Berenice (modern **Benghazi**), **Cyrene** itself, the capital, and Ptolemaïs (now **Tolmeta**).

Perdekop. *Village, southeastern Transvaal, South Africa.* The name is a form of Afrikaans *Paardekop,* "horses' hill," referring to a custom of keeping horses on hill slopes here when sickness prevailed among them in the lower pastures.

Petit-Bassam. See (1) **Grand Bassam**; (2) **Port-Bouët.**

Petit Popo. See **Aného.**

Petrusberg. *Town, western Orange Free State, South Africa.* The town was established on a farm in 1891 and named for its owner, *Petrus* Albertus Venter.

Petrus Steyn. *Town, northeastern Orange Free State, South Africa.* The town was established on a farm in 1914 and named for its owner, *Petrus Steyn.*

Petrusville. *Town, east central Cape Province, South Africa.* The town, south of the Orange River, takes its name from *Petrus* Jacobus van der Walt, owner of the farm on which it was developed by his sons in 1877.

Pfuru. See **Mount Darwin.**

Phalaborwa. *Town, northeastern Transvaal, South Africa.* The name refers to the local Mmakao people, who were known as the *Ba-Phalaborwa,* "better-than-the-south people." The town arose as one of the tribe's mining centers, with modern development dating only from 1951.

Pharos. *Peninsula, northern Egypt.* The name is that of a former island off Alexandria on which was located a famous lighthouse, one of the Seven Wonders of the World, built in about 280 BC. The name is of unknown origin, but gave that of the lighthouse itself. As a result, the Greek word for "lighthouse" was *pharos* and the Latin, *pharus.* In modern times, these have given the words for both "lighthouse" and "headlight" in various (mainly Romance) languages, such as French *phare,* Italian and Spanish *faro,* Portuguese *farol,* and the like. The original name is unlikely to be related to Greek *phanos,* "bright," "light," since the island name predates that of the lighthouse.

Philadelphia. *Village, southwestern Cape Province, South Africa.* The village, north of Cape Town, was founded by the Dutch Reformed Church in 1863 and given a biblical name (Revelation 1:11) popularly interpreted as meaning "brotherly love" (but actually meaning "loving the brethren").

Philae. *Island, Nile River, southeastern Egypt.* The island, just south of the Aswan Dam, has a name of Greek origin that has (falsely) become associated with *philos,* "loved," "pleasing." However, it actually represents the Coptic original *Pilak,* meaning "corner," "end," probably referring to the island's location on the border with Nubia. Arabic names for Philae include *jazīrat fīlah,* "island of Philae," and *jazīrat anas al-wujūd,* "island of Anas el-Wujud." The latter, with name traditionally interpreted as "delight of the world," is the hero of one of the tales in the *Arabian Nights,* who traces his beloved to the island, where she has been locked up by her father, only to find that she has escaped. Yet another name is *jazīrat al-birba,* "island of the temple," with reference to the famous Temple of Isis (removed to the nearby island of Agilka when Philae was submerged during construction of the Aswan Dam).

Philippeville. See **Skikda.**

Philippolis. *Town, southwestern Orange Free State, South Africa.* The town, the oldest in the province, was founded in 1823 by Dr. John *Philip* of the London Missionary Society to serve the Bushmen. It was given his name, using the Greek suffix *-polis* to mean "town" and perhaps to add a general biblical or classical flavor. (The New Testament has *Philippi,* and *Philippopolis* was the Greek name of Plovdiv, Bulgaria.)

Philipstown. *Town, central Cape Province, South Africa.* The town was laid out in 1863 and named for Sir *Philip* Edmond Wodehouse (1811–1887), governor of the Cape from 1861 to 1870.

Pico. *Island, central Azores.* The island has a Portuguese name meaning "peak." The reference is to the island's conical volcano of the same name, higher than any other mountain in the group. The volcano itself is called *Pico Alto,* "high peak."

Pienaar's River. *Town, central Transvaal, South Africa.* The town, established in 1908, takes its name from the river here, itself said to be named for a local pioneer surnamed *Pienaar.* The Afrikaans form of the placename is *Pienaarsrivier.*

Pietermaritzburg. *Capital of Natal, South Africa.* The city was established in 1838 and named for the Voortrekker (Afrikaner settler) leaders *Pieter* (Piet) Retief (1780–1838) (see **Piet Retief**) and Gerhardus Marthinus (Gerrit) *Maritz* (1798–1839). Both men died young: Retief treacherously murdered by the Zulu king Dingane; Maritz of injuries sustained in the war against the Zulus after Retief's death. The rather long and awkward name is popularly shortened to *Maritzburg.*

Pietersburg. *Town, north central Transvaal, South Africa.* The town was founded in 1884 and named for General *Pieter* Joubert (1834–1900), the soldier and statesman who commanded the Boer forces in the war of 1880–1881. See also **Paulpietersburg.**

Piet Retief. *Town, southeastern Transvaal, South Africa.* The town was established in 1882 and named commemoratively for the Voortrekker leader Pieter *(Piet) Retief* (1780–1838). See also **Pietermaritzburg.**

Piggs Peak. *Town, northwestern Swaziland.* The town takes its name from the prospector William *Pigg,* who discovered gold here in 1884. The discovery led to the establishment of *Pigg's Peak Mine,* the richest source of gold in the country's history.

Piketberg. *Town, southwestern Cape Province, South Africa.* The name refers to the military outpost or picket (Dutch *piket*) placed here in the 1670s to prevent possible Khoikhoin (Hottentot) inroads into the Cape. The present name was initially that of the nearby mountain (Dutch *berg*), and passed to the town on its foundation in 1835.

Pilanesberg. *Mountain, Bophuthatswana, South Africa.* The name means "Pilane's mountain," for *Pilane*, a Tswana chief who held territory here. His own name is said to mean "eland."

Pilgrims Rest. *Town, eastern Transvaal, South Africa.* The area here was established as a gold diggers' camp in about 1870, and was given an apparently punning name referring to the "pilgrims" (goldseekers) who settled here.

Pinetown. *Town, southeastern Natal, South Africa.* The town, west of Durban, was laid out on a farm in 1847 and in 1849 given its present name, for Sir Benjamin *Pine* (1809–1891), lieutenant-governor of Natal from 1849 to 1856 and governor from 1873 to 1875.

Pithom. See **El Tell el-Maskhutah.**

Plateaux. *Region, central Congo.* The region's name represents French *plateaux*, referring to the series of plateaus that extend here from the western mountains to the Congo River in the east.

Plettenberg Bay. *Coastal town, southern Cape Province, South Africa.* The seaside resort takes its name from the bay here, itself named for Joachim van *Plettenberg* (1739–1793), governor of the Cape from 1774 to 1785, who erected a beacon here in 1778. Portuguese explorers knew the bay by different names, such as *Angra dos Alagões*, "bay of lagoons," or *Bahia Formosa,* "beautiful bay."

Plumtree. *Village, southwestern Zimbabwe.* The village, on the border with Botswana, arose in 1897 when the railroad was built from South Africa northwards through Bechuanaland (modern Botswana) to Bulawayo, Rhodesia (Zimbabwe). Its name refers to a large marula tree here (see **Marula**).

Pniel. *Village, southwestern Cape Province, South Africa.* The village, east of Cape Town, was founded as a mission station in 1843 and given a biblical name, that of *Peniel* (Genesis 32:30), meaning "face of God."

Po. *Town, southern Burkina Faso.* According to legend, the town was founded around 1500 by Nablogo, a Mossi man who cultivated a field (*po*) here.

Podor. *Town, northern Senegal.* The town, on the Senegal River, is said to derive its name from French *pot d'or*, "pot of gold." The origin is suspect, although it is known that gold was at one time brought downriver to this point.

Pofadder. *Town, western Cape Province, South Africa.* The town arose as a mission station in 1875 and was named for the Korana chief Klaas *Pofadder,* whose own name is Afrikaans for "puff adder." The name was not to the liking of the white settlers who came here in 1889, so they changed it in 1917 to *Theronsville,* for T. P. *Theron,* a local politician. The original name was restored, however, in 1936.

Pofung. See **Mont aux Sources.**

Pomeroy. *Town, central Natal, South Africa.* The town takes its name from the British army officer Sir George *Pomeroy* Colley (1835–1881), governor of Natal from 1880 to 1881, who was killed in combat against the Boers.

Pondoland. *Former region, Transkei, South Africa.* The region took its name from the *Pondo* people who inhabited it. It existed as an official administrative territory from 1844 to 1910, when the Union of South Africa was formed and it ceased to exist. The Pondo are still here, however.

Pongola. *River, South Africa.* The river flows east along the border between Transvaal and Natal to unite with the Usutu and so form the Maputo in Mozambique. Its name represents the local word *phongolo,* "trough-like," since it is a lengthy river with few crossing places.

Ponta Delgada. *Town and port, São Miguel, Azores.* The town, on the south of the island, has a Portuguese name meaning "fine point," referring to the narrow headland originally here. A coastal village on the island of Flores has the same name.

Ponthierville. See **Ubundu.**

Pool. *Region, southeastern Congo.* The name comes from that of *Pool* Malebo, the lakelike expansion of the Congo River that forms the region's (and country's) southeastern border. The earlier name of the lake was *Stanley Pool,* for the British explorer, Sir Henry Morton *Stanley* (1841–1904), who discovered and named it in 1877. He duly recorded the event, the name itself being proposed by Frank Pocock, a member of his expedition: "Frank ... said, 'Why, I declare, sir, this place is just like a pool; as broad as it is long. There are mountains all round it, and it appears to me almost circular.' 'Well, if it is a pool, we must distinguish it by some name. Give me a suitable name for it, Frank.' 'Why not call it "Stanley Pool"?' ... In accordance with Frank's suggestion I have named this lake-like expansion of the river ... the Stanley Pool" (*Through the Dark Continent,* 1878). In 1972 the lake was renamed as now, the local name already being in use in neighboring Zaïre.

Pool Malebo. See **Pool.**

Port Alfred. *Town and port, southeastern Cape Province, South Africa.* The town was established in 1825 and originally named *Port Frances,* for the wife of Colonel Henry Somerset, son of Lord Charles Somerset, governor of the Cape. After the visit in 1860 of Prince *Alfred* (1844–1900), Queen Victoria's second son, the place was renamed in his honor. See also **Somerset East.**

Port Beaufort. *Coastal village, southwestern Cape Province, South Africa.* The seaside resort was founded in about 1816 and was so named by the governor of the Cape, Lord Charles Somerset (see **Somerset East**) for his father, the Duke of *Beaufort* (see **Beaufort West**).

Port Bell. *Town and port, southern Uganda.* The town, on the northern shore of Lake Victoria, southeast of the capital, Kampala, takes its name from Sir Hesketh *Bell* (1864–1952), first governor of Uganda. The town was founded in 1908, during his governorship (from 1907 to 1910).

Port-Bouët. *Town and port, southern Côte d'Ivoire.* The town, on the southern side of a lagoon opposite the capital, Abidjan, was so named in 1904 for the French admiral and explorer, Count Louis *Bouët*-Willaumez (1808–1871), governor of Senegal in 1843. The name replaced the earlier one of *Petit-Bassam* (see **Grand Bassam**).

Port Durnford. *Coastal village, eastern Natal, South Africa.* The village arose round an anchorage in about 1852 and is said to be named either for Midshipman E. P. *Durnford,* who surveyed the coast here in about 1822, or for the British army officer Anthony William *Durnford* (1830–1879), who went to South Africa in 1871 and was killed in the Zulu War. The latter's exploits appear to be too late for the name, however.

Port Edward. *Coastal village, southern Natal, South Africa.* The seaside resort was established in 1924 and named for *Edward,* Prince of Wales, later (briefly) King Edward VIII of England (1894–1972), and after his abdication more familiar as the Duke of Windsor.

Port Elizabeth. *City and port, southeastern Cape Province, South Africa.* The city arose as a military station founded in 1799. It was originally named *Port Frederick,* for *Frederick* Augustus, Duke of York and Albany (1763–1827), second son of King George III of England. In 1820, on the arrival of the Settlers (the 5000 British immigrants who came to Algoa Bay that year), it was renamed by Sir Rufane Donkin, acting governor of the Cape, for his late wife, *Elizabeth* Frances, née Markham, who had died two years earlier at the age of 28.

Porterville. *Town, southwestern Cape Province, South Africa.* The town was laid out on a farm in 1863 and named by its owner for William *Porter* (1805–1880), Irish attorney-general of the Cape from 1839 to 1866.

Port-Étienne. See **Nouadhibou.**

Port-Francqui. See **Ilebo.**

Port Fuad. *Town and port, northeastern Egypt.* The town and port at the northern end of the Suez Canal, opposite Port Said, was established in 1926 and named for *Fuad* I (1868–1936), first king of Egypt (from 1922) and youngest son of Ismail Pasha (see **Ismailia**). The Arabic name of the port is *būr fu'ād,* the first word of which represents English *port.* See also **Port Said, Port Taufiq.**

Port-Gentil. *City and port, western Gabon.* The present city arose from various French commercial houses established here at the mouth of the Ogooué River in the late 19th century. It takes its name from the French colonial administrator Émile *Gentil* (1866–1914), governor of the French Congo from 1904 to 1908.

Port Harcourt. *City and port, southern Nigeria.* The country's second largest port, on the Niger Delta, was founded in 1912 and named for the British colonial secretary, Lewis *Harcourt,* first Viscount Harcourt (1863–1922).

Port Herald. See **Nsanje.**

Port Louis. *Capital of Mauritius.* The city and port was founded in about 1736 by the French and named in honor of King *Louis* XV of France (1710–1774).

Port-Lyautey. See **Kenitra.**

Port Nolloth. *Town and port, northwestern Cape Province, South Africa.* The town, at the mouth of the Orange River, originally took its name from the bay here, as *Robbe Bay,* "seal bay." It was given its present name in 1855 by Sir George Grey, governor of the Cape, in honor of Commander M. S. *Nolloth,* captain of the ship HMS *Frolic,* which had carried out a survey of Namaqualand the previous year.

Porto Amélia. See **²Pemba.**

Porto Novo. *Capital of Benin.* The city and port was settled by the Portuguese in the 16th century as a center of the slave trade with a name meaning "new port." The port was "new" as a result of the merging of the two existing coastal villages.

Porto Santo. *Island, northeast of Madeira.* The island was discovered and settled by the Portuguese in the first half of the 15th century. They named the bay on its southern side *Porto Santo,* "blessed harbor," as it offered a safe anchorage. The island's main port, *Vila de Porto Santo* or *Porto Santo* (or just *Vila*), is on the bay.

Port Said. *City and port, northern Egypt.* The port, at the northern entrance to the Suez Canal, was founded in 1859 when construction of the canal began. It was named for *Said* Pasha (1822–1863), viceroy of Egypt, who in 1854 granted a concession for the enterprise to the French diplomat Ferdinand de Lesseps and who decided the site of the town. The Arabic name of the city is *būr saʿīd.* The first word of this represents English *port.* The second word is the proper Arabic form of *Said* Pasha's name, meaning "happy," "fortunate." Said Pasha was succeeded as viceroy by his nephew, Ismail Pasha (see **Ismailia**). See also **Port Fuad; Port Taufiq.**

Port St. Johns. See **Umzimvubu.**

Port Shepstone. *Town and port, southern Natal, South Africa.* The site here by the Indian Ocean was surveyed in 1867 and named *South Shepstone,* for Sir Theophilus *Shepstone* (1817–1893), secretary for native affairs from 1856 and administrator of Zululand from 1884. The town was created a full fiscal port in 1893 and given its present name then.

Port Sudan. *City and port, northeastern Sudan.* The city was built between 1905 and 1909 on the Red Sea coast to replace the historic Arab port of Suakin to the south, which by then was abandoned and choked with coral. It takes its name from **Sudan,** the country whose principal port it remains today. The Arabic name of the city is *būr sūdān,* the first word of which represents English *port.*

Port Taufiq. *Town and port, northeastern Egypt.* The town is the port for Suez at the southern end of the Suez Canal. It is named for Muhammed *Tawfiq* Pasha (1852–1892), eldest son of Ismail Pasha (see **Ismailia**), whom he succeeded as khedive of Egypt in 1879. The Arabic name of the town is *būr tawfīq,* the first word representing English *port.* See also **Port Said; Port Fuad.**

Portuguese Guinea. See **Guinea-Bissau.**

Portuguese West Africa. See **Angola.**

Portus Divinus. See **Oran.**

Portus Magnus. See (1) **Mers el-Kebir**; (2) **Oran.**

Port Victoria. *Village and port, southwestern Kenya.* The village, named for Queen *Victoria* of England, was originally planned as the terminus on Lake Victoria of the Uganda Railway.

Postmasburg. *Town, north central Cape Province, South Africa.* The town arose as a mission station of the London Missionary Society named *Sibiling.* A village then developed under the Afrikaans name of *Blinkklip,* "shining rock." Finally, the settlement received its present name in 1890, for the Rev. Dirk *Postma* (1818–1890), founder of the "Dopper" section of the Dutch Reformed Church in 1859.

Potchefstroom. *Town, southern Transvaal, South Africa.* The town, the oldest in the Transvaal, was founded in 1838 by the Boer leader Andries Hendrik *Potgieter* (1792–1852) (see **Potgietersrust**) and the name is apparently based on his. The origin of the elements *chef* and *stroom* remains uncertain. Some authorities trace them to the names of two other Boer leaders: *Scherl* and *Stockenstroom* (see **Stockenstroom**). But possibly *chef* means simply "leader," and *stroom* ("stream") refers to the Mooi River on which the town lies. A source for the name in Dutch *potscherf,* "potsherd," seems unlikely, although pottery fragments are said to have been found by the river here.

Potgietersrus. *Town, central Transvaal, South Africa.* The town arose in 1852 on a site named *Makapan's Poort,* for a local chief, *Makapan.* The new settlement was at first named *Vredenburg,* "town of peace," alluding to the reconciliation between the Voortrekker leaders Andries Hendrik Potgieter and Andries Pretorius, who had disagreed on policy. In 1858 the settlement was renamed *Piet-Potgietersrust,* for *Pieter*, son of Andries Hendrik Potgieter, who had been killed in 1854 at the entrance to Makapan's cave when fighting against the chief. The town was then abandoned for some years, following sickness and warring, and reestablished in 1870 with its present name. The final *-rus,* representing Afrikaans *rust,* "rest" (the *t* was dropped in 1939), marks the resting place of the murdered Pieter Potgieter.

Praia. *Capital of Cape Verde.* The city, on the south coast of the island of São Tiago, was founded by the Portuguese in the late 15th century and has a name that is the Portuguese word for "beach," "shore" (related to Spanish *playa* and French *plage*).

Praslin. *Island, northern Seychelles.* The second largest island in the group (after Mahé) is named for the French officer and diplomat Gabriel de Choiseul-Chevigny, Duc de *Praslin* (1712–1785), who reorganized the French navy in preparation for war with Britain. See **Seychelles** for the islands' French background.

Pretoria. *Capital of Transvaal, South Africa.* The city, the administrative capital of the country as a whole, was founded in 1855 and named for the Voortrekker leader Andries Wilhelmus Jacobus *Pretorius* (1798–1853) by his son, Marthinus Wessel Pretorius. The name of the province's capital appropriately, but only coincidentally, suggests Latin *praetorium,* the term for the official residence of the Roman governor of a province.

Prieska. *Town, north central Cape Province, South Africa.* The name has been recorded in various forms over the years, such as *Priskab* (1805), *Brieskap* (1822), and *Briesschap* (1854). All these are corruptions of the Korana words *beris*, "goat," and *ga,* "lost," so that the name literally means "place of the lost shegoat." The reference seems to be to a particular incident, perhaps when some goats were being driven across the Orange River here.

Prince Albert. *Town, southern Cape Province, South Africa.* The town was founded in 1843 and named for *Prince Albert* (1819–1861), consort of Queen Victoria of England.

Prince Alfred Hamlet. *Village, southwestern Cape Province, South Africa.* The village, northeast of Cape Town, was founded in 1861 and named for *Prince Alfred* (1844–1900), second son of Queen Victoria, after his visit to South Africa the previous year as a young midshipman in the Royal Navy.

Prince Edward Islands. *Islands, southern Indian Ocean.* The islands, which belong to South Africa, are situated some 1180 miles (1900 km) southeast of Cape Town. There are two islands in the group: *Prince Edward Island* itself (the smaller) and *Marion Island* (the larger). They were discovered in 1772 by the French explorer and surveyor *Marion* du Fresne, who named one *Île de l'Espérance* ("island of hope") and the other *Île de la Caverne* ("cave island"). He could not land on either, however, so gave the islands the joint name of *Îles des Froids* ("islands of cold"). Captain Cook then came on the islands in 1776, unaware of du Fresne's discovery, and named them *Prince Edward Islands* for *Prince Edward* Augustus (1767–1820), fourth son of King George III of England. He subsequently learned of du Fresne's expedition and renamed the southern island for him as *Marion Island*. After World War II, Britain and South Africa agreed that the island group should be annexed by South Africa. Marion was acquired in 1947, and Prince Edward in 1948.

Príncipe. *Island, São Tomé e Príncipe.* The island, in the Gulf of Guinea, was colonized by the Portuguese in the 15th century and named by them *Ilha do Príncipe,* "Prince Island," in honor of Prince *Afonso,* the future King Afonso V of Portugal (1432–1481).

Protem. *Village, southwestern Cape Province, South Africa.* The village, east of Cape Town, has a name that is a colloquial shortening of the Latin phrase *pro tempore,* "for the time being." The place was originally planned as a temporary railroad junction.

Ptolemaïs. See **Tolmeta.**

Pugu. *Village, eastern Tanzania.* The village, west of Dar es Salaam, has a name that is a local word for a hole in a sack. The reference is to a place located in a hollow, with its surrounding rice fields like rice spilling from a hole in a sack.

Pungo Andongo. *Village, west central Angola.* The second part of the name relates to the *N'Dongo* people who inhabited the region at one time. The first word is probably the name of a local headman or leader.

Qachas Nek. *Town and district, southeastern Lesotho.* The name commemorates *Ngasha (Qacha),* the San (Bushman) name for the son of chief Morosi. His own name means "hide away," since Nqasha used the *nek* (Afrikaans, "pass") as a refuge.

Qamata. *Town, Transkei, South Africa.* The name is believed to be a Xhosa adaptation of the name of a Khoikhoin (Hottentot) deity.

Qantara. See **El Qantara.**

Qena. *Town, eastern Egypt.* The town, east of the Nile River, has a name that is a corruption of its original Greek name of *Caene.* This represents Greek *kainē,* "new," since the town arose later than *Coptos* (now **Qift**), 14 miles (23 km) to the south.

Qift. *Town, eastern Egypt.* The town, on the east bank of the Nile River, was known to the ancient Egyptians as *Qebt,* which gave both its former name of *Koptos* or *Coptos* and its present name. This did not itself give the name *Copt* for an ancient Egyptian (or member of the Coptic Church), since this derives from Greek *Aiguptos,* "Egypt." It did become associated with the name, however. See also **Qena.**

Quathlamba. See **Drakensberg.**

Queenstown. *Town, eastern Cape Province, South Africa.* The town was founded in 1853 and named in honor of *Queen* Victoria of England (1819–1901).

Quelimane. *Town and port, eastern Mozambique.* The town has had its name recorded variously in the past as *Kilimane, Quilimane,* and *Quiliamo,* the last on a map of 1740. The name is popularly derived from English *kill man,* allegedly with reference to the town's unhealthy location on the left bank of the river. It probably represents Swahili *kilima,* however, meaning "mountain" (compare **Kilimanjaro**), or is the name of a tribe who themselves came from a mountain and settled here.

Que Que. See **Kwekwe.**

Quibala. *Town, western Angola.* The town, founded in 1928, has a local name meaning "great bald one," referring to stones here that resemble bald heads.

Qumbu. *Town, Transkei, South Africa.* The town, established in 1876, is said to have a Xhosa name originating during a tribal war when the corn was coming into full ear, with *amazimba aqumbu* meaning "the corn has budded," "the corn is swollen."

Quthing. *Village, southwestern Lesotho.* The former name of the village was *Moyeni,* meaning "windy place." Its present name is said to represent San (Bushman) *Phuthing,* "land of the *Baphuti,*" with reference to a local tribe. The name is also that of a river and district here.

Qwaqwa. *Bantustan, eastern Orange Free State, South Africa.* The Bantu homeland, bordering northern Lesotho, became self-governing in 1974 as the territory of the *BaSotho ba Borwa,* "Sotho people of the south." Its name means "whiter than white," referring to the light-colored sandstone hills here. The land was formerly known as *Witsieshoek,* the name of a settlement here. This means "Witsie's corner," for a chief called *Witzie* or *Whetse* who was defeated here in about 1857.

Rabat. *Capital of Morocco.* The name represents Arabic *ar-ribāṭ,* "the ribat," from *al,* "the," and *ribāṭ,* "ribat," a fortified Islamic monastery. (The word is related to *marabout* as a term for a Muslim holy man or hermit.) The city, on the Atlantic coast, arose on the site of such a monastery established in the 12th century by Abd-al-Mumin, founder of the Almohad dynasty of Muslims. Abu Yusuf Yaqub al-Mansur, his grandson, enlarged the town by building city walls and erecting what he intended to be the largest mosque in the world. At the same time he extended its name as *ar-ribāṭ al-fatḥ,* "ribat of the victory," commemorating his defeat of the Spanish army at Alarcos in 1195.

Rakops. *Village, central Botswana.* The village takes its name from that of *RaKopo,* a headman who settled here.

Ramatlabama. *Village, southeastern Botswana.* The village, on the border with South Africa, is said to take its name from a Tswana word meaning "to cross with legs apart," referring to an incident in which a local chief killed a lion at short range. Another origin, however, interprets the name as meaning "one who has settled down." The name is also that of the river here.

Ramokgwebana. *Village, northeastern Botswana.* The name derives from Tswana *mekgweba,* the word for the South African bustard or *korhaan (Otis afroides),* and refers to a person who hunts these birds.

Ramotswa. *Village, southeastern Botswana.* The village, south of Gaborone, has a Tswana name meaning "father of the village" or "guardian of the village." The place is the headquarters of the chief of the Bamalete people.

Ramsgate. *Coastal town, southeastern Natal, South Africa.* The seaside resort developed round a house built at the mouth of the

Bilanholo River here in 1922. The settlement was named *Ramsgate* for its proximity to **Margate**, since the two resorts have almost identical parameters to their namesakes in Kent, England: both are on the southeast coast, with Margate north of Ramsgate, and both are 4 miles (6 km) apart.

Randburg. *Town, southern Transvaal, South Africa.* The town, now a northwestern extension of Johannesburg, takes its name from the **Witwatersrand** here.

Randfontein. *Town, southern Transvaal, South Africa.* The town, west of Johannesburg, takes its name from the farm on which it was laid out in 1889. The Afrikaans name means "spring on the *Rand*," the latter being the short form of **Witwatersrand**, the rocky ridge here with Johannesburg at its center.

Ras. For names beginning thus, see the next word, as for Ras **Asir.**

Ras el Ma. *Village, south central Mali.* The village, between the Niger River and the Mauritanian border, has an Arabic name meaning "head of the water." The village lies at the source of a river that flows into nearby Lake Faguibine and of other streams that make their way south to enter the Niger.

Rawsonville. *Town, southwestern Cape Province, South Africa.* The town, northeast of Cape Town, was named in 1858 for Sir Rawson W. *Rawson*, colonial secretary at the Cape from 1854 to 1864.

Rayton. *Town, southern Transvaal, South Africa.* The town, east of the capital, Pretoria, was established in 1901 and named for Mrs. *Ray* Wollaston, wife of the general manager of the Montrose Diamond Mine here.

Reddersburg. *Town, south central Orange Free State, South Africa.* The town was founded in 1861 as a congregation of the Dutch Reformed Church. Its Afrikaans name is of religious origin and means "town of the Savior," from *redder,* "savior," and *burg,* "town."

Redelingshuys. *Village, southwestern Cape Province, South Africa.* The village, north of Cape Town, was founded by the Dutch Reformed Church in 1906 and named for J. N. *Redelingshuys*, who donated the land for the purpose.

Red Sea. *Sea, bordering northeastern Africa.* The sea forms the eastern seaboard of Egypt, Sudan, Eritrea, and Ethiopia, connecting with the Mediterranean in the north through the Suez Canal, and with the Gulf of Aden in the south through the strait of Bab el Mandeb. Its name has mostly been translated literally in both classical and modern languages. To the Romans it was thus *Mare rubrum* and to the Greeks either *Eruthra thalassa* or *Eruthros pontos.* The Arabic name for it is *al-baḥr al-aḥmar* (literally "the sea the red") and its Amharic name is *qăyyĕ bahr,* while French has *Mer Rouge,* German *Rotes Meer,* Russian *Krasnoye more*, and so on. However, the sea's Hebrew name is *yam sūf,* "sea of reeds." The reason for the color red remains disputed. The following are some of the theories proposed: (1) It is that of the algae *Trichodesmium erythraeum* in its waters and along its shores; (2) It is that of the sandstone along its coasts; (3) It refers to the Himarites, a people here whose own name means "red"; (4) "Red" means "south," just as "north" means "black." (Hence possibly the name of the *Black Sea.*) Although this last theory is favored by some modern scholars, the first explanation quoted seems the most likely. There are also those who point to the similarity between the English meaning of the Hebrew name and the English name itself, so that the *Red* Sea is "really" the *Reed* Sea! See also **Eritrea.**

Red Volta. See **Volta.**

Rehoboth. *Town, central Namibia.* The site was originally known as *Anis*, a local word meaning "steam," with regard to the hot springs here. In 1844 the settlement was given its present biblical name (Genesis 26:22), meaning appropriately "large spaces." The name is also that of a homeland here.

Reitz. *Town, northeastern Orange Free State, South Africa.* The town was founded in 1884 on a site originally known as *Singer's Post,* for a trader named *Singer.* The new development was at first known as *Amsterdam,* for the Dutch city, but was given its present name in 1889 when a village was personally proclaimed here by Francis William *Reitz* (1844–1934), president of the Orange Free State from 1889 to 1895.

Reivilo. *Town, northern Cape Province, South Africa.* The town was founded in 1883 as a parish of the Dutch Reformed Church and was originally named *Cathcart West,* presumably for **Cathcart** in the southeast of the province. This name was then changed to *Klein Boetsap,* "little Boetsap," for **Boetsap,** to the southeast. In 1927 the town assumed its present name, which is a reversal of the name of the local minister, the Rev. A. J. *Olivier.* The reason for this reversal is uncertain, unless it was intended to suggest some biblical name.

Rembo. *River, Gabon.* The river, in the west of the country, has a local name meaning simply "river." It appears to be related to the name of the **Limpopo.**

Réunion. *Island, Indian Ocean.* The island, in the Mascarene Islands east of Madagascar, and a French possession since 1642, was discovered by the Portuguese explorer Pedro de Mascarenhas in about 1513, and when first occupied by the French was called by them *Isle Mascareigne.* In 1649 it was renamed *Bourbon,* for the French royal house, but in 1793, at the time of the Revolution, it was further renamed *Réunion* to commemorate the reunion of the revolutionaries from Marseilles with the National Guard in Paris on August 10, 1792. Under Napoleon it was known from 1801 to 1810 as *Bonaparte.* In the latter year it was taken by the British and again renamed *Bourbon.* It was handed back to the French in 1815 on the defeat of Napoleon, and they retained the name, appropriate again for the restoration of the royal house of Bourbon. Finally, with the Revolution of 1848, it regained its former name *Réunion* and has retained it ever since. See also **Mascarene Islands.**

Rey Bouba. See **Bouba Njida National Park.**

Rhadamès. See **Gadamès.**

Rhodes. *Village, eastern Cape Province, South Africa.* The village was originally named *Rossville,* for the local Dutch Reformed Church minister, the Rev. David *Ross.* The name was then adjusted to commemorate Cecil *Rhodes,* who famously gave the name of *Rhodesia.*

Rhodesia. *Former name of Zambia and Zimbabwe.* The name is based on that of the British colonial administrator and financier Cecil John *Rhodes* (1853–1902), who in 1888 obtained by concession from Lobengula, king of the Matabele (Ndebele), the territory north of Bechuanaland (modern Botswana). In 1890 Queen Victoria granted Rhodes and others a charter to establish the British South Africa Company (BSAC), so entitling them to occupy territory, enter into diplomatic relations with local rulers, and carry out military expeditions. In May 1895 the territory claimed by Rhodes was first designated *Rhodesia.* Informed of the decision, Rhodes is said to have replied: "Has anyone else had a country called after their name? Now I don't care a damn what they do with me." Later, he reportedly confided to a friend: "Well, you know, to have a bit of country named after one is one of the things a man might be proud of." For some reason the name was pronounced in three syllables with the second stressed, "Rho*des*ia," instead of in two syllables with the first stressed, "*Rhodes*ia." In 1900 the BSAC split the Rhodesia Protectorate, as it was now called, into three: North Western Rhodesia and North Eastern Rhodesia lying north of the Zambezi River, and *Southern Rhodesia* lying south of it. In 1911 the first two of these became a single district, *Northern Rhodesia.* In 1964 Northern Rhodesia gained its independence as **Zambia**, while Southern Rhodesia (renamed simply *Rhodesia* that year) followed suit as **Zimbabwe** in 1980. In the latter case the changeover did not take place immediately, so that the country was known as *Rhodesia-Zimbabwe* for an interim period from April 21, 1979, to the declaration of independence on April 18, 1980. Cecil Rhodes is unique in being the only man for whom two countries have been named.

Rhodes Inyanga National Park. See **Inyanga.**

Ribeira Grande. *Town, Santo Antão, Cape Verde Islands.* The island's capital has a Portuguese name meaning "big river." This properly applies to the river at the mouth of which the town is situated. See also **Cidade Velha.**

Richards Bay. *Coastal town, southeastern Natal, South Africa.* The seaside resort, on the Indian Ocean, is named for the bay here, itself named for Sir Frederick William *Richards* (1833–1912), commander of the British forces that provided additional defense against the Zulus here in 1879. The Zulu name of the resort is *Cwebeni,* "at the lagoon." (Note: on some maps, including those in *The Times Atlas of the World*, 8th ed., 1990, the name of bay and resort appears incorrectly as "*Richard's Bay.*")

Richard's Garden. See **Richard Toll.**

Richard Toll. *Town, northwestern Senegal.* The name means "Richard's garden." The reference is to a French planter named *Richard,* survivor of an expedition on board the *Méduse*, who in 1821 was entrusted by Jacques-François Roger, governor of Senegal, to lay out an ornamental garden here on the left bank of the Senegal River. The second word of the name is Wolof *toll*, "field," "garden." The garden has now long reverted to nature. The alternate name *Richard's Garden* also exists.

[1]**Richmond.** *Town, central Cape Province, South Africa.* The town was established in 1844 and named for Charles Lennox, 4th Duke of *Richmond* and Lennox (1764–1819), father-in-law of Sir Peregrine Maitland (1777–1854), governor of the Cape from 1844 to 1847. Cf. [2]**Richmond.**

[2]**Richmond.** *Town, southern Natal, South Africa.* The town was founded in 1850 and is named for Charles Lennox, 4th Duke of *Richmond* and Lennox (1764–1819), father-in-law of Sir Peregrine Maitland (1774–1854), governor of the Cape from 1844 to 1847. It was originally known as *Beaulieu,* for the duke's seat at *Richmond,* Yorkshire, the town from which he took his title. Cf. [1]**Richmond.**

Riebeek East. *Village, southeastern Cape Province, South Africa.* The village was established in 1842 and takes its name from the Dutch pioneer Jan van *Riebeeck* (1618–1677), first commander of the Cape and the first important colonist in South Africa. The second word of the name distinguished the place from **Riebeek West.**

Riebeek-Kasteel. *Village, southwestern Cape Province, South Africa.* The village takes its name from the mountain here. Its own name means "Riebeeck's castle," referring to Jan van *Riebeeck,* first commander of the Cape (see **Riebeek East**). Just north of Riebeek-Kasteel is **Riebeek West.**

Riebeek West. *Village, southwestern Cape Province, South Africa.* The village, northeast of Cape Town, was established in 1858 and named for the nearby mountain of **Riebeek-Kasteel**, with the second word of the name distinguishing it from **Riebeek East.**

Rietbron. *Village, southern Cape Province, South Africa.* The village has an Afrikaans descriptive name meaning "reed spring."

Rif. See **Er Rif.**

Rift Valley. *Province, western Kenya.* The province takes its name from the **Great Rift Valley**, which traverses its western section from north to south. Six of Kenya's provinces have self-explanatory English names. The others are *Central, Coast, Eastern, North Eastern,* and *Western.* The seventh is **Nyanza.**

Río de Oro. *Region, southern Western Sahara.* The name is Spanish for "river of gold." In 1436 members of a Portuguese expedition discovered a vast stretch of water here that they took for a river. They named it *Rio de Ouro* for the golden color of the surrounding sands. The Spanish subsequently adopted the name when they occupied the region in 1884. Geographically, the name is that of the narrow bay on the Atlantic coast here. See also **Western Sahara** and **Saquía el-Hamra.**

Río Muni. *Continental province, western Equatorial Guinea.* The name was given by the Spanish for a river here, from *río,* "river," and a corrupt form of a local word meaning "silence." The name as a whole thus means "quiet river." The name was actually applied to the estuary of the Temboni, in the southwest of the country.

Ripon Falls. *Waterfall, Victoria Nile, south central Uganda.* The falls were discovered by the British explorer John Hanning Speke in 1862 and named for George Frederick Samuel Robinson, 1st Marquess of *Ripon* (1827–1909), then undersecretary of state for India, under whose auspices his expedition had been arranged by the Royal Geographical Society. In 1954 the falls were submerged by the Owen Falls Dam.

Rivers. *State, southern Nigeria.* The state is named for the many channels, known as *rivers,* that form an intricate network of waterways in the Niger Delta.

Riversdale. *Town, southern Cape Province, South Africa.* The town, founded in 1838, is named not for its topography but for the local commissioner and resident magistrate, Harry *Rivers* (1785–1861).

Riviersonderend. *Village, southwestern Cape Province, South Africa.* The village takes its name from the river here. Its own Afrikaans name translates as "river without end": an official report of 1712 refers to the location as "an endless number of small streams flowing into the river." The implication is that early explorers found difficulty in tracing the true source of the river among its many headstreams.

Rkiz, Lake. *Lake, southwestern Mauritania.* The name means "end," "extremity," referring to the fact that the lake is the end point of all the local rivers. At the northern end of the lake is the village *Sehout el Ma*, "end of the water."

Robben Island. *Island, off southwestern South Africa.* The island, in Table Bay, Cape Province, has a Dutch name meaning "seal island." Some of the seals here were used for food when visiting ships were unable to obtain livestock from the mainland.

Robertsfield. See **Robertsport.**

Robertson. *Town, southwestern Cape Province, South Africa.* The town was established in 1853 and named for Dr. William *Robertson* (1805–1879), a minister of the Dutch Reformed Church.

Robertsport. *Town and port, northwestern Liberia.* The town takes its name from Joseph Jenkins *Roberts* (1809–1876), a black American from Virginia, who was governor of the Liberia Commonwealth from 1842 to 1847 and first president of Liberia from 1848 to 1856. His name is also borne by *Robertsfield,* earlier *Robertsville,* north of Marshall, the site of *Roberts* International Airport.

Rodriguez. *Island, Mascarene Islands, east of Madagascar.* The easternmost of the Mascarene Islands was discovered by the Portuguese in 1645 and subsequently colonized by French settlers from Mauritius. It was probably named for its discoverer. It has also been known as *Diego Ruy's Island,* a name recorded on a map of 1752 in Latin form as *Insula Jacobi Roderici.* (*Ruy* is the short form of *Rodrigo,* of which *Rodríguez* is the patronymic.).

Roma. *Village, western Lesotho.* The village arose in 1862 as a Roman Catholic mission station, which came to be known by the local name of *Ha Ba-Roma,* "home of the Roman people." The name was adopted officially in 1877. *Roma* also happens to be the Latin name of Rome, the home of the Roman Catholic Church itself.

Rombo. *Island group, southwestern Cape Verde Islands.* The three small islands that comprise the group have a Portuguese name meaning "opening," referring to their location at the northern end of the strait between the larger islands of Brava and Fogo.

Rommani. *Town, northern Morocco.* The town, south of Rabat, has a name representing Arabic *ar-rummāni,* "the pomegranate tree." In the French colonial period the town was known for many years as *Marchand* (originally *Camp Marchand*), for the French soldier and explorer Jean-Baptiste *Marchand* (1863–1934), who in 1897 crossed Africa from Brazzaville in the Congo to Fashoda (now Kodok) in the Sudan, confronting the British in the latter town.

Roodeport. *City, southern Transvaal, South Africa.* The name is that of the farm on which the present city grew from a gold mining camp set up in 1888. The Afrikaans name means "red gate," referring to the red soil of the farm.

Rooiberg. *Mountain, northwestern Transvaal, South Africa.* The descriptive Afrikaans name means "red mountain." The *Rooiberge* mountains in southeastern Orange Free State, near the border with Lesotho, have an identical name.

Rorke's Drift. *Historic locality, northern Natal, South Africa.* The locality is that of the British defense against the Zulus in 1879 (as reenacted in the British 1964 movie, *Zulu*). The *drift* (ford) here took its name from one James *Rorke* who set up a trading post in 1860.

Rosetta. *Town, northern Egypt.* The town, in the northwestern Nile Delta, is famous for the *Rosetta*

Stone which provided the key to the decipherment of ancient Egyptian texts. Its name is a European form of its Arabic name, *rashīd.* This represents the name of the caliph Hārūn ar-*Rashīd,* who founded the town in about AD 800. The name itself means "rightly guided," from *rashada,* "to follow the right course." (See also **Er Rashidia**.)

Rosmead. *Village, central Cape Province, South Africa.* The village, east of Middelburg, was established in 1880 and was originally known as *Middelburg Road.* When the railroad reached here in 1883, the settlement was renamed for Sir Hercules George Robert Robinson, 1st Baron *Rosmead* (1824–1897), governor of the Cape from 1880 to 1889. He took his title from *Rosmead* in Ireland.

Rouxville. *Town, southern Orange Free State, South Africa.* The town was founded in 1864 and named for a local Dutch Reformed Church minister, the Rev. Pieter *Roux.*

Ruacana Falls. *Waterfall, Kunene River, Southern Africa.* The falls, at the eastern end of the river's course along the border between Namibia and Angola, have a name that is probably a Portuguese corruption of Herero *oruha hakahana,* meaning "hurrying of the waters." The current Portuguese name of the falls is *Quedas do Ruacaná.*

Ruanda. See **Rwanda.**

Rudolf, Lake. See Lake **Turkana.**

Rufisque. *Town and port, western Senegal.* The town just east of the capital, Dakar, has a name that appears to be a French corruption of Portuguese *Rio Fresco,* "fresh river," with reference to a small river that flows into the sea here. (Cf. **Fresco**.) At the same time the name may have been influenced by that of *Recife,* familiar to the Portuguese as one of the leading seaports of Brazil. Some Portuguese may even have given this name to the settlement for its corresponding location: Recife is near the easternmost point of South America while Dakar is close to the westernmost point of Africa.

Rusape. *Town, eastern Zimbabwe.* The local name means "sparing of its waters," "one that does not give," with reference to the irregular flow of the Lesape River to the west of the town.

Ruspina. See **Monastir.**

Rustenburg. *Town, western Transvaal, South Africa.* The town, founded in 1850, has an Afrikaans name which means literally "town of rest," from *rust,* "rest," and *burg,* "town." The precise reference for this is uncertain. It may relate to the rest taken here by the Voortrekkers after the defeat of Kumalo chief Mzilikazi's impis (Bantu warriors), or be based on a farm name, several of which end in *-rust* to denote "home," "settlement." Possibly the intention was simply to give a pleasant name to a place where people had made their home.

Ruwenzori. *Mountain range, Central Africa.* The range, between Lake Mobutu Sese Seko and Lake Edward and on the border between Uganda and Zaïre, has a local name popularly said to mean "lord of the clouds." The reference is to the cloud cover that often hides its summits. Alternately, although meteorologically on similar lines, some authorities derive the name from *ru-enzura,* meaning "of rain" (with *ru-shozi,* "mount," understood), referring to the very damp climate and heavy annual rainfall for which the range is notorious. The Ruwenzori have been identified with Ptolemy's "Mountains of the Moon," although this title is thought by some to have applied to the **Virunga Mountains.**

Rwanda. *Republic, Central Africa.* The country takes its name from its indigenous people, the *Vanyaruanda,* whose own name is of uncertain meaning. Prior to 1962, the present territory of Rwanda formed the northern part of *Ruanda-Urundi,* itself part of German East Africa from 1890. In the year stated Ruanda gained independence as a republic with the name *Rwanda,* while **Burundi** became an independent kingdom, retaining its name.

Sabi. See **Save.**

Sabie. *Town, eastern Transvaal, South Africa.* The town takes its name from the river here, its own name deriving from a local word meaning "sand." The river rises near the town, and flows east across the border with Mozambique, where the village of *Sabié* is also named for it. The river should not be confused with the *Sabi* (see **Save**).

Sabinyo. See **Virunga Mountains.**

Sá da Bandeira. See **Lubango.**

Safi. *Town and port, western Morocco.* The ancient town was originally settled by the Canaanites under the name of *Asfi.* This represents the same Berber word, meaning "river," that gave the names of both **Fès** and **Ifni.**

Saguía el-Hamra. See **Saquía el-Hamra.**

Sahara. *Desert, North Africa.* The name represents Arabic *ṣaḥrā',* "desert," the feminine of *aṣḥar,* "fawn-colored." A mid-17th century map of Africa, with Latin inscriptions, names the Sahara as "*LIBYA INTERIOR quae hodie SARRA appellatur quae vox idem quod desertum significat*" ("INNER LIBYA which today is called SARRA which word means the same as desert"). See also **Western Sahara.**

Sahel. *Region, North Africa.* The region is a belt of semidesert and sparse savannah extending from the Atlantic coast of Mauritania and Senegal in the west, across Mali, Burkina Faso and Niger, to Chad and the western part of Sudan in the east. The name represents Arabic *sāḥil* or *saḥil,* "border," "edge." The band forms a natural divide between the arid Sahara to the north and tropical West Africa to the south. The same Arabic word gave the name of the *Swahili,* as a "border" or coastal people, living mainly in Zanzibar.

Saint-Denis. *Capital of Réunion.* The city and port, on the north coast of the island, is named for the patron saint of France. (The same name is borne by the town that is now a northern suburb of Paris.)

Ste. Catherine, Pointe. *Cape, western Gabon.* The cape, southeast of Port-Gentil, was discovered by the Portuguese in the mid-15th century and named (as *Cabo de Santa Catarina*) for *St. Catherine,* presumably because they arrived here on her feastday (November 25). The present name has the corresponding French form.

St. Francis Bay. *Bay, southern Cape Province, South Africa.* It was probably this bay that was named *Golfo dos Pastores,* "gulf of the shepherds," by the Portuguese navigator Bartholomeu Dias when he discovered it in 1488. The present name, in its original Portuguese form of *Bahia de São Francisco,* was given by the explorer Manuel Perestrelo who visited the area in 1575. He may have arrived at this point on October 4, St. Francis' Day, or simply named it for his favorite saint.

St. Helena. *Island, southeastern Atlantic.* The volcanic island, some 1120 miles (1800 km) west of the Angolan coast, was discovered by the Portuguese navigator João da Nova Castela on May 21, 1502, the feastday of *St. Helena,* and named for the saint (the mother of Emperor Constantine I of Rome). The island was annexed by the British in 1659 and remains a British dependent territory today.

St. Helena Bay. *Bay, southwestern Cape Province, South Africa.* The bay, at the mouth of the Berg River, was originally named *Bahia de Santa Helena* by the Portuguese navigator Vasco da Gama in 1497, and this gave the present English name. Presumably da Gama gave the name for the saint, although he did not land here on May 21, the feastday of St. Helena, but on November 7.

St. Louis. *Island city and port, northwestern Senegal.* The city, the oldest French settlement in West Africa, was founded in 1659 at the mouth of the Senegal River and was the capital of Senegal until 1958. It was named notionally for King *Louis* XIV of France (1638–1715), but actually for his patron saint, *Louis* IX (1214–1270), as was *Saint Louis,* Missouri, USA. The oldest part of the city is on the island of the same name, and thus exactly mirrors the Île *Saint-Louis* in Paris, on the Seine, named for the same French saint and king.

St. Lucia, Lake. *Lake, northeastern Natal, South Africa.* The name was given by the Portuguese, who discovered a freshwater lagoon here in 1507 and named it *Santa Lucia,* possibly because they arrived here on December 13, feastday of *St. Lucy. St. Lucia Estuary* is the name of the mouth of the Tugela River, to the south.

St. Marks. *Village, Transkei, South Africa.* The village was founded in 1855 as a Church of England mission station and named for *St. Mark,* one of the four apostles. The name matched those of three other stations founded at the same time: *St. Matthew, St. Luke,* and *St. John.*

Sakassou. *Village, central Côte d'Ivoire.* The name is a Baule one meaning "cemetery," referring to the burial place of a local king or chief. There are several places so called.

Sakkara. See **Saqqara.**

Sal. *Island, northeastern Cape Verde Islands.* The northeasternmost island of the Cape Verde group is noted for its saltworks. Hence its Portuguese name, *Ilha do Sal,* "island of salt."

Salamanga. *Village, southern Mozambique.* The village was established in 1909 and has a local name representing a combination of *ku-sala,* "to be," and *manga,* "lie," "falsehood." The story goes that people of the Zulu king Shaka invited others here in about 1830 to a feast, and when all the guests had drunk, slaughtered them. From this event the conclusion was drawn that the invitation, and the feast, "was a lie."

Saldanha Bay. See **Table Bay.**

Salé. *Town and port, northwestern Morocco.* The town, across the Bou Regreg River from Rabat, of which it is a suburb, has a name of Berber origin meaning "rock."

Salem. *Village, southeastern Cape Province, South Africa.* The village was established by Methodists in 1820 and given a biblical name meaning "peace." At a local level this referred to a reconciliation between sects.

Salisbury. See **Harare.**

Salisbury Channel. *Channel, western Lake Victoria, Uganda.* The channel, north of the Sese Islands, takes its name from the British prime minister Lord *Salisbury* (see **Harare**).

Sandton. *Town, southern Transvaal, South Africa.* The town, now a northern district of Johannesburg, was created as a municipality in 1969 and given a name that was a blend of those of the existing suburbs of *Sandown, Sandhurst,* and *Bryanston.*

Sango. *Village, southeastern Zimbabwe.* The name is a Shona one, meaning "bush," "veldt." The village was established in 1955 as the railroad station of *Vila Salazar,* when the rail link to Lourenço Marques (now Maputo), Mozambique, was opened. This original name was given in honor of the Portuguese dictator António de Oliveira *Salazar* (1889–1970).

Sanitatas. *Watersource, northwestern Namibia.* The waterhole has a name that is said to be of Herero origin and to mean "place where seed came up."

Sannieshof. *Village, southwestern Transvaal, South Africa.* The Afrikaans name means "Sannie's garden," and was given to the village by a local postmaster for his fiancée, *Sannie* de Beer, whom he married in 1904. When the railroad reached the village subsequently, the name was changed to *Roosville,* for Tielman *Roos* (1879–1935), deputy prime minister of South Africa. The original name was so familiar, however, that it was officially readopted in 1952.

San-Pédro. *Town and port, southwestern Côte d'Ivoire.* The name, Spanish for "St. Peter," is said to refer to one *Pedro,* a companion of the Portuguese navigators João de Santarém and Pero de Escobar, who landed on the coast here in 1497.

Santa Cruz de Tenerife. *City and port, west central Canary Islands.* The city, on the northern coast of the island of **Tenerife**, was founded by the Spanish in 1494. Its name, meaning "Holy Cross," is commonly found in Spanish and Portuguese overseas possessions. The second part of the name distinguishes this Santa Cruz from others, but especially from *Santa Cruz de la Palma* on the island of La Palma.

Santa Isabel. See **Malabo.**

Santa Luzia. *Island, northern Cape Verde Islands.* The island, between São Vicente and São Nicolau, is said to be so named because it was discovered on December 13, 1461, the feastday of *St. Lucy.*

Santa Maria. *Island, eastern Azores.* The easternmost island of the Azores was reputedly settled by the Portuguese official Gonçalo Velho Cabral on August 15, 1432, the feastday of the Assumption of the Blessed Virgin *Mary,* and so named for her. Compare **São Jorge, São Miguel.**

Santa Maria, Cabo de. *Cape, southeastern Angola.* The name, meaning "St. Mary's cape," was given by Portuguese explorers some time in the late 15th or early 16th century. It is not clear why this particular saint was chosen, although the name of the Virgin Mary was frequently given to places discovered or founded by European Catholics.

Santo Antão. *Island, northwestern Cape Verde Islands.* The northernmost island of the group was discovered by the Portuguese in 1461 and is said to be so named because they reached it on June 13, the feastday of *St. Antony* of Padua, a saint popular in Portugal. Compare **São Nicolau.**

Santo António de Zaire. See **Soyo.**

Sanyati. See **Umniati.**

Sao Hill. *Village, southern Tanzania.* The name is said to represent either a local form of greeting, *sau yu nyenye,* or to be a form of English *scientist*, referring to the arrival here of Lord Chesham and other European settlers in the 19th century.

São Jorge. *Island, central Azores.* The island was discovered by the Portuguese some time between 1450 and 1453 and was presumably named for the feastday of *St. George* (April 23), when a landing or settlement was made. Compare **São Miguel.**

São Miguel. *Island, eastern Azores.* The largest island of the group was reputedly settled by the Portuguese official Gonçalo Velho Cabral on May 8, 1444, a feastday of *St. Michael,* and so named for him. Compare **Santa Maria, São Jorge.**

São Nicolau. *Island, northern Cape Verde Islands.* The island was discovered by the Portuguese in 1461 and is said to be so named because they reached it on December 6, the feastday of *St. Nicholas.* But they would hardly have taken six months to arrive here after sighting **Santo Antão**!

São Salvador. See **Mbanza Kongo.**

São Tiago. *Island, southern Cape Verde Islands.* The island was discovered by the Genoese navigator, António da Noli, in the service of Prince Henry of Portugal, on May 1, 1456, the feastday of *St. James* the Less, and was named for the saint. (The name is the equivalent of the more familiar Spanish *Santiago.*)

São Tomé. *Island, off west coast of Africa.* The island, in the Gulf of Guinea, has been part of the republic of *São Tomé e Príncipe* since 1975. Its name, Portuguese for "St. Thomas," refers to its date of discovery by the Portuguese: December 21, 1471, the feastday of *St. Thomas.* See also **Príncipe.**

São Vicente. *Island, northwestern Cape Verde Islands.* The island is named for *St. Vincent* on whose feastday, January 22, it is said to have been discovered in 1492.

Sapele. *Town, southern Nigeria.* The town, a port on the Benin River, is a sawmilling center. It takes its name from the *sapele* tree (*Entandrophragma cylindricum*), the wood of which, similar to mahogany, is used for furniture.

Saqqara. *Village, northern Egypt.* The village, near Memphis, is noted for its mastabas (ancient mudbrick tombs) and pyramids. Its name probably derives from the tribal leader *Beni Soqar.* However, it may be no coincidence that it is similar to that of *Sokaris,* Egyptian god of the dead, who was worshipped here. The name is also spelled *Sakkara.*

Saquía el-Hamra. *Region, northern Western Sahara.* The region takes its name from the intermittent river so called, its own name representing Arabic *sāḳiya al-ḥamra,* "the red canal," with reference to the red sands here. (In North Africa the *ḳ* of the Arabic word is pronounced more like *g.* Hence the alternate form of the name as *Saguía el-Hamra.*) A *sakia* (spelling varies) is also the term for the waterwheel with buckets attached used for drawing water from wells or pits in North Africa, and especially in Egypt. See also **Western Sahara** and **Río de Oro.**

Sarafere. *Village, south central Mali.* The name is a corruption of Fulani (Peul) *Saré-Faran,* itself a translation of Songhai *Faran-Koïra,* "village of the *Faran,*" referring to a local tribe.

Sasolburg. *Town, northern Orange Free State, South Africa.* The town was laid out in 1950 to serve the South African Coal, Oil and Gas Corporation, and its name is based on *SASOL,* the acronym of the Afrikaans name of this company, *Suid-Afrikaanse Steenkool-. Olie- en Gaskorporasie.*

Sassandra. *Town and port, southwestern Côte d'Ivoire.* The port is at the mouth of the river of the same name, on the southwest coast. Its name represents a contraction of *Santo Andrea,* "St. Andrew," given by the Portuguese explorers João de Santarém and Pero de Escobar when they landed here on November 30, 1497, *St. Andrew*'s day.

Saurimo. *Town, northeastern Angola.* The name is a corruption of *Sa Urimbo,* itself a distortion of the title of a chief formerly here. He was called *Sa Visgo,* literally "lord of the catapult," referring to his method of catching birds.

Save. *River, Southern Africa.* The river rises in Zimbabwe (where it is known as the *Sabi*), then flows eastward into Mozambique, forming the border between the districts of Manica and Sofala to the north and Gaza and Inhambe to the south to enter the Mozambique Channel. Most authorities agree that its name derives from the local word *missaba,* "sand," as for the **Sabie** River, although it may be a corruption of a local word *shave* or *shavi,* meaning "foreign spirit," "strange presence," or else be linked with that of *Sofala* itself.

Savé. *Town, south central Benin.* The name is said to be a corruption and shortening of Nagol *Tcha-lo-bé,* "hitting with the knife," from *tcha,* "hit," *lo,* "with," and *bé,* "knife," "machete." The reference is to the weapons used by local people.

Sawmills. *Village, western Zimbabwe.* The name is self-descriptive, referring to the local teak industry here in the Gwaai Forest.

Schuckmannsburg. *Village, northeastern Namibia.* The village, at the eastern end of the Caprivi Strip, was founded as a military encampment in 1909 and named for Baron Bruno von *Schuckmann,* governor of German South-West Africa (present **Namibia**) from 1907 to 1910.

Schweizer-Reneke. *Town, southwestern Transvaal, South Africa.* The locality here was originally known as *Mamusa,* for the Korana chief David *Massouw,* who had his stronghold at this point. The town was established in 1888 and named for two officers: Captain Constantin Alexander *Schweizer* (1837–1885) and Field-Cornet C. N. *Reneke,* who both lost their lives in a battle with Massouw's people in 1885.

Scottburgh. *Coastal town, southeastern Natal, South Africa.* The seaside resort was founded in 1860 and named for Sir John *Scott* (1814–1898), lieutenant-governor of Natal from 1856 to 1864.

Sebakwe. *River, Zimbabwe.* The river, a tributary of the Munyati in the center of the country, has a name representing the local word *tshibagwe,* "place of maize."

Sébékoro. *Village, southwestern Mali.* The village, west of the capital, Bamako, has a name meaning "near the borassus," from Mande or Bambara *sébé,* "borassus" (a type of sugar palm), and *koro,* "near."

Seeheim. *Village, southern Namibia.* The village, a railroad junction on the Great Fish River, has a German name meaning literally "sea home." When the river flooded, an island formed so that the houses were surrounded by water, resembling a seaside settlement.

Seeis. *Village, central Namibia.* The village, east of the capital, Windhoek, has a Khoikhoin (Hottentot) name meaning "small face," "small cheek," with reference to the appearance of a mountain here.

Ségou. *Town, southwestern Mali.* The town, on the Niger River, derives its name from Mande *segu,* "enclosure," "fortified village."

Sehithwa. *Village, northwestern Botswana.* The name is said to be of

Herero origin and to mean "[place] where people meet."

Sehlabathebe National Park. *National park, southeastern Lesotho.* The game reserve, on the border with South Africa, has a local name said to mean "plateau of the shield," referring to some legendary battle here, in which a tribe won a victory by "piercing the shield" of an enemy.

Sehout el Ma. See Lake **Rkiz.**

Sekoma. *Village, southern Botswana.* The local name means "licking," said to apply to the custom of licking powdered food here.

Selebi-Phikwe. *Town, eastern Botswana.* The name of the mining town combines those of two adjacent places. *Selebi* is said to mean "place of waterholes," and *Phikwe* "mound of sticks left after clearing land."

Selous Game Reserve. *Game reserve, southeastern Tanzania.* The reserve is named for the English big game hunter and naturalist, Frederick Courteney *Selous* (1851–1917), who explored southeastern Africa and who was killed here when serving as an army officer in World War I.

Selukwe. See **Shurugwi.**

Sena. *Village, central Mozambique.* The name of the village, on the Zambezi River, is said to be a corruption of *Siona* or *Shona*, although it does not refer to the Shona people. The meaning of the name is uncertain. One theory claims that it may be an Arab borrowing of the name of *Sana'a*, that of the capital of what is now Yemen.

Senegal. *Republic, West Africa.* The country takes its name from the river that marks its northern border with Mauritania. This itself may either derive from an ancient town called *Sanghana* or preserve the name of the Berber *Zenaga* people. Alternately, it could represent some African word meaning "navigable." The Arabic name for the river is *as-sinigal.* The Wolof have a traditional story to explain the name. An explorer reached the river and, pointing, asked some fishermen what it was called. They replied "*li suñu gal le*," "That's our boat."

Senegambia. *Region, West Africa.* The region, mostly in Senegal, takes its name from the **Senegal** and **Gambia** rivers, between which it lies. The name first appeared in 1765, when Senegal merged with the British posts on the Gambia River. As such, Senegambia was the first British Crown Colony in Africa.

Senekal. *Town, east central Orange Free State, South Africa.* The original name of the town was Afrikaans *De Put*, "the well," for the farm on which it was established in 1877. The present name derives from that of Frederik Petrus *Senekal* (1815–1866), who fought in the Basuto wars of 1858 and 1865–1866, losing his life in the latter.

Sengwa. *River, Zimbabwe.* The river flows into Lake Kariba in the northwest of the country. Its name is said to be of Chishankwe origin meaning "to be disliked," "to be hated." The reference is to its treacherous current, making people wary of crossing it.

Sennar. *Town, eastern Sudan.* The town, on the Blue Nile, takes its name from the ancient kingdom formerly here between this river and the White Nile. The name itself, also spelled *Sannar*, is said to have evolved from a full form *Darsennār*, meaning "land of fire," presumably with some local reference. It is unlikely to represent Turkish *sınır*, "boundary," "frontier," as sometimes explained.

Serowe. *Village, eastern Botswana.* The village takes its name from the *serowa*, the local word for the small, sweet edible bulb of the plant species *Ceropegia,* which grows here.

Serpa Pinto. See **Menongue.**

Serule. *Village, eastern Botswana.* The name is said to mean "place where the load was put down," presumably with reference to some particular incident here.

Sesfontein. *Village, northwestern Namibia.* The Afrikaans name, meaning "six springs," is a translation of the Khoikhoin (Hottentot) name *Nanious.*

Sesheke. *Town, southern Zambia.* The town, on the Zambezi River, which here forms the border with Namibia, has a local name said to mean "white sand."

Sétif. *Town, northern Algeria.* The name represents Arabic *sṭīf*, going back through Roman *Sitifis* to some Punic name of uncertain meaning. *Sétif* is the French form of the name, which is also found as *Stif.*

Seychelles. *Island republic, Indian Ocean.* The islands, east of Tanzania, were discovered by the Portuguese in 1502 and given the name (or its equivalent) *The Seven Sisters.* (The number is arbitrary: there are actually 85.) In 1742 Bertrand-François Mahé, Comte de la Bourdonnais, then governor of Île de France (future Mauritius), sent Captain Lazare Picault to explore the group. He named them *La Bourdonnais* for his patron. In 1756 the French staked a claim to the islands, and named them *Séchelles* for the French finance minister, Jean Moreau de *Séchelles.* The present form of the name (coincidentally but appropriately suggesting "seashells") was introduced by the British, to whom the islands were ceded in 1815. See also **Mahé, Praslin, Silhouette.**

Seymour. *Town, southeastern Cape Province, South Africa.* The town was originally called *Elands Post*, for the animals here. Its present name honors Colonel Charles *Seymour,* military secretary to Sir George Cathcart, governor of the Cape (see **Cathcart**).

Sfax. *City and port, eastern Tunisia.* The present name is a form of Arabic *ṣafāqs* or *ṣafāks*. The meaning of this is uncertain, though according to some sources it represents a term for a species of cucumber. The town was already in existence in the 7th century, and arose on the site of the Roman settlement of *Taparura.* Again, the origin of this is unclear.

Shaba. *Province, southeastern Zaïre.* The name represents Swahili *shaba*, "copper," referring to the rich deposits of this metal (and many others) here. Until 1972 the province had the name *Katanga*, from a Hausa word meaning "ramparts," "structures," with reference to the old capital, Yoruba.

Shabani. See **Zvishavane.**

Shakawe. *Village, northwestern Botswana.* The name is a local one, said to be that of a type of tree used for medicinal purposes.

Shamva. *Town, northeastern Zimbabwe.* The town takes its name from the *tsamvi*, a species of wild fig that grows here. It was originally known as *Abercorn,* for James Hamilton, 2d Duke of *Abercorn* (1838–1913), first president of the British South Africa Company.

Shari. *River, Central Africa.* The river, flowing northwest from the Central African Republic to Lake Chad, Chad, has a local name meaning simply "river." *Ubangi-Shari* was the former name of the **Central African Republic** itself. See also **Ubangi.**

Sharm el-Sheikh. *Town and resort, northeastern Egypt.* The town, at the southern end of the Sinai Peninsula, is named for the bay on which it lies. Its own Arabic name, more accurately *sharm ash-shaykh*, means "inlet of the sheikh." The inlet's Hebrew name is *Mifraz Shlomo,* "bay of Solomon," referring to the ships of the biblical king Solomon, said to have passed here on their route from Eziongeber, in the Gulf of Aqaba, to the land of Ophir (1 Kings 9:26–28). An actual town named *Ofira* was built on the bay in the 1970s.

Shashe. *River, Southern Africa.* The river, a tributary of the Limpopo, forms part of the border between southwestern Zimbabwe and northeastern Botswana. Its name is said to derive from the local phrase *shaya ishe*, "without a chief," denoting that the territory here was at one time ungoverned. There is a village of the same name on the Botswana side of the border.

Shellen. *Village, eastern Nigeria.* The village, on the Gongola River, has a local name said to mean "wood," "hidden place."

Shimoni. *Town, southern Kenya.* The town, near the coast, is famous for its caves and is named for them, from Swahili *shimo,* "cave."

Shire. *River, Southern Africa.* The river, in southern Malawi and central Mozambique, flows south from Lake Malawi (Nyasa) into the Zambezi. Its name, pronounced "Shirry," is of uncertain origin but may be a Nyanja word meaning "woodland," "undergrowth," implying that the source of the river is far inland. The river gave the name of the *Shire Highlands,* the hill country of southern Malawi, and of the village of *Chire,* southwestern Mozambique. The latter has the Portuguese spelling of the river name.

Shoshong. *Village, eastern Botswana.* The Tswana name, which is also that of the hills here, refers to the type of tree known as *Leswaswa,* common locally.

Shurugwi. *Town, central Zimbabwe.* The town, founded in 1899, is said to take its name from a nearby bare oval granite hill that resembled a pigpen (*shurugwi*) of the local Venda people. Until 1982 the name was spelled *Selukwe.*

Sicca Veneria. See **Le Kef.**

Sidi Abd el-Rahman. *Coastal town, northern Egypt.* The Arabic name of the Mediterranean resort is more accurately represented as *saydī ʿabd ar-raḥmān*, from *saydī*, "sir," "my lord" (also giving *El Cid* as the title of the Spanish warrior hero), and the personal name *ʿabd ar-raḥmān* ("servant of the merciful," i.e., of Allah), that of a local Muslim holy man. The *Sidi* that begins many placenames in North Africa is often followed by the name of a marabout whose tomb is in the place mentioned. See, for instance, **Sidi-bel-Abbès, Sidi Bou Said**. (English *marabout* derives from Arabic *murābiṭ*, literally "garrisoned one," that is, a member of a Muslim community living in a *ribat*. See **Ribat**.)

Sidi-bel-Abbès. *City, northwestern Algeria.* The town was founded in 1843 as a French military outpost and was the headquarters of the French Foreign Legion from then until 1962. Its name relates to the local marabout *Sīdī bel ʿAbbās,* whose tomb is here (see **Sidi Abd el-Rahman**).

Sidi Bou Said. *Coastal town, northeastern Tunisia.* The town, just north of Carthage and northeast of Tunis, takes its name from the 13th century marabout around whose tomb it arose. See **Sidi Abd el-Rahman.**

Sidi Ifni. *Town and port, southwestern Morocco.* The town was the capital of the former Spanish protectorate of **Ifni**, as well as of subsequent territories of this name down to 1969. Its own name thus refers to its official status in this respect, with the first word representing Arabic *saydī,* literally "sir," "my lord."

Sidra, Gulf of. *Bay, northern Libya.* The broad inlet of the Mediterranean, known in Arabic as *khālij surt*, and formerly to the Romans as *Syrtis Major*, has a name meaning "sandbank," referring to the large one in the sea here, a navigational hazard and the cause of several shipwrecks. The name is of Greek origin, and ultimately derives from *surō,* "I drag," "I sweep away." The coast here borders the section of the Sahara known as the *Surt Desert*, with a name of identical origin, while on the coast itself is the town of *Surt*. A similar but smaller sandbank, known to the Romans as *Syrtis Minor*, lay further west in what is now the Gulf of Gabès, on the east coast of Tunisia.

Sierra Leone. *Republic, West Africa.* The name as it stands means "lion mountains," from Spanish *sierra*, "mountain chain," and *león*, "lion." It was recorded in 1462 as *Serra da Leão* in this sense by the Portuguese navigator Pedro de Sintra. An earlier record of 1457, however, was made by the Venetian navigator Alvise Ca' da Mosto, which in translation reads, in part, "...and named this mountain Serre-Lionne, because of the great noise here from the fearful sound and claps of thunder that are always over it, constantly surrounded by storm clouds." The name thus apparently refers to storms over the range of hills that surrounds what is now Freetown harbor, not to the actual roaring of lions. (A third theory attributes the "roaring" to the sound of surf breaking over reefs here.) Lions in any case do not frequent this part of Africa, even if they once did, although three lions appear on the republic's coat of arms.

Sihota. *Village, southeastern Cape Province, South Africa.* The village, on the Great Kei River, has a Xhosa name said to mean "secluded place."

Silhouette. *Island, western Seychelles.* The island, northwest of Mahé, takes its name from Étienne de *Silhouette* (1709–1767), the French controller of finance who succeeded Jean Moreau de Séchelles (see **Seychelles**). Silhouette's brief career in this post (1757), or a portrait of him in outline, resulted in the satirical use of his name for a shadow image, or *silhouette*. The bestowal of his name on an island, typically seen in outline, is thus fortuitously appropriate.

Silsila. *Ancient quarries, southeastern Egypt.* The quarries, by the Nile River midway between Idfu and Aswan, take their name from the hills here, themselves known in Arabic as *Jebel es-Silsila*, "chain of hills."

Silva Porto. See (1) **Bié**; (2) **Kuito**.

Simonstown. *Town, southwestern Cape Province, South Africa.* The town, an important naval base, takes its name from *Simon* van der Stel (1639–1712), first governor of the Cape (from 1691 to 1699), who visited the bay here in 1687. The British landed here in 1795, but the settlement became known as *Simon's Town* only after the second British occupation in 1806.

Sinai. *Peninsula, northeastern Egypt.* The peninsula, geographically in Asia (not Africa) but politically in Egypt, takes its name from Mount *Sinai* in its southern region. The name comes from Hebrew *sīnay*, itself probably representing *Sin*, the name of the moon god of the Sumerians, Akkadians, and ancient Arabians. Its Arabic name is *jabal mūsa*, "mountain of Moses," and the mountain is referred to in the Bible by the parallel names *Mount Sinai* and *Mount Horeb*. (Although now thought of as a Jewish name, *Moses* may well be a name of Egyptian origin.) There is another *Jebel Musa* at Ceuta, northern Morocco, where jointly with the Rock of Gibraltar in Europe it forms the so-called "Pillars of Hercules."

Sinoe. See **Greenville.**

Sinoya. See **Chinhoyi.**

Sirakoro. *Village, southwestern Mali.* The village, west of the capital, Bamako, has a name meaning "by the baobab," from Mande or Bambara *sira*, "baobab," and *koro*, "near."

Siteki. *Town, eastern Swaziland.* The Siswati name of the town literally means "place of marriage," a favorable name for a location with a kind climate and fertile land.

Siwa. *Town, northwestern Egypt.* The name of the town represents ancient Egyptian *sekht-am*, "palm land." Olive trees and date palms still provide the region's chief source of income. The name is also that of the oasis in which the town is located. Some Egyptologists have linked the name with that of Suez, although this is usually interpreted differently.

Skeleton Coast National Park. *National park, northwestern Namibia.* The game reserve extends south along the Atlantic coast for some 300 miles (480 km) from the Angolan border. Its name is a popular one for the seaboard between Cape Fria and Cape Cross, and is as appropriate today as it has ever been: "It was only there [at Cape Fria] that we realised how aptly named the Skeleton Coast is, since it is littered with the bleached bones of whales and seals and men. The ocean off Namibia was once full of whales, but the men who hunted them were lured to their deaths by the treacherous Atlantic fogs. One hundred years later, the wooden ribs of their ships now mingle with the ribs of the whales they pursued" (Isabel Wolff, "Seasoned by the Sun," *The Times Magazine*, June 5, 1993).

Skikda. *Town and port, northeastern Algeria.* The present town was founded by the French in 1838 and named *Philippeville*, for King Louis-*Philippe* of France (1773–1850), then reigning. After Algeria gained independence in 1962, the present name was adopted, as a reversion to the local form of the original name *Rusicade*, that of the 4th century port on which the modern town arose. The meaning of this is uncertain, although it is possible the initial syllable may represent Arabic *ra's*, "headland," referring to some nearby cape.

Skipskop. *Coastal village, southwestern Cape Province, South Africa.* The seaside resort has an Afrikaans name that means "ships' hill," apparently with reference to the many ships wrecked here in the past.

Skoenmakerskop. *Coastal village, southeastern Cape Province, South Africa.* The literal meaning of the Afrikaans name is "shoemaker's hill," although the origin may actually be in the surname *Skoenmaker* or *Shoemaker*. A local legend tells how a soldier of this name deserted and settled here, just south of Port Elizabeth.

Slave Coast. *Section of coast, West Africa.* The name came to apply to the coast between the Niger and Volta estuaries, in modern Nigeria, Benin, Togo, and Ghana. It was mainly from this region that in the 16th to 19th centuries European traders shipped black slaves to America and the West Indies for work in the plantations.

Slurry. *Village, southwestern Transvaal, South Africa.* The name means what it says, and refers to the liquid mixture of limestone and other materials used in the manufacture of cement at the large cement works here, east of Mafikeng.

Smithfield. *Town, southeastern Orange Free State, South Africa.* The town was established in 1849 and was originally named *Smith Town* or *Smith Field*, for Sir Harry *Smith* (1787–1860), governor of the Cape from 1847 to 1852. (See also **Harrismith**.) This became *New Smithfield*, then finally the *New* was dropped to give the present name.

Sneeuberg. *Mountain range, south central Cape Province, South Africa.* The Afrikaans name means "snow mountain," and probably translates the Khoikhoin (Hottentot) name, *Nogore*, referring to the snow cover here which can last until early November, that is, until late spring.

Soa Pan. *Salt pan, northeastern Botswana.* The pan, the easternmost in the Makgadikgadi salt basin (see **Kalahari**), takes its name from Khoikhoin (Hottentot) *soa*, "salt." The village of *Sua* here takes its name from the pan.

Soavinandriana. *Town, central Madagascar.* The Malagasy name means "favored by the monarch," from *sòa*, "good," "pleasant," and *andrìana*, "prince," "sovereign."

Socotra. *Island, off northeastern Africa.* The island, east of Ethiopia, belongs to Yemen. Its name is of Sanskrit origin and represents an original form *dvīpa sukhatara*, "fortunate island" (literally "island more pleasant").

Soda Lake. See Lake **Natron**.

Sofala. *Province, southeastern Mozambique.* For the origin of this name, see **Nova Sofala**, also **Save**.

Sokolo. *Village, south central Mali.* There are various villages of the name, one of the most important being north of Ségou. The origin is in a Mande word meaning "hole," "breach," implying a new settlement.

Sokoto. *Town, northwestern Nigeria.* The town takes its name from the sultanate once here that formed the Fulah empire. The region developed under Berber and Arab influence, and the name is of Arabic origin, representing *sūḳ*, "market." (Cf. **Es Souk, Souk el Arba du Rharb**.) The name is also that of a state and river here.

Somabhula. *Village, central Zimbabwe.* The name derives from that of *Shamaburu*, a famous elephant hunter here at one time, in the region south of Gweru.

Somalia. *Republic, northeastern Africa.* The name of the country remains of uncertain origin, though it is clearly that of the indigenous people. There are four hypotheses; that it derives: (1) From a Cushitic word meaning "dark," "black," referring to the color of the people's skin; (2) From a local phrase *soo mal*, meaning "go and milk," implying a welcome given to visitors, who are offered milk by their hosts (although an expression of this kind is hardly likely to be adopted as a placename); (3) From the name of a tribal chief; (4) From Arabic *zamlā*, "cattle," for the relative abundance of livestock in this region. See also **Somaliland**.

Somaliland. *Region, East Africa.* The name is a general term for the extensive region between the Equator and the Gulf of Aden where the Somali people are indigenous. In practice this means **Somalia** itself together with Djibouti and southeastern Ethiopia. As a historic name, *Somaliland* was formerly familiar for both British Somaliland and Italian Somaliland, which united in 1960 to form Somalia.

Somerset East. *Town, southeastern Cape Province, South Africa.* The town was established in 1825 on the tobacco farm owned by Lord Charles Henry *Somerset* (1767–1831), governor of the Cape from 1814 to 1826. *East* was added to the name subsequently to distinguish the town from **Somerset West**.

Somerset West. *Town, southwestern Cape Province, South Africa.* The town was founded in 1822 as a church community and was named for Lord Charles Henry *Somerset* (1767–1831), governor of the Cape from 1814 to 1826. When **Somerset East** was founded three years later, *West* was added to the original *Somerset* to distinguish the two places, one in the southeast of the province, the other in the southwest.

Souk el Arba du Rharb. *Town, northern Morocco.* The town, south of Tangier, has a name meaning "Wednesday market of the west," from Arabic *sūḳ*, "market," *el*, "the," *arbʿa*, "Wednesday" (literally "four"), French *du*, "of the," and Arabic *ṛarb*, "west." Many Moroccan villages are named for the days of the week on which they hold their market. Others would be (with slight variations in spelling): *Souk el Had*, "Sunday market" (literally "one," as the first day of the week), *Souk el Tnine,* "Monday market" ("two"), *Souk el Tleta*, "Tuesday market" ("three"), *Souk el Khemis*, "Thursday market" ("five"), and *Souk el Sebt*, "Saturday market" ("Sabbath"). There are few markets in Morocco on Friday, Islam's holy day. Places named for markets usually have a distinguishing suffix, as here.

Sousse. *City and port, northeastern Tunisia.* The ancient port was founded by the Phoenicians in the 11th century BC, and was originally known as *Hadrumetum*, a name of uncertain meaning. When the Vandals conquered it in the 5th century AD it became *Hunericopolis*, for *Huneric*, son of the Vandal king Genseric. After the Byzantine invasion of the 6th century it was further renamed *Justinianopolis*, for the Byzantine emperor *Justinian* I. The source of the present name is not clear. It may be of Berber origin and relate to the names of *Marsa Susa* in Libya, also on the coast, or even to the plain (and river) *Sous* in southern Morocco. Any connection with the biblical *Susa*, the ancient city north of the Persian Gulf, is highly unlikely.

South Africa. *Republic, Southern Africa.* Africa's southernmost country has its historical beginnings in the expeditions here of the Portuguese navigators Bartholomeu Dias and Vasco da Gama in the 15th century, and in those of the English and Dutch in the 17th. The purely geographical name developed gradually from then on, and was well established by the 19th century for this part of the continent. As official names, the *Union of South Africa* came into being in 1910, and the *Republic of South Africa* in 1961. The Afrikaans name of the country is *Suid-Afrika.* Its African name, *Azania*, introduced by the African National Congress, is of classical origin and initially applied to East Africa. It derives from the same root word as that behind **Zanzibar**, so that the meaning is "land of the blacks." (For a similar meaning, see **Guinea; Sudan.**)

Southern Desert. See **New Valley.**

Southern Rhodesia. See **Zimbabwe.**

South West Africa. See **Namibia.**

Soutpan. *Village, central Orange Free State, South Africa.* The Afrikaans name means "salt pan," with reference to the large one south of the village. Cf. **Soutpansberg.**

Soutpansberg. *Mountain range, northern Transvaal, South Africa.* The Afrikaans name means "salt pan mountain," referring to the large salt pans at the northern edge of the range.

Soweto. *Complex of townships, southern Transvaal, South Africa.* The black townships, some 26 in number southwest of Johannesburg, were established in 1963 and given a name that is an acronym of the collective name *South Western Townships.* The name happens to suggest a local African word.

Soyo. *Town, northwestern Angola.* The town has a name that is a shortened form of *Sonyo Sohio,* "province of the Kongo [people]." For several years until 1980 the town was known by the Portuguese name of *Santo António de Zaire,* for *St. Anthony,* patron saint of the Portuguese capital, Lisbon. Soyo is situated in the province of Zaïre. (See **Zaïre.**)

Spanish Guinea. See **Equatorial Guinea.**

Speke Gulf. *Gulf, Lake Victoria, northern Tanzania.* The large inlet, in the southeastern corner of the lake, is named for the British explorer John Hanning *Speke* (1827–1864), who reached the southern end of Lake Victoria in 1858. The name was given by the British explorer Henry Morton Stanley, as recorded in his account of his descent of the Congo, *Through the Dark Continent* (1878): "I set sail on the 8th of March, 1875, eastward along the shores of the broad arm of the lake which we first sighted, and which henceforward is known, in honour of its first discoverer, as Speke Gulf."

Spion Kop. *Hill, western Natal, South Africa.* The Afrikaans name, properly *Spioenkop,* means "spy hill," referring to the hill's potential as a vantage point. It is historically famous for the battle of 1900 in the second Boer War in which the British lost over 1700 dead, while the Boers lost only 50. There is another hill of the same name in southern Transvaal, south of Johannesburg.

Spitzkopje. *Mountain, western Namibia.* The name is a combination of German *Spitz,* "point," and Dutch *kopje,* "hill." There are several mountains of the name in Southern Africa, such as, in South Africa itself, *Spitskop* in southwestern Orange Free State, and *Spitskop* in southern Cape Province, in the Groot-Swartberge.

Springbok. *Town, northwestern Cape Province, South Africa.* The town takes its name from South Africa's national animal, the *springbok* (the antelope *Antidorcas marsupialis*), formerly found in this region in large herds, though now mostly restricted to game reserves. The town was laid out in 1862 and was at first known as *Springbokfontein,* "springbok spring." This was shortened to its present form in 1911.

Springfontein. *Town, southern Orange Free State, South Africa.* The town was established on a farm in 1904 and has an Afrikaans name meaning literally "springing spring." The reference is to a spring that bubbles or flows freely.

Springs. *City, southern Transvaal, South Africa.* The town takes its name from that of the farm, *The Springs,* on which it arose in 1887. The reference is to the many springs of water here. The city owes its prosperity not to its water, however, but initially to its coal, discovered in 1887, and subsequently its gold, first mined in 1908.

Stampriet. *Town, east central Namibia.* The original Afrikaans name of the town was *Stamprietfontein*, literally "stamp reed spring." The reference is to the reed-bordered spring found here in early settlement days.

Standerton. *Town, southeastern Transvaal, South Africa.* The town was established in 1878 on plotlands initially known as *Stander's Drift* (from Afrikaans *drift*, "ford"). It adopted its present name in the year stated, for Commandant Adriaan H. *Stander* (1817–1896), owner of the farm on which the original plotlands were laid out.

Stanford. *Village, southwestern Cape Province, South Africa.* The village was established on a farm in 1857 and named for its former owner, Sir Robert *Stanford.*

Stanger. *Town, eastern Natal, South Africa.* The town, laid out in 1873, takes its name from Dr. William *Stanger* (1811–1854), first surveyor-general of Natal. The Zulu name for the place was *KwaDukuza*, "place of the lost person," since the site was a maze of huts. As such, it was the capital of Chief Chaka (Shaka), founder of the Zulu Empire in 1816.

Stanley, Mount. *Mountain, Ruwenzori Range, east central Africa.* The peak, on the border between Zaïre and Uganda, was reached by the British explorer Sir Henry Morton *Stanley* in 1888, and is named for him.

Stanley Pool. See **Pool.**

Stanleyville. See **Kisangani.**

Steelpoort. *Village, eastern Transvaal, South Africa.* The village and railroad terminus originally bore the Afrikaans name of *Olifantspoort*, "elephant's pass," explaining as referring to the killing of an elephant here and the theft of its tusks. This in turn is said to have given the present name, literally "steal pass." But this origin is almost certainly anecdotal.

Stefanie, Lake. See Lake **Turkana.**

Steinkopf. *Village, western Cape Province, South Africa.* The original site here was known by the Afrikaans name of *Bijzondermeid*, literally "strange maid," a translation of its Nama name, *Tarrakois*. The reference seems to have been to a girl or woman of unknown origin found here by early settlers. A missionary station was set up here in 1818 and given its present name, for Karl Friedrich Adolf *Steinkopf* (1773–1859), a German priest who donated generously to the mission.

Stellaland. See **Vryburg.**

Stellenbosch. *Town, southwestern Cape Province, South Africa.* The town was founded in 1679 by Commander Simon van der *Stel* (1639–1712), first governor of the Cape (from 1691 to 1699). He inspected the outposts of the Dutch East India Company, allocated land to the colonists, and named the place for himself, with *bosch* the Dutch word for "bush," "forest." See also **Simonstown.**

Sterkfontein Caves. *Caverns, southern Transvaal, South Africa.* The Afrikaans name of the caverns, an important archaeological site west of Johannesburg, means "strong spring," referring to a steadily flowing spring nearby.

Sterkstroom. *Town, eastern Cape Province, South Africa.* The town, founded in 1875, has an Afrikaans name meaning "strong stream," referring to the current of the Hex River nearby.

Steynsburg. *Town, east central Cape Province, South Africa.* The town grew round a church of the Dutch Reformed Church built here in

1872 and takes its name from Douwe Gerbrandt *Steyn*, grandfather of South African statesman Paul Kruger (see **Kruger National Park**).

Steynsrus. *Town, north central Orange Free State, South Africa.* The Afrikaans name of the town, founded in 1910, means "Steyn's rest," and was given in honor of Marthinus Theunis *Steyn* (1857–1916), last president of the Orange Free State. The name was originally *Steynsrust.*

Steytlerville. *Town, southern Cape Province, South Africa.* The town was established by the Dutch Reformed Church in 1876 and originally named *Steytlerton*, for the Rev. Abraham Isaac *Steytler* (1840–1922), an influential minister nicknamed the "Dutch Reformed Pope." The name was later modified to its present form.

Stif. See **Sétif.**

Stormsvlei. *Town, southwestern Cape Province, South Africa.* The Afrikaans name means "storm marsh," referring to the swamp that forms here after heavy rainfall on the banks of the Riviersonderend.

Strand. *Town and resort, southwestern Cape Province, South Africa.* The town, on the coast southeast of Cape Town, arose in about 1850 on a site originally called *Van Ryneveld's Town*, for D. J. *van Ryneveld*, magistrate of Stellenbosch, owner of land here. The location also became known as *Somerset Strand,* "Somerset beach," for its proximity to **Somerset West**. In 1918, at the request of the townsfolk, the name was shortened to *The Strand*, and although this was officially abbreviated further in 1937 to *Strand*, the town today is always referred to as "The Strand."

Strydenburg. *Town, east central Cape Province, South Africa.* The town was founded by the Dutch Reformed Church in 1892 and given an Afrikaans name meaning "town of strife." The reference is to an initial dispute regarding the choice of site.

Stutterheim. *Town, southeastern Cape Province, South Africa.* The town arose from a mission station set up in 1837. In 1857 a fort named *Döhne Post* was built, its name given for J. L. *Döhne*, the first missionary. The name was soon after changed to its present form, for Major-General Carl Gustav von *Stutterheim* (1815–1871), commander of the British-German Legion who had built the fort.

Sua. See **Soa Pan.**

Sudan. *Republic, northeastern Africa.* The name represents Arabic *sūdān*, a short form of *balad as-sūdān*, "land of the blacks," from *balad*, "land," *al*, "the" (here *as* before *s*), and *sūdān*, plural of *aswad*, "black" (cf. **Guinea**, and comment on *Azania* under **South Africa**). There are currently two applications for the name. The first is to the region of Africa that extends across the continent from the west coast to the Abyssinian Highlands (Ethiopia), otherwise the area north of the Equator that is inhabited by black peoples under Muslim influence. (The people are distinguished as "black" by contrast with the lighter-skinned Arabs, to the north.) The second, more recent, application is to the modern republic, whose former name (from 1899 to 1956) was *Anglo-Egyptian Sudan*. Modern Mali, under French rule, was formerly known as *French Sudan* (from 1890 to 1958).

Suez. *City and port, northeastern Egypt.* The name represents Arabic *as-suways*, from the Egyptian *suan*, "beginning." Already in the 7th century AD the town was the terminal point of the canal connecting the Red Sea with the Nile. From 1869 the city and port has also been the southern terminus of the Suez Canal, opened that year. (Its northern terminal is Port Said.) Some Egyptologists have linked the name with that of the oasis of **Siwa**, in northwestern Egypt, although this usually has another interpretation.

Sukuma. *Region, northeastern Tanzania.* The name is an ethnic one, for the *Sukuma* people who inhabit this region, south of Lake Victoria. Their name means "northern ones," by contrast with the **Nyamwezi** south of them, to which they are very similar. Together, the Sukuma and Nyamwezi make up almost a quarter of the population of Tanzania.

Sundays. *River, South Africa.* The river rises in central Cape Province and flows south to enter the sea at Algoa Bay. Its name, in Afrikaans *Sondags*, is popularly said to refer to its historic function as a border of an area where the Sabbath had to be strictly observed. It is more likely, however, that it represents the name of a pioneer family who settled in the region. The lower reach of the river has the local self-descriptive name *t'Nuka t'Kamma*, "grassy river."

Surt. *Coastal town, northern Libya.* The town, also known as *Sirte*, has a name of the same origin as that of the Gulf of **Sidra** (or *Sirte*) on which it lies. Just south of the town is the section of the Sahara known as the *Surt* (or *Sirte*) Desert.

Sutherland. *Town, southwestern Cape Province, South Africa.* The town, west of Beaufort West, was founded in 1858 by the Dutch Reformed Church and named for a local minister, the Rev. Henry *Sutherland* (1790–1879). The name happens to be appropriate for a place in the south of the province and of South Africa as a whole.

Swaershoek. *Region, southeastern Cape Province, South Africa.* The region, between Cradock and Somerset East, has an Afrikaans name meaning "brothers-in-law glen," referring to the related Du Plessis, Erasmus, Jordaan, and Malan families who live here.

Swakopmund. *Town and resort, western Namibia.* The town was laid out in 1897 when a German military base was established here. Its name means "mouth of the Swakop," the latter being the river that enters the sea here. Its own name represents Khoikhoin (Hottentot) *tsoa-xoub*, from *tsoa*, "hole," and *xoub*, "excrement," referring to the deposits of mud and waste that it leaves along its banks after flooding.

Swartberg. *Mountains, southern Cape Province, South Africa.* The Afrikaans name, meaning "black mountain," translates the Khoikhoin (Hottentot) name *Nogareb*, with the same meaning. The reference is to the dark appearance of the mountains.

Swartkops. *River, southeastern Cape Province, South Africa.* The Afrikaans name of the river northwest of Port Elizabeth means "black hills," referring to the dark-colored hills through which it flows. The name is also that of a village here.

Swartruggens. *Town, western Transvaal, South Africa.* The Afrikaans name, meaning "black backs," refers to the dark-colored ridges of the hills here.

Swaziland. *Kingdom, South Africa.* The country, between South Africa to the west and Mozambique to the east, takes its name from its indigenous people, the *Swazi.* This was the name given by the Zulus to the race whose own name for themselves is *Swati*, from *Mswati*, originally the name of a 16th century king. His own name perhaps means "rod," "stick." However, the name is specifically related not to him but to

Chief *Mswati* II (c. 1820–1868), who became king in 1840 and who was the son of Sobhuza I, founder of the Swazi nation. The Swazis themselves were a Nguni clan originally called *Ngwane*, and this name is now in current use as an alternate indigenous name for the country. It comes from their chief, *Ngwane* III, who in about 1750 led a group of Dlamini-Nguni to settle in this southeastern region of Africa. Cf. **KaNgwane.**

Swellendam. *Town, southwestern Cape Province, South Africa.* Town, southwestern Cape Province, South Africa. The town was founded in 1747 and named for Hendrik *Swellengrebel* (1700–1760), governor of the Cape from 1739 to 1751, and his wife Helena, née ten *Damme.*

Sydney-on-Vaal. *Town, northern Cape Province, South Africa.* The name of the town, west of Kimberley, is of disputed origin. The latter part refers to its location on the *Vaal* River. The first part may refer to one *Sidney* Mendelssohn, a local landowner, or to *Sydney* Shippard, a district lawyer.

Syrtis Major. See Gulf of **Sidra.**

Syrtis Minor. See Gulf of **Sidra.**

Tabankulu. *Village, Transkei, South Africa.* The village, established in 1894, has a Xhosa name meaning "big mountain," with reference to the mountainous terrain here.

Table Bay. *Inlet, southwestern Cape Province, South Africa.* The bay, an inlet that forms the harbor of Cape Town, was visited by the Portuguese in about 1503, when they named it *Aquada de Saldanha*, "watering place of Saldanha," for the navigator Antonio *de Saldanha*, who anchored here then. In 1601 a Dutch fleet under Joris van Spilbergen named it with its present name (Dutch *Tafelbaai*) for the **Table Mountain** that overlooks it. When the bay gained its new name, the name *Saldanha Bay* was transferred to another bay some 60 miles (100 km) to the north.

Table Mountain. *Mountain, southwestern Cape Province, South Africa.* The mountain, south of Cape Town, was originally named *A Meza*, "the table," by Portuguese navigators of the 15th century. The name refers to the virtually horizontal layers of sandstone that give it its distinct flat-topped shape. The mountain, moreover, has its own cloud cover, known locally as "the Tablecloth," which forms when the wind is in the southeast. The Dutch version of the name, *Tafelberg*, is first recorded in the early 17th century. (A colloquial name for the mountain is *Devil's Peak*, from the legend that the cloud cover is caused by the tobacco smoke of Van Hunks, a Dutch pirate sea captain who once lost a smoking contest here with the Devil.) See also **Table Bay.**

Tafelberg. See **Table Mountain.**

Tagdempt. See **Tiaret.**

Talak. *Region, northwestern Niger.* The Tamashek (Berber) name means "clay," referring to the soil of the plain here.

Talana. *Village, west central Natal, South Africa.* The Zulu name means "little shelf," referring to a nearby hill with a flat top.

Tamaran. See **Canary Islands.**

Tamat Edderit. *Watersource, northwestern Niger.* The name is that of a spring, mountain, and valley. The Tamashek (Berber) meaning is "gum tree of fatness."

Tananarive. See **Antananarivo.**

Tanatave. See **Toamasina.**

Tanezrouft. *Desert region, North Africa.* The region of the Sahara, lying in southern Algeria and northern Mali, takes its name from Tuareg *tanezruft*, "waterless desert." The region lacks not only water but also vegetation, and was long shunned by travelers, with the first European crossing made (by a Frenchman) only in 1913.

Tanganyika. *Lake, Central Africa.* The lake was discovered by the British explorer Sir Richard Burton in 1858, and he explained its name as deriving from the local phrase *kou tanganyika*, meaning "to join," "to meet," referring to a place where waters meet or tribes gather. Another theory derives the second part of the name from the *nyika* nut (*Trapa natans*), a type of water chestnut, whose plants float on the lake in great masses. Sir Henry Morton Stanley, who surveyed the lake in 1876, also endeavored to establish the origin of the name: "I made many attempts to discover whether the Wajiji knew why the lake was called Tanganika. They all replied they did not know, unless it was because it was large, and canoes could make long voyages on it. They did not call small lakes Tanganika, but they call them Kitanga. . . . Nika is a word they could not explain the derivation of. . . . One day, while translating into their language English words, I came to the word 'plain,' for which I obtained *nika* as being the term in Kijiji. As Africans are accustomed to describe large bodies of water as being like plains, 'it spreads out like a plain,' I think that a satisfactory signification of the term has finally been obtained in 'the plain-like lake'" (*Through the Dark Continent*, 1878). Stanley adds that the Wakawendi name for the lake was *Msaga*, "tempestuous one." Later, the name was that of the British mandated territory formed in 1920 out of British-occupied German East Africa and in 1964 uniting with **Zanzibar** to form the republic of **Tanzania.**

Tangier. *City and port, northern Morocco.* The ancient city, on the Strait of Gibraltar, was a Phoenician trading post in the 15th century BC. Its name is generally linked with that of *Tingis,* son of the mythological giant Atlas, which itself probably represents a Phoenician word meaning "river." However, the name may actually mean "harbor." The city's name has been (and still sometimes is) popularly spelled *Tangiers*, by association with **Algiers**, to the east.

Tanis. *Ancient city, northern Egypt.* The historic city, located in the eastern part of the Nile Delta and at one time the capital of Egypt, has a name of uncertain origin. Its Egyptian name was *Djāni,* and it is mentioned in the Bible as *Zoan* (Numbers 13:22).

Tanzania. *Republic, East Africa.* The republic was formed in 1964 on the union of **Tanganyika** and **Zanzibar**. The name represents equally (and thus fittingly) the first syllables of their own names, and has the Latin-style suffix *-ia* implying "land." The name is said to have been proposed by Sir Cosmo Parkinson of the Colonial Office.

Taolagnaro. *Town and port, southern Madagascar.* The name derives from a southern dialect form of Malagasy, and represents *taolo*, "bones," and *gnaro*, "many." The town is said to have arisen on a site where many human remains were found. It was founded by the French in 1643 and originally had the name *Port-Dauphin*, from the title (*dauphin*) of the eldest son of the king of France who was heir to the throne. In the year stated this was Louis XIV.

Tarfaya. *Town and port, southwestern Morocco.* The town is said to take its name from Arabic *ṭarfā*, "tamarisk," a shrub found on many coastal sites in North and northwest Africa. The present town was founded at the end of the 19th century by a British trader and was originally known as *Port Victoria.* It was occupied by Spain in 1916 and became the extraterritorial capital of the Spanish Sahara. From 1950 to 1958 it was renamed *Villa Bens* or *Cabo Yubi.* The former name commemorated Francisco *Bens* Argandoña, ruler of the Río de Oro Dependent Protectorate (later Spanish Sahara) from 1903 to 1912. The latter name is that of the nearby peninsula of *Cap Juby.*

Tarkastad. *Town, eastern Cape Province, South Africa.* The town was established in 1862 and took the name of the *Tarka* River on which it stands. This in turn may represent the Khoikhoin (Hottentot) name *Taraxalal,* meaning "place rich in women."

Tataouine. *Town, southeastern Tunisia.* The full Berber name of the town is *Foum Tataouine,* meaning "mouth of the springs."

Taung. *Village, Bophuthatswana, South Africa.* The Tswana name derives from that of the *Tau* tribe, who formerly had their home here. Their own name means "lion," and is probably in turn that of a chief so called.

Tchai-Tchai. See **Xai-Xai.**

Tchaourou. *Village, central Benin.* The name is a corruption of *Tchaouilou,* meaning "place where the horses have a caparison [*tchaou*]."

Teebus. *Village, east central Cape Province, South Africa.* The Afrikaans name means "tea caddy," referring to the shape of a nearby hill. To the north of this is another hill named *Koffiebus,* "coffee caddy."

Telimélé. *Village, western Guinea.* The village, founded in 1903, has a name representing Fula (Peul) *teli* and Susu *meli,* both words for the tree *Erythrophtaeum guineense.*

Tell el Amarna. *Ancient city, northern Egypt.* The city, on the right bank of the Nile, was built in about 1375 BC by Amenhotep IV as the new capital of his kingdom when he abandoned his worship of Amon and devoted himself to that of Aton, at the same time changing his name to Akhetaton. Its name means "mound of the Amra," from Arabic *tell,* "mound," "hill," and *Amra,* the name of a local Bedouin tribe.

Tell el-Kebir. See **El Tell el-Kebir.**

Tell el-Maskhutah. See **El Tell el-Maskhutah.**

Tenerife. *Island, west central Canary Islands.* The largest island of the group takes its name from the volcano that is its highest point. This in turn represents Guanche *Chinerfe.* The origin of the name is uncertain, although it could either be that of a Guanche chief or have the meaning "snow mountain." The Romans knew Tenerife as *Nivaria,* "snowy one." (The Guanche were the local people of the Canary Islands before their extermination by the Spanish after the Spanish conquest of the islands in 1405.)

Terceira. *Island, central Azores.* The island has a Portuguese name meaning "third," allegedly because it was the third island of the group to be discovered or settled. The first two were **Santa Maria** and **São Miguel.** Terceira was originally named *Ilha de Jesus Cristo,* from the day of its Easter discovery, March 21, 1450.

Tete. *Town and province, western Mozambique.* The name represents the Chisema word *tete,* meaning "reed," "canebrake." The town lies on the Zambezi River.

Tétouan. *City, northern Morocco.* The city, the former capital of Spanish Morocco, has a name that is a Spanish corruption of Berber *tittawin,* the plural of *tit,* "spring."

Teyateyaneng. *Town, northwestern Lesotho.* The town takes its name from the *Teya-Teyane* River near which it stands. The river's own name represents local words meaning "flowing sands."

Thaba Bosiu. *Mountain, eastern Lesotho.* The mountain is venerated as the site where the Basuto nation was founded. The settlement here of the same name was the capital of Basutoland (now Lesotho) until 1869, when the present capital, Maseru, was founded 11 miles (19 km) to the west. Its name means "mountain of night," said to refer to the fact that the mountain appears to grow in size at night.

Thaba Nchu. *Village and mountain, Bophuthatswana, South Africa.* The village takes its name from the mountain, which has a Sotho name meaning "black mountain," with reference to its dark appearance.

Thaba Putsoa. *Mountain range, western Lesotho.* The name, that of the highest mountain in the range, is of Sotho origin and means "blue mountain," with reference to its appearance. The name spread from the individual peak to the whole range.

Thabazimbi. *Town, northwestern Transvaal, South Africa.* The name is that of the mountain here, which has a Sotho name meaning "iron mountain." The town owes its existence to the establishment of the Iron and Steel Corporation (ISCOR) at this site in 1919.

Thamaga. *Village, southeastern Botswana.* The Tswana name means "red and white ox," referring to the coloring and appearance of a hill here.

Thamalakane. See **Maun.**

Thebes. *Ancient city, east central Egypt.* The historic city, on the west bank of the Nile at the point where Luxor now stands, derives its name from Semitic *teba*, "chest," "box." Its Egyptian name was *Wāset*, from the sacred *was* or scepter. It was also *Nīt* or *Nīūt*, meaning "city" (that is, of the god Amon). The latter gave its biblical name of *No* (Jeremiah 46:25). At one time its Greek name was *Diospolis*, "city of Zeus," since Zeus was equated with Amon. The Egyptian city gave its name to its namesake in Greece, the chief city of Boeotia, founded by the Phoenician Cadmos but destroyed in the 4th century BC by Alexander the Great.

Theunissen. *Town, central Orange Free State, South Africa.* The town was established in 1907 and was originally named *Smaldeel*, "narrow portion," after a farm here. It was subsequently given its present name in honor of Commandant Helgaardt *Theunissen*, the original owner of the farm.

Thiès. *Town, western Senegal.* The name of the town, east of Dakar, represents a local pronunciation of French *caisse*, "case," "crate." The reference is to a depot where crates of materials were stored from around 1885 during construction of the Dakar to St. Louis railroad. The present town grew from the depot, and is still an important rail center.

Thohoyandu. *Capital of Venda, South Africa.* The town has a Venda name meaning "head of an elephant," with symbolic reference to the power that this animal represents. The town was planned before the independence of Venda in 1979, and construction began in 1980.

Thomson's Falls. See **Nyahururu.**

Thysville. See **Mbanza-Ngungu.**

Tiaret. *Town, northern Algeria.* The town, formerly also known as *Tagdempt*, arose as an Arab settlement in the 7th century. Its name is said to mean "lioness."

Tiassalé. *Village, southern Côte d'Ivoire.* There are various explanations of the name. One derives it from a river spirit, *Tiassa*, another sees it as a corruption of Baule *gyassalé*, "the rocks are there," and a third takes it from *tiassalé*, "it is forgotten," the remark made by a local queen on leaving the place.

Tibesti Mountains. *Mountain group, northwestern Chad.* The group takes its name from the *Tibu*, a Berber people of the Sahara. Their own name is said to mean "bird," referring either to their "whistling" speech or to their speed in running. More prosaically, their name has also been derived from the local words *tu*, "mountain," and *bu*, "inhabitants," as they are hill dwellers.

Tichitt. *Village, east central Mauritania.* The village is said to have been founded in the 12th century by the Almohad patriarch Abd al-Mumin who was blind when leading his people here in migration. When they arrived at the appointed place he sniffed a pinch of moist clay and cried "*Tü chutu*," "This suits me." The present name then evolved from these words.

Tiflet. *Town, northern Morocco.* The name is a contraction of Berber *tifelfelt*, "pepper," itself a borrowing of Arabic *filfil*.

Tigré. *Province, northern Ethiopia.* The province, bordering Eritrea, takes its name from the indigenous *Tigré* peoples. The origin of their own name is uncertain.

Tih, Gebel el. *Plateau, northeastern Egypt.* The name is that of the plateau in the central Sinai Peninsula. The Arabic meaning is "mountain [of] the wanderings," as a short form of the full name, *jabal et-ṭīh-beni-isrāʾīl*, "mountain [of] the wanderings [of the] sons [of] Israel." The reference is to the biblical wanderings of the "children of Israel" before entering the Promised Land (Numbers 14).

Tillabéri. *Town, southwestern Niger.* The town, on the Niger River northwest of the capital, Niamey, has a Songhai name meaning "[place of] *Tila* the great," from the name of a local chief and *beri*, "big." This contrasts with the nearby village of *Tilakeïna*, "[place of] Tila the small."

Timbo. *Town, west central Guinea.* The town, in the Fouta Djalon mountains, has a Mande name meaning literally "level way out," from *ti*, "straight," "level," and *bo*, "way out," "exit." The reference is to the location of the town by a hill at the edge of a plain.

Timbuktu. *Town, central Mali.* The town, legendary for its remoteness, derives its name from Tuareg *tim-buktu*, said to be the name of an old slavewoman, meaning "woman with a big navel," left to guard valuable objects here while the Tuareg were tending their flocks to the north. Alternately, the origin may lie in Berber *tin*, "place of," and either a female name *Buktu* or an Arabic word meaning "dune." Timbuktu was settled by Tuaregs in the early 11th century.

Timsah, Lake. *Lake, northeastern Egypt.* The lake, traversed by the Suez Canal, has a name that represents Arabic *buḥaira at-timsāḥ*, "lake [of] the crocodile."

Tiourourt. *Watersource, western Mauritania.* The springs, near the coast south of the capital, Nouakchott, have a name representing Zenaga *taourouert*, "gum trees."

Tizi-n-Talrhemt. *Village, northern Morocco.* The village takes its name from the pass here through the High Atlas mountains. Its name is a Berber one meaning "pass of the she-camel."

Tizi-Ouzou. *Town, northern Algeria.* The first part of the town's name is the Berber word for "pass," found in the names of many places in North Africa (e.g., **Tizi-n-Talrhemt**). The second word is the name of a species of flowering broom that grows (or grew) in the pass where the town is located.

Tiznit. *Town, southwestern Morocco.* The name of the town derives from a Berber word for "basket," this itself being the name of a spring here near the Great Mosque.

Tlemcen. *City, northwestern Algeria.* The city, capital of an Arab kingdom from the 12th to the late 14th century, has a name that is a French corruption of Berber *tilimsàn*, the plural of *talmist*, "spring." The earlier name of the town, as a Roman settlement in the 4th century, was *Pomaria*, from the plural of Latin *pomarium*, "orchard." The Berbers later renamed it **Agadir**, as for the city in Morocco. In due course this merged with the nearby Almoravid military settlement of *Tagrart*, meaning "camp," founded in the 11th century. The resulting union finally adopted its present name in the 13th century.

Toamasina. *City and port, eastern Madagascar.* The name is said to represent a combination of Malagasy *tòa*, "as if," and *màsina*, "holy" (also "salt"). The story goes that King Radama I, reigning in the early 19th century, saw sea water for the first time and, on tasting it, exclaimed, "How salty it is!" But this is almost certainly a legend devised to explain the name, which even so may well have a sense based on "salt." The French knew the port as *Tamatave,* a corruption of its Malagasy name. When the Portuguese first visited the town in the 17th century, they corrupted its name to *São Tomás*, "St. Thomas."

Tobruk. *Town and port, northeastern Libya.* The name represents Arabic *ṭubruq*, a corruption of the port's Greek name, *Antipurtos*, "opposite the tower," from *anti*, "opposite," and *purtos*, "tower." The bay here was sheltered from the wind by an island opposite a tower on the shore.

Togo. *Republic, West Africa.* The region was so named in 1884 by the German explorer and government official Gustav Nachtigal. He took the name from that of a small coastal village where he had signed a treaty with the local people. The original name of the village, now *Togoville*, is said to have been *Miayi To Godo*, "we shall go beyond the hill," although it is much more likely to have been adopted from that of nearby Lake *Togo*. Its own name probably comes from Ewe *to*, "water," and *go*, "bank," "shore."

Tokwe. *River, Zimbabwe.* The river, in the southeast of the country, has a name meaning "river that sweeps away," referring to its regular flooding.

Toliary. *Town and port, southwestern Madagascar.* The name represents Malagasy *Tòleara.* The origin of this is explained as follows. A foreign traveler in Madagascar asked a native in a canoe where he was going to land. The man thought he was being asked where there was a mooring place, so replied "*tòly eròa*," "the moorage down there." This was then corrupted to the present name.

Tolmeta. *Coastal town, northeastern Libya.* The present town stands on the site of ancient *Ptolemaïs,* so named in the 3rd century BC for *Ptolemy* III, king of Egypt, who united Cyrenaica with Egypt. The current name, and its Arabic equivalent, *ṭulmaythah*, are corruptions of the original.

Tongaat. *Town and resort, eastern Natal, South Africa.* The town, north of Durban, was founded in 1849 and was originally named *Victoria*, for Queen *Victoria* of England (1819–1901). After the second Boer War (also known as the South African War) of 1899–1902, the name was changed to its present form, deriving from that of the *Tongati* River here. Its own Zulu name is said to come from the trees on its banks, the fruits of which are known as *thonga*.

Tonkoui, Mount. *Mountain, western Côte d'Ivoire.* The name of the peak represents Dan *tonkpi*, "big mountain."

Toteng. *Village, northern Botswana.* The name derives from *Letota*, the name of the abandoned home of chief *Letsholathebe* I, and in turn based on his own name.

Touba. *Village, west central Senegal.* The name is found both here and elsewhere in West Africa, for example for villages in northwestern Guinea and southwestern Mali. The meaning is "favorable," ultimately from Arabic *ṭaiyib*, "good," with the name itself given under Islamic influence.

Toukoto. *Village, southwestern Mali.* The village, northwest of the capital, Bamako, has a name meaning "near the forest," from Mande *tu*, "forest," and *koto*, "near." The implication is that the place is protected by the forest.

Toumodi. *Town, south central Côte d'Ivoire.* The name means literally "buying before eating," from Baule *to*, "to buy," *mo*, "before," and *ndi*, "to eat." The local inhabitants had a reputation for meanness, or at best prudence, and demanded payment from visitors before giving them a meal.

Touna. *Village, southern Mali.* The village, southeast of Ségou, has a name meaning "near the termitarium," based on Mande *tu*, "termitarium" (the nest of a colony of termites).

Touws River. *Town, southwestern Cape Province, South Africa.* The town takes its name from the river, whose own name is of Khoikhoin (Hottentot) origin, meaning "ash river," presumably referring to the appearance of the soil here.

Transkei. *Bantustan, Cape Province, South Africa.* The name of the Bantu homeland, declared an independent state in 1976, is derived from Latin *trans*, "across," and *Kei*, the name of the river (usually called the *Great Kei*) across which it lies from the south. The name was probably modeled on that of **Transvaal.** See also **Ciskei** and **Kei**.

Transvaal. *Province, northeastern South Africa.* The province was formed in 1877 when Britain annexed the territory then known as the South African Republic. Its name derives from Latin *trans*, "across," and **Vaal**, the name of the river across which it lies from the south. The river now forms its southern border with the Orange Free State. (An earlier name of this type was that of *Transorangia*, a Boer settlement "beyond the Orange" that existed in the southern part of the present Orange Free State from 1824 to 1848.) Cf. **Transkei.**

Trappes Valley. *Village, southeastern Cape Province, South Africa.* The village takes its name from Captain Charles *Trappes* (1776–1828), founder of the nearby town of Bathurst.

Triangle. *Village, southeastern Zimbabwe.* The name refers to the sugarcane plantations here laid out experimentally in the form of a triangle by the Scottish immigrant

Thomas Murray MacDougall (1881–1964).

Trichardt. *Village, southeastern Transvaal, South Africa.* The village was founded as a settlement of the Dutch Reformed Church and named for Carolus Johannes *Trichardt* (1811–1901), son of the Voortrekker leader Louis Trichardt, who himself gave his name to **Louis Trichardt**, in the north of the province.

Tripoli. *Capital of Libya.* The name, in the form *Tripolis*, was originally that of a Phoenician colony founded in what is now northwestern Libya in about the 7th century BC. Its name refers to its three main cities, and derives from Greek *treis*, "three," and *polis*, "city." The modern city and port of *Tripoli* stands on the site of Oea, one of the three. The other two, which no longer survive, were Leptis Magna and Sabratha. The Arabic name of the city is *ṭarābulus al-gharb*, "Tripoli of the west," as distinct from its namesake, also originally a Phoenician colony, the port of *Tripoli* in Lebanon, which is *ṭarābulus ash-shām*, "Tripoli of Syria." See also **Tripolitania.**

Tripolitania. *Region, northwestern Libya.* The original region of the name was the Roman province created in AD 297 (with two others) out of the much larger province of **Africa**. It took its name from the three chief cities that were historically part of the original Phoenician colony of *Tripolis* (see **Tripoli**). In modern times the name became familiar as that of the territory in northwestern Libya gained by Italy from Turkey in 1912 and under Italian rule until World War II. See also **Tripoli.**

Tristan da Cunha. *Island group, South Atlantic.* The group name is that of three small islands, about halfway between South Africa and South America, that were discovered in 1506 by the Portuguese navigator *Tristão da Cunha* (1460–1540) and named for him. (Individually, the name applies to the largest and northernmost island. The other two, both uninhabited, are respectively *Inaccessible* and *Nightingale.* A fourth island, *Gough*, is associated with the group.) The group remained a vaguely Portuguese possession until 1816, when the islands were annexed by the British.

Tristão, Îles. *Island group, western Guinea.* The islands, near the border with Guinea-Bissau, are named for the Portuguese explorer Nuño *Tristão* (died 1443), discoverer of Cape Blanc, killed while investigating the Rio de Oro. See also **Nunez.**

Trompsburg. *Town, southern Orange Free State, South Africa.* The town was originally known as *Jagersfontein Road*, for **Jagersfontein**, to which the road from here led. It was then named *Hamilton*, for Sir *Hamilton* John Goold-Adams (1858–1920), acting governor of the Orange River Colony from 1901 to 1905 and governor from 1907 to 1910. This name was transferred to a railroad junction near Bloemfontein, and the town was given its present name to commemorate Jan and Bastiaan *Tromp*, owners of the farm on which it had been originally established in 1891.

Tsavo East National Park. *National park, southern Kenya.* Taken together, *Tsavo East National Park* and the rather smaller *Tsavo West National Park*, to the southwest, form one of the largest game reserves in the world. They take their name from the *Tsavo* River that flows between them. Its own name is a local (Kamba) word meaning "slaughter," referring to some historic intertribal battle here.

Tses. *Village, southern Namibia.* The village has a name of Nama origin that is said to mean "place of daylight."

Tsévié. *Town, southern Togo.* The town, north of the capital, Lomé, has a name traditionally explained as follows. In one of the many wars that formerly took place in Togo, a group of young men working in the fields near present-day Tsévié fled to Anlo, the chief Ewe town and the one that has the greatest historical importance both for the Togolese and for subsequent German and English colonists. The king of Anlo invited the elderly people who had stayed behind to come as well. They replied: "*ayi le tsetsem vivivi, eyata mimele vava ge o*," "The beans are about to grow, so we cannot come." The name of modern Tsévié derives from the first syllables of the two words *tsetsem vivivi.*

Tshabong. *Village, southern Botswana.* The name is a Tlhaping one and means "place from where people have fled," probably with reference to its isolated location.

Tshaneni. *Town, northeastern Swaziland.* The name is a shortened form of Siswati *etshaneni*, "at the rock," with reference to a prominent rock in the town.

Tshesebe. *Village, eastern Botswana.* The name of the village derives from that of the sassaby or tshesebe (*Damaliscus lunatus*), a type of large antelope also known as the bastard hartebeest, at one time common here.

Tsholotsho. *Village, southwestern Zimbabwe.* The name is properly that of a dried-up lake here, called by the San (Bushmen) *Tshololo Njowe*, "head of an elephant," apparently with reference to its shape.

Tsiafajavona. *Mountain, central Madagascar.* The mountain has a Malagasy name meaning "[place] that is always in the mist."

Tsinjoarivo. *Village, east central Madagascar.* The village, on the eastern heights of the Ankaratra mountains, has a Malagasy name appropriate for its lofty location, meaning "overlooking a thousand."

Tsitsikamma Forest and Coastal National Park. *National park, southern Cape Province, South Africa.* The park, on the coast west of Port Elizabeth, has a Khoikhoin (Hottentot) name meaning either "bright water," referring to the many streams here, or "waters begin," with similar reference to the abundance of rivers and streams.

Tsodilo Hills. *Hills, northwestern Botswana.* The hills have a local name meaning "steep." They are situated in groups known to the San (Bushmen) as "Man, Woman, and Child."

Tsolo. *Village, Transkei, South Africa.* The Xhosa name means "pointed," and refers to a number of peaked hills nearby. The village was established in 1876.

Tsomo. *Village, Transkei, South Africa.* The village, established in 1877, is named for the local river. Its own name derives from that of *Tsomo,* a Xhosa chief who formerly had his kraal where the bridge now crosses the river.

Tsumeb. *Town, northern Namibia.* The town developed on a site known to the Herero as *oTjisume*, "place of algae," with reference to the surface outcrops of copper ore here, resembling algae. This name was corrupted by the San (Bushmen) to *Sumeb* and then by Europeans to its present form. Copper ore was discovered here in 1851 by the English anthropologist and explorer, Sir Francis Galton, and a mine opened in 1900. The town remains the chief copper-mining center in the country.

Tugela. *River, central Natal, South Africa.* The river rises in Mont aux Sources and, through a series of falls (the *Tugela Falls*), flows east to the Indian Ocean. Its name is a Zulu word meaning "startling one," presumably referring either to the falls or to the river's unpredictable flow or appearance at some point.

Tulbagh. *Town, southwestern Cape Province, South Africa.* The town, northeast of Cape Town, is in an area originally named *Waveren* by Simon van der Stel, commander of the Cape (see **Simonstown**), for one of his Dutch relations, Oetgens van *Waveren*. The Dutch Reformed Church founded a settlement here in 1743 and the resulting village was named *Roodezand*, "red sand." The present name was given in 1804 to commemorate Ryk *Tulbagh* (1699–1771), governor of the Cape from 1751 to his death.

Tuli. *Village, southern Zimbabwe.* The village is famous for its historical site of *Fort Tuli*, the first defense post built in Rhodesia by the pioneers who crossed the Limpopo in 1890. Its name, which is also that of the river on which it stands, was originally *Uhtuli*, representing the Ndebele word for "dust."

Tunis. *Capital of Tunisia.* The present city and port, on the Mediterranean, was founded in about 1000 BC as a suburb of ancient Carthage, rising to power from the late 7th century AD after the capture of Carthage by the Arabs. Its Greek name was *Tunēs*, said to derive from an Ahaggar (see **Ahaggar**) dialect word meaning "lying down," and by extension "spending the night." If this is so, the general sense would be something like "encampment." The name has also been associated with that of *Tanith*, the chief goddess of Carthage, herself linked with Astarte. The precise origin of the name is uncertain. *Tunis* was equally the name of the Berber state that became a Roman province of Africa in the 2d century AD and that was the forerunner of modern **Tunisia.**

Tunisia. *Republic, North Africa.* The country takes its name from **Tunis**, its capital. Since *Tunis* was also the name for the ancient state and province here, some languages today have the same name for both country and capital, for example Spanish *Túnez* and Russian *Tunis.*

Turkana, Lake. *Lake, East Africa.* The long, narrow lake, mainly in Kenya in the Great Rift Valley, takes its name from the local *Turkana* tribe, a people of Hamitic origin. The origin of their name is uncertain. The lake is still sometimes known by its old colonial name, *Lake Rudolf.* It was discovered in 1888 by the Hungarian explorer Count Samuel Teleki and the Austrian explorer L. von Höhnel, who named it in honor of the Austrian crown Prince *Rudolf* (1858–1889), son of Francis Joseph I, emperor of Austria. The Maasai know the lake as *Embasso Narok*, "black lake." Northeast of Lake Turkana is Lake *Chew Bahir*, in southwestern Ethiopia. This was also named by Teleki, as *Lake Stefanie*, for Rudolf's wife (married 1881), Princess *Stefanie* of Belgium (died 1945). This colonial name is also still sometimes found on maps. The Maasai name for it is *Embasso Ebor*, "white lake."

Tutume. *Village, eastern Botswana.* The village takes its name from the seasonal watercourse here, whose own name is of Tswana origin and represents the sound of water bubbling out of the ground.

Tweeling. *Town, northeastern Orange Free State, South Africa.* The name is Afrikaans for "twins," referring to two hillocks locally.

Tweespruit. *Town, eastern Orange Free State, South Africa.* A settlement for British soldiers was established here in the early years of the 20th century and was named for the confluence of two streams at the site, from Afrikaans *twee*, "two," and *spruit*, "stream."

Tylden. *Village, southeastern Cape Province, South Africa.* The village is named for Captain Richard *Tylden* (1819–1855), of the Royal Engineers, who led a campaign against the Tembu people in 1851.

Tzaneen. *Town, northern Transvaal, South Africa.* The name of the town is of uncertain origin. It may represent Karanga *dzana*, "to dance," with some local reference, or relate to Tsonga *tsana*, a shrub used for making baskets. It is probably tribal in origin, and perhaps actually means "place where people gathered."

Ubangi. *River, Central Africa.* The river is formed by the confluence of the Bomu and the Uele on the northern border of Zaïre, from which point it flows west and south along the border with Zaïre and the Central African Republic into the Congo. Its Bantu name means "land of the rapids," from *u*, "land," and *bangi*, "rapid." The rapids also gave the name of the mixed *Bangi* peoples who inhabit this riverine region. Cf. **Bangui**. The combined names of the Ubangi and Shari rivers gave the former name (*Ubangi-Shari*) of the **Central African Republic.**

Ubangi-Shari. See **Central African Republic.**

Ubombo. *Village, northern Natal, South Africa.* The village takes its name from the mountain chain here. Its own name derives from the Zulu word *lubombo*, meaning "high ridge." See also **Lebombo Mountains.**

Ubundu. *Town, northeastern Zaïre.* The town, on the Congo River south of Kinshasa, takes its name from the local *Bundu* or *Bundi* people. For some years until 1966 the town bore the colonial name of *Ponthierville*, for the Belgian infantry officer Pierre *Ponthier* (1858–1893), killed in armed conflict with Arab slave traders.

Uganda. *Republic, East Africa.* The name means "land of the Ganda," from Swahili *u*, "land," and *Ganda*, the country's most numerous people.

Ugie. *Town, eastern Cape Province, South Africa.* The name was given to the region by a Scottish missionary in 1863, since the landscape reminded him of that round the *Ugie* River in his homeland. The town itself was established in 1885.

Uis. *Village, northwestern Namibia.* The name is of Khoikhoin (Hottentot) origin and means "place of brackish water."

Uitenhage. *Town, southern Cape Province, South Africa.* The town formed part of the district of Graaff-Reinet in 1804 and was named for J. A. *Uitenhage* de Mist (1749–1823), commissioner-general from 1803 to 1804.

Ujiji. *Town, western Tanzania.* The town, on the eastern shore of Lake Tanganyika, has a name meaning "land of the Jiji," from Swahili *u*, "land," and *Jiji*, a local people.

Ukerewe. See Lake **Victoria.**

Ulco. *Town, northern Cape Province, South Africa.* The town has important limeworks, and its name is an acronym for the *U*nion *L*ime *Co*mpany that operates them.

Ulundi. *Capital of KwaZulu, South Africa.* The town, also the former capital of Zululand, has a Zulu name denoting its status. It means "high place," and refers specifically to King Cetewayo's royal kraal, established in 1873 but burned down in 1879 when Cetewayo was defeated in the Zulu War.

Umbogintwini. *Coastal settlement, southeastern Natal, South Africa.* The name of the industrial area southwest of Durban is Zulu in origin and is that of the river here, properly the *Embokodweni*, "[river] of round stones."

Umfolozi Game Reserve. *Game reserve, KwaZulu, South Africa.* The name is that of the river here, and is said to mean either "river of fiber," with reference to the wild fig trees yielding bark for sewing fiber, or "erratic one," referring to the river's zigzag course.

Umfuli. *River, Zimbabwe.* The river, in the northwest of the country, has a name that is a form of *Mumvuri*, "river of shade," referring to the many trees along its banks.

Umguza. *Village, western Zimbabwe.* The name, also that of the river here, means "calabash snuffbox," that is, the gourd shell of the calabash tree used as such a box. The reference may be either to an incident of some kind, or else to the appearance of a local natural feature.

Umhlali. *Town, southeastern Natal, South Africa.* The town, near the coast northwest of Durban, takes its name from the river here. It is of Zulu origin and is said to mean either "resting place" or to refer to some wild orange trees (*Strychnos spinosa*) growing locally. If the former, the reference could be to the stay here of king Shaka, founder of the Zulu nation, before continuing to Umzimkulu.

Umhlanga Rocks. *Coastal settlement, southeastern Natal, South Africa.* The seaside resort, northeast of Durban, derives its name from the *Mhlanga* River here, whose own name comes from a Zulu word meaning "river of reeds."

Umkomaas. *Coastal settlement, southeastern Natal, South Africa.* The seaside resort, southwest of Durban, takes its name from the river here. The name is Zulu in origin and means either "gatherer of the waters" or, more probably, "place of cow whales." The latter refers to the frequent calving of whales in the river.

Umniati. *Village, central Zimbabwe.* The name is a corruption of *Munyati*, that of the river on which the village is located. The meaning is "river of buffaloes."

Umsweswe. *Village, central Zimbabwe.* The village, south of Kadoma, takes its name from the river on which it lies. The river's name is properly *Muzvezve,* meaning "sluggish river," "slow river," with *zvezve* (or *sweswe*) an imitative word representing the sound of someone walking with dragging feet.

Umtali. See **Mutare.**

Umtata. *Capital of Transkei, South Africa.* The town developed from a military post set up in 1882. It is named for the river (also spelled *Mtata* or *Mthatha*) on which it stands. The river's own name is probably a Xhosa word for a type of sneezewood (*Pteroxylon inerme*) that grows on its banks.

Umtentweni. *Coastal village, southern Natal, Southern Africa.* The seaside resort, northeast of Port Shepstone, derives its name from that of the river here, itself named for the *mtentweni* grass that grows along its banks.

Umvoti. *River, South Africa.* The river, rising in central Natal and flowing east to the Indian Ocean, has a Zulu name meaning "quiet river," "slow-flowing river."

Umzimkulu. *River and villge, southern Natal, South Africa.* The river forms the eastern border of Transkei, where the village of the same name is located, and flows southeast to enter the Indian Ocean at Port Shepstone. Its name is a Zulu word meaning "great place," from *umzi,* "place," and *kulu,* "great." The reference is not to the river but to an important residence of a chief here. The village was laid out in 1884 on a site that already operated as a trading center.

Umzimvubu. *River, South Africa.* The river rises in the Drakensberg near the meeting-point of the borders between Transkei, Lesotho, and Natal, and then flows southeast through Transkei to enter the Indian Ocean at Port St. Johns. Its Zulu name means "place of the hippopotamus," from *umzi,* "place," and *vubu,* "hippopotamus."

Umzingwani. *River, Zimbabwe.* The river rises in the southern part of the country and flows south to enter the Limpopo where this forms the border between Zimbabwe and South Africa. Its proper name is *Mudzingwani,* "river with small beginnings," referring to its inconspicuous source streams.

Umzinto. *Town, southern Natal, South Africa.* The town, southwest of Durban, derives its name from Zulu *umenziwezinto,* "kraal of achievement." The town arose round the sugar company that was established here in 1858.

Umzumbe. *Coastal town, southern Natal, South Africa.* The town is at the mouth of the *Mzumbe* River, and takes its name from it. The name is of Zulu origin and is said to mean either "dangerous river" or "winding river."

Unango. *Village, northwestern Mozambique.* The name is that of the mountain here, itself said to mean "clitoris," referring to its shape. The British Admiralty publication, *A Handbook of Portuguese Nyasaland,* issued in London in 1917, refers to "the imposing double peak of Unangu [about 5,000 ft.]."

Underberg. *Village, southwestern Natal, South Africa.* The name is descriptive of the site of the village at the foot of the Drakensberg. It arose round a railroad terminus built in 1916.

Uniondale. *Town, southern Cape Province, South Africa.* The town arose in 1865 as the amalgamation (union) of two separate villages named respectively *Hopedale* and *Lyon.* Hence its name.

Unyamwezi. See **Nyamwezi.**

Upington. *Town, northern Cape Province, South Africa.* The town developed from a mission station founded here in 1871. It was at first known as *Olijvenhoutsdrift,* "olive wood ford," but was renamed in 1884 for Sir Thomas *Upington* (1844–1898), prime minister of the Cape from 1884 to 1886, who visited it that year. The town's Khoikhoin (Hottentot) name is *Kharaes,* meaning "place of gravel." The reference is to the gravelly bed of the Orange River here.

Upper Egypt. *District, central Egypt.* The name traditionally applies to the valley of the Nile from El Minya in the north to the border with Sudan in the south. Here the terrain is generally higher than in the Nile Delta. Cf. **Lower Egypt.**

Upper Volta. See **Burkina Faso.**

Usakos. *Town, western Namibia.* The name is said to derive from a Nama word meaning "to grasp by the heel." The reference may be to the sticky clay by the spring here which makes walking difficult for people and animals. The town was founded in 1905 on a farm bought in order to mine copper.

Usutu. *River, central Swaziland.* The river, properly divided into the

Great Usutu and Little Usutu, has a Zulu name representing *uSutu*, "dark brown," referring to the color of the water. Some authorities link this name with the *Sotho* people of **Lesotho**.

Utica. *Ancient city, North Africa.* The historic settlement, northwest of Carthage in what is now Tunisia, has a name of Phoenician origin said to mean either "colony" or "old." The name would thus probably be related either to Hebrew *ʿatoq*, "to advance," "to move," or to Hebrew *ʿattīq*, "ancient." If the sense is "old," then it is to Utica that **Carthage** was perhaps by comparison the "new town." The city was founded by the Tyrians in about 1101 BC.

Utrecht. *Town, northwestern Natal, South Africa.* The town was laid out in 1854 and given its name two years later for the city in the Netherlands.

Uvongo Beach. *Coastal settlement, southern Natal, South Africa.* The seaside resort, between Port Shepstone and Margate, was established in about 1920. Its name is that of the river here, deriving from Zulu *ivungu*, from the verb *vungazela*, meaning "to make a rumbling sound." The reference is to the noise made by a waterfall on the river near the beach.

Vaal. *River, South Africa.* The river rises in the Drakensberg and flows west, forming the border between *Transvaal* and the Orange Free State, to empty into the Orange River in the northern Cape. It has a name of Afrikaans origin, from *vaal*, "pale" (related to German *fahl* and English *fallow*, as well as *pale* itself). This describes the gray color of its waters when in full flood and carrying silt, and in turn is almost certainly a translation of the Khoikhoin (Hottentot) name for the river, which is *ki-garep*.

Valley of the Kings. *Ancient burial site, east central Egypt.* The site, near Thebes, is famous for the tombs of the pharaohs (kings of Egypt) of the 18th, 19th, and 20th dynasties, that is, from 1567 BC to about 1085 BC. The Arabic name of the site, or more exactly of the valley in which the tombs are located, is *bībān al-mulūk*, "gates of the kings," from *bībān*, plural of *bāb*, "gate," *al*, "the," and *mulūk*, plural of *malik*, "king." To the southwest of the Valley of the Kings is the *Valley of the Queens,* where queens (and a few royal princes) of the 19th and 20th dynasties are buried. The Arabic name of the valley is *bībān al-ḥarīm*, "gates of the harem." (Arabic *ḥarīm* is the actual source of English *harem* and means literally "that which is prohibited.")

Valley of the Queens. See **Valley of the Kings.**

Vanderbijlpark. *Town, southern Transvaal, South Africa.* The steel-producing town, south of Johannesburg, was laid out in 1944 under the direction of Dr. Hendrik Johannes *van der Bijl* (1887–1948) as a new settlement for workers at the South African Iron and Steel Corporation (ISCOR), when that company was unable to expand further in Pretoria. It was thus named for him, with *park* added to denote its "garden city" plan.

Van Reenen. *Village, western Natal, South Africa.* The village, near the Orange Free State border, takes its name from *Van Reenen's Pass* across the Drakensberg here. This was itself named for Frans *van Reenen* (1816–1914), owner of a farm at its foot, who planned its route.

Vanrhynsdorp. *Town, western Cape Province, South Africa.* The town was established in 1887 on the farm owned by Petrus Benjamin *van Rhyn*, and is named for him, with Afrikaans *dorp* meaning "settlement."

Van Stadensrus. *Town, southeastern Orange Free State, South Africa.* The town was laid out in 1920 and is named for its founder, M. H. *van Staden*, with the last part of the name representing Afrikaans *rust*, "rest," "home."

Vanwyksdorp. *Village, southwestern Cape Province, South Africa.* The name means "Van Wyk's settlement," and is for the local *Van Wyk* family.

Vatomandry. *Town and port, eastern Madagascar.* The Malagasy name means "rock that sleeps," presumably because a local cliff or crag resembles a sleeping person.

Velddrif. *Coastal village, southwestern Cape Province, South Africa.* The fishing village has an Afrikaans name referring to the ford over the river here that took the road north from the region known as the *Sandveld*, "sandy field," so called for the sandy nature of its soil.

Vélingara. *Town, southern Senegal.* The town, near the border with Gambia, is said to have a name meaning "come, it is good," from Fulani (Peul) *veli*, "good," "favorable," and *ngara,* "come."

Venda. *Bantustan, northern Transvaal, South Africa.* The Bantu state, near the border with Zimbabwe, takes its name from the *Venda* people who were led here from the north in the 18th century by Chief Dimbanyika. Their name is said to mean either "world" or "land." The state was granted its independence in 1979.

Ventersburg. *Town, north central Orange Free State, South Africa.* The town was laid out in 1859 on a farm owned by the Voortrekker P. A. *Venter*, and is named for him. See also **Venterstad**.

Ventersdorp. *Town, southern Transvaal, South Africa.* The town, west of Johannesburg, was established in 1866 on a farm and named for its owner, Johannes *Venter.*

Venterstad. *Town, eastern Cape Province, South Africa.* The town was established in 1875 on a farm owned by Johannes J. T. *Venter* and is named for him. The original name was *Ventersburg*, but this was later altered to avoid confusion with **Ventersburg** in the Orange Free State. The last part of the name is thus Afrikaans *stad*, "city," not *burg*, "town."

Vereeniging. *Town, southern Transvaal, South Africa.* The town, south of Johannesburg on the Orange Free State border, arose from the discovery of coal here in 1878. A company was formed to exploit it, and was given the Dutch name *De Zuid-Afrikaansche en Oranje Vrijstaatsche Kolen- en Mineralen-Mijn Vereeniging*, "The South Africa and Orange Free State Coal and Mineral Mining Association." Mining operations began in 1879 and when a town was founded in 1882 it was named with the last word of the company's title.

Verga, Cape. *Cape, western Guinea.* The name represents Portuguese *Cabo de Verga*, "rod cape," presumably for the promontory's thin shape.

Verhuellpolis. See **Bethalie.**

Verkeerdevlei. *Town, east central Orange Free State, South Africa.* The Afrikaans name means literally "reverse marsh," referring to a stream here that flows in the opposite direction to all other streams.

Verkykerskop. *Village, northeastern Orange Free State, South Africa.* The literal meaning of the Afrikaans name is "farlooker's hill," implying a hill that can serve as a lookout post. Compare **Spion Kop.**

Verneukpan. *Village, west central Cape Province, South Africa.* The village takes its name from the pan or lake here. Its own name means literally "cheat pan," referring either to the mirages experienced here or to the fact that after rainfall the apparently large area of water lasts only a few weeks.

Vert, Cape. See **Cape Verde.**

Verulam. *Town, eastern Natal, South Africa.* The town, north of Durban, was founded in 1850 by a group of Methodist settlers who were brought to South Africa from St. Albans, England, under the patronage of Lord Grimston, Earl of *Verulam.* The earl took his title from the ancient Roman station of *Verulamium*, near St. Albans.

[1]**Victoria.** *Capital of Seychelles.* The city and port, on the island of Mahé, was founded in 1841 and named (originally as *Port Victoria*) for Queen *Victoria* of England (1819–1901), who had come to the throne four years previously.

[2]**Victoria.** *Town and port, western Cameroon.* The town was founded by Baptist missionaries in 1858 and named for Queen *Victoria* of England (1819–1901). It is now more usually known by its indigenous name of *Limbe.*

[3]**Victoria.** *Village, western Guinea.* The village, a former British possession on the estuary of the Nuñez River, owes its name to Queen *Victoria*, in whose reign (1837–1901) it arose.

Victoria, Lake. *Lake, East Africa.* The lake is divided among the three countries that surround it: Kenya, Uganda, and Tanzania. It was discovered by the British explorer John Hanning Speke on July 30, 1858, and named by him for Queen *Victoria* of England (1819–1901). (Speke may also have intended to commemorate his discovery as a personal *victory.*) Its alternate name is *Victoria-Nyanza*, the second part of which is simply the Bantu word for "lake." (Cf. Lake **Nyasa**). The Arabs knew the lake as *Ukerewe*, "land of the Kerewe," from the *Kerewe* people who inhabited the island of this name in the southeastern sector of the lake. A current local name for the lake is *Nalubale*, "abode of the great spirit," perhaps suggested by the waterspouts that sometimes occur. When the three countries achieved independence, proposals were made for a new, indigenous name. They included *Uhuru*, "freedom," "independence" (a word especially associated with Kenya), *Shirikisho*, "union," and *Umoja*, "unity." However, the colonial name remains.

[1]**Victoria Falls.** *Waterfall, Zambezi River, Southern Africa.* The falls, on the border between Zimbabwe and Zambia, were discovered by the British explorer David Livingstone on November 16, 1855, and named by him for Queen *Victoria* of England (1819–1901). The indigenous (Kalolo-Lozi) name for the falls is *Mosi-oa-tunya*, "the smoke that thunders."

[2]**Victoria Falls.** *Town, southwestern Zimbabwe.* This town is just south of, and is named for, the falls (see previous entry).

Victoria Nile. See **Nile.**

Victoria Nyanza. See Lake **Victoria.**

Victoria West. *Town, central Cape Province, South Africa.* The town was laid out on a farm here in 1844 and named *Victoria* for the queen of England, who had come to the throne in 1837. *West* was added in 1855 to distinguish the town from the district of *Victoria East*, Ciskei, itself established in 1847.

Vila António Enes. See **Angoche.**

Vila Cabral. See **Lichinga.**

Vila da Maganja. *Village, north central Mozambique.* The village was established in 1914 and is named for the *Maganja* people, who had come here from Lake Malawi. An earlier settlement on the site was known as *Vila João Coutinho*, for the Portuguese naval minister, explorer, and statesman, *João* de Azevedo *Coutinho*.

Vila de João Belo. See **Xai-Xai.**

Vila de Porto Santo. See **Porto Santo.**

Vila Fontes. See **Caia.**

Vila Gamito. *Village, western Mozambique.* The village, on the border with Zambia, was established in 1937 and is named for the Portuguese army officer and governor of Tete, António Candido Pedroso *Gamito* (1806–1886).

Vila General Machado. See **Camacupa.**

Vila Gouveia. See **Catandica.**

Vila Junqueiro. See **Guruè.**

Vila Luísa. See **Marracuene.**

Vila Machado. *Village, central Mozambique.* The village was established in 1898 and was originally known as *Nova Fontesvila*, for the Portuguese marquis *Fontes* Pereira de Melo. But it was simultaneously known by the English name of *Bamboo Creek*, and this was the name of the railroad station here. The present name derives from that of General Joaquim José *Machado* (1847–1925), governor of Mozambique from 1914 to 1915. He also gave his name to **Machadodorp**, South Africa.

Vilanculos. *Coastal village, southeastern Mozambique.* The name is that of a tribe formerly here, the *Vilanculo* people.

Vila Nova Sintra. *Town, Brava, Cape Verde Islands.* The Portuguese name of the chief town on the island of Brava means "new town of Sintra," referring to *Sintra*, the royal resort near Lisbon, Portugal.

Vila Pinto Teixeira. See **Mabalane.**

Vila Robert Williams. See **Caála.**

Vila Teixeira da Silva. See **Bailundo.**

Vila Vasco da Gama. *Village, western Mozambique.* The village, established in 1924, is named for the famous Portuguese navigator, *Vasco da Gama* (1460–1524). The founding of the village coincided with the quadricentennial of his death.

Viljoensdrif. *Village, northern Orange Free State, South Africa.* The coal-mining village, on the Vaal River, takes its name from J. H. *Viljoen*, who operated a ferry across the Vaal at this point in 1857. The ford (Afrikaans, *drif*) here was closed by President Paul Kruger in 1895 to prevent merchandise going through to the Rand, thus forcing people to use a railroad some miles away.

Viljoenshof. *Village, southwestern Cape Province, South Africa.* The village, southeast of Cape Town, was originally given the Afrikaans name of *Wolfgat*, "wolf hole," perhaps referring to hyenas who made their home here. The name was later changed to honor D. J. *Viljoen*, minister of the Dutch Reformed Church at nearby Bredasdorp for 30 years to 1934. Afrikaans *hof* means literally "court," "garden."

Viljoenskroon. *Town, northern Orange Free State, South Africa.* The town was established on a farm in 1921 and named for its owner, J. J. *Viljoen*, and his horse *Kroon* ("Crown").

Villa Bens. See **Tarfaya.**

Villa Cisneros. See **Ad Dakhla.**

Villiers. *Town, northeastern Orange Free State, South Africa.* The town was laid out on two farms in 1882 and named for their owner, L. B. de *Villiers.*

Villiersdorp. *Town, southwestern Cape Province, South Africa.* The town was established in 1844 and named for its founder, Field-Cornet Pieter Hendrik de *Villiers*, Afrikaans *dorp* meaning "settlement," "town."

Virginia. *Town, central Orange Free State, South Africa.* The name of the town has an apparently anecdotal origin which nevertheless has documented support. When American engineers were surveying the railroad running across a farm here in 1890, they carved the name "Virginia" on a boulder. This name was then given to the railroad siding when it was built two years later. The present town developed around the siding.

Virunga Mountains. *Mountain range, east Central Africa.* The volcanic range, extending along the borders of Zaïre, Rwanda, and Uganda, has a local name, probably of Swahili origin, meaning "volcanoes." The alternate name of the range, *Mufumbiro*, preferred in Uganda, means "that which cooks." Individual volcanoes have Rwandan names, such as *Sabinyo* "old man with large teeth") and *Muhavura* ("landmark," "guide"). The range also gave the name of the *Virunga National Park*, northeastern Zaïre, a game preserve and gorilla sanctuary established in 1925. This was originally called the *Albert National Park* (French: *Parc National Albert*), for *Albert* I, King of the Belgians (1875–1934), but was renamed in 1972. The range is thought by some to have been Ptolemy's famous "Mountains of the Moon," from the physical appearance of the summits. They are referred to as such, for example, by the British explorer John Hanning Speke in his *Journal of the Discovery of the Source of the Nile* (1863). The title is more usually assigned to the **Ruwenzori**, however.

Vishoek. See **Fish Hoek.**

Volksrust. *Town, southern Transvaal, South Africa.* The town was established in 1888 and has an Afrikaans name meaning "people's rest." This is said to have been given to the settlement by Dorothea de Jager, wife of Field-Cornet G. W. J. de Jager, since burghers (Boer citizens) had rested here after the battle of Majuba in 1881.

Volta. *River, West Africa.* The chief river of Ghana is formed by the confluence of the *Black Volta* and the *White Volta* in the north central region of the country. Its name represents Portuguese *Rio da Volta*, meaning "river of turning," either because it was the point where a Portuguese expedition turned back, or (more likely) because the river has many bends and loops. The name first appeared on a map in 1471. The *Black Volta* and *White Volta*, so named for the comparative color of their water, both rise in **Burkina Faso** (hence that country's previous name of *Upper Volta*). There is also a *Red Volta*, as a tributary of the White Volta.

Volubilis. *Ancient town, northern Morocco.* The former chief inland city of the Roman province of Mauretania Tingitana has a name that suggests Latin *volubilis*, "turning." However, the name is actually a Roman corruption of the Berber word *walili*, meaning "bay-tree."

Vosburg. *Town, central Cape Province, South Africa.* The town was founded on a farm in 1895 and named for its owners, the *Vos* family.

Vrede. *Town, northeastern Orange Free State, South Africa.* The town was established in 1863 and given an Afrikaans name meaning "peace," referring to the settlement of a dispute over the siting of the town.

Vredefort. *Town, northern Orange Free State, South Africa.* The town was established in 1876 and given an Afrikaans name meaning "fort of peace." The reference appears to be some kind of settlement or agreement, possibly one between the Orange Free State and the Transvaal, since the town is close to the border between these provinces.

Vredenburg. *Town, southwestern Cape Province, South Africa.* The town was laid out in 1883 by a spring named *Procesfontein*, "lawsuit spring," and at first bore this name, referring to a dispute between two men over ownership of the spring. When the first church was consecrated here the present name was given, meaning "town of peace."

Vryburg. *Town, northern Cape Province, South Africa.* The town was founded in 1883 as the capital of *Stellaland*, a miniature republic set up by Boer adventurers the previous year, and taking its name from a comet (Latin *stella*, "star") visible at the time. Its burghers (citizens) called themselves "free burghers" (Dutch *vryburgers*), hence the name. Stellaland itself was absorbed into Bechuanaland and the South Africa Republic (modern Transvaal) in 1884.

Vryheid. *Town, northwestern Natal, South Africa.* The town was established in 1884 as the capital of a new republic here known simply as the *New Republic.* Hence the name, which is the Afrikaans word for "freedom." The republic was incorporated into the South Africa Republic (modern Transvaal) in 1887.

Wa. *Town, northwestern Ghana.* The town takes its name from the *Wala* people who migrated to this part of Ghana from Mali.

Wadi Natrun. *Watercourse, northern Egypt.* The name represents Arabic *wādi al-natrūn*, "river of natron," referring to the salt deposits here. Cf. Lake **Natron**.

Wagadugu. See **Ouagadougou.**

Wakkerstroom. *Town, southeastern Transvaal, South Africa.* The Afrikaans name is that of a stream here, meaning literally "awake stream," as a translation of its local name, *Utaka.* When the town was first laid out in 1859 it was named *Marthinus Wesselstroom*, for *Marthinus Wessel* Pretorius (1819–1901), first president (in 1856) of the South African Republic, and the son of Andries Wilhelmus Pretorius, who gave the name of **Pretoria**. This name was subsequently shortened to *Wesselstroom*, then altered to its present form.

Walfish Bay. See **Walvis Bay.**

Walmer. *Residential district, southeastern Cape Province, South Africa.* The district, a western extension of Port Elizabeth, is named for *Walmer* Castle, Kent, England, seat of the Duke of Wellington (see **Wellington**).

Walvis Bay. *Town and port, western Namibia.* The port takes its name from the bay on which it is located. This is an English translation of Afrikaans *Walvisbaai*, from *walvis*, "whale" (compare it with the obsolete English *whalefish*), and *baai*, "bay." The coastal region here on the Atlantic has long been a whaling center. The name also occurs in the form *Walfish Bay.*

Wankie. See **Hwange.**

Warden. *Town, northeastern Orange Free State, South Africa.* The town was established in 1912 and is said to be named either for Major Henry D. *Warden*, British resident of the Orange River Sovereignty from

1845 to 1852 or, more probably for his son, Charles Frederick *Warden, landdrost* (district magistrate) at nearby Harrismith.

Warmbad. *Town, southwestern Namibia.* The Afrikaans name means literally "warm bath," referring to a hot water spring here that attracted early settlers. The Khoikhoin (Hottentot) name for the spring was */Ai-//gams*, "hot water." (The unusual characters denote clicks.) A mission was established here in 1805 and was itself known as *Blijde Uitkomst*, "happy deliverance." It changed hands several times and was eventually superseded by a German garrison in 1894, after which the present settlement developed.

Warmbaths. *Town, central Transvaal, South Africa.* The town was laid out in 1882 and originally named *Hartingsburg*, for Professor Pieter *Harting* (1812–1885), a pro-Boer spokesman in the Netherlands. The local name *Warmbaths* was already in use, however, for the hot spring here, and this was officially adopted in 1903. The Afrikaans form of the name is *Warmbad* (compare **Warmbad**, Namibia).

Warrenton. *Town, northeastern Cape Province, South Africa.* The town was established in 1884 and named for Sir Charles *Warren* (1840–1927), soldier and archaeologist.

Wartburg. *Village, central Natal, South Africa.* The name is of religious significance. It is that of the castle of *Wartburg* in Germany, overlooking Eisenach, where Martin Luther began his translation of the Bible into German in 1521.

Wasbank. *Village, northwestern Natal, South Africa.* The village takes its name from the river here. The Afrikaans name means "wash shelf," and is said to refer to the regular washing that formerly took place here on the slabs of rock. The Zulu name of the river is *Busi*, "dominant one."

Waterberg. *Village, north central Namibia.* The village takes its Afrikaans name from that of the plateau here, itself meaning "water mountain." The reference is to the many springs on the hill slopes.

Waterval-Boven. *Town, southeastern Transvaal, South Africa.* The town was established in 1895 and has a Dutch name describing its location, "above the waterfall." Cf. **Waterval-Onder.**

Waterval-Onder. *Village, southeastern Transvaal, South Africa.* The village is just east of **Waterval-Boven** (q.v.), and has a descriptive name contrasting with it, meaning "below the waterfall." The railroad station here was originally called *Waterval-Beneden*, "beneath the waterfall," but this wrongly described the actual location, so was modified to the present name.

Wazzan. See **Ouezzane.**

Wedza. *Village, south central Zimbabwe.* The name is said to derive from that of the mountains here, and to mean "place of wealth," referring to their rich supplies of iron ore. However, an anecdotal origin is also current: the name represents the Chishona word *hwedza*, meaning "tomorrow," the reply given to certain non-Shona travelers when they asked for directions.

Weenen. *Town, central Natal, South Africa.* The town was laid out in 1838 near the scene of the Zulu massacre of Piet Retief's party of 182 Voortrekkers that same year. Hence its name, Afrikaans for "weeping."

Weissrand Mountains. *Plateau, south central Namibia.* The plateau is seen as a long line of white cliffs when viewed from the west. Hence its German name, meaning "white ridge," which may have been translated from a Khoikhoin (Hottentot) original.

Welkom. *Town, north central Orange Free State, South Africa.* The town was founded soon after 1846 when gold was discovered in the province. It was laid out on a farm of the same name, Afrikaans for "welcome." The name was appropriately propitious for a site that promised wealth.

Wellington. *Town, southwestern Cape Province, South Africa.* The Huguenots settled here in 1688 and named the region *Limiet Vallei,* "limit valley," implying a place at the extreme point of civilization, some 60 miles (96 km) from the Cape of Good Hope. The French later changed this name to *Val du Charron,* "valley of the cartwright." The town was eventually established in 1840. Sir George Napier, governor of the Cape, wished it to be named for himself, but a town of this name had already been founded. He therefore chose the present name in honor of Arthur Wellesley, Duke of *Wellington* (1769–1852), hero of the battle of Waterloo (1815). This was further fitting in that the Cape as yet had no town of the name. See also **Walmer.**

Welwitschia. See **Khorixas.**

Wepener. *Town, southern Orange Free State, South Africa.* The town was established in 1866 with the aim of maintaining order in the region after the territory here had been annexed to the Orange Free State. It was named for Commandant Louw *Wepener* (1812–1865), killed here in battle the previous year.

Wesselsbron. *Town, northwestern Orange Free State, South Africa.* The town was founded in 1920 and named for Cornelis J. *Wessels,* who commanded the siege of Kimberley in 1899. Afrikaans *bron* means "spring."

Western. See (1) **Barotse;** (2) **Copperbelt.**

Western Desert. *Desert region, west central Egypt.* The conventional English name translates Arabic *aṣ-ṣaḥrā' al-garbīyah,* literally "the desert the west." The desert, actually a part of the Libyan Desert, extends from the border with Libya in the west to the Nile in the east, and is considerably larger than the **Eastern Desert.**

Western Sahara. *Territory, northwestern Africa.* The disputed territory, along the Atlantic coast west of Mauritania and south of Morocco, was a Spanish overseas province from 1958 to 1975 and was known as *Spanish Sahara* during this period. In 1975 it was partitioned between Morocco and Mauritania, Morocco taking the northern region of **Saquía el-Hamra** and Mauritania the southern region of **Río de Oro**. In 1976 the whole territory was designated the "Saharan Arab Democratic Republic" (SADR) by Polisario, the guerrilla movement created in 1973 to set up an independent state here. (Its name is an abbreviation, a partial acronym, of Spanish *Frente Popular para la Liberación de Saquía el-Hamra y Río de Oro,* "Popular Front for the Liberation of Saquía el-Hamra and Río de Oro.") In 1979 Mauritania renounced its claim, although Polisario continued to oppose Morocco's annexation. In 1993 a UN referendum calling for a straight choice between independence or integration with Morocco was discussed by Polisario and the Moroccan government, but talks collapsed in midyear. When independence is eventually gained, Western Sahara will almost certainly take a new name.

Westminster. *Village, eastern Orange Free State, South Africa.* The village was founded after the second Boer War (1899–1902) by Hugh Richard

Arthur Grosvenor, 2d Duke of *Westminster* (1879–1953), to provide accommodation for British ex-soldiers, and was named for him.

West Nicholson. *Village, southern Zimbabwe.* The village was founded in 1898 and named for the gold mine here that had developed from the earlier *Nicholson* Reef, itself named for Andrew *Nicholson,* a prospector. The first word of the name must have been added to distinguish this mine from another further east.

Westonaria. *Town, southern Transvaal, South Africa.* The town, southwest of Johannesburg, originally comprised the two townships of *Veterspost* and *Westonaria.* They combined in 1948 under the former name, but on gaining municipal status in 1952 the latter name was adopted, mainly to avoid confusion with existing names beginning *Venters-* such as *Ventersburg,* **Ventersdorp**, and *Venterstad. Westonaria* is intended to represent the words "western area," for the company that developed the original township, *Western Areas* Ltd.

White Nile. *Section of Nile River, northeastern Africa.* The name is that of the **Nile** proper as it flows northward through Sudan to meet its chief tributary, the **Blue Nile**, at Khartoum. When in flood, from June to September, the river carries a considerable amount of material in suspension. This gives its waters a whitish hue. Hence the name, which translates Arabic *al-baḥr al-abyaḍ*, from *al*, "the," *baḥr*, "sea," "river," and *abyaḍ*, "white."

White River. *Town, eastern Transvaal, South Africa.* The town was established as a settlement for demobilized soldiers after the second Boer War (1899–1902). It took the name of the farm on which it was laid out, with the farm's name in turn deriving from that of the river here, itself a translation of its local name *Manzemhlope*, "white water."

White Volta. See **Volta.**

Whittlesea. *Town, Ciskei, South Africa.* The town was established in 1849 and named for the village in England that was the birthplace of Sir Harry Smith (see **Harrismith, Smithfield**), governor of the Cape, *Whittlesea* (now *Whittlesey*), Cambridgeshire.

Wilberforce Island. *Island, southern Nigeria.* The island is a region of land surrounded by the channels of the Niger Delta (see **Rivers**). Its name commemorates William *Wilberforce* (1759–1833), the British politician who brought about the abolition of the slave trade and of slavery itself in the British empire. The Niger enters the Atlantic on the **Slave Coast.**

Wilgedorp. See **Lichtenburg.**

Williston. *Town, southwestern Cape Province, South Africa.* The town arose as a mission station in 1845 and was originally named *Amandelboom*, "almond tree," allegedly because the first missionaries pitched their tents under such a tree. In 1919 the town was given its present name, in honor of Colonel Hampden *Willis*, colonial secretary for the Cape in 1883.

Willowmore. *Town, southern Cape Province, South Africa.* The town was established in 1862 on a farm named *The Willows*, itself so named for its owner, *William Moore*, and a blend of both names was devised to give that of the town.

Winburg. *Town, central Orange Free State, South Africa.* The town was laid out on a farm in 1841 and was at first named *Wenburg*. This can be interpreted as "winning town," and relate either to a battle victory or to the settlement of a dispute over the siting of the town. The name was subsequently modified to its present form.

Windhoek. *Capital of Namibia.* The city, in the center of the country, has a name that suggests Afrikaans *windhoek*, "wind corner," although high winds are infrequent here. The name was apparently first used by the Nama leader Jonker Afrikaner, who founded a settlement on the site of the present city in 1840. He himself came from the village of *Winterhoek*, near Tulbagh, Cape Province, South Africa, and perhaps adopted (and adapted) the name from there. The original Nama name of the city was *Aigams* or *Eikams*, from *ais*, "fire," and *gami*, "water," referring to the hot springs here.

Windsorton. *Village, northern Cape Province, South Africa.* The village was founded as a diamond diggers' camp in 1869 and was at first given the biblical name of *Hebron* (Genesis 13:18), meaning "place of the covenant." It was later renamed for its developer, P. E. *Windsor*. The Khoikhoin (Hottentot) name of the village is *Chaib*, "place of kudu."

Winterton. *Village, western Natal, South Africa.* The village was laid out in 1905 and was originally named *Springfield.* In 1910 it was renamed as now for the Hon. Henry Daniel *Winter* (1851–1927), minister of agriculture in Natal from 1899 to 1906.

Witbank. *Town, south central Transvaal, South Africa.* The industrial town was established in 1903 and has an Afrikaans name meaning "white shelf," with reference to a slab of light-colored rock near the present railway station.

Witsieshoek. See **Qwaqwa.**

Witvlei. *Village, east central Namibia.* The Afrikaans name, meaning "white marsh," is a translation of Herero *Omataura* and Nama *!uri-!khuwis* (literally, "white water pan"). (The unusual characters in the latter name represent clicks.) A German military mission was set up here in 1898 and the village developed from it.

Witwatersrand. *Rocky ridge, southern Transvaal, South Africa.* The ridge, containing the richest gold deposits in the world, has an Afrikaans name meaning "white waters ridge," from *wit*, "white," *water*, "water," and *rand*, "edge," "ridge." The name originally applied to the watershed between the Vaal River and the Limpopo, and was later extended. The name is colloquially shortened to *The Rand*, and it was this that gave the name of the *rand*, South Africa's standard unit of currency, with reference to the goldmining here.

"W" National Park. *National park, West Africa.* The official name of the game park that is mainly in southwestern Niger but that extends across the border into Burkina Faso and Benin is, since these are all French-speaking countries, *Parc National du "W" du Niger*, "national park of the 'W' of the Niger." The "W" refers to the many bends of the Niger River here. In the French name, *W* is thus pronounced in the French fashion, as *double vé.*

Wolmaransstad. *Town, southwestern Transvaal, South Africa.* The town arose in 1884 from a community that had grown around a trading store. It was named for Jacobus M. A. *Wolmarans*, a member of the executive council of the Transvaal.

Wolseley. *Town, southwestern Cape Province, South Africa.* The town was founded in 1875 and originally named *Ceres Road*, for its location on the road to that town. It was subsequently renamed for Sir

Garnet Joseph *Wolseley* (1833–1913), a British commander in the Zulu War of 1879.

Wonder Gorge. *Valley, central Namibia.* The valley, a gorge of the Lunsemfwa River above its confluence with the Mkushi, has a descriptive name referring to the "wonderful" view here. The name is said to have been given in about 1912 by the English local government official, E. Knowles Jordan.

Wooldridge. *Village, Ciskei, South Africa.* The village is named for Colonel J. W. *Wooldridge*, an officer under Major-General von Stutterheim (see **Stutterheim**).

Worcester. *Town, southwestern Cape Province, South Africa.* Thc town was laid out in 1820 and was named by Lord Charles Somerset, governor of the Cape, for his brother, the Marquess of *Worcester.*

World's View. *Hillsite, southwestern Zimbabwe.* The site in the Matopo Hills is famous for being selected by Cecil Rhodes (see **Rhodesia**) as his burial place, and was described by him as having "a view of the world." Its earlier Matabele (Ndebele) name was *Malindidzimu*, "place of spirits."

Wuppertal. *Village, southwestern Cape Province, South Africa.* The village arose in a valley here in 1830 as a station of the Rhenish Missionary Society, and was named for the *Wuppertal*, "valley of the Wupper River," in Germany, the location of the town of Barmen, where the Rhenish Missionary Institute had its headquarters. (The German industrial town of Wuppertal arose only in 1930.)

Xai-Xai. *Town and port, southern Mozambique.* The name has been spelled in the past as *Chai-Chai* and *Tchai-Tchai* and is said to be a local plural form of Portuguese *cheia*, "flood" (pronounced "shaya"), with reference to the formerly frequent floods here at the mouth of the Limpopo River. But the name may be an entirely African one, perhaps meaning "kill, kill," referring to some battle here. From 1897 the town was named *João Belo* or *Vila de João Belo*, for *João Belo* (1876–1928), the Portuguese ship's captain who held various posts in Mozambique for about 30 years, having arrived there as a midshipman in 1896.

Xhora. See **Elliotdale.**

Xinavane. *Village, southern Mozambique.* The name derives from Changana *nàva*, "to spread," "to propagate," as of creeping plants. The reference is to fertile land, where anything that is planted will grow well.

Yamoussoukro. *Capital designate of Côte d'Ivoire.* The Baule name means "Yamusa's house," from *Yamusa* (here in its French form, *Yamoussou*), founder of the village here, and *kro*, "house," "village." The city was officially designated capital (in place of Abidjan) in 1983, though the full transfer is not yet complete. It is the birthplace of the republic's former president (from 1960), Félix Houphouët-Boigny (1905–1993).

Yaoundé. *Capital of Cameroon.* The name of the city represents Duala *Yawonde*, derived from the name of the *Ewondo* people. The meaning of their own name is uncertain. The city was founded as a German military post in 1888, and became the capital in 1960. The name is also spelled *Yaunde.*

Yatenga. *Province, northwestern Burkina Faso.* The province takes its name from the northern Mossi kingdom that was founded here in about 1540. It in turn was named for its founder, *Yadega*, so that the state was called *Yadega tenga*, "Yadega's land." This was later shortened to *Yatenga.*

Yaunde. See **Yaoundé.**

Yelimané. *Village, western Mali.* The village, near the border with Mauritania, owes its name to Islamic influence. It represents Arabic *al-imām*, "the imam" (the title of the Muslim priest who leads prayers in a mosque, as well as that of various Muslim officials).

Yola. *Town, eastern Nigeria.* The town derives its name from the Fulfulde word *yolde*, used for a settlement on rising ground, as Yola originally was when founded in 1841 as a Fulani (Peul) war camp.

Yorubaland. *Former kingdom, southwestern Nigeria.* The kingdom took its name from the *Yoruba* people who still inhabit this part of Africa. Their own name is said to mean "meeting-place," or literally "I go meet," referring to the many dialects that they speak.

Zaïre. *Republic, south Central Africa.* The country's name is an alternate one for the **Congo** River, which today forms its western border with the Congo itself. It represents Kikongo *nzai*, a coastal dialect form of *nzadi*, "river." The country's present name is the sixth it has had in the 20th century. The others were: *Congo Free State* (1885–1908), *Belgian Congo* (1908–1960), *Congo (Léopoldville)* (1960–1964), *Congo* (in full, *Democratic Republic of the Congo*) (1964–1965), and *Congo (Kinshasa)* (1965–1971). The parenthetic additions to the fourth and sixth names refer to the country's capital, **Kinshasa** (formerly *Léopoldville*). Neighboring *Congo* (formerly *People's Republic of the Congo*) was for some time similarly identified as *Congo (Brazzaville).*

Zambezi. *River, Central and East Africa.* The river, rising in Zambia and flowing generally eastward to enter the sea in Mozambique, has a name based on the same indigenous root word, *za*, "river," that gave the name of **Zaïre**. It can therefore be understood generally to mean "great river." When the Portuguese explorer Vasco da Gama discovered the river in 1498 he named it *Rio dos Boms Sinaes*, "river of good signs," since he saw it as promising trade in ivory, gold, and slaves (compare **Ivory Coast, Gold Coast, Slave Coast**). The river's original local (Ndebele) name was *Egwembeni*, meaning "place of the boats."

Zambézia. *Province, central Mozambique.* The province takes its name from the **Zambezi** River, which forms its southern border with Sofala.

Zambia. *Republic, Southern Africa.* The former *Northern Rhodesia* (to 1964) takes its present name from that of the **Zambezi** River, which forms its southern border with Zimbabwe. The earlier name, *Zambesia*, of the same origin, was used by the British South Africa Company for the territory from 1888 to 1894.

Zamfara. *River, northwestern Nigeria.* The river takes its name from the territory that existed here from about 1200 to 1902. This was itself named from its inhabitants, the *Zamfarawa*, "men of *Fara*," referring to a local princess.

Zanzibar. *Island off coast of East Africa.* The name is an ancient one for the east coast of Africa that today lies in Tanzania and Kenya. It represents a combination of *Zengi* or *Zenj*, the name of a local people, from *zang*, "black," and Arabic *barr*, "land," "coast." (Compare *Malabar* in southwestern India, meaning "land of mountains.") The name has also been popularly linked with Arabic *zinjfīl*, Latin *zingiber*, or Greek *zingiberis*, "ginger," presumably by association with the cloves for which the island is famous. Today the name is found in both that of the island and in that of the city and port of *Zanzibar* on the island's west coast. An earlier form of the name was *Zanguebar*, especially as applied to the Arab and Persian mainland territory with a capital at Kilwa Kivinje, now in Tanzania. See also *Azania* (in the **South Africa** entry) and **Tanzania.**

Zaria. *City and former state, north central Nigeria.* The city was founded in about 1536 by Bakwa Turunku, queen of the Hausa kingdom of *Zazzau*, itself founded in the early 11th century and having a name meaning "sword." The queen named the town for her younger daughter, *Zaria*. Bakwa was succeeded by her elder daughter, Amina, a powerful and warlike ruler, who was in turn succeeded by Zaria. When the town became Zazzau's capital in about 1578, in place of the earlier Turunku, the state adopted the same name.

Zastron. *Town, southern Orange Free State, South Africa.* The town was laid out in 1876 and named for the maiden name, *Zastron*, of Lady Johanna Sibella Brand, wife of the Orange Free State president, Sir Johannes (Jan) Brand (see **Brandfort**). She was the daughter-in-law of the Lady Brand who gave the name of **Ladybrand.**

Zeerust. *Town, western Transvaal, South Africa.* The town was laid out in 1867 on a farm owned by Diederik J. Coetzee, and for this reason was at first known as *Coetzee-Rust*, "Coetzee's home" (from Afrikaans *rust*, literally "rest"). This was later shortened to the present form, as if the first part of the name were Afrikaans *zee*, "sea."

Zemmour. *Region, eastern Western Sahara.* The region, near the border with Mauritania, has a name representing Zenaga *azamur*, "wild olive."

Ziguinchor. *Town, southwestern Senegal.* The town, a port on the Casamance River near the border with Guinea-Bissau, is said to take its name from the *Iziguicho* people who once lived here. According to some sources, however, the name means "sit and weep with us," from Mande *sigi*, "sit," and Creole *tior*, "weep," allegedly referring to the embarkation of slaves here. A local (Diola) name for the town is *Ebeubeu*, "town of whites."

Zimbabwe. *Republic, southeastern Africa.* The former *Southern Rhodesia* (to 1964) and *Rhodesia* (from then to 1980) takes its present name from the ruined fortified settlement in the center of the country that was probably at one time the capital of an extensive empire. The name represents *Zimba we bahwe*, "houses of stones," from Bantu *zimba*, "houses," plural of *imba*, and *bahwe*, "stones." The ruins themselves are generally known as *Great Zimbabwe* to distinguish them from a small and more recent group of ruins some 8 miles (13 km) away, known as *Little Zimbabwe*. The name is not unique to these particular ruins, and is found as a generic term for similar ancient stone ruins elsewhere in southern Africa, for example in Mozambique. See also **Rhodesia.**

Zinder. *Town, southern Niger.* The town was founded in 1740 by a Bornuan hunter (see **Bornu**) and is said to be named for him. However, other sources derive the name from a local dialect word *zundum* meaning "big," referring to large rocks nearby.

Zoar. *Village, southwestern Cape Province, South Africa.* The village arose as a mission station in 1817 and was named for the biblical town of *Zoar* (Genesis 13:10), whose own name means "little."

Zomba. *Town, southern Malawi.* The former capital of Malawi (to

1975) was established as a planters' settlement in 1885 and proclaimed a town in 1900. It has a Nyanja name meaning "locust," no doubt because these insects are common here. The name primarily applies to Mount *Zomba*, on whose slopes the town lies.

Zululand. See **KwaZulu.**

Zuwarah. *Town and port, northwestern Libya.* The name is said to derive from an Arabic word meaning "deceived." A legend is told how two farmers walked together to a village, but that when one suggested they return, the other refused, saying he liked the place and intended to remain there. The first man, finding himself alone, then said "*zauart ahlia*," "You deceived me," and this gave the name.

Zvishavane. *Town, south central Zimbabwe.* The town, formerly known as *Shabani*, was founded in about 1913 around an abestos mine. Its local name refers to the mine, and represents the Rozvi word *shava*, "red-brown of iron oxides."

Zwartland. See **Malmesbury.**

Zwelitsha. *Capital of Ciskei, South Africa.* The town was established in 1948 to accommodate the employees of the Good Hope Textile Corporation, and was given a Xhosa name meaning "new world."

Glossary

The following glossary of terms occurring in the present work is designed to assist the interpretation of African placenames not entered individually in the dictionary. Particular emphasis is placed on Arabic name elements, chiefly found in North Africa, as these can occur in different forms but have identical (or similar) meanings.

ābār (Arabic), wells
abyār (Arabic), wells
adrar (Berber), mountains
aguelt (Berber), well
aïn (Arabic), spring, well
angra (Spanish), bay
anou (Berber), well
ʿaqabat (Arabic), pass
ʿayn (Arabic), well
baai (Afrikaans), bay
bāb (Arabic), strait, gate
bādiyah (Arabic), desert
bahiret (Arabic), lagoon
baḥr (Arabic), river, sea
baḥra (Arabic), lagoon
baḥrat (Arabic), lake
bandar (Arabic), port, harbor, inlet
bannaanka (Somali), plain, area
barqā (Arabic), hill
bas, basse (French), lower
baṭīn (Arabic), depression
-berg (Dutch, German, Afrikaans), mountain
bi'ār (Arabic), wells
bidʿ (Arabic), waterhole
bir (Arabic), spring, well
birk, birkat, birket (Arabic), well, lake
bordj (Arabic), fort
borj (Arabic), fort
bron (Afrikaans), spring
buheirat (Arabic), lake
cabo (Spanish, Portuguese), cape, headland
cachoeira (Portuguese), waterfall
cap (French), cape, headland
capo (Italian), cape, headland
chalb (Arabic), watercourse
chebka (Arabic), hill
chott (Arabic), salt lake, marsh
-dal (Afrikaans), valley
djebel (Arabic), mountain
djibāl (Arabic), mountains
dooxo (Somali), valley
-dorp (Afrikaans), village
dūr (Arabic), mountains
erg (Arabic), desert with dunes
fajj (Arabic), watercourse
fulayj (Arabic), watercourse
garet (Arabic), hill
gebel (Arabic), mountain
gezāir (Arabic), islands
gezīret (Arabic), islands
ghadfat (Arabic), watercourse
ghadīr (Arabic), well
ghard (Arabic), sand dunes
ghubbat (Arabic), bay
ghubbet (Somali), bay
groot (Dutch, Afrikaans), big
gubed (Somali), bay
guelta (Arabic), well
ḥadabat (Arabic), plain
ḥadh, ḥadhat (Arabic), sand dunes
ḥafar (Arabic), plain
hamada, hamadet (Arabic), plateau, desert
ḥammād, ḥammadah (Arabic), plateau, plain

ḥarrat (Arabic), lava field
hassi (Arabic), well
ḥasy (Arabic), well
hawr (Arabic), lake
ḥazm (Arabic), plateau
ḥiṣn (Arabic), fort
idd (Arabic), well
idhan (Arabic), sand dunes
ʿidwet (Arabic), mountain
île (French), island
ilha (Portuguese), island
irhzer (Berber), watercourse
ʿirq (Arabic), sand dunes
isla (Spanish), island
jabal (Arabic), mountain
jāl (Arabic), ridge
jasiired (Somali), island
jazā'īr (Arabic), islands
jazīrat (Arabic), island
jbel (Arabic), mountain
jebel (Arabic), mountain
jibāl (Arabic), mountains
jiddat (Arabic), gravel plain
jūn (Arabic), bay
kaap (Afrikaans), cape
karīf (Arabic), well
kathīb (Arabic), sand dunes
kebīr (Arabic), big
kereb (Arabic), hill, ridge
khabāri (Arabic), rainpools
khabb (Arabic), depression between dunes
khabr, khabrah (Arabic), rainpool, waterhole
khalīg, khalīj (Arabic), bay, gulf
khashm (Arabic), mountain
khawr (Arabic), inlet
khor (Arabic), inlet
klein (Afrikaans, German), small
kloof (Afrikaans), gorge
kōm (Arabic), mound
kop (Afrikaans), hill
kūlet (Arabic), hill
laaq (Somali), river
lagoa (Portuguese), lagoon
madīnat (Arabic), town, city
mamarr (Arabic), pass
manāqīr (Arabic), hills
marsā (Arabic), anchorage, inlet
masabb (Arabic), estuary
mashāsh (Arabic), well
maṣṭabet (Arabic), tomb
maʿṭan (Arabic), well
mersa (Arabic), anchorage, inlet
mīnā' (Arabic), port, harbor
minqār (Arabic), hill
mishāsh (Arabic), well
mont (French), mountain
monte (Italian, Spanish, Portuguese), mountain
mudiriyat (Arabic), province
mushāsh (Arabic), well
nafūd (Arabic), desert, dune
nahr (Arabic), river
naqb (Arabic), pass
nasb (Arabic), hill, mountain
nieu (Afrikaans), new
nieuw (Dutch), new
oued (Arabic), dry riverbed
pointe (French), point, cape
qaʿ (Arabic), depression
qabr (Arabic), tomb
qalamat (Arabic), tomb
qalīb (Arabic), well
qarārar (Arabic), depression
qāret (Arabic), hill
qoor (Somali), bay
qoz (Arabic), hill
qulbān (Arabic), wells
qūr (Arabic), hills
qurayyāt (Arabic), hills
qurnat (Arabic), peak
qurūn (Arabic), hills
ramlat (Arabic), sands
rās (Arabic), point, cape, headland
rass (Somali), point, cape, headland
rijm (Arabic), hill, spur
rio (Portuguese), river
río (Spanish), river
rivier (Afrikaans), river
rujm (Arabic), hill, spur
sabkhat (Arabic), salt flat
sadd (Arabic), dam
ṣaghīr (Arabic), small
sahl (Arabic), plain
ṣaḥrā' (Arabic), desert
san, santa, santo (Spanish, Italian, Portuguese), saint
sāniyat (Arabic), well
são (Portuguese), saint
sayḥ (Arabic), gravel plain
sebkra (Arabic), salt flat
shaʿīb (Arabic), watercourse
shāriʿ (Arabic), street

sharm (Arabic), inlet
shaṭṭ (Arabic), river, estuary
shiqāq (Arabic), depression between dunes
shuqqat (Arabic), depression between dunes
sint (Dutch, Afrikaans), saint
souk (Arabic), market
-*stad* (Afrikaans), town
suhūl (Arabic), plain
sūḳ (Arabic), market
sūq (Arabic), market
tall (Arabic), hill
tallāt (Arabic), hills
taraq (Arabic), hill
tassili (Berber), plateaus
tell (Arabic), hill
teniet (Arabic), pass
thamad (Arabic), cistern, well
tilat (Arabic), hill
tilemsi (Berber), pool, well
tirʿat (Arabic), canal
tizi (Berber), pass
tulūl (Arabic), hills
ʿuqlat (Arabic), well
ʿurayq (Arabic), sand ridge
ʿurūq (Arabic), area of dunes
ʿuyūn (Arabic), springs
vila (Portuguese), small town
ville (French), town
wādī (Arabic), river, valley of seasonal watercourse
wāḥat (Arabic), oasis
webi (Somali), river

Appendix I: The Exploration of Africa

The following summary is intended to serve as a chronological guide to the exploration of Africa by non-Africans, from the earliest times to the end of the 19th century. Each item is given in the following form: date(s), nature of exploration; exploring state or country; explorer(s) or patron. For sake of uniformity, an expedition or passage by land or river is termed a "journey" and one by sea a "voyage."

15th c. BC. Journeys south and up Nile as far as 5th cataract: Egypt/royal military commanders of 18th dynasty.

No later than 8th c. BC. Exploration of entire northern seaboard of Africa and Strait of Gibraltar: Phoenicia/unknown seafarers.

Before 594 BC. Three-year voyage round Africa: Egypt/Phoenician seafarers.

About 525 BC (or, according to some sources, 5th c. BC). Voyage from Carthage along west coast of Africa to point beyond Cape Vert (perhaps Gulf of Guinea): Carthage/Hanno.

2d c. BC. Arrival in Canary Islands: Spain/Cadiz fishermen.

About 20 BC. Journey to Fezzan oases (central Sahara): Rome/Balbus.

About AD 42. Traverse of High Atlas: Rome/Paulinus.

About AD 50–100. Voyage along east coast of Africa to Zanzibar: Rome/Greek seafarers.

About 60. Journey up White Nile to point south of latitude 10°N: Rome/unknown soldiers.

About 340. First Christian mission to Ethiopia: Byzantium/St. Frumentius.

8th–9th centuries. Arrival at Comoro Islands, Madagascar, and Mozambique coast: Iraq/Arabian seafarers.

1060s. Traverse of Sahara from Atlas Mountains to Niger River (as military campaign to Mali): Morocco/Berber military commanders.

1312–41. Second arrival in Canary Islands: Italy and Portugal/Genoese seafarers.

1344 or 1345. Arrival in Madeira: Italy/unknown seafarers.

1352–53. Traverse of western Sahara to Niger River (from south to north) and central Sahara: Morocco/ibn-Battuta.

1431–35. Arrival in Azores: Portugal/naval commanders under Henry the Navigator.

1434–57. Voyage south along west coast of Africa to latitude 10°N; arrival at Cape Vert, Senegal and Gambia rivers, Bissagos Islands: Portugal/naval commanders under Henry the Navigator.

1456–62. Arrival at Cape Verde Islands: Italy, Portugal/Cadamosto, Noli, Afonso.

About 1461–73. Voyage southeast along coast of Africa to Gulf of Biafra and south to latitude 2°S; arrival at Mt. Cameroon and islands in the Gulf of Guinea: Portugal/Cintra, Costa, Santarem, Sequeira, Fernando Po.

1482–86. Voyage down west coast of Africa to latitude 22°S; arrival at lower reaches of Congo River: Portugal/Cão.

1487–88. Arrival at south coast of Africa and Cape of Good Hope: Portugal/Bartholomeu Dias.

1489–93. Voyage from Horn of Africa down east coast to latitude 20°S and journey north from there to Ethiopia: Portugal/Covilhã.

1497–98. Second voyage from Europe to India round Africa; circumnavigation of African coastline completed: Portugal/Vasco da Gama.

1500. First visit by Europeans to Madagascar: Portugal/Diogo Dias.

1501–07. Arrival at Ascension Island, St. Helena, Amirante Islands, Seychelles, and Mascarene Islands: Portugal/Nova, Mascarenhas, and others.

1511–15. Journey across Sahara to Niger River and Lake Chad: Morocco/Leo Africanus.

About 1570. Exploration of lower Zambezi River: Portugal/Barreto.

1613. Exploration of Lake Tana and upper reaches of Blue Nile: Portugal/Paez.

1616. Arrival at Lake Nyasa (Malawi) and Ruvuma River: Portugal/Bocarro.

1648–61. Exploration of eastern Madagascar: France/Flacourt.

1652–62. Arrival at Cape mountains and Great and Little Karoo: Holland/Riebeeck and others.

1714–16. Exploration of Senegal River region: France/Brüe.

1760–61. Journey south of Orange River; arrival at Namaqualand plains: Holland/Cape colonists.

1769–72. Exploration of Abyssinian Highlands: Britain/Bruce.

1787. Exploration of Cunene Ruver region: Portugal/Lacerda.

1791–92. Arrival at Namib Desert: Holland/Cape colonists.

1795–97, 1805–06. Journey from mouth of Gambia River to upper Niger River; journey along Niger from Ségou to Bussa rapids: Britain/Mungo Park.

1812. Arrival at source of Limpopo River and Witwatersrand watershed: Britain/Campbell.

1818–23. Exploration of upper reaches of Gambia, Senegal, and Niger rivers to Fouta Djallon plateau: France, Britain/Mollien, Lang.

1822–25. Double traverse of Sahara; exploration of Lake Chad and Chad-Niger watershed: Britain/Denham, Clapperton.

1827–28. Traverse of West Africa from Sierra Leone to Morocco: France/Caillé.

1830. Exploration of lower reaches of Niger and Benue rivers: Britain/Lander brothers.

1836–40. Exploration of region between Orange and Vaal rivers, of that between Vaal and Limpopo (Transvaal), and of Drakensberg: South Africa/Pretorius, Retief, and other Boer leaders.

1837–48. Exploration of Ethiopian uplands: France/Abbadie brothers.

1848–49. Exploration of Mt. Kilimanjaro and other mountains of Kenya: Germany/Krapf, Rebmann.

1849–54. Traverse of Kalahari Desert; exploration of upper reaches of Zambezi River: Britain/Livingstone.

1849–55. Exploration of river system of Angola: Hungary/Magyar.

1850–53. Traverse of Kalahari and Damaraland uplands: Sweden/Andersson.

1850–55. Exploration of Sahara, Lake Chad, upper reaches of Benue River, and central Sudan to Niger River: Britain, German/Richardson, Overweg, Barth.

1852–53. Traverse of Africa from Benguela (Angola) to mouth of Ruvuma River: Portugal/Silva Porto.

1854–56. Traverse of Central Africa from Luanda (Angola) to mouth of Zambezi River; arrival at Victoria Falls: Britain/Livingstone.

1856–63. Exploration of Lake Tanganyika; arrival at Lake Victoria and Victoria Nile River: Britain/Burton, Speke, Grant.

1859–61. Exploration of lakes Nyasa and Chilwa completed: Britain/Livingstone.

1864. Arrival at Albert Nile River and Lake Albert: Britain/Baker.

1865–70. Systematic exploration of Madagascar: France/Grandidier (*père*).

1867–71. Arrival at lakes Mweru and Bangweulu and of Lualaba River (upper Congo): Britain/Livingstone.

1869–74. Arrival at Tibesti Mountains (Chad): Germany/Nachtigal.

1870. Exploration of Uele River (with Bomu forming Ubangi): Germany/Schweinfurth.

1873–75. Traverse of Central Africa between latitudes 6°30′S and 12°30′S and exploration of terrain here; exploration of Lake Tanganyika completed: Britain/Cameron.

1875–77. Arrival at Kagera River, Lake Edward, and Ruwenzori Range; journey down Congo River from upper reaches to mouth: Britain and USA/Stanley.

1875–92. Exploration of Ogooué River region and tributaries of Congo River: France/de Brazza.

1877–79. Traverse of Africa from Angola to Mozambique; exploration of Cubango River region: Portugal/Serpa Pinto.

1878–83. Exploration of Great Rift Valley; arrival at Lake Rukwa: Britain/Thomson.

1880–83. Exploration of Uele River and section of watershed between Nile and Congo rivers: Russia/Yunker.

1883–1900. Exploration of Sahara and of Shari and Ubangi rivers: France/Foureau.

1884–86. Exploration of Kasai River: Germany/Wissman.

1888. Arrival at Lake Rudolf: Hungary/Teleki.

1892–97. Exploration of Horn of Africa and Juba River region: Italy/Bottego.

1894. Arrival at Lake Kivu: Germany/von Götzen.

1897–99. Exploration of region of Lake Rudolf, and of Juba, Sobat, and Omo rivers: Russia/Bulatovich.

1898–1902. Exploration of western and southern Madagascar: France/Grandidier (*fils*).

Appendix II: Official Names of African Countries

The official names of African countries on January 1, 1993, in their translated English and indigenous forms, were as follows:

Country	*Official Name*	*Official Indigenous Names*
Algeria	Democratic and Popular Republic of Algeria	al-Jumhūrīyah al-Jazā'irīyah ad-Dīmuqrāṭīyah ash-Shaʿbīyah (Arabic)
Angola	Republic of Angola	República de Angola (Portuguese)
Benin	Republic of Benin	République du Bénin (French)
Botswana	Republic of Botswana	Republic of Botswana (English)
Burkina Faso	Burkina Faso	Burkina Faso (French)
Burundi	Republic of Burundi	Republika y'u Burundi (Rundi); République du Burundi (French)
Cameroon	Republic of Cameroon	République du Cameroun (French); Republic of Cameroon (English)
Cape Verde	Republic of Cape Verde	República de Cabo Verde (Portuguese)
Central African Republic	Central African Republic	République Centrafricaine (French)
Chad	Republic of Chad	Jumhūrīyah Tshad (Arabic); République du Tchad (French)
Comoros	Federal Islamic Republic of the Comoros	Jumhūrīyat al-Qumur al-Ittihādīyah al-Islāmīyah (Arabic); République Fédérala Islamique des Comores (French)
Congo	Republic of the Congo	République du Congo (French)
Côte d'Ivoire	Republic of Côte d'Ivoire	République de Côte d'Ivoire (French)

Country	*Official Name*	*Official Indigenous Names*
Djibouti	Republic of Djibouti	Jumhūrīyah Jībūtī (Arabic); République de Djibouti (French)
Egypt	Arab Republic of Egypt	Jumhūrīyah Miṣr al-ʿArabīyah (Arabic)
Equatorial Guinea	Republic of Equatorial Guinea	República de Guinea Ecuatorial (Spanish)
Ethiopia	Ethiopia	YeĒtiyop'iya (Amharic)
Gabon	Gabonese Republic	République Gabonaise (French)
Gambia	Republic of the Gambia	Republic of the Gambia (English)
Ghana	Republic of Ghana	Republic of Ghana (English)
Guinea	Republic of Guinea	République de Guinée (French)
Guinea-Bissau	Republic of Guinea-Bissau	República da Guiné-Bissau (Portuguese)
Kenya	Republic of Kenya	Jamhuri ya Kenya (Swahili); Republic of Kenya (English)
Lesotho	Kingdom of Lesotho	Lesotho (Sotho); Kingdom of Lesotho (English)
Liberia	Republic of Liberia	Republic of Liberia (English)
Libya	Socialist People's Libyan Arab Jamahiriya	al-Jamāhīrīyah al-ʿArabīyah al-Lībīyah ash-Shaʿbīyah al-Ishtirākīyah (Arabic)
Madagascar	Democratic Republic of Madagascar	Repoblika Demokratika Malagasy (Malagasy); République Démocratique de Madagascar (French)
Malawi	Republic of Malawi	Republic of Malawi (English)
Mali	Republic of Mali	République du Mali (French)
Mauritania	Islamic Republic of Mauritania	al-Jumhūrīyah al-Islāmīyah al-Mūrītānīyah (Arabic)
Mauritius	Republic of Mauritius	Republic of Mauritius (English)
Morocco	Kingdom of Morocco	al-Mamlakah al-Maghribīyah (Arabic)
Mozambique	Republic of Mozambique	República de Moçambique (Portuguese)
Namibia	Republic of Namibia	Republic of Namibia (English)
Niger	Republic of Niger	République du Niger (French)
Nigeria	Federal Republic of Nigeria	République du Niger (French)

Country	*Official Name*	*Official Indigenous Names*
Rwanda	Republic of Rwanda	Republika y'u Rwanda (Rwanda); République Rwandaise (French)
São Tomé e Prīncipe	Democratic Republic of São Tomé e Prīncipe	República Democrática de São Tomé e Prīncipe (Portuguese)
Senegal	Republic of Senegal	République du Sénégal (French)
Seychelles	Republic of Seychelles	Repiblik Sesel (Creole); Republic of Seychelles (English); République des Seychelles (French)
Sierra Leone	Republic of Sierra Leone	Republic of Sierra Leone (English)
Somalia	Somali Democratic Republic	Jamhuuriyadda Dimuqraadiga Soomaaliya (Somali); Jumhūrīyah aṣ-Ṣūmāl ad-Dīmuqrāṭīyah (Arabic)
South Africa	Republic of South Africa	Republiek van Suid-Africa (Afrikaans); Republic of South Africa (English)
Sudan	Republic of the Sudan	Jumhūrīyat as-Sūdān (Arabic)
Swaziland	Kingdom of Swaziland	Umbuso weSwatini (Swazi); Kingdom of Swaziland (English)
Tanzania	United Republic of Tanzania	Jamhuri ya Muungano wa Tanzania (Swahili); Republic of Tanzania (English)
Togo	Republic of Togo	République Togolaise (French)
Tunisia	Republic of Tunisia	al-Jumhūrīyah at-Tūnisīyah (Arabic)
Uganda	Republic of Uganda	Republic of Uganda (English)
Western Sahara	Western Sahara	[no official indigenous name]
Zaïre	Republic of Zaïre	République du Zaïre (French)
Zambia	Republic of Zambia	Republic of Zambia (English)
Zimbabwe	Republic of Zimbabwe	Republic of Zimbabwe (English)

Appendix III: Language and Religion

The following is a guide to the languages spoken in the different countries of Africa. In most cases the official languages, here indicated in *italics*, are European, and thus of colonial origin. It goes without saying that these have had a bearing on a particular country's placenames, and still influence the spelling of African names today (for example, the French spellings in francophone West Africa). Countries whose official religion is Islam are indicated by an asterisk. A religious background of this kind can equally influence placenames. Population figures (as of 1992) are given to the nearest 100,000. "Local," with reference to languages, means "African," "non-European."

ALGERIA* (26.4 million). About 80 percent of the population speak *Arabic*. There are also about 2 million Berber speakers, while in the south, in parts of the Sahara, about 10,000 Tuaregs speak Tamashek. French is still spoken by the rapidly declining European community and by many educated Algerians, but has retained its importance for commerce and tourism.

ANGOLA (10.6 million). The official language is *Portuguese*. The chief local languages are Umbundu, with about 3 million speakers in the center of the country, and Mbundu, with about 1.8 million speakers in the north. In the far north, around 1 million people speak Kongo, and a similar number speak Chokwe in the northeast.

BENIN (4.9 million). The official language is *French*. The main local language and lingua franca is Fon, with around 1 million speakers in the south of the country. About 500,000 people speak Burba in the north, and a similar number speak Yoruba along the eastern border with Nigeria.

BOTSWANA (1.3 million). The official languages are *English* and *Tswana*. In the west there are a dwindling number of San (Bushman) speakers.

BURKINA FASO (9.5 million). The official language is *French*. The most important local language is More (sometimes also called Mossi), with about 4 million speakers. Gourma is spoken in the east, Fulani (Peul) and Tuareg (Tamashek) in the north, and Dyula in the west.

BURUNDI (5.6 million). Virtually the whole population speaks *Rundi* (also called Kirundi or Urundi, or Rwanda in Rwanda), and this is the official language, together with *French*. Swahili serves as a lingua franca.

CAMEROON (12.6 million). *French* and *English* are both official languages, although not many people speak the latter. There are a large number of local languages, most of them of the Bantu family, especially in the south. They include

Fang, with almost 2 million speakers, Bamileke, with about 1.6 million, and Duala, with around 1.3 million. A form of pidgin English serves as a lingua franca.

CAPE VERDE (0.3 million). The official language is *Portuguese*, with most of the population speaking a Creole dialect of this.

CENTRAL AFRICAN REPUBLIC (2.9 million). The official language is *French*, while *Sango*, at one time the language of a single tribe along the banks of the Ubangi River, is now an official lingua franca.

CHAD (5.9 million). The official languages are *French* and *Arabic*, the latter serving as a lingua franca. There are around 100 other local languages, including Sara, in the south, with around 750,000 speakers.

COMOROS* (0.5 million). The official language is French, while a form of Swahili is spoken by many people.

CONGO* (2.7 million). The official language is *French*. The main local languages are Kongo, spoken by about half the population, and Teke, having around 500,000 speakers.

CÔTE D'IVOIRE (12.9 million). The official language is *French*. There are about 70 local languages, the most important including Dyula and Senufo, spoken in the north, Agni and Akar (Baule), in the southeast, and Malinke, in the northwest.

DJIBOUTI (0.5 million). The two official languages are *Arabic*, spoken by about 12 percent of the population, and *French*, spoken by only around 4 percent. The two main local languages are Somali, spoken by about 45 percent of the population (the Issa), and Afar, spoken by about 40 percent.

EGYPT* (55.9 million). Almost the entire population speaks *Arabic*, the official language. Several varieties of colloquial Arabic exist.

EQUATORIAL GUINEA (0.4 million). The official language is *Spanish*. In continental Río Muni, the main local language is Fang, spoken by about 75 percent of the population, while on the island of Bioko most people speak Bubi.

ERITREA (3.5 million). The two main languages in use for business, and those taught in schools, are English and Arabic. There are also nine indigenous languages, including Afar, Tigré, and Tigrinya.

ETHIOPIA (50.3 million). The official language is *Amharic*, spoken by about 25 percent of the population and widely used as a lingua franca. Tigrinya and Tigré are spoken in the north. Arabic is also widely understood, and Italian is still found in places. Coptic (a form of Egyptian) survives in liturgical use, but is otherwise a dead language, preserved only in some placenames.

GABON (1.2 million). The official language is *French*. Around 40 Bantu languages are also current, the most important being Fang, spoken by around 30 percent of the population.

GAMBIA (0.9 million). The official language is *English*. Local languages include Malinke, with around 400,000 speakers, Fulani (Peul), with around 100,000, Wolof, with 75,000, and Dyola and Soninke, 50,000 each.

GHANA (15.2 million). The official language is *English*, spoken by about 1 million people as a second language. The chief local language is Akan, spoken by around

45 percent of the population. More and Ewe are also fairly widely found, while Hausa is the lingua franca in the north.

GUINEA (7.2 million). The official language is *French*. The main local languages are Fulani (Peul), spoken by about 40 percent of the population, mostly in the central part of the country, Malinke, in the north, spoken by about 25 percent, and Susu, in the southwest, spoken by about 10 percent of the population.

GUINEA-BISSAU (1.0 million). *Portuguese* is the official language, with a dialect form of this serving as a lingua franca. Local languages include Balante, spoken by about 30 percent of the population, Fulani (Peul), spoken by around 20 percent, and Malinke.

KENYA (27.0 million). The official languages are *Swahili*, widely used as a lingua franca, and *English*. Major Bantu languages are Kikuyu, spoken by about 20 percent of the population, Luo, spoken by about 14 percent, Luya, with around 13 percent of speakers, and Kamba, with about 11 percent. Maasai is found along the border with Tanzania, while Turkana is spoken in the northwest.

LESOTHO (1.8 million). Both *Sotho* and *English* are official languages, the former being spoken by almost all indigenous inhabitants. Zulu is another local language, spoken by about 15 percent of the population.

LIBERIA (2.8 million). The official language is *English*, with a form of pidgin English spoken by about 70 percent of the population. The main local languages are Kpelle and Kru.

LIBYA* (4.4 million). Most of the population speak *Arabic*, the official language. Some Tuareg (Tamashek) speakers are also found in the west.

MADAGASCAR (12.8 million). The official languages are *Malagasy*, spoken by almost the entire population, and *French*, still widely understood from colonial times.

MALAWI (9.5 million). *English* and *Nyanja* are the official languages, with the latter spoken by about a third of the population and serving as a lingua franca.

MALI (8.4 million). The official language is *French*. Bambara is the most important local language, with around 2 million speakers, and serving as a lingua franca.

MAURITANIA* (2.1 million). The official language is *Arabic*, spoken by about 70 percent of the population, sometimes in dialect form. French is still important, while Fulani (Peul) is spoken by about 150,000 people in the south.

MAURITIUS (1.1 million). The official language is *English*, though it is spoken very little. The lingua franca of the country is Creole French, spoken by about 30 percent of the population. Although two inhabitants out of three are from India or Pakistan, the languages they speak have had virtually no influence on placenames.

MOROCCO* (26.2 million). The official language, *Arabic*, is spoken by about 65 percent of the population. There are also about 5 million Berber speakers, mainly in the mountain regions. French and Spanish are still understood by many, especially in towns.

MOZAMBIQUE (14.8 million). The official language is *Portuguese*. The two main local languages are Makua, spoken in the north by around 6 million people, and Tsonga, with about 2 million speakers in the south.

NAMIBIA (1.5 million). The most widespread local language is Ambo, spoken by the Ovambo in the north. In the eastern and central parts of the country Herero is also found. The main languages spoken by whites are Afrikaans and *English*, the latter being the country's official language. German is also still spoken in places.

NIGER (8.3 million). The official language is *French*, while Hausa, spoken by about half the population, is the leading local language. Dyerma, spoken by about 23 percent of the population, is found mainly in the southwest, while Fulani (Peul), with around 15 percent of speakers, is in the northern and central regions, where Tuareg (Tamashek) is also found.

NIGERIA (89.6 million). Africa's most populous country has the greatest number of different languages. The official language is *English*. The chief local languages are Hausa, with about 20 million speakers, mainly in the north, Yoruba, spoken in the southwest by about 17 million, and Ibo, with about 13 million speakers in the southeast. There are as many as 400 other local languages, some with just a small number of speakers.

RWANDA (7.3 million). The two official languages are *Rwanda*, spoken by almost everyone, and *French*, with speakers much fewer in number. Swahili serves as a commercial language. Rwanda is also spoken in Burundi, where it is known as Rundi.

SÃO TOMÉ E PRÍNCIPE (0.1 million). The official language is *Portuguese*, but most people speak a Portuguese-based Creole.

SENEGAL (7.7 million). The official language is *French*. Wolof is the main local language, spoken by around 35 percent of the population, mainly in the west of the country. Other languages include Fulani (Peul), Serer, Dyola, and Malinke.

SEYCHELLES (0.1 million). The official languages are *English* and *French*, but French Creole is spoken everywhere and serves as a lingua franca.

SIERRA LEONE (4.4 million). The official language is *English*. There are many others. Mende is the most important, with around 1 million speakers in the southern half of the country.

SOMALIA* (7.9 million). *Somali* and *Arabic* are the two official languages, while Italian and English are still widely understood.

SOUTH AFRICA (32.0 million). The two official languages are *Afrikaans* and *English*, the former spoken by about 60 percent of the white and most of the colored (mixed race) population, the latter by about 40 percent of whites. Zulu is the leading language of blacks, with about 4 million speakers in Natal. Approximately the same number speak Xhosa, found chiefly in Transkei. Tswana has about 2 million speakers, mostly in the north of the country near the border with Botswana. Sotho, with about 1.5 million speakers, is found in the region surrounding Lesotho, while there are around 500,000 speakers of Swazi in the area adjoining Swaziland.

SUDAN* (30.0 million). Over half the population speak *Arabic*, the official language, chiefly in the northern part of the country. A dialect of Nubian is spoken by around 500,000 people in the central region, while another dialect of this same language has around 175,000 in the north. Beja has about 500,000 speakers in the east bordering the Red Sea, and Darfurian around 175,000 in the west.

SWAZILAND (0.8 million). Almost the whole black population speaks *Swazi*, which is now an official language, together with *English*.

TANZANIA (25.8 million). The two official languages are *Swahili*, spoken by almost everybody, and *English*, widely used for commercial purposes. Most of the many local languages are of the Bantu family, with Swahili dominant in Zanzibar and serving as a lingua franca.

TOGO (3.7 million). The official language is *French*. Of the local languages, Ewe is the most important, spoken by around 20 percent of the population, mainly in the south.

TUNISIA* (8.4 million). The official language, *Arabic*, is spoken almost everywhere, while French is still found in official circles. Berber speakers are also found in places.

UGANDA (17.2 million). The official language is *English*. Of the local languages, Ganda (Luganda) is the most important, and is spoken by around 16 percent of the population. Swahili is widely used as a lingua franca, as also are English and Ganda themselves.

WESTERN SAHARA (0.2 million). Hassaniyah, a dialect of Arabic, is the main language. It is also spoken in Mauritania.

ZAÏRE (41.1 million). The official language is *French*. Kongo is spoken by about 15 percent of the population, mainly in the west, Lingala by about 25 percent, mostly as a second language, but as a first language in the north and northwest, Luba by about 15 percent, mainly in the southeast, and Swahili by around 30 percent, for the most part as a second language, but as a first language chiefly in the northeast.

ZAMBIA (8.3 million). The official language is *English*. Bemba is the main local language, spoken in the northeast of the country by about 25 percent of the population. Tonga, in the south, is spoken by around 12 percent of the population, and the same percentage has Nyanja as a first language in the eastern and central regions.

ZIMBABWE (9.9 million). The official language is *English*, spoken chiefly by whites. Of the local languages, Shona is the most important, and is spoken by over half the population. Ndebele, spoken by around 8 percent, is found almost entirely in the southwest.

Appendix IV: Independence Dates

The following table gives the independence dates of African countries. It will be seen that the independence movement as a whole took off in 1960, the year of British prime minister Harold Macmillan's prophetic "wind of change" speech. This contrasts with the situation in 1914, at the outbreak of World War I, when all countries of Africa except Ethiopia and Liberia were under colonial rule. A declaration of independence does not, of course, necessarily guarantee a permanent abrogation of tyranny and oppression. But it is a key event in a country's history and one that often results in the symbolic adoption of new and indigenous placenames, and even in some cases a new name for the country itself.

Background information on Africa's few remaining *dependent* states follows the table.

Country	*Date of Independence*
Algeria	July 5, 1962
Angola	November 11, 1975
Benin	August 1, 1960
Botswana	September 30, 1966
Burkina Faso	August 5, 1960
Burundi	July 1, 1962
Cameroon	January 1, 1960
Cape Verde	July 5, 1975
Central African Republic	August 13, 1960
Chad	August 11, 1960
Comoros	July 6, 1975
Congo	August 15, 1960
Côte d'Ivoire	August 7, 1960
Djibouti	June 27, 1977
Egypt	February 28, 1922
Equatorial Guinea	October 12, 1968
Eritrea	May 24, 1993
Ethiopia	(Oldest independent state)
Gabon	August 17, 1960

Country	*Date of Independence*
Gambia	February 18, 1965
Ghana	March 6, 1957
Guinea	October 2, 1958
Guinea-Bissau	September 24, 1973
Kenya	December 12, 1963
Lesotho	October 4, 1966
Liberia	July 26, 1847
Libya	December 24, 1951
Madagascar	June 26, 1960
Malawi	July 6, 1964
Mali	September 22, 1960
Mauritania	November 28, 1960
Mauritius	March 12, 1968
Morocco	March 2, 1956
Mozambique	June 25, 1975
Namibia	March 21, 1990
Niger	August 3, 1960
Nigeria	October 1, 1960
Rwanda	July 1, 1962
São Tomé e Príncipe	July 12, 1975
Senegal	April 4, 1960
Seychelles	June 29, 1976
Sierra Leone	April 27, 1961
Somalia	July 1, 1960
South Africa	May 31, 1961
Sudan	January 1, 1956
Swaziland	September 6, 1968
Tanzania	April 26, 1964
Togo	April 27, 1960
Tunisia	March 20, 1956
Uganda	October 9, 1962
Western Sahara	(Yet to be determined)
Zaïre	June 30, 1960
Zambia	October 24, 1964
Zimbabwe	April 18, 1980

Dependent States

Western Sahara is the territory for which independence is most obviously outstanding. When this happens, it will very likely adopt an indigenous name. (See its main entry for a fuller account.)

Western Sahara was formerly Spanish Sahara, and it is Spain who has retained the greatest number of African possessions to date. (Spain has always had the advantage of being geographically the closest country in Europe to Africa: the Strait of Gibraltar, separating the two continents, is a mere eight miles wide at its narrowest point.) On the African mainland, Spain still holds the two towns of Ceuta and Melilla, on the Moroccan coast. As island territory, Spain's most important possession is the Canaries. Smaller island settlements held by Spain include Alhucemas and Velez, also on the Moroccan seaboard, and the Chafarinas, a group of three islands near the border with Algeria.

Portugal, also geographically close, has the important island territories of Madeira and the Azores, in the North Atlantic. In the South Atlantic, held by Britain, are Ascension Island, St. Helena, and Tristan da Cunha. In the Indian Ocean, France still holds the major island possession of Réunion, as well as several small uninhabited islands off Madagascar. (Uninhabited, but not unnamed: Bassas da India, Europa, Îles Glorieuses, Juan de Nova, and Tromelin.) In the Comoros, France still holds Mayotte: the island voted to remain a French territory after Comoros itself gained independence.

Select Bibliography

Hundreds if not thousands of books have been written on Africa. The following are books and articles that have a direct or general relevance for the study of the continent's placenames. (The *Rough Guides* are more useful in this respect than many other current tourist publications, and belie their casual title.) Some of the books are old. Even so, and when necessarily used with caution, they have information of interest and value to contribute.

Four books by African authors on African personal names (three of them on Nigerian names) are included because the interrelationship between personal names and placenames is very close. Many places in Africa are named for individuals, and the meaning of such placenames is therefore ultimately the meaning of the personal names themselves.

Since placenames involve history, I felt it would also be useful to include one general book on the subject, for any desired background reading. I have chosen Roland Oliver's *The African Experience* as one of the best books about Africa to appear in recent times. The author, an acknowledged expert on African affairs, writes easily and elegantly about the entire span of human history across the African continent, from the birth of humanity over a million years ago in the high grasslands of East Africa to the release of Nelson Mandela in South Africa in 1990.

Readers wishing to pursue the study of African placenames in greater detail are referred to the bibliographies included in some of the titles below, in particular that in *African Ethnonyms and Toponyms* (pp. 187–196).

Titles in languages other than English are provided with an English translation.

Adams, Edwin. *The Geographical Expositor, or, Names and Terms Occurring in the Science of Geography, Etymologically and Otherwise Explained.* London: Longman & Roberts, 1856.

African Ethnonyms and Toponyms. (The General History of Africa: Studies and Documents: No. 6.) Paris: Unesco, 1984.

Asante, Molefi Kete. *The Book of African Names.* Trenton, N.J.: Africa World Press, 1991.

Automobile Association. *Road Atlas and Touring Guide of Southern Africa,* 4th ed. Johannesburg: Automobile Association, 1974.

Báguena Corella, Luis. *Toponimia de la Guinea Continental Española* ("Placenames of continental Spanish Guinea"). Madrid: Cons. Sup. Invest. Cient., Inst. Est. Afr., 1947.

Bates, Oric. "On certain North African place-names prefixed with *Rus.*" *Cairo Scientific Journal*, Vol. 6, 1912.

Berlyn, Philippa. *Lore and Legend of Southern Rhodesia Place Names.* Salisbury: Chief Information Officer, Division of Native Affairs, Southern Rhodesia, 1960.

Blackie, Christina. *Geographical Etymology: A Dictionary of Place-Names Giving Their Derivations*, 3d rev. ed. London: John Murray, 1877.

Bulpin, T. V. *Discovering Southern Africa,* 3d ed. Cape Town: Books of Africa, 1983.

Cabral, António. *Dicionário de nomes geográficos de Moçambique: sua origem* ("Dictionary of geographical names of Mozambique: their origin"). Lourenço Marques: Empresa Moderna, 1975.

Calderini, Aristide. *Dizionario dei nomi geografici e topografici dell'Egitto Greco-Romano* ("Dictionary of the geographical and topographical names of Graeco-Roman Egypt"). Cairo: Società reale geografica dell'Egitto, 1935.

Campani, Romeo. "La terminologia geografica degli Arabi con speciale riguardo alla toponomastica della Libia" ("The geographical terminology of the Arabs with special respect to the toponymy of Libya"). *La Géographie,* Vol. 3, 1915.

Castillejo, R. "Toponimias y términos del lenguaje popular de origen africano" ("Placenames and colloquial terms of African origin"). *Divulgaciones Etnológicas*, VI, 1957.

Cherpillod, André. *Dictionnaire étymologique des noms géographiques* ("Etymological dictionary of geographical names"), 2d ed. Paris: Masson, 1991.

Dauzat, A. "Quelques notes de toponymie du Nord-Cameroun" ("Some notes on the placenames of North Cameroon"). *Bulletin de la Société d'études camerounaises.* No. 4, November 1943.

Desanges, Jehan. "Deux études de toponymie de l'Afrique romaine" ("Two studies of the placenames of Roman Africa"). *Les Cahiers de Tunisie*, Nos. 57–60, 1967.

Dresch, J. "Toponymie nord-africaine" ("Placenames of North Africa"). *L'Information géographique,* No. 15, 1951.

Egli, Johann Jacob. *Nomina Geographica* ("Geographical names"), 2d rev. ed. Leipzig: F. Brandstetter, 1893.

Ellingham, Mark, and Shaun McVeigh. *Morocco: The Rough Guide*, 3d ed. Bromley: Harrap Columbus, 1990.

Engeln, Oscar Diedrich von. *The Story Key to Geographic Names.* New York: D. Appleton, 1924.

Essien, Okon. *Ibibio Names: Their Structure and Their Meanings.* Ibadan: Daystar Press, 1986.

Flutre, Louis-Fernand. *Pour une étude de la toponymie de l'A.-O.F.* ("A study of the placenames of French West Africa"). Dakar: Université de Dakar, 1957.

Fontaine, Alfred L. "Régions et sites anciens intéressant la Sociéte d'études historiques et géographiques de l'Isthme de Suez" ("Ancient regions and sites and interest to the Society for the Historical and Geographical Study of the Isthmus of Suez"). *Bulletin de la Société d'études historiques et géographiques de l'Isthme de Suez*, Vol. 1, 1948.

Graesse, Johann Gustav Theodor, and Friedrich Benedict. *Orbis latinus, oder Verzeichnis der wichstigsten lateinischen Orts- und Ländernamen* ("The Latin world, or a register of the most important Latin names of places and countries"). Berlin: Transpress, 1980.

Grandidier, Alfred. "Des principaux noms de lieux de Madagascar et leur signification" ("The chief placenames of Madagascar and their meaning"). *Bulletin de la Société de géographie commerciale de Paris*, No. 17, 1895.

Griffiths, Ieuan L. L. *The Atlas of African Affairs,* 2d ed. London: Routledge, 1993.

Gromyko, A. A., chief ed. *Afrika: entsiklopedicheskiy spravochnik* ("Africa: an encyclopedic reference guide"). 2 vols. Moscow: Sovetskaya Entsiklopediya, 1986-87.

Holt, Basil Fenelon. *Place-names in the Transkeian Territories*. Johannesburg: Africana Museum, 1963.

Houis, M. "Quelques Données de toponymie ouest-africaine" ("Some information on West African placenames"). *Bulletin de l'Institut Français Afrique Noire*. Vol. 20, Nos. 3-4, July-October 1958.

Hudgens, Jim, and Richard Trillo. *West Africa: The Rough Guide*. Bromley: Harrap Columbus, 1990.

Hugon, Anne. *The Exploration of Africa: From Cairo to Cape*. London: Thames and Hudson, 1993.

Kane, Robert S. *Africa A to Z*, rev. ed. New York: Doubleday, 1972.

Kirchherr, Eugene C. *Place Names of Africa, 1935-1986: A Political Gazetteer*. Metuchen, N.J. Scarecrow, 1987.

Lester, K. J., *et al.*, eds. *Reader's Digest Atlas of Southern Africa*. Cape Town: Reader's Digest Association, 1984.

Losique, Serge. *Dictionnaire étymologique des noms de pays et de peuples* ("Etymological dictionary of the names of countries and peoples"). Paris: Klincksieck, 1971.

McCrea, Barbara, and Tony Pinchuck. *Zimbabwe and Botswana: The Rough Guide*. Bromley: Harrap Columbus, 1990.

McEvedy, Colin. *The Penguin Atlas of African History*. London: Penguin Books, 1980.

Matthews, C. M. *Place Names of the English-Speaking World*. London: Weidenfeld & Nicolson, 1972.

Mauny, R. "Noms de pays d'Afrique occidentale" ("Names of countries in West Africa"). *Présence africaine*. Nos. 34-35, 1961.

Mercier, Gustave. "La Langue libyenne et la toponymie antique de l'Afrique du nord" ("The Libyan language and the historic placenames of North Africa"). *Journal asiatique*. No. 205, 1924.

Mill Hill Fathers. "Derivations of Some Teso Place-names." *The Uganda Journal*, Vol. 16, No. 2, September 1952.

Morris, Peter, Daniel Jacobs, Charles Farr, and Adrian Fozzard. *Tunisia: The Rough Guide*, 3d ed. Bromley: Harrap Columbus, 1992.

Mostyn, Trevor, ed. *The Cambridge Encyclopedia of the Middle East and North Africa*. Cambridge: Cambridge University Press, 1988.

Mota, Avelino Teixeira da. *Toponimos de origem portuguesa ma costa Ocidental de Africa desde o Cabo Bojador ao Cabo de Santa Caterina* ("Placenames of Portuguese origin on the West coast of Africa from Cape Bojador to Pointe Sainte-Catherine"). Bissau: Contribuição do Centro de Estudos Luso-Brasileiros, 1950.

Müller, Franz. "Erklärung einiger ostafrikanischer Ortsnamen" ("Explanation of some East African placenames"). *Mittheilungen des Seminars für orientalische Sprachen an der Königlichen Friedrich Wilhelms-Universität zu Berlin*, Vol. 3, 1900.

Nicolas, J. P. "Questions de toponymie" ("Questions of toponymy"). *Études camerounaises*. Supplement to Nos. 21-22, 1948.

Nienaber, Petrus Johannes. *Suid-Afrikaanse Pleknaamwoordeboek* ("South African placename dictionary"). Cape Town: Tafelberg, 1972.

Nikonov, V. A. *Kratkiy toponimicheskiy slovar'* ("Concise toponymical dictionary"). Moscow: Mysl', 1966.

Odelain, O., and R. Séguineau. *Dictionary of Proper Names and Places in the Bible.* New York: Doubleday, 1981.

Odinot, Paul. "Notes de toponymie marocaine" ("Notes on Moroccan placenames"). *La Géographie.* No. 71, January-May 1939.

Oduyoye, Modupe. *Yoruba Names: Their Structure and Their Meanings.* Ibadan: Daystar Press, 1972.

Oliver, Roland. *The African Experience.* London: Weidenfeld & Nicolson, 1991.

_______, and Michael Crowder, eds. *The Cambridge Encyclopaedia of Africa.* Cambridge: Cambridge University Press, 1981.

Pellegrin, Arthur. *Essai sur les noms de lieux d'Algérie et de Tunisie* ("Essay on the placenames of Algeria and Tunisia"). Tunis: S.A.P.I., 1949.

Perkins, A. *A Manual of the Origin and Meaning of Geographical Names.* New York: G. Savage, 1852.

Pesenti, Gustavo. "Raccolta di leggende sull'origine di alcune località della Libia" ("Collection of stories on the origin of some places in Libya"). *Bollettino della Società Geografica Italiana.* Vol. 99, 1912.

Phillips, Tracy. "Etymology of Some African Names." *Geographical Journal.* Vol. 110, Nos. 1-3, January-March, 1948.

Raper, P. E. *A Dictionary of Southern African Place Names,* 2d ed. Johannesburg: Jonathan Ball, 1989.

Reader's Digest Illustrated Guide to Southern Africa, 3d ed. Cape Town: Reader's Digest Association, 1982.

Reyniers, P. "Signalisation et toponymie en Tunisie et Tripolitaine" ("Signposting and placenames in Tunisia and Tripolitania"). *Revue internationale d'onomastique,* No. 1, 1961.

Richardson, Dan, and Karen O'Brien. *Egypt: The Rough Guide.* Bromley: Harrap Columbus, 1991.

Roden, D. "Some Geographical Implications from the Study of Ugandan Placenames." *East African Geographical Review.* No. 12, April 1974.

Room, Adrian. *Dictionary of World Place Names Derived from British Names.* London: Routledge, 1989.

_______. *Place-Name Changes: 1900–1991,* 2d ed. Metuchen, N.J.: Scarecrow Press, 1993.

_______. *Place-Names of the World.* Sydney: Angus & Robertson, 1987.

Rosenthal, Eric. *Encyclopedia of Southern Africa,* 7th ed. Cape Town: Juta, 1978.

Shann, G. N. "Tanganyika Place Names of European Origin." *Tanganyika Notes and Records,* No. 54, March 1960.

Sibree, James, ed. "Malagasy Place-names." *The Antananarivo Annual and Madagascar Magazine.* No. 22, Christmas 1898.

Snoxall, R. A. "Some Buganda Place-names." *Bulletin of the Uganda Society,* No. 2, 1944.

Spiess, C. "Bedeutung einiger Städte- und Dorfnamen in Deutsch-Togo" ("The meaning of some town and village names in German Togo"). *Globus.* No. 89, 1906.

Stewart, John. *African States and Rulers: An Encyclopedia of Native, Colonial and Independent States and Rulers Past and Present.* Jefferson, N.C.: McFarland, 1989.

Sturmfels, Wilhelm, and Heinz Bischof. *Unsere Ortsnamen* ("Our placenames"). Bonn: Dümmlers, 1961.

Taylor, Isaac. *Names and Their Histories.* London: Rivington, Percival, 1896.

_______. *Words and Places.* Edited with corrections and additions by A. Smythe Palmer. London: George Routledge, 1907.

Thomas, H. B., and Ivan R. Dale. "Uganda Place Names: Some European Eponyms." *The Uganda Journal.* Vol. 17, No. 2, September 1953.

Trillo, Richard. *Kenya: The Rough Guide.* Bromley: Harrap Columbus, 1991.

Tubiana, Joseph. "Éléments de toponymie éthiopienne (Tigre)" ("Elements of Ethiopian [Tigre] placenames"). *Journal Asiatique.* Vol. 244, 1956.

Ubahakwe, Ebo. *Igbo Names: Their Structure and Their Meanings.* Ibadan: Daystar Press, 1981.

Velten, C. "Erklärung einiger ostafrikanischer Ortsnamen" ("Explanation of some East African placenames"). *Mittheilungen des Seminars für orientalische Sprachen an der Königlichen Friedrich Wilhelms-Universität zu Berlin.* Vol. 1, 1898.

Webster's New Geographical Dictionary. Springfield, Mass.: Merriam-Webster, 1988.

Wilcocks, Julie. *Countries and Islands of the World*, 2d ed. London: Clive Bingley, 1985.

Zhuchkevich, V. A. *Toponimika* ("Toponymy"). Minsk: Vysshaya Shkola, 1965.